Key Words in Multicultural Interventions

Key Words in Multicultural Interventions

A DICTIONARY

EDITED BY
Jeffery Scott Mio,
Joseph E. Trimble,
Patricia Arredondo,
Harold E. Cheatham,
and David Sue

GREENWOOD PRESS
Westport, Connecticut • London

Library of Congress Cataloging-in-Publication Data

Key words in multicultural interventions : a dictionary / edited by
  Jeffery Scott Mio . . . [et al.].
    p. cm.
  Includes bibliographical references and index.
  ISBN 0–313–29547–6 (alk. paper)
    1. Cross-cultural counseling—Dictionaries. 2. Psychotherapy—
Dictionaries. I. Mio, Jeffery Scott.
  BF637.C6K493   1999
  303.48'2'03—dc21   99–14839

British Library Cataloguing in Publication Data is available.

Library of Congress Catalog Card Number: 99–14839
ISBN: 0–313–29547–6

First published in 1999

Greenwood Press, 88 Post Road West, Westport, CT 06881
An imprint of Greenwood Publishing Group, Inc.
www.greenwood.com

Printed in the United States of America

The paper used in this book complies with the
Permanent Paper Standard issued by the National
Information Standards Organization (Z39.48–1984).

10 9 8 7 6 5 4 3 2 1

Contents

Preface

It has often been said that the words people use give one a sense of who they are, what they value and believe, how they choose to express themselves, and their knowledge of language. Words, then, give us clues about the whim and fancy of people. Also, it can be said that one of the best ways to understand an academic field is to become intimately familiar with its vocabulary. Indeed, academic disciplines have developed unique words, idioms, lexicons, terms, concepts, and constructs to describe, explain, discuss, and promote understanding. Some scholars have suggested that one of the best ways to understand an academic discipline is to trace its development by carefully studying its idiosyncratic terms. Astute observers of human behavior even suggest that one can discern a person's profession by the words they use.

For many cultural and tribal groups, certain words have spiritual qualities. These often highly revered words are thought to have a living quality—a life and spiritual force of their own. These words typically are reserved for use by shamans, religious leaders, sorcerers, and healers. Some shamans, for example, will seek wisdom and guidance through use of an archaic language, a language learned through relationships and instructions from spiritual guides. Some tribal groups believe that if one speaks ''sacred words'' without the authority to do so, shame, illness, and even death may come to pass. Hence, sacred or living words are rarely written but passed on through oral tradition from one generation to the next. Sacred words are unrevealed to all but a select few, and their archaic origins remain embedded in the folk customs of the community. Yet sacred words and their corresponding archaic language are firmly imprinted in the lifeways and thoughtways of many cultural groups; such words may have a strong relationship with multicultural counseling but for apparent reasons are beyond the scope of this dictionary.

The contents of this volume contain words that are typically used in the field of multicultural counseling and psychotherapy. This is a wordbook or more precisely a dictionary, a reference book containing an alphabetical list of words, terms, concepts, and theories that form a significant portion of the language of the field.

The major objective of this dictionary is to provide definitions accompanied with specialized information about their origins and usage; references are provided to assist the reader in learning more about the terms and those responsible for their development.

The idea for this wordbook originated with Paul Pedersen in 1993, a well-known pioneer in the development of the field of multicultural counseling. At the time, Professor Pedersen realized that the field of multicultural counseling was growing and expanding. Along with the growth in interest in the field, an academic-specific vocabulary emerged. Words and terms were borrowed from other academic disciplines such as anthropology, sociology, history, social welfare, and psychiatry to describe actions, thoughts, and emotions that emerged in the course of counseling clients from unique ethnic groups and cultural backgrounds. The newly emerging "fourth force" in psychology also created its own vocabulary (Pedersen, 1998). Because of the widespread emergence of the language of multicultural counseling, Professor Pedersen decided that a dictionary must be initiated and published. Moreover, the executive board of Division 45, the Society for the Psychological Study of Ethnic Minority Issues of the American Psychological Association, formally endorsed this project and encouraged its development. Many of Division 45's executive board members were even part of the planning and implementation of this project. All involved at these early stages of development felt that it would be an important contribution to the field to help develop a common language around which we all could agree.

Initial activities consisted of the daunting and tedious tasks of poring and searching through journal articles, book chapters, monographs, conference proceedings, and books for multicultural counseling topics and the words and terms to discuss and describe. Words were selected and compiled from the multitude of sources and initially circulated among a small core group of Professor Pedersen's colleagues including (among many others) Patricia Arredondo, Thomas Parham, Derald Wing Sue, and Joseph Trimble. In turn, these psychologists added terms they considered important to the field, and with this activity the list of dictionary terms grew extensively. Eventually, Professor Pedersen turned the dictionary project over to Jeff Mio, Joseph Trimble, and Patricia Arredondo; Harold Cheatham and David Sue joined the editorial team later on in the project's evolution.

Editors were assigned a list of terms and asked to find contributors who could research and write the definitions; in some cases, editors were able to assign words to certain contributors who actually first coined or developed a word or term. Contributors were asked to follow a firm set of guidelines as follows: (1)

each definition was to be limited to about one page (350–400 words); (2) contributors had the freedom to format the definition in a style that best suited their background, expertise, and interests; however, they had to provide information that answered the following questions: Where did the word come from? What are the alternative definitions? What is the preferred definition and why? What one or two primary sources can one find to further examine the term? Examples were provided to the contributors to assist them in writing up their assigned words. In the end, many terms were left undefined. Some contributors were not able to write their assigned terms; some did not comply with the written instructions. Thus, editorial decisions needed to be made as to whether these terms were important enough to be categorized as "necessities" for a dictionary of this kind, or if the terms were important but not absolutely essential for inclusion. Some of these terms were left unchanged, so the reader will notice marked differences between these terms and other terms that followed our instructions. Some of these terms were modified or elaborated by one of the editors, but these definitions may still appear to be much less researched than other definitions. Where terms were left undefined by their assigned authors but considered essential, one of the editors or editors' designees wrote the definitions in an expedited manner. Although care was taken to write complete definitions, these definitions may have emerged quite differently had the time not been as compressed as it was near the completion of this project.

Contributors put a great deal of effort and time in researching and writing their assigned words; however, no doubt others may disagree with the definition and all of its attendant elements. This is to be expected and actually welcomed. The majority of our contributors relied on published materials to research the words; in a few instances, interviews were conducted with authorities to help track down the origin of a word and assist in clarifying its meaning. Often, newly composed technical terms are included in unpublished speeches or manuscripts; these so-called "fugitive sources" are known to a select handful of people, and thus commonly are not widely available for review and scrutiny. Knowledge of these sources can contribute to further understanding of the meaning and origins of words contained in this dictionary. Furthermore, the definitions can serve as a point of reference for further debate about the different ways the words can be used. The debates and discussions may assist in developing new terms or new nuances of the terms. Contributors definitely approached the terms with points of view that reflect where the field (or at least a significant portion of the field) is with respect to the terms. We anticipate that debates of the appropriateness of these points of view are not only inevitable, we deem these debates to be welcome.

The editors want to use this occasion to thank the contributors for their definitions and the tedious work they put into researching and writing them. Additionally, we want to extend our gratitude to Professor Paul Pedersen for continuing to stay with the project even though he had to pass it on. And we certainly want to extend our highest appreciation and gratefulness to Nita Romer, our editor at Greenwood Publishing Group. She stayed with us throughout the long and sometimes difficult task of meeting (and missing) deadlines, helping us in making the transition to a revised collection of editors, and giving us assurance that she would not abandon us even though sometimes we thought we would never complete this book.

Reference

Pedersen, P. (Ed.). (1998). *Multiculturalism as a fourth force*. Philadelphia: Taylor and Francis.

Joseph E. Trimble, Bellingham, Washington
Jeffery Scott Mio, Pomona, California
March 1999

Key Words in Multicultural Interventions

A

ABNORMAL—Bulhan (1985) summarized the five approaches used in the field of mental health either alone or in combination with each other to define *abnormal behavior*: (1) The statistical approach identified normality with conformity to the behaviors of the majority in the society. This approach vindicates the majority against the minority. (2) The subjective distress approach relies on personal accounts. This is useful since it takes into account personal experience. (3) The medical "disease" approach emphasizing an imbalance in biochemical processes. (4) The "cultural relativist" approach emphasizes the variability of definition, criterion, and symptom expression between cultures. (5) The ideal states approach assumes that we expect that everyone embodied or approximated some ideal standard; an individual's inability to do so is then considered "abnormal." Marsella's (1982) account of the history defining the universality of normal and abnormal behavior dates back to the early 1930s with the writings of cultural anthropologists. These early anthropologists were the first to challenge the assumption of the universality of normal behavior. Marsella summarized earlier studies (e.g., Benedict, 1934; Hallowell, 1934) that espoused the relativity of normal behavior based on studies of culture and personality. Marsella (1982) concluded from numerous empirical studies that "we can no longer impose an arbitrary standard of 'abnormality' and 'normality' derived from one cultural group upon another. . . . Normality and abnormality must be considered within a cultural context" (p. 365). A preferred definition espoused by Chin, De La Cancela, and Jenkins (1993) defines *abnormality* using cultural context as the defining criteria. According to Chin et al., "rather than searching for universal norms as criteria for evaluating behavior, we need to look at norms as culturally specific. . . . In psychotherapy we should . . . define the context first

before we interpret a particular behavior as pathological [abnormal] or adaptive''
(p. 77).

References

Benedict, R. (1934). Anthropology and the abnormal. *Journal of General Psychology,*
    10, 59–80.
Bulhan, H. A. (1985). *Franz Fanon and the psychology of oppression.* New York: Ple-
    num.
Chin, J. L., De La Cancela, V., & Jenkins, Y. (1993). *Diversity in psychotherapy: The*
    politics of race, ethnicity, and gender. Westport, CT: Praeger.
Hallowell, A. (1934). Culture and mental disease. *Journal of Abnormal and Social Psy-*
    chology, 29, 1–9.
Marsella, A. J. (1982). Culture and mental health: An overview. In A. J. Marsella & G.
    M. White (Eds.), *Cultural conceptions of mental health and therapy* (pp. 359–
    388). Boston: D. Reidel.

Leslie C. Jackson

ABORIGINALITY—The state or quality of being in existence, as the inhab-
itant of a country, region, land, or territory, since its most remote or ancient
periods of antiquity, so far as scientific or historical records can account or
confirm. The term *aboriginality* is most commonly used to designate the populace who occupied a particular land, especially Australia, before the invasion
of European settlers (Coolwell, 1993). Aboriginal cultures are in many parts of
Africa, America, and Australia, where Europeans began to explore and establish
colonies more than 500 years ago (Easton, 1960). The term *aboriginality* is a
derivative of its root word *aborigine*, which is derived from the words *ab* and
origine (or origin). The first recorded use of the words ab and origine combined
was by Latimer in 1537. In its original context, aborigine meant ''of origin,''
or from the beginning (Simpson & Weiner, 1989). Ten years later in 1547,
Harrison used the word aborigine to distinguish native populations from immigrants and settlers (Simpson & Weiner, 1989). When European exploration
and colonization became increasingly prevalent in the mid- to late centuries of
this millennium (approximately 1500–1900), designating indigenous populations
of the regions that settlers claimed as ''territory,'' became the context in which
aboriginality was most frequently used (Easton, 1960). Many aboriginal peoples
were regarded by White settlers as inferior or subhuman. According to Carlisle
(1989), it is remarkable there remains living aborigines, especially in Australia,
as estimated millions were killed as a result of European imperialism. Many
others were forced to abandon good or fertile land and made to relocate to barren
land or designated reservations. Many aboriginal cultures have been successful
in gaining restitution or reparations for years of mistreatment and oppression
(Toldson, 1995). Synonyms of aboriginality include *native* and *indigenous.*
Aboriginality is most commonly used to designate natives of Austrailia. However, since many Africans and Americans are also referred to as aboriginal,
authors should specify the geographical location when using this term in

publications. Also, aboriginality is an encompassing term and should not be used to describe any one or a few aboriginal cultures. In other words, if one is referring to the Mecassans of Australia, the Cherokees of North America, or the Acholi of East Africa, the proper name, as assigned by that particular ethnic group, should be employed. The American Psychological Association (1994) explicitly states that when addressing a particular culture, one should make every effort to ensure that he/she used the ethnic label that the ethnic group accepts most.

References

American Psychological Association. (1994). *The publication manual of the American Psychological Association* (4th ed.). Washington, DC: Author.
Carlisle, R. (Ed.). (1989). *The illustrated encyclopedia of mankind.* New York: Marshall Cavendish.
Coolwell, W. (1993). *My kind of people: Achievement, identity and aboriginality.* St. Lucia, Queensland: University of Queensland Press.
Easton, S. (1960). *The twilight of European colonialism, a political analysis.* New York: Holt, Rinehart and Winston.
Simpson, J. A., & Weiner, E.S.C. (Eds.). (1989). *The Oxford English dictionary* (2nd ed.). Oxford: Oxford University Press.
Toldson, I. A. (1995). HR 40: The history of the struggle for Black reparations in America. *Encobra Magazine, 4,* 18–21.

Ivory Achebe Toldson

ACCULTURATION—Refers to the process of adjustment—the borrowing, acquiring, and adopting of cultural traits from a host society by people who have migrated from another society (Szapocznik, Scopetta, Kurtines, & Aranalde, 1978). Baron (1991) conceptualized the process of acculturation as a multidimensional and multidirectional process whereby immigrant groups incorporate both overt and covert cultural characteristics of the dominant culture. According to Baron, overt cultural characteristics such as dress, language usage, eating habits, and celebrations are more easily incorporated into a new set of patterns and can be more easily observed than covert characteristics such as beliefs, attitudes, values, and feelings. Moreover, several personal, social, and demographic variables affect the rate at which acculturation occurs. For example, personal motivation for assimilating into the dominant culture, degree of contact with other groups, and age affect acculturation rates. In general, younger persons acculturate more rapidly than older ones. Because youngsters tend to acculturate more rapidly than their parents, this process often exacerbates intergenerational differences. Clinical experience with migrant groups indicates that the acculturation process often results in family disruption within this population. Studies of acculturative differences in self and family role perception have found strong support for the hypothesis that one of the mechanisms that generate family disruption within migrant groups is the occurrence of intergenerational differences in rates of acculturation (Kurtines & Miranda, 1980). Families who experience the greatest distress are those in which the levels of acculturation within the family unit are most discrepant. For example, acculturative change has been correlated with the decline in the high esteem parental roles have occupied in traditional Latino families (Kurtines & Miranda, 1980). Researchers also have found that family conflict resulting from different rates of acculturation has increased the tendency among some Latino youth groups to participate in social networks characterized by antisocial activities, including drug abuse and other delinquent behavior (Szapocznik, Ladner, & Scopetta, 1979). Given these findings, it is clear that understanding the concept of acculturation is central to counseling migrant groups in general and Latino groups in particular.

References

Baron, A. (1991). Counseling Chicano college students. In C. C. Lee & B. L. Richardson (Eds.), *Multicultural issues in counseling: New approaches to diversity* (pp. 171–184). Alexandria, VA: American Association for Counseling and Development.

Kurtines, W. M., & Miranda, L. (1980). Differences in self and family role perception among acculturating Cuban American college students: Implications for the etiology of family disruption among migrant groups. *International Journal of Intercultural Relations, 4*, 167–184.

Szapocznik, J., Ladner, R. A., & Scopetta, M. A. (1979). Youth drug abuse and subjective distress in a Hispanic population. In G. M. Beschner & A. S. Friedman (Eds.), *Youth drug abuse: Problems, issues, and treatment* (pp. 493–511). Lexington, MA: D.C. Heath.

Szapocznik, J., Scopetta, M. A., Kurtines, W. M., & Aranalde, M. A. (1978). Theory and measurement of acculturation. *Interamerican Journal of Psychology, 12*, 113–130.

Gerardo M. Gonzalez

ACCULTURATIVE STRESS—The experience of psychological difficulties as a consequence of changes in one's sociocultural surroundings caused either by entry into a new culture or by the encroachment of a new culture on an already existing culture. It can be best understood as a negative reaction to encroaching Westernization or modernization. Difficulties can range from mildly pathological to serious mental health problems and corresponding psychosomatic symptoms (Berry, 1975). John Berry (1971) first used the term in 1971, however the term was often alluded to in earlier anthropological and sociological writings. Park (1928) spoke about a relation between migration and marginality. Gillin, as quoted by Keesing (1953), maintained that for any society undergoing acculturation, one can expect to experience some confusion and lack of stability where rapidly recurring alterations of conditions will produce random behavior, disorganization, apathy, and withdrawal. Acculturative stress varies considerably from one individual to the next, because people react to change and situations in different ways. Basically, the more similar one's behavior is to the encroaching group, the less adjustment necessary, and thus less stress will be experienced. Also, individuals within a society who are more independent of the congruity of the society will be more independent of the incongruity and conflict arising from acculturation (Berry, 1975).

References

Berry, J. W. (1971). Ecological and cultural factors in spatial perceptual development. *Canadian Journal of Behavioural Science, 3*, 324–336.
Berry, J. W. (1975). Ecology, cultural adaptation, and psychological differentiation: Traditional patterning and acculturative stress. In R. Brislin, S. Bochner, & W. Lonner (Eds.), *Cultural perspectives in learning* (pp. 207–228). Beverly Hills, CA: Sage.
Keesing, F. M. (1953). *Culture change: Analysis and bibliography of anthropological sources to 1952.* Stanford, CA: Stanford University Press.
Park, R. E. (1928). Human migration and marginal man. *The American Journal of Sociology, 33*, 881–893.

Joseph E. Trimble

ADAPTATION—A process that enhances or strengthens the endurance, survival, and stability of individuals and their social system through a reciprocal exchange and the mutual adjustment of culture and environment. In its most general definition, adaptation implies that things are naturally modified to fit new conditions. Among humans, these modifications alter individuals' physiological and psychological attributes, while amending existing social and environmental conditions (Winthrop, 1991). The first time the word adaptation was used in a publication was by Healy (1610) in his translation of St. Augustine's *The City of God* (Simpson & Weiner, 1989), which was used to describe the action or process of fitting or suiting one thing to another. Following the publication of Darwin's (1859) *The Origin of Species*, the term adaptation acquired a deeper, more philosophical meaning. Darwin noted the ubiquitous adaptations in every part of the organic world. This use of the word made adaptation synonymous with survival and fitness and spawned broad research addressing whether adaptability is inherent and/or disproportionally distributed across individuals or subgroups of individuals (e.g., race, gender). Currently, the term adaptation is used in both biological and behavioral sciences. Biological sciences are concerned with the organic modifications by which an organism adjusts to its environment (Alland & McCay, 1973). In counseling and psychotherapy, adaptation is concerned with the total set of societal dynamics and psychosocial ramifications that accompany an individual's (or group of individuals') adjustment to a new environment. Cross-cultural adaptation in counseling and psychotherapy is specifically concerned with human beings' psychocultural development when two or more cultural groups share the same surroundings (Adelman, 1988). According to Cross (1995), immersion into a new culture often challenges one's view of self and the world, as he/she is confronted with a different set of values, customs, and beliefs (see ACCULTURATION). The consequences of this cultural immersion often includes psychological stress

(Oberg, 1960) or "culture shock" (Cross, p. 676). Successful cultural adaptation generally entails holding steadfast to one's original values, customs, and beliefs, while maintaining a positive regard for surrounding cultures who reciprocate accordingly, in an environment that proportionately and impartially accommodates each cultural group. Thus, in a mutual, influential exchange of cultural norms, and a collective alteration of the constitution of the environment, each culture will be invested with, and enhanced by, a broader cultural perspective that strengthens cultural adaptation.

References

Adelman, M. B. (1988). Cross-cultural adjustment: A theoretical perspective on social support. *International Journal of Intercultural Relations, 12*, 183–204.

Alland, A., & McCay, B. (1973). The concept of adaptation in biological and cultural evolution. In J. J. Honigmann (Ed.), *Handbook of social and cultural anthropology* (pp. 143–178). Chicago: Rand McNally.

Augustine, St. (1610). *[De civitate Dei]. The city of God* (J. Healey, Trans.). London: Dent & Co.

Cross, S. E. (1995). Self-construals, coping, and stress in cross-cultural adaptation. *Journal of Cross-Cultural Psychology, 26*, 673–697.

Darwin, C. (1859). *The origin of species*. London: John Murray.

Oberg, K. (1960). Culture shock: Adjustment to new cultural environments. *Practical Anthropology, 7*, 177–182.

Simpson, J. A., & Weiner, E.S.C. (Eds.). (1989). *The Oxford English dictionary* (2nd ed.). Oxford: Oxford University Press.

Winthrop, R. H. (Ed.). (1991). *Dictionary of concepts in cultural anthropology*. Westport, CT: Greenwood Press.

Ivory Achebe Toldson

ADDICTION—"There have been many definitions offered over the years for the term *drug addiction*, and this term has been so widely used and discussed that it has passed into that group of terms that elude precise definition" (Ray & Ksir, 1990, p. 27). Although it has been known for thousands of years that certain drugs have the power to "enslave men's minds," the "classic" conception of addiction did not evolve until the nineteenth century when certain opiates (i.e., opium and morphine) became widely used. Much later, it was recognized that alcohol, sedatives, and tranquilizers also produce most of the symptoms of "classic" addiction (Goode, 1993). According to Goode, *classic addiction* is based on the fact that if a person takes a certain drug in sufficient quantity over a sufficiently long period of time and then stops taking it abruptly, the user will experience the physical symptoms known as withdrawal. Although practically every drug ingested by humans has been termed "addicting," it has been recognized that certain drugs do not produce the physical sickness associated with withdrawal when their use is discontinued. These drugs, such as LSD and marijuana, are not addicting in the "classic" sense of the word. Recognizing that just because a drug is not physically addicting in the classic sense of the word does not mean that it is not dangerous. In the early 1950s, the World Health Organization adopted the term "drug dependence" as a way of extending the concept of addiction to drugs that are not physically addicting (Goode, 1993). During the 1960s, when the use of drugs became a public issue, it became popular among a growing group of interested scientists to refer to drugs like marijuana, amphetamines, and cocaine as producing psychological dependence, whereas heroin was thought to produce a true addiction, including physical dependence. More recently, however, this view has been challenged by a series of animal and human experiments, which clearly showed that drugs, such as amphetamines and cocaine, could easily be used as reinforcers of behavior and that this might be the basis for what is called psychological addiction (Ray & Ksir, 1990). Moreover, Ray and Ksir suggest that "Psychological dependence, based on reinforcement, is apparently the real driving force behind even narcotic addiction, and tolerance and physical dependence are less important contributors to the basic problem" (p. 29). In general, discussions of addiction today usually include some reference to the concepts of tolerance, physical dependence, and psychological dependence. Tolerance refers to a phenomenon seen with most drugs in which repeated exposure to the same dose of the drug results in diminishing effects. The American Psychiatric Association (1994) provides diagnostic criteria for "psychoactive substance dependence" that includes tolerance and physical dependence among its determinants. These definitions are meant to be applied to the pattern of use once called drug addiction. However, it is generally recognized that the exact manner in which addiction does or does not appear in each individual depends on that person's history, personality, and the social and economic setting (Ray & Ksir, 1990).

References

American Psychiatric Association. (1994). *Diagnostic and statistical manual of mental disorders* (4th ed.). Washington, DC: Author.
Goode, E. (1993). Addiction and dependence. In E. Goode (Ed.), *Drugs, society, and behavior* (8th ed., pp. 30–34). Guilford, CT: Dushkin.
Ray, O., & Ksir, C. (1990). *Drugs, society and human behavior*. St. Louis, MO: Times/Mirror/Mosby.

Gerardo M. Gonzalez

AFFIRMATIVE ACTION—Consists of sets of institutionalized policies, procedures, and programs designed and implemented to ensure the eradication of past negative actions through which certain citizens were denied equal opportunity for full participation and success in all U.S. societal institutions. *Affirmative action* is an intentional good-faith effort to reverse the ills of the past. It is, as Washington and Harvey (1989) suggested, the corollary of benign neglect. The forerunner to affirmative action policies appears to be President Franklin Roosevelt's Executive Order 8802 (1941) requiring nondiscrimination by employers receiving government defense contracts. The earliest direct reference to the concept of affirmative action apparently is in President Lyndon B. Johnson's "Great Society" speech (1965). In proposing an economic reconstruction, Johnson's intent was to move the nation from equality as a concept to equality as a fact. Affirmative action is enunciated also in terms of societal goals to insure equal opportunity as set forth in the report of the President's Commission on Higher Education (1947): "Thus the social role of education in a democratic society is to insure equal liberty and equal opportunity to differing individuals and groups" (p. 5).

Note

    From Cheatham, H. E. (1991). Affirming affirmative action. In H. E. Cheatham and Associates (Eds.), *Cultural pluralism on campus* (pp. 9–21). Washington, DC: American College Personnel Association. Reprinted with permission of The American College Personnel Association.

References

President's Commission on Higher Education for American Democracy. (1947). *A report of the President's Commission on Higher Education: Vol. 1. Establishing the goals*. Washington, DC: Author.
Washington, V., & Harvey, W. (1989). *Affirmative rhetoric, negative action: African American faculty at predominantly White institutions* (Report No. 2). Washington, DC: George Washington University.

Harold E. Cheatham

AFRICAN AMERICAN—Customarily identifies any individual, or characteristics associated with any person, who has a lineage that can be traced to any region of Africa, south of the Sahara, and who is a citizen of the United States, usually as a result of the historical Transatlantic slave trade. Conceivably, this term identifies any person of immediate or remote African ancestry who resides in any part of the Americas; however, African American is rarely used in any way that deviates from the former definition. African American appeared for the first time in the title of a published document in Alexander's (1981) *Elijah Muhammad on African American Education: A Guide for African American and Black Studies Programs*. However, the term African American became prevalent following the establishment of the first Ph.D. program in African American Studies at Temple University in Philadelphia (Jackson, 1988). "African American" received national attention when 75 African American leaders, meeting to discuss a Black agenda, collectively expressed the preference for African American as opposed to Black to identify Americans of African descent (Edelin, 1989; Zibler, 1995). Jesse Jackson, speaking on behalf of the group, declared that Black is "baseless," while African American has "cultural integrity" (Edelin, 1989, p. 76). This assembly spawned several movements both to promote and abridge the use of African American. Advocates asseverated that, in this term, Black Americans finally had an ethnonym that resonated with their cultural heritage and would be in impetus to a cultural renaissance (Ackerman, 1989).

Opponents alleged that Black Americans, by continuing to devote time and energy to trivial semantics, would be less engaged in more urgent issues, such as crime and unemployment, and handle them with laxity (McNulty, 1989). Today, African American remains one of the most widely used terms to identify persons of African ancestry in counseling and psychotherapy publications. The American Psychological Association (1994) established that while the terms Negro and Afro-American were archaic and inappropriate for publication, both African American and Black are acceptable terms. Further, documents written in APA style format should have no hyphen between African and American.

References

Ackerman, P. (1989). "African American": A new opportunity for teaching. *Education Week, 8,* 24–25.

Alexander, E. (1981). *Elijah Muhammad on African American education: A guide for African American and Black studies programs.* New York: ECA Associates.

American Psychological Association. (1994). *The publication manual of the American Psychological Association* (4th ed.). Washington, DC: Author.

Edelin, R. (1989). African American or Black: What's in a name? *Ebony, 44,* 76–80.

Jackson, R. (1988). First Ph.D. program in African American studies. *Black Collegian, 29,* 20.

McNulty, H. (1989). Hazards of labeling: African American, black or Black? *Editor & Publisher, 122,* 5–37.

Zilber, J. (1995). "Black" versus "African American": Are Whites' political attitudes influenced by the choice of racial labels? *Social Science Quarterly, 76,* 655–664.

Ivory Achebe Toldson

AFROCENTRICITY—A worldview, quality of being, or state of consciousness that is held by people who use the history, culture, and antiquities of Africa as the vantage point or preeminent axiom through which their reality is constructed or interpreted. The Afrocentric worldview shares its origins with humanity, as human beings are naturally inclined to be partial toward their land of origin (Shujas & Lomotey, 1996). However, Afrocentrism as a formal construct is a more recent manifestation of intellectuals from continental Africa and of the African diaspora in response to European colonization and imperialism that mandated the promotion and maintenance of the *Eurocentric* (see entry) worldview among people of African descent. Diop, a Senegalese scholar, has been cited as the progenitor of Afrocentricity (Ekwe-Ekwe & Nzegwu, 1994; Spady, 1978). By demonstrating unique aspects of the lifestyle, history, linguistic patterns, and antiquities of Africa, Diop (1978) proclaimed the cultural continuity of Africa, broadened the perspectives of African intellectuals worldwide, and served as a catalyst for Black philosophical change. This international insurgence of African scholars endeavoring to resist White supremacy, and reaffirm racial and ethnic identity, lead to an epochal movement to construct paradigms and principles based on African continuity (Spady, 1978). Afrocentricity is the culmination of these ideologies, perspectives, and philosophies that were spawned by people of color desirous of adopting a worldview devoid of bias and more congruous with the intrinsic nature of Black people worldwide. As a worldview, Afrocentricity is distinguished from an ideology or philosophy in that it defines a peoples' conception of universal truths and serves as the fundamental basis for the construction of reality (Carruthers, 1980). Among the scholars who emerged during the Afrocentric rennaisance was Asante (1987; 1988) who identified Afrocentricity as a "transforming agent" that enables individuals to realize their true selfhood. He further suggested that people of African descent were born out of the conscious of "others" and needed to transform this origin into a consciousness of self (Asante, 1988). This concept had a profound impact on Black peoples' perception of the educational and social development of African Americans. Many social scientists and educators received Asante's principles as an edict for infusing Afrocentric tenets into every aspect of African American life (Dunn, 1993; Morgan, 1991; Schiele, 1994). Counseling and psychotherapy researchers and practitioners are concerned principally with the implications of Afrocentricity for the cognitive and psychosocial development of people of African descent. Dei (1994) asserted that Afrocentricity could be legitimized within epistemological constructs. By noting relevant connections of African cultural patterns to various themes of the Afrocentric perspective, such as collective responsibility, African aesthetics and spirituality, and harmony with nature, Dei avowed that Afrocentricity is an inherent quality of all people of African descent. Psychologists (e.g., Cross, 1991; Jackson, 1975) aver that Afrocentricity is a vital stage in the development of African American identity (see BLACK IDENTITY DEVELOPMENT). The Afrocentric stage of development is typified as cultivation, reaffirmation, and deeper reverence for African heritage and culture. This change in perspective, according to Cross (1991) and Jackson (1975), inevitably ushers a broader understanding and greater appreciation of other world cultures.

References

Asante, M. K. (1987). *The Afrocentric idea*. Philadelphia: Temple University Press.
Asante, M. K. (1988). *Afrocentricity*. Trenton, NJ: Africa World Press.
Carruthers, J. H. (1980). Reflections of the history of the Afrocentric worldview. *Black Books Bulletin, 7*, 4–25.
Cross, W. (1991). *Shades of Black*. Philadelphia: Temple University Press.
Diop, C. A. (Ed.). (1978). *The cultural unity of Black Africa: The domains of patriarchy and matriarchy in classical antiquity*. Chicago: Third World Press.
Dunn, F. (1993). The educational philosophies of Washington, Du Bois, and Houston: Laying the foundations for Afrocentrism and multiculturalism. *Journal of Negro Education, 62*, 24–34.
Ekwe-Ekwe, H., & Nzegwu, S. (1994). *Operationalising Afrocentrism*. London: International Institute for Black Research.
Jackson, B. (1975). Black identity development. *Journal of Educational Diversity and Innovation, 2*, 19–25.

Morgan, G. D. (1991). Africentricity in social science. *Western Journal of Black Studies, 15,* 197–206.

Schiele, J. H. (1994). Afrocentricity: Implications for higher education. *Journal of Black Studies, 25,* 150–169.

Shujas, M., & Lomotey, K. (1996). Afrocentricity. In J. Salzman, D. Smith, & C. West (Eds.), *Encyclopedia of African American culture* (pp. 79–80). New York: Simon & Schuster Macmillan.

Spady, J. (1978). Afterword. In C. A. Diop (Ed.), *The cultural unity of Black Africa: The domains of patriarchy and matriarchy in classical antiquity* (pp. 209–233). Chicago: Third World Press.

Ivory Achebe Toldson

ALASKA NATIVE—A term referring to the aboriginal inhabitants of Alaska, who settled there at least 11,000 years ago. *Alaska Native* can be divided into three groups: the Aleuts, the Yupik and the Inupiat, and the Indians. Aleuts inhabit the Alaska Peninsula and the Aleutian Islands in Southwestern Alaska. Western and Northern Alaska are inhabited by Yupik and Inupiat Eskimos. Ethnologically, Aleuts and Eskimos are not considered Indians but they have always been treated as such for the purposes of federal Indian policy. (See 53 Interior Decisions 593, 1932.) The final category of Alaska Native is comprised of Indians. There are three goups of Indians: the Tlingits in Southeastern Alaska, the Haidas also in Southeastern Alaska, and the Athabascans, who live in interior Alaska. Most pertinent to the definition of the Alaska Native was the recognition of Native rights in 1971, when the U.S. Congress approved the Alaska Native Claims Settlement Act. At this point, Alaskans of one-fourth or more native ancestry were given ownership of 12 percent of the state's territory (44 million acres) as well as $962.5 million for relinquishing their rights to the remaining land. Although they did not receive either land or money directly, they became ''shareholders'' in the regional and village corporations that were mandated by the legislation. The corporations then invested the government money in enterprises such as fish processing plants, pipeline maintenance companies and hotel management (Conlan, 1994). It is important to recognize that as with the term American Indian, the U.S. Census Bureau definition also recognizes as Alaska Native anyone who declares that he/she is Native, thus allowing for self-identification. In fact, many of the methods used for legally determining American Indian status are also used to determine Alaska Native (see AMERICAN INDIAN). This definitional category in no way captures the rich culture of those indigenous to Alaska, their hunting and survival skills needed in such a cold area, their ceremonies, dances, arts and crafts, nor their stuggle for the survival of their traditions and villages.

References

53 Interior Decisions 593. (1932, February 24). *Status of Alaskan Natives.* Washington, DC: Author.

Conlan, R., & Editors of Time–Life Books. (1994). *People of the ice and snow* (American Indian Series). Alexandria, VA: Time–Life Books.

Recommended Readings

Aponte, J., & Crouch, R. (1995). The changing ethnic profile of the United States. In J. Aponte, R. Rivers, & J. Woh (Eds.), *Psychological intervention and treatment of ethnic minorities* (pp. 1–18). Needham Heights, MA: Allyn & Bacon.
Burch, E. (1988). *The Eskimos: Echoes of the ancient world*. Norman: University of Oklahoma Press.
Dumond, D. E. (1987). *The Eskimos and Aleuts*. London: Thames and Hudson.
Getches, D., Wilkinson, C. F., & Williams, R. A., Jr. (1998). *Federal Indian law. Rights of Alaska Natives and Native Hawaiians*. St. Paul, MN: West Group.
Landgon, S. J. (1987). *The Native people of Alaska*. Anchorage, AK: Greatland Graphics.
Pamela Jumper Thurman

ALIENATION—Legally, alienation refers to the sale or transfer of any possession; from a sociological perspective, alienation refers to separation from work, society, or self and includes the concept of group or self-identification. And from a psychological perspective, alienation refers to psychological withdrawal or mental illness (Ludz, 1973). The term originally derived from Middle French and was later adapted into the Latin language. The idea of alienation traces back to the third century when Plotinus described it as an unfolding process of Divine power down into material existence (Conger, 1977). However, the term did not become popular until the nineteenth century when Karl Marx used it to refer to alienated labor. Marx described alienation as a person's loss of creativity and identity in a work force controlled by capitalism, but in need of socialism. In addition, Emile Durkheim used alienation to refer to an anomie or a separation from traditional norms of society and religion such as individualism. Anomie and alienation are sometimes used synonymously; however, they do differ historically and behaviorally (Ludz, 1973). From a psychoanalytic perspective, Sigmund Freud believed alienation was caused by the separation of the conscious and unconscious mind (Marcson, 1970). However, alienation is also used to describe feelings of dissociation.

References

Conger, J. (1977). Alienation: An overview. In B. Wolman (Ed.), *International Encyclopedia of psychiatry, psychology, psychoanalysis, and neurology* (Vol. 1, pp. 430–433). New York: For Aesculapius Publishers, Inc., by Van Nostrand Reinhold.
Ludz, P. (1973). Alienation as a concept in the social sciences. *Current Sociology, 21*, 9–124.
Marcson, S. (1970). *Automation, alienation and anomie*. New York: Harper & Row.
Joseph E. Trimble and Heather K. Mertz

ALLOCENTRISM—The tendency for individuals to place the collective's needs over their own needs. According to Triandis (1989), "*individualism and* *collectivism* should be used to characterize cultures and societies, the terms *idiocentric* and *allocentric* should be used to characterize individuals'' (p. 509). Thus, allocentrism is the conceptual equivalent to collectivism at the individual—as opposed to societal—level, and can be construed as a personality trait as opposed to a societal norm. Allocentric individuals living in collectivistic societies know what cultural/societal expecations are of them. Since most people in such societies are allocentric, cooperative, harmonious relations are expected. However, allocentric individuals living in individualistic societies can experience a great deal of stress as a result of their own behaviors tending to assume cooperation from others, but this cooperative tendency is not returned. Thus, such individuals can either be taken advantage of or be disappointed when others do not respond in a cooperative manner. On the other hand, allocentric individuals report feeling much more social support than do idiocentric individuals. Triandis and his colleagues (e.g., Bontempo, Lobel, & Triandis, 1990; Triandis, 1989, 1995; Triandis, Bontempo, Villareal, Asai, & Lucca, 1988; Triandis, Leung, Villareal, & Clack, 1985) have discussed such mismatches of cooperative styles. However, most researchers do not use the term allocentrism, applying instead the term collectivism to both individuals and societies.

References

Bontempo, R., Lobel, S., & Triandis, H. (1990). Compliance and value internalization in Brazil and the U.S. *Journal of Cross-Cultural Psychology, 21*, 200–213.

Triandis, H. C. (1989). The self and social behavior in differing cultural contexts. *Psychological Review, 96*, 506–520.

Triandis, H. C. (1995). *Individualism and collectivism.* Boulder, CO: Westview.

Triandis, H. C., Bontempo, R., Villareal, M. J., Asai, M., & Lucca, N. (1988). Individualism and collectivism: Cross-cultural perspectives on self–ingroup relationships. *Journal of Personality and Social Psychology, 54*, 323–338.

Triandis, H. C., Leung, K., Villareal, M. J., & Clack, F. L. (1985). Allocentric versus idiocentric tendencies: Convergent and discriminant validation. *Journal of Research in Personality, 19*, 395–415.

Jeffery Scott Mio

AMERASIANS—First introduced by Buck (1930), the term refers to a specific classification of children of intergroup mating. Historical and political events have influenced the use of the word Amerasian. After World War II, the term specifically applied to the progeny of Japanese ''war brides'' and American military personnel from World War II (Spickard, 1989). With the end of the Vietnam War in 1975, the term came to refer to people having Vietnamese mothers and American fathers. However, the term Amerasian can be generalized, for wherever the U.S. has become involved in Asia (such as Korea, Phillippines, Thailand, Taiwan), there are people of part-American descent (Valverde, 1992). Amerasians have been characterized in several ways: as byproducts of exploitative sexual unions resulting from social, psychological, and physical domination of colonialists over members of indigenous or colonized groups (Rex, 1971/1983; Williams, 1992), as marginal people caught between the politics of two nations that differ in race, culture, and philosophy (Valverde, 1992), and as multiculturalists who are creating a third culture by embracing Eastern and Western values, beliefs, and behaviors in all aspects of their lives (Williams, 1992).

References

Buck, P. (1930). *East wind, west wind*. New York: John Day.

Rex, J. (1983). *Race relations in sociological theory*. London: Routledge & Kegan Paul. (Original work published in 1971)

Spickard, P. R. (1989). *Mixed blood: Intermarriage and ethnic identity in twentieth-century America*. Madison: University of Wisconsin Press.

Valverde, K.L.C. (1992). From dust to gold: The Vietnamese Amerasian experience. In M.P.P. Root (Ed.), *Racially mixed people in America* (pp. 144–161). Newbury Park, CA: Sage.

Williams, T. K. (1992). Prism lives: Identity of binational Amerasians. In M.P.P. Root (Ed.), *Racially mixed people in America* (pp. 280–303). Newbury Park, CA: Sage.

MaryAnna Domokos-Cheng Ham

AMERICAN—Originally applied to a resident of America, encompassing North and South America, named after explorer Amerigo Vespucci. Now, this term is most commonly applied to residents of the United States of America. Within the field of multiculturalism, this term is used in two different ways: (1) American is used as a compound noun, consisting of a noun plus a modifier and joined by a hyphen, as in African-American, Anglo-American, and so on. This compound noun gives credit to the individual's cultural ancestry. 1990 Census figures indicate the following populations for each culturally derived subgroup: Native-American (descendants of the original inhabitants), 1.9 million; Asian-American (descendants of Chinese and Japanese immigrants who arrived between 1860 and 1920, plus more recent immigrants from those countries and from Southeast Asia and Korea; this is the most rapidly growing ethnic group), 7 million; African-American (mostly descendants of slaves), 11 million; Hispanic-American (for the most part, recent immigrants from Mexico and Central and South America; this is the second fastest growing ethnic group), 22 million; European-American, most of the remainer of the population. Total 1990 population was 254 million (*Grolier's Multimedia Encyclopedia*, 1993). (2) American is used as a description of the dominant culture, e.g., having a strong American identity aligns oneself with European-Americans; a Latina identity is in contrast to an American identity. Persons with a strong American identity are often described as very American, American-identified, or having familiarity with the American culture (Felix-Ortiz de la Garza, Newcomb, & Myers, 1995).

References

Felix-Ortiz de la Garza, M., Newcomb, M. D., & Myers, H. F. (1995). A multicultural measure of cultural identity for Latino and Latina adolescents. In A. M. Padilla

(Ed.), *Hispanic psychology: Critical issues in theory and research.* Thousand Oaks, CA: Sage.

Grolier's Multimedia Encyclopedia. (1993). Software Toolworks, Inc.

Michele Harway

AMERICAN INDIAN—An imposed ethnic category with many complex implications that continue to be controversial. The term is primarily reflective of indigenous, native people who comprise over 500 tribes living in the United States. Yet, American Indians are a very diverse ethnic group with different languages, traditions, and orientations. The 1990 U.S. Census indicates that there are approximately 1.8 million Indians, less than 1 percent of a population of 250 million people. However, it is significant to note that many Indian people refuse to participate in the U.S. Census for a variety of reasons. Further complicating the issue is the fact that many people are biracial, triracial, or multiracial, with mixed blood of Blacks, Whites, Hispanics, and other populations and may choose not to identify in only one ethnic category. This suggests that, in fact, census figures may not give a true reflection of the actual number of. American Indians. Taylor (1984) estimates that between 10 million and 20 million people in the United States have some Indian blood. Historically, the term American Indian was a generalized gloss given to the Arawak, a now extinct tribe, by Christopher Columbus who thought he had reached India (Trimble & Fleming, 1989). Thus, the term has become widely accepted. Throughout history and the making and breaking of various treaties, the Federal Government has developed a unique relationship with American Indians, which has led the U.S. Congress to establish a legal definition for American Indians. This has allowed federal entities such as the Bureau of Indian Affairs (BIA), the Indian Health Service (IHS), and the Department of Education a point from which to establish who is entitled to government and treatied services. The BIA defines an Indian as one who is (1) an enrolled or registered member of a federally recognized tribe, or (2) at least one-fourth Indian or more in blood quantum and can legally demonstrate that fact to BIA officials. This legal demonstration may consist of birth records of the individual and his/her ancestors. The U.S. Census Bureau definition differs in that it recognizes as American Indian anyone who declares that he/she is Indian, while the Department of Education (1982) allows one to be counted as Indian if he/she is a descendant of anyone who was at one time a member of a tribe. However, to qualify for federally funded educational assistance, one must be able to document one-quarter blood quantum. It is important to recognize that many tribes have established their own blood quantum requirement. For some, such as the Western Cherokee, it is a traceable roll number (indicating someone in the ancestral line who was recognized by and documented on tribal rolls as a Cherokee); for others, the blood quantum requirement may vary from one quarter to one half. Pavar (1992) offers an ethnographic definition of American Indian as an ethnological sense that a person is an Indian and only if that person has more than one half Indian blood. He also presents a legal definition and a federal two-part test defining Indian as (1) one who must have some Indian blood, and (2) the Indian community must recognize him/her as an Indian. Finally, Svennson (1973, p. 9) suggests that "Indianness is a state of being, a cast of mind, a relationship to the Universe. It is undefinable."

References

Pavar, S. L. (1992). *The rights of Indians and tribes: The ACLU guide to Indian and tribal rights.* Carbondale and Edwardsville: Southern Illinois University Press.
Svennson, F. (1973). *The ethnics in American politics: American Indians.* Minneapolis: Burgess.
Taylor, T. W. (1984). *The Bureau of Indian Affairs.* Boulder, CO: Westview.
Trimble, J., & Fleming, C. (1989). Providing counseling services for Native American Indians: Client, counselor, and community characteristics. In P. Pedersen, J. Draguns, W. Lonner, & J. Trimble (Eds.), *Counseling across cultures* (3rd ed., pp. 177–204). Newbury Park, CA: Sage.
United States Department of Commerce. (1994). *1990 U.S. census of population: Characteristics of American Indians by tribe and language* (1990, CP-3-7). Washington, DC: U.S. Government Printing Office.
United States Department of Education. (1982). *A study of alternative definitions and measures relating to eligibility and service under Part A of the Indian Education Act.* Unpublished report. Washington, DC: United States Department of Education.

Recommended Reading

Snipp, C. M. (1989). *American Indians the first of this land.* New York: Russell Sage Foundation.

Pamela Jumper Thurman

AMOK OR AMUCK—A state of madness brought on by stress or grief, followed by depression, confusion, and worry, often found among males. *Amok* manifests in a self-induced trance that evolves into a frenzy of violence and killing. Sometimes if the frenzy occurs in Malaysian public settings, people in the crowd will cry "amok, amok." Some people attribute this state of madness to a Mohammedan suicidal taboo that eventually wounds or kills the afflicted person. Amnesia and depression will commonly follow if the person suffering from amok survives. This term also means "to run wild." The word originated within the Malay language in Southeast Asia in the mid-1500s. It originally described the courageous vow men took during battle to sacrifice their own lives to defeat the enemy. Within the twentieth century, researchers have associated amok with various meanings ranging from an "epileptic dream state" to psychosis (Murphy, 1972). This behavior is used as a coping strategy for stress without being negatively judged by modern society. It is yet undetermined if this condition is cultural-specific, but some researchers have found similar cases in Kenya, New Guinea, and the Phillipines (Newman, 1964; Salisbury, 1968; Langness, 1969).

References

Langness, L. (1969). Possession in the New Guinea Highlands. *Transcultural Psychiatric Research Review, 6,* 95–100.

Murphy, H. (1972). History and the evolution of syndromes: The striking case of latah and amok. In M. Hammer, K. Salzinger, & S. Sutton (Eds.), *Psychopathology: Contributions from the Biological, Behavioral and Social Sciences* (pp. 33–55). New York: Wiley.

Newman, P. (1964). Wild man behavior in a New Guinea Highlands community. *American Anthropologist, 66,* 1–19.

Salisbury, R. (1968). Possession in the New Guinea Highlands: A review of literature. *International Journal of Social Psychiatry, 14,* 85–94.

Joseph E. Trimble and Heather K. Mertz

ANGLO-AMERICAN—Is a combination of a term of Latin origin (Anglo), which is derived from England and the English. The original usage of the compound forms denoted people of English origin or descent now living temporarily or permanently elsewhere, as in Anglo-Canadian, an English person living in Canada, or Anglo-Indian, an English person living in India, and so on. Anglo-American came to be used to depict an American whose language, ancestry, and culture were English. The shortened term Anglo is now employed to distinguish Americans of any European heritage from citizens of color and White peoples of Hispanic derivation. The evolution of this usage requires some understanding of the historical development of certain racial terminology. An Anglo-Saxon (Latin, Angli-Saxones, common in Latin documents down to 1100) was a member of one of the Germanic peoples (Angles, Saxons, and Jutes) who settled in Britain in the fifth and sixth centuries, and who were dominant in England until the Norman Conquest of 1066. Subsequent practice included the rhetorical usage of Anglo-Saxon for English in a wider ethnological sense so as to avoid the historical restriction of English as distinct from Scottish or Irish. By the 1840s, the use of Anglo-Saxon had been extended to refer to any persons of Teutonic descent who resided in Britain, whether of English, Scottish, or Irish birth, and subsequently, its colonies and dominions in America. Origin of the usage of the term Anglo lies in the early supremacy of Anglo-Saxons in the development of the colonies. The English were conceived as the founders, the settlers, the "formative population" (Higham, 1975) rather than as immigrants. The English dominated, numerically and politically, in the development of the fledgling nation. Ultimately, the language, political systems, patterns of work and settlement, and mental habits became regarded as the mainstream, accepted normative patterns. No fewer than 61 percent of the White population of the United States in 1790 were Anglo-Saxon English and 99 percent were Protestant (Steinberg, 1989). Other White, non-English speaking ethnic immigrants, such as the Italians, Greeks, Jews, Slavs, Scandinavians, and Poles, or English-speaking Catholics like the Irish, were regarded as aliens and were not privy to the power, status, nor participation in the intellectual voice. These non-British immigrants were subjected to a forced assimilation and acculturation, and obligated to adapt to English rule and dominance of both politics and culture, to the extent that a journalistic source of the era refered to the "Anglo-Saxonizing amalgamation mill" of the United States. Additionally, in the 1800s, many in the United States were committed to the justificaiton of the enslavement of Blacks and the rapidly spreading obliteration of the Indians. The emergence of the use of the word "White" arose to distinguish the European explorers, traders, and settlers from the indigenous Native Americans and Africans with whom they came into contact, even before permanent British settlement occurred in North America. Through the process of "racialization," which signifies the "extension of a racial meaning to a previously racially unclassified relationship, social practice, or group" (Gordon & Newfield, 1996, p. 179), "White" became the term of self-identity which evolved from earlier concepts of Christian, English, and free. Anti-Indian and anti-African thought played a large role in the development of "American racial Anglo-Saxonism" which Horsman (1981) asserts was intellectually dominant by the 1850s. The notion of the "White man's burden" illustrates the racism of a culture that asserted that the Anglo-Saxon was the root stock of the "American Way" and that other racial and ethnic stocks were incapable of producing the ideals. This was fed by the absorption of Western European ideas and support from the intellectual community via theories that promulgated racial classification. Throughout the history of the nation, and the subsequent dilution of some of the earlier ethnic distinctions among White Americans, the early Anglo-Saxon supremacy became generalized into a broader "Euro-American ethnocentricity" (White & Parham, 1990). One result has been institutional racism, wherein the policies, procedures, and priorities of the normative group result in unequal goals, status, access to goods and services, and blocking of economic opportunities and outcomes. The legacy of this monocultural hegemony of the White sensibility has been the oppression and subordination of non-White Americans. The powerlessness of nondominant minorities has led to minority distrust, suspicion, and hostility of the Anglos who have historically been politically less vulnerable than their minority counterparts.

References

Gordon, A., & Newfield, C. (1996). *Mapping multiculturalism.* Minneapolis: University of Minnesota Press.
Higham, J. (1975). *Send these to me.* New York: Atheneum.
Horsman, R. (1981). *Race and manifest destiny: The origin of American racial Anglo-Saxonism.* Cambridge, MA: Harvard University Press.
Jordan, W. D. (1968/1977). *White over Black: American attitudes toward the Negro.* New York: Norton.

Kallen, H. (1956). *Cultural pluralism and the American idea: An essay in social philosophy.* Philadelphia: University of Pennsylvania Press.
Roediger, D. R. (1991). *The wages of whiteness.* New York: Verso.
Steinberg, S. (1989). *Race, ethnicity and class in America.* Boston: Beacon.
White, J. L., & Parham, T. A. (1990). *The psychology of Blacks: An African-American perspective* (2nd ed.). Englewood Cliffs, NJ: Prentice-Hall.

Christine A. Bates

ARCTIC HYSTERIA—A state of hysteria or irrational behavior that manifests in stages of withdrawal, excitement, convulsions and deep sleep, and recovery where amnesia of hysteria is common (Wallace, 1961). The excitement or hysteria stage includes irrational behavior such as running naked into the cold snow drifts or ice, breaking or throwing things, and yelling obscenities. Belief has it that a psychiatrist interpreted and popularized the term into its meaning today, but in its original form, *pibloktoq* of the Inuit language means "not himself" (Foulks, 1973). Writings dating back to 1870 have reported instances of *pibloktoq* among the Alaskan Eskimos, but later have included Eskimos of North America and Greenland in the Arctic and subarctic regions. Novakovsky (1924) argues that Arctic hysteria only occurs among the people of Greenland and Siberia and should be termed "Hysterica Siberica." However, Siberia does have a similar behavior referred to as *amurakh* or *latah* (see *LATAH*). Arctic hysteria is considered to be a cultural-specific disorder that affects mostly adult females in smaller communities. One hypothesis states that the hysteria manifests itself among those women whose husbands have rejected or abused them, increasing the women's need for love and attention (Brill, 1913). Freeman, Foulks, and Freeman (1978) found among North Alaskan males that the hysteria was an acute dissociative experience stemming from failure to separate and individualize oneself from childhood. Wallace (1961), however, believes these psychological symptoms are caused by nutritional factors, particularly, a calcium deficiency.

References

Brill, A. (1913). Piblokto or hysteria among Peary's Eskimos. *Journal of Nervous Mental Disorders, 40,* 514–520.
Foulks, E. (1973). The Arctic hysterias of the North Alaskan Eskimo. *Abstracts International, 33,* 2905B.
Freeman, D., Foulks, E., & Freeman, P. (1978). Child development and Arctic hysteria in the North Alaskan Eskimo male. *Journal of Psychological Anthropology, 1,* 203–210.
Novaskovsky, S. (1924). Arctic or Siberian hysteria as a reflex of the geographic environment. *Ecology, 5,* 113–127.
Wallace, A. (1961). Mental illness, biology and culture. In F.L.K. Hsu (Ed.), *Psychological anthropology: Approaches to culture and personality* (pp. 225-295). Homewood, IL: Dorsey.

Joseph E. Trimble and Heather K. Mertz

ASIAN AMERICAN—A term used to classify more than 25 different groups, including Chinese, Japanese, Filipino, Korean, Vietnamese, Cambodian, Laotian, Hmong, and Asian Indian, that is based on their common origins in Asia, sharing of similar cultural values, and having similar physical features (Uba, 1994). The use of the term Asian American began in the late 1960s alongside the civil rights movement (Uba, 1994) and replaced the disparaging labels of Oriental, Asiatic, and Mongoloid. Paralleling the civil rights movement was the onset of Asian American studies programs on college and university campuses (Chan, 1991). Traditional Asian culture emphasizes Confucianistic principles which value the importance of specific roles and the determination of these roles in relationships (Shon & Ja, 1982). Key concepts in understanding Asian culture are obligation, especially unspoken, and shame, which help reinforce expectations of society and an individual to act properly (Shon & Ja, 1982). In 1990, Asian Americans numbered 7,272,662, or 2.9 percent of the population in the United States (same as Asian Pacific Americans; see ASIAN PACIFIC AMERICAN). The diversity of these ethnically distinct subgroups outweighs their similarities (Auerbach, 1994). Furthermore, individual differences make it difficult in making generalizations about the subgroups (Sue & Sue, 1990). The ethnic subgroups and individuals within these groups have vastly different experiences with migration, acculturation level, primary language (Sue & Sue, 1990), religion, socioeconomic status, cultural values, education, and ethnic identity (Sue & Kirk, 1973). One of the drawbacks of using the umbrella term Asian American is losing sight of these individual differences among Asian Americans and thus, the creation of stereotypes. Historically, stereotypes, such as the "yellow peril," sly, and deceitful, have been negative. Although the current major stereotype of Asian Americans, the "model minority," appears positive, the drawbacks include a lack of financial support for Asian-American communities and a tendency to pit Asian Americans against other ethnic minority groups. Furthermore, Asian Americans have been victims of horrendous discrimination, including internment camp detainment, murder, and assault (Sue & Sue, 1990). Sue and Sue (1990) further note that examination of the status of Asian Americans does not support the "successful minority" label.

References

Auerbach, S. (1994). Asian American population—diversity within. In S. Auerbach (Ed.), *Encyclopedia of multiculturalism* (Vol. 1, pp. 196–203). North Bellmore, NY: Marshall Cavendish.

Chan, S. (1991). *Asian Americans: An interpretive history*. Boston: Twayne Publishers.

Shon, S., & Ja, D. (1982). Asian families. In M. McGoldrick, J. K. Pearce, & J. Giordano (Eds.), *Ethnicity and family therapy* (pp. 208–228). New York: Guilford.

Sue, D. W., & Kirk, B. (1973). Differential characteristics of Japanese-American and Chinese-American college students. *Journal of Counseling Psychology, 20*, 142–148.

Sue, D. W., & Sue, D. (1990). *Counseling the culturally different: Theory and practice* (2nd ed.). New York: Wiley.

Uba, L. (1994). *Asian Americans: Personality patterns, identity, and mental health.* New York: Guilford.

Julie Eiko Kobayashi-Woods

ASIAN AMERICAN PSYCHOLOGICAL ASSOCIATION (AAPA)—A nonprofit, professional organization that was established to advance the welfare of Asian Americans through research and service to the Asian community (Yabusaki, 1997). The AAPA seeks to develop and apply theories of Asian American psychology, educate individuals about the sociopsychological issues faced by Asian Americans, and influence public policy that would better meet the needs of the Asian community, such as improvement of mental health services (Yabusaki, 1997). In addition, this organization is designed to further the advancement of Asian Americans. Another major focus of the AAPA is the education and training of Asian American psychologists through a mentoring program by which younger members receive support and advice of more established members (Leong, 1995; Asian American Psychologist, 1994). The AAPA, the only national organization for Asian Americans in the Social and Behavioral Sciences, was founded in December 1972 by a group of concerned Asian American mental health professionals in California (Asian American Psychologist, 1994; Leong, 1995). This association started with a handful of active members and currently includes more than 500 members from various regions of the United States. Over the years, the AAPA has been an influential source to the American Psychological Association (APA) and the National Institute of Mental Health by providing guidance and feedback regarding Asian American psychological issues (Leong, 1995). The first president of AAPA, Dr. Derald Sue, participated in and was a chairperson of APA's Committee for Equal Opportunity in Psychology (CEOP), which was a forerunner to the Board of Ethnic Minority Affairs (BEMA; currently, the Committee on Ethnic Minority Affairs, CEMA). Furthermore, the Minority Fellowship Program was partially established by the CEOP. Membership in the AAPA is open to individuals and organizations who support the interests and purposes of the Association (*Asian American Psychologist*, 1997).

References

Asian American Psychologist (1994, Spring/Summer). Phoenix, AZ: Asian American Psychological Association.

Leong, F. (1995). History of Asian American psychology. *Asian American Psychological Association Monograph Series, 1.*

Yabusaki, A. (Ed.). (1997, February). *Asian American Psychologist: A newsletter of the Asian American Psychological Association.* Phoenix, AZ: Asian American Psychological Association.

Julie Eiko Kobayashi-Woods

ASIAN PACIFIC AMERICAN (APA) [ASIAN PACIFIC ISLANDER (API)]—An American whose ethnic heritage is linked to an Asian nation or a Pacific Island. This term is related to *Asian American*, but it is more inclusive in that it includes those from Pacific island countries, states, and territories. The formal coinage of the term Asian American reportedly occurred during the student–faculty strike at San Francisco State University in 1968 (Tong, 1995). The more inclusive term of Asian Pacific American has evolved in recent years, with no specifically identified origin. It is a demographic term used primarily for census classification purposes. It should not be viewed in terms of cultural homogeneity. In fact, they are greatly diversified in geographic origins, migration patterns, languages, religious, and ethnic heritages. However, in the context of American society, they share the following salient characteristics: (a) frequent targets of anti-Asian discrimination; (b) sharing, to a different degree, the teaching of Confucian social order and a collectivistic value; and (c) sharing the importance of family (Chen & True, 1994; Fairbank, 1992). Asian Pacific Americans are the fastest growing and newest immigrant group of the mosaic of the American population. In 1990, there were 7,272,662 APAs which represented 2.9 percent of the entire U.S. population. Ninety-five percent of APA population is comprised of more than 28 separate groups of peoples of Asian ancestry. They are Chinese, Filipino, Japanese, Asian Indian, Korean, Thai, Vietnamese, and others. The separate Pacific groups include peoples from Hawaii, Samoa, Guam, Tahiti, and more than 20 other Pacific islands (U.S. Bureau of Census, 1988). Chinese and Filipino were the early settlers in America around 1760. Japanese and Koreans followed a few decades later. Most of the APAs, especially peoples from the Southeastern Asian countries, did not migrate to the U.S. until the 1970s. Despite extreme hardships and cruel discrimination, APA pioneers had made significant contributions in railroad construction, farming, mining, fishery, and trade in Hawaii and Western U.S. states (Mark & Chih, 1982). Asian American educational attainment is striking. In 1990, 40 percent of Asian Americans age 15 and over had at least four years of college, nearly double the figure of non-Hispanic Whites. In 1989, the median income of an Asian American family was $35,900—3 percent higher than the median income of $35,000 of a non-Hispanic White family. However, the per capita income of the Asian population was $14,000 compared with $14,900 for Whites, and Asians lagged behind Whites in terms of income for comparable education. The lower financial return per year of education may reflect the lingering discrimination against APA workers (O'Hara & Felt, 1991). APAs may have suffered from both the most blatant racial discrimination in institutional practices and the most extreme victimization in terms of physical violence and personal abuse. In 1882, the United States Congress passed the Chinese Exclusion Act, which initially denied the entry of Chinese laborers, despite the fact that Chinese laborers were overtly recruited years before to help build the railroads and mine the mines. This law was later broadened to any person of Chinese ancestry. It took 61 years to repeal this racist act in 1943. Anti-Asian sentiments were epitomized when Japanese

Americans were interned during World War II while their sons and daughters were serving in the Armed Services in the European battleground. Resulting from a combination of both negative media images and racial stereotyping, APAs are often identified with many demeaning labels such as: Oriental, Chink, Jap, Chinaman, Gook, Dink, Slanteyes, Banana, Yellow peril, and others. In recent years, APAs have been equally troubled by a reversed stereotyping, such as *super minority* or *model minority*, often leading to divisiveness when compared with other ethnic minorities.

References

Chen, S. A., & True, K. (1994). Asian/Pacific Island Americans. In L. D. Eron, J. H. Gentry, & P. Schlegel (Eds.), *Reason to hope: A psychological perspective on violence and youth* (pp. 145–162). Washington, DC: American Psychological Association.

Fairbank, J. (1992). *China: A new history*. Cambridge, MA: Harvard University Press.

Mark, D.M.L., & Chih, G. (1982). *A place called Chinese America*. Washington, DC: Organization of Chinese Americans, Inc.

O'Hara, W. P., & Felt, J. C. (1991). *Asian American: America's fastest growing minority group*. Washington, DC: Population Research Bureau.

Tong, B. R. (1995). Asian American psychology: A critical introduction. In K. P. Monteiro (Ed.), *Ethnic psychology* (pp. 117–126). Dubuque, IA: Kendall/Hunt.

S. Andrew Chen

ASSIMILATION—The process by which a person or group of a minority culture comes to adopt or accept the beliefs, values, attitudes, and behaviors of the majority or dominant culture to the complete extent that a person or group no longer retains the specific characteristics or loyalties which identify him/her to the minority culture (Fairchild, 1944; LaFromboise, Coleman, & Gerton, 1993; Park & Burgess, 1921; Rose, 1956). Tracing its origins to the late 1600s (Sayegh & Lasry, 1993), sociologists and anthropologists began to commonly use this term in the 1920s and 1930s to describe the processes and results of first-hand contact between two cultural groups. In his critical analysis of this concept, Gordon (1964) identified several subprocesses of assimilation: (1) *cultural or behavioral assimilation (acculturation)*; (2) *structural assimilation*; (3) *marital assimilation (amalgamation)*; (4) *identification assimilation*; (5) *attitude receptional assimilation*; (6) *behavioral receptional assimilation*; and (7) *civic assimilation*. To date, there is still a certain degree of confusion about the terms *assimilation* and *acculturation*. At times, these two terms are used to describe the same process, while in other usages, their descriptions, rather than being identical, tend to overlap. Social scientists now use the term assimilation to describe a more linear, unidirectional, and unidimensional process where a person or group chooses to relinquish or abandon the specific qualities of the minority culture to more fully adopt or acquire the beliefs, values, attitudes, and behaviors of the majority culture (Berry & Annis, 1974; Berry, 1988; Sadowsky, Lai, & Plake, 1991). In contrast, the term acculturation is used to describe a more complex, bidirectional, and multidimensional process where a person or group chooses to retain the essential qualities of the minority culture and yet also to adopt the most functional elements of the majority culture to provide the greatest congruence for this person or group to live in these two separate and distinct cultural worlds (Leong & Chou, 1994; Nagata, 1994; Rogler, Cortes, & Malgady, 1991; Sadowsky et al., 1991).

References

Berry, J. W. (1988). Acculturation and psychological adaptation: A conceptual overview. In J. W. Berry & R. C. Annis (Eds.), *Ethnic psychology: Research and practice with immigrants, refugees, native people, ethnic groups and sojourners* (pp. 41–51). Berwyn, PA: Swets North America.

Berry, J. W., & Annis, R. C. (1974). Acculturative stress: The role of ecology, culture, and differentiation. *Journal of Cross-Cultural Psychology, 5*, 382–405.

Fairchild, H. P. (1944). *Dictionary of sociology.* New York: Philosophical Library.

Gordon, M. M. (1964). *Assimilation in American life.* New York: Oxford University Press.

LaFromboise, T., Coleman, H., & Gerton, J. (1993). Psychological impact of biculturalism: Evidence and theory. *Psychological Bulletin, 14*, 395–412.

Leong, F.T.L., & Chou, E. L. (1994). The role of ethnic identity and acculturation in the vocational behavior of Asian Americans: An integrative review. *Journal of Vocational Behavior, 44*, 155–172.

Nagata, D. (1994). Assessing Asian American acculturation and ethnic identity: The need for a multidimensional framework. *Asian American and Pacific Islander Journal of Health, 2*, 108–124.

Park, R. E., & Burgess, E. W. (1921). *Introduction to the science of sociology.* Chicago: University of Chicago Press.

Rogler, L. H., Cortes, D. E., & Malgady, R. G. (1991). Acculturation and mental health status among Hispanics. *American Psychologist, 46*, 585–597.

Rose, A. M. (1956). *Sociology: The study of human relations.* New York: Alfred A. Knopf.

Sadowsky, G. R., Lai, E.W.M., & Plake, B. S. (1991). Moderating effects of sociocultural variables on acculturation attitudes of Hispanics and Asian Americans. *Journal of Counseling and Development, 70*, 194–203.

Sayegh, L., & Lasry, J. (1993). Immigrants' adaptation in Canada: Assimilation, acculturation, and orthogonal cultural identification. *Canadian Psychology, 34*, 98–109.

Phillip D. Akutsu

ATAQUE (DE NERVIOS)—Term used to describe a cultural specific syndrome seen in Spanish-speaking people of the Caribbean Islands (Cuba, Dominican Republic, Puerto Rico), and Hispanic/Latino immigrants to the United States. *Ataque* represents culturally sanctioned responses to acute stressful experiences, particularly relating to grief, loss, fear, and family conflict. A variety of physical symptoms ranging from trembling to loss of consciousness, chest tightness, and spells are part of ataque. The person may begin to shout, swear, strike out at others, fall to the ground, and experience convulsive body movements. These symptoms elicit support from the person's social network expressed through focusing attention on the afflicted person, praying over them, and interventions that resolve the conflict which triggered the ataque. The person usually regains consicousness and does not remember the ataque. *Ataque* is of short duration and is frequently resolved without need for medical intervention (Oquendo, Horwath, & Martinez, 1989).

Reference

Oquendo, M., Horwath, E., & Martinez, A. (1989). *Ataque de nervios*: Proposed diagnostic criteria for a culture specific syndrome. *Culture, Medicine and Psychiatry, 16*, 367–376.

Sandra I. Lopez-Baez

B

BACKLASH—The word backlash first appeared in English in 1815 (Merriam Webster, 1997) and referred to the sudden backward movement of mechanical gears. In the early part of the twentieth century, a second definition appeared in Webster's Dictionary which described backlash as ''a strong adverse reaction (as to a recent political or social development)'' (Merriam Webster, 1997, p. 84). In contemporary American usage, the term backlash appears to refer to recurring attempts by the privileged class to rescind recently won rights and liberties gained by an underpriviledged group or class. This latter interpretation became part of American consciousness after journalist Susan Faludi published her 1991 book, *Backlash: The Undeclared War Against Women.* In it, Faludi describes backlash as ''a powerful counterassault on women's rights . . . an attempt to retract the handful of small and hard-won victories that the feminist movement [managed] to win for women'' (Faludi, 1991, p. xviii). According to her thesis, a reaction against the ''women's movement'' was first noted during the Victorian Age and appeared again in the early 1900s, the early 1940s, and the 1970s. The backlash derives not from a conspiracy but from a number of sources including the popular press, the ''New Right,'' fundamentalist ideology, pop psychology, anti-feminists (male and female), and even ''scientific'' findings. The general consensus among these sources is that feminism has made women's lives miserable and is responsible for ''female burnout,'' the ''infertility crisis,'' and the ''marriageable male shortage'' which would all disappear if women would just get back into the kitchen and the nursery. Although not described explicitly in contemporary literature, the term backlash could apply to recent counterassaults on undocumented workers, affirmative action programs, abortion clinics, same-sex marriage, and other proposed equal rights' legislation for gays, lesbians and bisexuals, Native American-run casinos, and people with disabilities.

Reference

Faludi, S. (1991). *Backlash: The undeclared war against American women*. New York: Crown.
Merriam-Webster's Collegiate Dictionary (10th ed.). (1997). Springfield, MA: Merriam-Webster.

Monica D. Lange

BARRIERS TO EFFECTIVE CROSS-CULTURAL COUNSELING AND PSYCHOTHERAPY—Characteristics of the therapist or client, or of the therapist–client interaction or larger environmental context, that reduce the accuracy of assessment or attenuate intervention outcome. Historically, concerns about barriers to effective cross-cultural counseling and psychotherapy were anticipated by recognition of culture-bound syndromes (late 1800s), the cultural relativism of normality (1930s), and biases of Western diagnostic methods used in epidemiological studies (1950s; Marsella, 1993). However, it was not until the 1960s that community mental health programs expanded to provide services to ethnic minorities and made evident the deficiencies of traditional interventions as practiced in the field (Rogler, Malgady, Constantino, & Blumenthal, 1987). Since then, various schools of cross-cultural counseling and psychotherapy (e.g., multicultural counseling, cultural psychiatry, cross-cultural behavior therapy) have hypothesized specific barriers to effective service delivery (Kleinman, 1977; Sue & Sue, 1990; Tanaka-Matsumi, Seiden, & Lam, 1996), and empirical evidence has been reviewed (Sue, Zane, & Young, 1994). Some barriers proposed include *culture-bound values* (e.g., verbal/emotional/behavioral expressiveness), *class-bound values* (e.g., long-term goal setting), and *language variables* (e.g., monolingual English orientation; Sue & Sue, 1990). Another is what Kleinman (1977) termed the *category fallacy*, or the tendency to apply categories from one's own culture (e.g., Western diagnoses) to the behavior of patients from another. Lòpez (1989) similarly warned that when a client's behavior is not evaluated in relation to norms of his/her own cultural reference group, the result may be overpathologization or minimization of symptom severity, and overdiagnosis or underdiagnosis. Proposed remedies to these barriers include *cultural sensitivity training* (Leong & Kim, 1991), *negotiation of client–therapist communication strategies and symptom meaning* (Higginbotham, West, & Forsyth, 1988), and *determination of culturally relevant problems, controlling variables, target behaviors, interventions, and procedures for outcome monitoring* (Tanaka-Matsumi et al., 1996).

References

Higginbotham, H. N., West, S. G., & Forsyth, D. R. (1988). *Psychotherapy and behavior change: Social, cultural and methological perspectives*. New York: Pergamon.

Kleinman, A. (1977). Depression, somatization and the "new cross-cultural psychiatry." *Social Science and Medicine, 11,* 3–10.

Leong, F.T.L., & Kim, H.H.W. (1991). Going beyond cultural sensitivity on the road to multiculturalism: Using the intercultural sensitizer as a counselor training tool. *Journal of Counseling and Development, 70,* 112–118.

Lòpez, S. R. (1989). Patient variable biases in clinical judgment: Conceptual overview and methodological considerations. *Psychological Bulletin, 106,* 184–203.

Marsella, A. J. (1993). Sociocultural foundations of psychopathology: An historical overview of concepts, events and pioneers prior to 1970. *Transcultural Psychiatric Research Review, 30,* 97–142.

Rogler, L. H., Malgady, R. G., Constantino, G., & Blumenthal, R. (1987). What do culturally sensitive mental health services mean? *American Psychologist, 42,* 565–570.

Sue, D. W., & Sue, D. (1990). *Counseling the culturally different: Theory and practice* (2nd ed.). New York: Wiley.

Sue, S., Zane, N., & Young, K. (1994). Research on psychotherapy with culturally diverse populations. In A. E. Bergin & S. L. Garfield (Eds.), *Handbook of psychotherapy and behavior change* (4th ed., pp. 783–817). New York: Wiley.

Tanaka-Matsumi, J., Seiden, D. Y., & Lam, K. N. (1996). The Culturally-Informed Functional Assessment (CIFA) Interview: A strategy for cross-cultural behavioral practice. *Cognitive and Behavioral Practice, 3,* 215–233.

Douglas Y. Seiden

BASQUE—One of five distinct cultural regions in Spain which is divided into three provinces. The Basque people live on the northern coastline and in the Pyrenees, and speak a language all their own—unrelated to Latin or any other Romance language. The Basque call themselves *Eskualdunak* and call their homeland *Eskual Herria* or *Euzkadi*, thought to be a derivative of the Basque word for "sun" (Gallop, 1970). In the United States, Basques came in large numbers to California in 1849. Many had been living in Central and South America, particularly Chile, and had immigrated to California after Mexico ceded "Alta California" to the United States in the Treaty of Guadalupe Hidalgo on February 2, 1848 (Douglass & Bilbao, 1975). This migration occurred because of gold in California and because of California's easy access to the ocean. Later, Basques immigrated to the Buffalo, New York, area between 1902 and 1920. Currently, over 50,000 Basques live in the United States, with the largest concentration in the American West.

References

Douglass, W. A., & Bilbao, J. (1975). *Amerikanuak: Basques in the new world.* Reno: University of Nevada Press.

Gallop, R. (1970). *A book of the Basques.* Reno: University of Nevada Press.

Cindy Yee and Jeffery Scott Mio

BICULTURAL—Often used interchangeably with *biracial*. In considering these terms, there are at least two areas worthy of attention. First, the term can refer to a person who is biracial, produced through the intermarriage of two parents from different ethnicities and/or races. Second, bicultural can refer to anyone who is a product of two cultures or even microcultures and moves between two cultural norms and expectations. The Puerto Rican woman is bicultural because she is a product of at least two different microcultures: Puerto Rican and woman, given that gender and the Puerto Rican culture dictate social expectations and behaviors. The product of intermarriage is the more common usage of the term. Social conditions and interactions among different ethnic groups have expanded, giving permission and acceptance to interracial marriages and partnerships which in turn have produced bicultural and/or biracial children. Gibbs (1989) wrote that a population of young people with unique characteristics, potential problems, and special needs was emerging which needed attention because of their ambiguous ethnicity and their need to define their identity. Root (1990) stated that because of society's treatment of races as being unequal, those with mixed ethnicities become marginalized.

References

Gibbs, J. T. (1989). Biracial adolescents. In J. T. Gibbs & L. N. Huang (Eds.), *Children of color* (pp. 322–350). San Francisco: Jossey-Bass.

Root, M.P.P. (1990). Resolving "other" status: Identity development of biracial individuals. In M.P.P. Root & L. S. Brown (Eds.), *Diversity and complexity in feminist therapy* (pp. 185–205). New York: Harrington Park.

Adelaida Santana Pellicier

BILINGUAL—The ability to read, write, speak, and/or understand two different languages; it can also be used as a noun to describe someone who has that ability. Historically, however, many different definitions have been employed due to the inclusion of additional criteria, such as *proficiency, language acquisition, frequency of language use*, and the distinction between *expressive and receptive skills* (Abudarham, 1987). In psychology, bilingualism has been studied at both individual and societal levels of analysis. At the individual level, researchers have been concerned with the acquisition, development, use, and consequences of a second language. For example, the possible association between bilingualism and intelligence has been much researched (Edwards, 1994). In clinical and counseling psychology, empirical findings demonstrate that the language of inquiry directly affects the diagnosis (Edgerton & Karno, 1971; Malgady, Rogler, & Constantino, 1989; Marcos, Ureuyo, Kesselman, & Alpert, 1973), assessment (Lopez & Taussig, 1991), and psychotherapy treatment of clients (Sue, Fujino, Hu, Takeuchi, & Zane, 1991). In society, controversy has surrounded the use of English by U.S. immigrants (Wagner, 1981). As stated by Hakuta and Garcia (1989), the policy debate concerns how long, how much, and how intensely native language instruction should be used to best educate students with limited English ability. Research has focused on the efficacy of different teaching methods as well as community opposition to bilingual education. Hakuta and Garcia (1989) noted that program evaluations typically concentrate on linguistic factors rather than other indicators of academic achievement, such as grade point average or dropout rates.

References

Abudarham, S. (1987). Terminology and typology. In S. Abudarham (Ed.), *Bilingualism and the bilingual: An interdisciplinary approach to pedagogical and remedial issues* (pp. 1–14). Berkshire, England: Nfer-Nelson.
Edgerton, R. B., & Karno, M. (1971). Mexican-American bilingualism and the perception of mental illness. *Archives of General Psychiatry, 24,* 286–290.
Edwards, J. (1994). *Multilingualism.* New York: Routledge.
Hakuta, K., & Garcia, E. E. (1989). Bilingualism and education. *American Psychologist, 44,* 374–379.
Lopez, S. R., & Taussig, I. M. (1991). Cognitive–intellectual functioning of Spanish-speaking impaired and nonimpaired elderly: Implications for culturally sensitive assessment. *Psychological Assessment: A Journal of Consulting and Clinical Psychology, 3,* 448–454.
Malgady, R. G., Rogler, L. H., & Constantino, G. (1989). Ethnocultural and linguistic bias in mental health evaluation of Hispanics. *American Psychologist, 42,* 228–234.
Marcos, L. R., Ureuyo, L., Kesselman, M., & Alpert, M. (1973). The language barrier in evaluating Spanish-American clients. *Archives of General Psychiatry, 29,* 655–659.
Sue, S., Fujino, D. C., Hu, L. T., Takeuchi, D. T., & Zane, N.W.S. (1991). Community mental health services for ethnic minority groups: A test of the cultural responsiveness hypothesis. *Journal of Counseling Psychology, 59,* 533–540.
Wagner, S. T. (1981). The historical background of bilingualism and biculturalism in the United States. In M. Ridge (Ed.), *The new bilingualism: An American dilemma* (pp. 29–52). Los Angeles: University of Southern California Press.

Jonathan Kaplan

BILINGUAL EDUCATION—The use of two languages, one of which is the mother tongue and the other is English, as mediums of instruction for any or all parts of the school curriculum for a student population in a program. It is the term found in the education literature prior to 1973. Bilingual education programs were expanded to incorporate the cultural background of the students into the curriculum with the reauthorization of the Bilingual Education Act in 1974. This marked the beginning of the use of the term *bilingual bicultural education.* Currently, the term bilingual education is preferred. Bilingual education in the United States has its roots in the late seventeenth century. It was used by some local schools up until the late nineteenth century when there was a backlash against immigrants, which also led to a decline in bilingual education. It was virtually eradicated in the United States and its colonies during World Wars I and II. Modern bilingual education got started again with the 1963 Coral Way Elementary School experiment in Dade County, Florida, with the influx of Cubans to Miami after the Cuban Revolution (Cordasco, 1976). English as a

Second Language (ESL) Programs have often been confused as a form of bilingual education. ESL is a method developed in the 1930s to teach English to foreign diplomats and university students, but it does not involve the use of the mother tongue.

Reference

Cordasco, F. (1976). *Bilingual schooling in the United States: A sourcebook for educational personnel.* New York: McGraw-Hill.

Maria Rodriguez

BIRACIAL—Utilized to describe persons who by virtue of their biological parents' racial identities are of two distinctly different racial backgrounds (Gibbs, 1989). The 1967 repeal of the antimiscegenation laws in the United States was followed by an increase in births of persons of biracial heritage, thus challenging long-standing beliefs regarding the biological, social, and moral meaning of race (Root, 1992). It has been estimated by population experts and multiracial support networks that there are at least a million biracial persons in the United States (Funderburg, 1994). Other terms related to biracial are multiracial, interracial, miscegenation, and mixed marriage (see entries for these terms).

References

Funderburg, L. (1994). *Black, White, other: Biracial Americans talk about race and identity.* New York: Morrow.
Gibbs, J. T. (1989). Biracial adolescents. In J. T. Gibbs & L. N. Huang (Eds.), *Children of color: Psychological interventions with minority youth* (pp. 322–350). San Francisco: Jossey-Bass.
Root, M.P.P. (Ed.). (1992). *Racially mixed people in America.* Newbury Park, CA: Sage.

Kelley R. Kenney

BLACK AMERICAN—Used to define or identify any person, or anything pertaining to (e.g., Black American music) people who are of African origin or descent, and are citizens or long-term residents of America, especially the United States. With an estimated population of 33 million, 12.6 percent of the American population, Black Americans constitute the largest non-White ethnic group in the United States (*Statistical Abstract of the United States*, 1995). The progenies or victims of the transatlantic slave trade comprise the majority of contemporary Black Americans. During the period from 1619–1863, millions of Africans were involuntarily relocated from various regions of West Africa to the newly established English colonies of North America (Asante, 1991). Casualties of this trade consisted of many different African ethnic groups including Congo, Yoruba, Wolof, and Ibo. The Black American population is the aggregate of these groups, consolidated into one race, bound by a common struggle against racial oppression and distinguished by cultural dualism. Du Bois (1969) illustrated cultural dualism in his observation that the Black American has "two souls, two thoughts, two unreconciled strivings; two warring ideals in one dark body, whose dogged strength alone keeps it from being torn asunder" (p. 23). The term Black is the world's oldest and most widely used ethnonym for people of African descent. Before the recorded birth of Christ, King Solomon used the term Black as an expression of homage toward his African wife with the phrase, "You are Black and comely" (Mills & Wilson, 1995, p. 1279). Subsequent documentation of Black are present in historic and momentous publications including Shakespeare's (1591/1924) notion, "Black men are pearls in 'beauteous' ladies eyes" (p. 57), and Pepys (1661) who wrote, "I found her to be a pretty, modest, Black woman" (p. 103). Clearly, Black often was used endearingly in early literature. However, as this term emerged into the Western world, where European settlers subjected people of color to the tyrannical cruelties of slavery and racial oppression, White racists made many attempts to reduce Black to a term of indignation and reproach. As a result, for centuries many Africans in America, experiencing Black in its connotation of subordination and despair, objected to the use of the term Black American. The use of designations such as Colored, Negro, and Afro-American became more popular. In the 1960s–1970s, during the Black Power revolution, Americans of African origin began to empower Black Americans to redefine and reaffirm racial and ethnic culture and identity (Meier, 1970). Phases and slogans such as "Black is Beautiful," "Black Pride," and "Black is Back" became increasingly popular as African Americans fought to overcome the vestiges of slavery and give reverence and adulation to their natural, physical attributes and cultural heritage (Smith, 1995). Today, Black American remains one of the two most commonly used terms to identify Americans of African descent (African American is the other; see entry). According to the American Psychological Association (1994), Black American and African American are the only two terms appropriate for use in publications written in APA style format. It is relatively unimportant, and contingent upon the subjective judgment of the author, whether or not to use African American and Black American in publications. As a practitioner of counseling and psychotherapy, however, it is often important to determine the clients' preference before using either of these terms in a clinical setting.

References

American Psychological Association. (1994). *The publication manual of the American Psychological Association* (4th ed.). Washington, DC: Author.

Asante, M. (1991). African Americans. In T. O'Leary (Ed.), *Encyclopedia of world cultures* (Vol. 1, pp. 10–17). Boston: G. K. Hall.

Du Bois, W.E.B. (1969). *The souls of Black folk*. New York: New American University Press.

Meier, A. (1970). *Black protest of the sixties*. Chicago: Quadrangle Books.

Mills, W., & Wilson, R. (1995). *Mercer commentary on the Bible*. Macon, GA: Mercer University Press.

Pepys, S. (1661). *The diary of Samuel Pepys: A new and complete transcription* (R. Latham & W. Matthews, Trans.). Berkeley: University of California Press.

Shakespeare, W. (1591/1924). *Two gentlemen of Verona* (K. Young, Trans.). New Haven, CT: Yale University Press.

Smith, K. (1995). *The Harlem cultural/political movements, 1960–1970: From Malcolm X to "Black is beautiful."* New York: Gumbs & Thomas.

Statistical Abstracts of the United States (115th ed.). (1995). Washington, DC: U.S. Bureau of the Census.

Ivory Achebe Toldson

BLACK IDENTITY DEVELOPMENT—A lifelong, natural, progressive process among Black people, marked by a series of gradual changes in one's subjective view of reality that succeed one another in a relatively fixed way, and ultimately lead toward a more elevated understanding and appreciation of Black heritage and culture. Although many Black psychologists have varying interpretations of the successive stages of Black identity, each avers that the development of Black people is not embedded in mental illness or self-hate, but is a natural inclination to oppose mis-education, and reaffirm and internalize Black culture, heritage, folkways, or identity. The quest for a bona fide cultural identity has been ubiquitous in the lives and experiences of "New Africans" or African Americans since the earliest stages of Black American history (Cross, 1971). Throughout the years of enslavement, and the worst periods of racial oppression, there is evidence of Black people in America striving to reject imposed inferiority and progress toward a more positive, cultivated regard for oneself. The lives and experiences of Harriet Tubman, Nat Turner, and Malcolm X are exemplars of this phenomenon. As a formal construct, *Black Identity Development* was spawned by the 1960s' Black Power movement. During this period, there was a renaissance of Black sociologists and psychologists striving to construct a paradigm to explain African American adaptation, and contravene prevailing theories that portrayed Blackness as synonymous to mental impairment. The Nigrescence models born of this renaissance are set forth in the works of Banks (1981), Cross (1971), Gay (1984), Helms (1986), Jackson (1975), Milliones (1980), Parham (1989), Thomas (1971), and Toldson and Pasteur (1975). Typically, Nigrescence models have four or five stages, through which an individual of African descent undergoes a series of cognitive and behavior changes. Through these gradual phases or transitions, one's identity evolves from a previous state, characterized by the internalization of subjugation, to a sublime state, whereby one exudes confidence and efficacy in self and culture (Cross, 1971). When using Nigrescence models in counseling and psychotherapy, the most important consideration is that interviewing style should be modified to match the client's ethnic level of awareness or the client's internal frame of reference (Ivey, 1993).

References

Banks, J. A. (1981). The stages of ethnicity: Implications for curriculum reform. In J. A. Banks (Ed.), *Multiethnic education: Theory and practice* (pp. 129–139). Boston: Allyn & Bacon.

Cross, W. E. (1971). The Negro-to-Black conversion experience: Toward a psychology of Black liberation. *Black World, 20*, 13–27.

Gay, G. (1984). Implications of selected models of ethnic identity development for educators. *The Journal of Negro Education, 54*, 43–53.

Helms, J. E. (1986). Expanding racial and identity theory to cover counseling process. *Journal of Counseling Psychology, 33*, 62–64.

Ivey, A. (1993). *Counseling and psychotherapy: A multicultural perspective* (3rd ed.). Needham Heights, MA: Allyn & Bacon.

Jackson, B. (1975). Black identity development. In L. Golubschick & B. Persky (Eds.), *Urban social and educational issues* (pp. 158–164). Dubuque, IA: Kendall/Hall.

Milliones, J. (1980). Construction of a Black consciousness measure: Psychotherapeutic implications. *Psychotherapy: Theory, Research and Practice, 17*, 175–182.

Parham, T. A. (1989). Cycles of psychological nigrescence. *The Counseling Psychologist, 17*, 197–226.

Thomas, C. (1971). *Boys no more*. Beverly Hills, CA: Glencoe Press.

Toldson, I. L., & Pasteur, A. (1975). Developmental stages of Black self-discovery: Implications for using Black art forms in group interaction. *Journal of Negro Education, 44*, 130–138.

Ivory Achebe Toldson

BORIQUÉN—A Spanish term meaning "the land of the brave lord," which the native Taíno Indians (see TAÍNO) gave to Puerto Rico. Puerto Ricans call one another *Boricua* (from *Boriquén*) as a form of bonding that reaffirms their ancient roots (Pane, 1973).

Reference

Pane, F. R. (1973). Account of the antiquities or customs of the Indians. In K. Wagenheim & O. J. Wagenheim (Eds.), *The Puerto Ricans*. New York: Anchor Books.

Cindy Yee

BRACEROS—Mexican immigrants recruited to work on a temporary basis in the United States. The term derived from the Spanish word *brazo*, meaning "arm" (De Varona, 1996). Braceros literally translates into someone who works with his arms, or a "hired hand." The Bracero Program was initiated in the United States in August 1942, after many male American workers went to fight during World War II, and the country was in desperate need of farm and industrial laborers to replace them (Bean & Tienda, 1987). The program was also designed, albeit with limited success, to ensure fair and humane treatment of Mexican workers in the United States. Mistreatment and discrimination in Texas was so extensive, in fact, that the Mexican government actually barred its citi-

zens from working there (De Varona, 1996). By the end of the bracero agreements in 1964, over 4 million Mexican nationals had come to the United States
as temporary workers (Ganster, 1996).

References

Bean, F. D., & Tienda, M. (1987). *The Hispanic population of the United States*. New
    York: Russell Sage Foundation.
De Varona, F. (1996). *Latino literacy: The complete guide to our Hispanic history and
    culture*. New York: Henry Holt.
Ganster, P. (1996). Bracero. In B. A. Tenenbaum, G. M. Magassy, M. Karasch, J. J.
    TePaske, & R. L. Woodward, Jr. (Eds.), *Encyclopedia of Latin American history
    and culture* (Vol. 1, pp. 403–404). New York: Charles Scribner's Sons.

Cindy Yee

C

CAMBODIAN AMERICAN—Since 1979, approximately 150,000 Cambodian refugees have settled in the United States (Carl, 1995; Crystal, 1995). Most live in California, Massachusetts, and Washington. Cambodian Americans are members of one of the youngest ethnic groups in America with a median age of 19.4 years. Cambodian Americans often remained outsiders to the new country and only about 20 percent have become naturalized citizens. Adapting to the American economy has been difficult. In Cambodia, most were farmers, while in the United States, many settled in cities. Forty-two percent of the Cambodian families live below the poverty line. Cambodian Americans face special mental and physical health problems resulting from their tragic recent history. Between 1975 and 1979, the brutal *Khmer Rouge* regime ruled Cambodia. Upward of 2 million of the country's 7 million people died or were killed due to the Khmer Rouge regime. As a result, many Cambodian Americans suffer from physical and emotional trauma (Sack & Clarke, 1996). Traditional music, dance, wood carving, painting, and silk weaving are of high value, and a great emphasis is placed on maintaining this link with their heritage. Also, traditional and important means of education occur through the use of proverbs. The family is extremely important to Cambodian Americans, and young children are especially treasured. Women often occupy a key position in the household and are in charge of the family budget and other family assets. In 1990, about 25 percent of Cambodian American households were headed by women. Buddhism is the traditional religion of Cambodia. One of the main beliefs is that all worldly things are considered changing and impermanent. Consequently, being attached to worldly things will lead to suffering as the soul goes through the cycle of rebirth. Meditation and a morally disciplined life can enable a believer to overcome desires and optimally acheive *Nirvana*, a state of perfect peace and enlightenment. The belief in *karma*, a concept meaning that present situations are determined by past lives and that good fortune is a result of virtuous past lives while bad fortune is a result of flawed or impure past lives, has often led Cambodians to wonder if their current suffering is the result of a collective fault of the nation.

References

Carl, B. L., III. (1995). Cambodian Americans. In R. J. Vecoli (Ed.), *Gale encyclopedia of multicultural America* (Vol. 1, pp. 227–237). New York: Gale Research.
Crystal, E. (1995). Cambodian Americans. In F. Ng (Ed.), *The Asian American encyclopedia* (pp. 163–166). New York: Marshall Cavendish.
Sack, W. H., & Clarke, G. N. (1996). Multiple forms of stress in Cambodian adolescent refugees. *Child Development, 67*, 107–116.

Rakefet Richmond

CARE/CAREGIVING—The term *care* appeared as early as the thirteenth century, and was commonly used in Shakespearean works in the 1600s (Simpson & Weiner, 1989). Care means to look after, or to provide for. The term caregiving is currently used primarily in gerontological literature and is used to describe the informal care of a sick, disabled, or elderly family member in the home (Stephens & Christianson, 1986). Duties performed include day-to-day housework and personal attention including feeding, transport from bed to commode, and bathing. Caregiving may also include staying with a person who requires supervision over daily tasks. The relationship that the caregiver has to the person cared for often influences the types of tasks that are undertaken. Stephens and Christianson (1986) reported that spouses and children are more likely than other relatives to engage in such activities as meal preparation and shopping. A division of labor based on gender also seems to exist in that sons of disabled persons tend to manage their finances, while daughters tend to provide a wider range of support services. In the 1970s, many people started paying attention to the fact that caring of this genre was common and that these caregivers were often unable to accept paid employment due to the extent of their caregiving in the home (Tulloch, 1991). In the 1980s, it became evident that these individuals needed support in the work they were doing. It was also found that caregivers can suffer from tremendous stress as a result of their caregiving (Belsky, 1990). Stress can be exacerbated by a number of factors, including a poor relationship with the individual cared for prior to the illness and a lack of appreciation accorded to the caregiving services or caregiver (see ETHNOCARING).

References

Belsky, J. K. (1990). *The psychology of aging* (2nd ed.). Pacific Grove, CA: Brooks/ Cole.
Simpson, J. A., & Weiner, E.S.C. (Eds.). (1989). *The Oxford English dictionary* (2nd ed.). Oxford: Oxford University Press.

Stephens, S. A., & Christianson, J. B. (1986). *Informal care of the elderly*. Lexington, KY: Lexington Books.

Tulloch, S. (Ed.). (1991). *The Oxford dictionary of new words: A popular guide to words in the news*. Oxford: Oxford University Press.

La Verne A. Berkel

CAREER DEVELOPMENT—Used to describe and explain the systematic changes in a person's vocational behavior observed over time. The term is used interchangeably with *vocational development* and *life-span planning*, although *career development* is the preferred usage. It was a concept developed as part of a developmental theoretical perspective to explain vocational choice as an ongoing process rather than a single, independent decision. The work of Ginzberg, Ginzberg, Axelrod, and Herma in the early 1950s, later expanded by Donald Super (cited in Axelson, 1993), constitute the pioneer work in career development theory. Vocationally related behaviors came to be viewed as important aspects of general human development, which could be observed in different ways at different developmental life stages. Most career development theories have emerged out of mainstream cultural values and experiences, and research has been conducted primarily on the middle class and White males. This has limited the generalizability of these theories for special populations such as ethnic and racial minorities, who have different social-psychological experiences. Some theorists have recognized the possible influence of race, ethnicity, and socioeconomic status on the process of career development, but they do not explain how this occurs.

Reference

Axelson, J. A. (1993). *Counseling and development in a multicultural society*. Monterey, CA: Brooks/Cole.

Maria Rodriguez

CAUCASIAN—See WHITE.

CENTRAL AMERICAN—Those individuals from Belize, Guatemala, El Salvador, Honduras, Nicaragua, and Costa Rica. Although these countries were part of the Spanish conquest during the 1520s to 1690s, there remains considerable ethnic and cultural diversity among the people of this region. For example, about half of Guatemala's population is Indian and speak a variety of indigenous languages, whereas in Costa Rica there remains a strong European influence with many of its people speaking English as the dominant language. In El Salvador, Honduras, and Nicaragua there is a *mestizo* ethnic element heavily influenced by the Black and Black Indian populations of the Caribbean coastal areas (Millett, 1991, p. 318). Central Americans have quickly become one of the fastest growing immigrant groups. It is estimated that approximately 1.3 million

Central Americans, particularly from El Salvador, Nicaragua, Guatemala, and Honduras, have migrated to the United States (U.S. Bureau of the Census, 1993).

References

Millett, R. (1991). Central America: Background to the crisis. In J. Knippers Black (Ed.), *Latin America: Its problems and its promise* (2nd ed., pp. 317–345). Boulder, CO: Westview.

U.S. Bureau of the Census. (1993). *Hispanic Americans today*. Current Population Reports. (P23:183). Washington, DC: U.S. Government Printing Office.

Azara L. Santiago-Rivera

CHAMORRO—Indigenous people of the Mariana Islands. In Spanish literature, this term literally meant *man with a shorn head*, perhaps of Iberian origin. *Chamorro* is akin to the Basque terms *sumur* and *sumurr tender*. History has divided the people of the Mariana Islands into Chamorros from Guam (a territory of the United States since 1898) and the Northern Marianas (a commonwealth of the United States since 1975). What remains consistent in Chamorros' historical experience is 300 years of colonization from Spain and most recently the United States. In the 1990 U.S. Census, the Chamorros (commonly referred to as *Guamanians*) represent the third largest Pacific Island group in the United States. Of the 133,000 people living on Guam, over 57,000 claim Chamorro ethnicity. Chamorros live in every state in the United States (over 50,000 Guamanians and Northern Mariana Islanders), with the largest concentration living in California. Given these figures, the total number of Chamorros in the United States, including the territory of Guam, exceeds 107,000. There is much confusion regarding the identity of Chamorros. After World War II, the term Guamanian was used to distinguish the Chamorros from Guam and those from the Northern Marianas. In addition to using the term Guamanians to differentiate the different political status, the term has been recently used in a looser sense to account for all people living on Guam regardless of their ethnicity or national origin. The erroneous usage of the term Guamanians has precipitated the concern for Chamorro identity.

Reference

Shimizu, D. (1982). *Mental health needs assessment: The Guamanians in California*. Unpublished doctoral dissertation, University of Massachusetts.

Patricia Taimanglo Pier

CHANGE AGENT—Refers to any entity that purposefully works for shifts from the status quo. Egan (1985) describes the agent as, ''anyone who plays an important part in designing, redesigning, running, renewing or improving any system, subsystem or program'' (p. 12). The referent may be an individual or class of individuals, such as a therapist or counselor, consultant or teacher, or it may be a system or subsystem which works for change, churches, schools, civil rights organizations, families, community organizations, or political parties. Given the many possible agents, the literature on this topic is quite varied. Sample articles on this topic would include Atkinson, Thompson, and Grant's (1993) article on counseling ethnic minorities, Kline's (1995) article on community psychology and school consultation, Pearce and Osmond's (1996) article on change in organizational settings, and Stokols' (1986) article on change via research. The change agent looks at the institutional environment that creates stress and maintains pathology and seeks to bring about health by changing an unhealthy setting. As is evident from this broad array of topics, modification and adaptation can come in many ways and through many different techniques.

References

Atkinson, D., Thompson, C., & Grant, S. (1993). A three-dimensional model for counseling racial/ethnic minorities. *The Counseling Psychologist, 21*, 257–277.

Egan, G. (1985). *Change agent skills in helping and human service settings.* Monterey, CA: Brooks/Cole.

Kline, M. (1995). Looking from the outside in: A community psychologist's reflections on school consultation. *Journal of Educational and Psychological Consultation, 6*, 287–293.

Pearce, C., & Osmond, C. (1996). Metaphors for change: The ALPS model of change management. *Organizational Dynamics, 24*, 23–35.

Stokols, D. (1986). The research psychologist as social change agent. *American Journal of Community Psychology, 14*, 595–599.

John Moritsugu

CHARREADA—Mexico's national sport, the rodeo, where *charros* (Mexican cowboys) participate in riding competitions and perform a variety of sometimes dangerous stunts and rope tricks. Usually there is live music from mariachi or other traditional bands and food, followed by dancing. The standard charreada has nine events, which include such specialties as a sliding stop on a horse, tripping a bull by its own tail, and bull riding (Wooden & Ehringer, 1996). Traditional charreadas had ten such events. Since the 1980s, charreadas have become increasingly popular in the Western United States. According to Wooden and Ehringer (1996), "[t]he charreada helps maintain cultural traditions and provides entertainment, but it also serves the Mexican-American community in other ways. Many Mexican-American families encourage their sons to get involved with the charreada as an alternative to neighborhood gangs and drugs. Fathers who competed as youngsters in the charreadas in Mexico now have the opportunity to teach their offspring to be charros" (pp. 203–204). Hence, through charreadas, families are able to strengthen their ties to one another, and the children are able to gain respect from their peers in socially desireable manners.

Reference

Wooden, W. S., & Ehringer, C. (1996). *Rodeo in America: Wranglers, roughstock, and paydirt*. Lawrence: University Press of Kansas.

Cindy Yee and Jeffery Scott Mio

CHICANOS—A derivation of the term *Mejicanos/Mexicanos*, popularized in civil rights and political activities particularly in the Southwest United States. According to Padilla (1995), these were/are university educated individuals who prefer the term Chicano/a to Mexican American or Hispanic. It is a statement about ethnic identity, self-determination, and self-authorization. Descriptively, the term is reserved to "indicate people of Mexican descent who were born in the United States or Mexico but were raised in the U.S. and as such are a native minority" (Padilla, 1995, p. 90). The term Mexican descendents is more inclusive because it refers to Chicanos as well as to recent immigrants. However, individuals self-identify with a more specific ethnic term such as Chicano, la raza, Mexicano, Mexican and so forth. Because the term is used based on personal preference, levels of acculturation, assimilation, and other demographic factors, generalizations about Chicanos cannot be assumed. Garza and Gallegos (1995) speak of Chicanos as a "multicultural group of people, with a greater influence from the Mexican and Anglo culture as well as from a number of other different cultures and subcultures" (p. 13). Being Chicano involves a "multidimensional ethnic identity including national origin, culture and language, race and color, and minority status" (Hurtado & Gurin, 1995, p. 92).

References

Garza, R. T., & Gallegos, P. I. (1995). Environmental influences and personal choice: A humanistic perspective on acculturation. In A. M. Padilla (Ed.), *Hispanic psychology* (pp. 3–14). Thousand Oaks, CA: Sage.
Hurtado, A., & Gurin, P. (1995). Ethnic identity and bilingualism attitudes. In A. M. Padilla (Ed.), *Hispanic psychology* (pp. 89–103). Thousand Oaks, CA: Sage.
Padilla, A. M. (Ed.). (1995). *Hispanic psychology*. Thousand Oaks, CA: Sage.

Patricia Arredondo

CHINCATE—A derrogatory term used by Mexicans to express prejudice towards Chinese immigrants, especially used after the passage of the Chinese Exclusion Act of 1882 in the United States. Many Chinese immigrants moved to Mexico and took away jobs from Mexican citizens. Mexicans who defended the rights of these Chinese immigrants were called the derrogatory term *Chinero* by other Mexicans (Hu-DeHart, 1980).

Reference

Hu-DeHart, E. (1980). Immigrants to a developing society: The Chinese in Northern Mexico. *Journal of Arizona History, 21*, 275–312.

Cindy Yee

CHINESE AMERICAN—An American of Chinese ancestry. They were the first Asian settlers in the United States, which occurred around the 1860s. They worked in the gold mines, fisheries, farms factories, trades, and laundries. In the 1860s, more than 12,000 Chinese laborers participated in the construction of the Pacific section of the Transcontinental railroad (Mark & Chih, 1982). After the Civil War ended in 1865, followed by a rising rate of unemployment, the Chinese labor forces soon were targets of expulsion and persecution. They were harassed with discriminating laws and ordinances depriving their rights to work and to live. From the 1870s to the 1890s, massacres and assaults against Chinese erupted in Los Angeles, California (1871), Snake River, Oregon (1877), Denver, Colorado (1880), Rock Spring, Wyoming (1885), Tacoma, Washington (1885), and other cities. The sentiment behind these hostile anti-Chinese sentiments was epitomized in the passage of the Chinese Exclusion Act of 1882, which prohibited the entry of any Chinese laborer. In 1888, it was changed to the exclusion of *any* person of Chinese ancestry. This unprecedented legislative exclusion of a single ethnic group from immigration to the United States lasted 61 years. It was repealed in 1943, only when Chinese and Americans were allies during World War II (Mark & Chih, 1982). The second wave of migration of Chinese occurred after the immigration reform in 1965. The Chinese American population has almost doubled every decade since the 1960s. According to the 1990 U.S. Census, there were 1,645,472 Chinese Americans representing 22.6 percent of the Asian Pacific Island American population and .7 percent of the total U.S. population (Gall & Gall, 1993). More than 50 percent of Chinese Americans reside in Western costal states, while approximately 30 percent live in Eastern and Mid-Atlantic states. Despite persistent discrimination, Chinese Americans have been quite successful in educational and socioeconomic areas. They have been recognized for outstanding achievements in science, education, arts, sports, business, medicine, law, and other endeavors. Given that 90 percent of Chinese Americans are foreign born, these accomplishments have signified great progress in language proficiency, acculturation, and political empowerment (Chen, 1988). As an example of political empowerment, on November 5, 1996, for the first time in the history of the United States, a Chinese American, Gary Locke, was elected the governor of a mainland state (Washington).

References

Chen, S. A. (1988). Chinese Americans: Their plights and challenges. *Community Psychologist, 21,* 36–37.

Gall, S. B., & Gall, T. L. (1993). *Statistical record of Asian Americans.* Detroit: Gale Research, Inc.

Hill, H. M., Soriano, F. I., Chen, S. A., & LaFromboise, T. D. (1994). Sociocultural factors in the etiology and prevention of violence among ethnic minority youth. In L. D. Eron, J. H. Gentry, & P. Schlegel (Eds.), *Reason to hope: A psychological perspective on violence and youth* (pp. 59–97). Washington, DC: American Psychological Association.

Mark, D.M.L., & Chih, G. (1982). *A place called Chinese America*. Washington, DC: Organization of Chinese Americans, Inc.

S. Andrew Chen

CHINESE EXCLUSION ACT—In response to the great shortage of the workforce due to the Civil War (1861–1865) and the rapid development of the "Wild West," Chinese laborers were recruited mostly from the Quantong Province of China. From the very beginning, the Chinese migrants were welcomed by the White Anglo-Saxon Protestant community. After the Civil War was over and the country was experiencing an unemployment crisis, the Chinese quickly became the scapegoat of both the economic depression and social strife of the country. On May 16, 1882, the 47th Congress of the United States Senate and the House of Representatives passed an unprecedented act to suspend the immigration of Chinese laborers for the next 10 years, called the *Chinese Exclusion Act*. The House vote was 201 yeas, 37 nays, and 51 absent. Six years later, this Act was broadened to include any person of Chinese ancestry with exemption of officials, students, teachers, tourists, and merchants. The Chinese Exclusion Act was renewed in 1892 and was extended indefinitely in 1902 (Takaki, 1989). The Chinese Exclusion Act provided a legitimate basis for both the institutional discrimination in laws and ordinances and also violent massacres, assaults, and physical abuses against Chinese Americans (see CHINESE AMERICANS). The Chinese community, led by the Chinese Six Company, challenged the 1882 Chinese Exclusion Act. The community protested in society as well as tested the Act in the courts. None of these community actions produced any direct results in repealing the Act. The Chinese population sharply reduced from 105,456 in 1880, to 89,863 in 1900, and to 61,639 in 1929 ((Mark & Chih, 1982). In 1943, after 61 years, President Franklin D. Roosevelt signed a congressional resolution to repeal the most discriminating law against a single ethnic group in the history of the United States. This was done in the context of World War II, when the United States and China were allies against Japan.

References

Mark, D.M.L., & Chih, G. (1982). *A place called Chinese America*. Washington, DC: Organization of Chinese Americans, Inc.
Takaki, R. (1989). *Strangers from different shores*. Boston: Little, Brown.
United States Congress. (1882). *United States Statutes*. Vol. 22, p. 58.

S. Andrew Chen

CIVIL RIGHTS—Refers to the constitutional and legal rights enjoyed by the citizens of a nation. These rights are an individual's claims to social freedom. In the United States, they are guaranteed by the Constitution and other legal statuses and usually refer either to life, liberty, or property (Gould & Kolb, 1964; Salzman, Smith, & West, 1996). Throughout the history of the United States, the status of an individual or group of individuals usually determined the extent to which they were allowed to exercise their civil rights. For example, White men historically have been accorded civil rights more so than have White women or ethnic and racial minorities. Since the nineteenth century, African Americans and some Whites have fought for an end to discrimination in civil rights on the basis of race. The Civil Rights Act of 1875, for example, banned legal racial discrimination and ensured equal access to all public places for all citizens. Although the discussion of civil rights frequently takes place rather exclusively in the context of African Americans' struggle for equality in this country, the Civil Rights Movement of the 1950s and 1960s benefited all racial and ethnic minorities (Smallwood, 1994). The women's liberation movement and gay rights movement have also been active in ensuring that these groups enjoy the civil rights due them based on their citizenship rather than on gender or sexual orientation, respectively. The term civil liberties is often confused with civil rights. Although the two terms are related, they are not synonymous. Gould and Kolb (1964) differentiated the two by stating that civil liberties become civil rights once they are enforced through judicial action. In 1947, the President's Committee on Civil Rights outlined the essential rights of all Americans as being *personal rights* (safety and security), *political rights* (citizenship), *civil liberties* (freedom of conscience and expression), and *equality of opportunity*.

References

Gould, J., & Kolb, W. L. (Eds.). (1964). *A dictionary of the social sciences.* Toronto: The Free Press of Glencoe.
Salzman, J., Smith, D., & West, C. (Eds.). (1996). *Encyclopedia of African-American culture and history* (Vol. 2). New York: Simon & Schuster.
Smallwood, J. (1994). The civil rights movement. In F. N. Magill (Ed.), *Survey of social science: Sociology series* (Vol. 1, pp. 265–270). Pasadena, CA: Salem.

La Verne A. Berkel

CLASS-BOUND—The term *class* is used to describe a group of people having a similar social status and can be defined objectively (amount of income) or subjectively (kind of occupation; Simpson & Weiner, 1989). The term currently is used in social theory, although it has political roots dating back to the seventeenth century (Bauman, 1996). Discussions of class tend to focus on people's position in either the upper, middle, or lower classes of society. Studies in political behavior have shown that a person's class can influence his/her value system (Gould & Kolb, 1964). When a person's class shapes his/her values, beliefs, and behaviors, this is referred to as *class-bound*. Class-bound values, beliefs, and behaviors can be a source of conflict in the multicultural counseling relationship. Sue and Sue (1990) elaborate on this issue by stating that minority clients are often in the lower classes and that their class-bound values may differ from those of the therapist who is often from a White, middle-class background. These class-bound values may include communication patterns. For example, poorer people have been documented as having less verbal and more nonverbal communication patterns. This is in direct contrast to the middle-class values of more intricate verbal language (Sue & Sue, 1990). Class-bound expectations of counseling may also differ. Whereas poorer people may have material needs such as adequate housing and may expect more immediate relief to their distress, middle-class individuals may desire long-term intrapsychic change (Sue & Sue, 1990). Sue and Sue summarized the class-bound values of Western culture as being unstructured approaches to problems, long-range goals, and strict adherence to time schedules. With the ever-present threat of class-bound conflicts between a therapist and client, counselors must be careful not to pathologize their clients who have values, beliefs, and behaviors that are the result of their social status.

References

Bauman, Z. (1996). Class. In A. Kuper & J. Kuper (Eds.), *The social science encyclopedia* (2nd ed., pp. 90–94). London: Routledge.

Gould, J., & Kolb, W. L. (Eds.). (1964). *A dictionary of the social sciences*. Toronto: The Free Press of Glencoe.

Simpson, J. A., & Weiner, E.S.C. (Eds.). (1989). *The Oxford English dictionary* (2nd ed.). Oxford: Oxford University Press.

Sue, D. W., & Sue, D. (1990). *Counseling the culturally different: Theory and practice* (2nd ed.). New York: Wiley.

La Verne A. Berkel

COMMUNITY—Rappaport (1977) generally defines *community* as "a subgroup within society, which is perceived or perceives itself as distinct in some respects from the larger society" (p. 3). Discussions about community as a psychological concept originated as part of the community mental health and community psychology movements. Initial definitions emerged out of social ecology which emphasized the interactions between persons and their environments. In his description of four ecological principles, Kelly (1966) refers to a community as a group of similar individuals with common interests who share a defined area. Community can be conceptualized in two primary ways: (1) as a particular geographic area; and (2) as a network of social relationships and resources (Heller, 1989; Heller, Price, Reinharz, Riger, & Wandersman, 1984; MacMillan & Chavis, 1986). Community as a geographic location can refer to the immediate residential environment (the block), the walking-distance neighborhood (elementary school district), a particular region within a city or the entire city (Heller et al., 1984). The community as a geographic area can also be defined in terms of the demographic characteristics of the residents (e.g., ethnicity, age), the land use and quality of housing (e.g., single family homes, industry), and the institutional and organizational composition of the community (e.g., churches, schools, social services; Hunter & Riger, 1986). Community as a social network refers to the formal and informal relationships we have with others which may or may not fall along geographic lines. It involves a person's relations with relatives, friends, neighbors, co-workers and acquaintances, the activities in which these individuals engage, the various roles they play, and functions they serve (e.g., friendship, social support, tangible support; Heller, 1989; Heller et al., 1984). A third major aspect of community has to do with the psychological sense of community, or the "feeling" of the relationship (Heller et al, 1984; Hunter & Riger, 1986). This refers to the internal sense of belongingness and connection. Sarason (1974) describes the four main ingredients of a sense of community as "the perception of similarity to others, an acknowledged interdependence by giving or doing for others what one expects from them, the feeling that one is part of a larger dependable and stable structure" (p. 157). MacMillan and Chavis (1986) describe a similar set of principles or elements of sense of community: (1) membership, which involves a feeling of belongingness and a sense of relatedness; (2) influence, which refers to whether an individual can affect the group and whether the group can exert some power on the larger systems that contain it; (3) a sharing and fulfillment of values and needs; and (4) a shared emotional connection.

References

Heller, K. (1989). The return to community. *American Journal of Community Psychology, 17*, 1–16.

Heller, K., Price, R. H., Reinharz, S., Riger, S., & Wandersman, A. (1984). *Psychology and community change: Challenges of the future.* Pacific Grove, CA: Brooks/ Cole.

Hunter, A., & Riger, S. (1986). The meaning of community in community mental health. *Journal of Community Psychology, 14*, 55–71.

Kelly, J. G. (1966). Ecological constraints on mental health services. *American Psychologist, 21*, 535–539.

MacMillan, D., & Chavis, D. (1986). Sense of community: A definition and theory. *Journal of Community Psychology, 14*, 6–23.

Rappaport, J. (1977). *Community psychology: Values, research, and action.* San Francisco: Holt, Rinehart and Winston.

Sarason, S. B. (1974). *The psychological sense of community: Prospects for community psychology.* San Francisco: Jossey-Bass.

Lori Barker-Hackett

COMPADRAZCO—Often referred to as "co-parentage" (Hauberg, 1974, p. 137), this is a cultural custom in which parents select a *compadre* (godfather) and a *comadre* (godmother) for their child's baptism. These individuals can be close friends of the family or relatives. Quite often, an individual who holds a position of considerable importance in a given community is chosen (Grebler, Moore, & Guzman, 1970). *Compadrazco* has been characterized as serving both a religious and socioeconomic function originating from Spain and the influence of Catholicism (Hauberg, 1974). The compadres (godparents) become part of the extended family support system in many Latino cultures (e.g., Puerto Rican, Mexican, and Cuban), and are expected to participate in the care of the child.

It has been argued that this is a Spanish custom adopted by the indigenous people of many of the countries colonized by Spain (Mirandé, 1985).

References

Grebler, L., Moore, J. W., & Guzman, R. C. (1970). *The Mexican American people.* New York: The Free Press.
Hauberg, C. A. (1974). *Puerto Rico and the Puerto Ricans.* New York: Twayne.
Mirandé, A. (1985). *The Chicano experience: An alternative perspective.* Notre Dame, IN: University of Notre Dame Press.

Azara L. Santiago-Rivera

CONFORMITY STAGE—Stage one of a five-stage identity model called the *Minority Identity Development (MID)* model which provides a developmental, process-oriented perspective (Atkinson, Morten, & Sue, 1989) on racial/cultural identity development. This model was refined and elaborated on by Sue and Sue (1990), called the *Racial/Cultural Identity Development Model (R/CID)*. According to these models, the *Conformity Stage* suggests minorities prefer and adopt the dominant cultural values over their own. Individuals at this stage depreciate their physical and cultural characteristics, including their minority group, perceiving it to be negative. They believe it is more desirable to imitate those positive and desirable characteristics of the dominant culture (i.e., White culture), rather than characteristics associated with the minority group. Individuals exhibit appreciating attitudes and beliefs by respecting, emulating, and admiring the dominant culture, and at the same time, discriminating against other minorities, thus striving for identification with the White culture. This stage is similar to the *passive-acceptance stage* (Jackson, 1970), the *preencounter stage* (Cross, 1971; Hall, Cross, & Freedle, 1972), the *conformity (pre-encounter) status* (Helms, 1995), and the *questioning/confusion phase* (Collins, 1996). The *MID* model roughly parallels Phinney's (1990) three-stage model of identity formation (Uba, 1994) and the five-status People of Color Racial Identity Ego Statuses and Information-Processing Strategies (IPS) developed by Helms (1994, 1995; Helms & Piper, 1994).

References

Atkinson, D. R., Morten, G., & Sue, D. W. (1989). *Counseling American minorities: A cross-cultural perspective.* Dubuque, IA: W. C. Brown.
Collins, J.L.F. (1996). *Biracial Japanese American identity: Hapa, double or somewhere in between.* Unpublished doctoral dissertation, The Fielding Institute, Santa Barbara, CA.
Cross, W. E. (1971). The Negro-to-Black conversion experience: Toward a psychology of Black liberation. *Black World, 20,* 13–27.
Hall, W. S., Cross, W. E., & Freedle, R. (1972). Stages in the development of Black awareness: An exploratory investigation. In R. Jones (Ed.), *Black psychology* (pp. 156–165). New York: Springer-Verlag.

Helms, J. E. (1994). Racial identity and career assessment. *Journal of Career Assessment*, 2, 199–209.

Helms, J. E. (1995). An update of Helms's White and people of color racial identity models. In J. G. Ponterotto, J. M. Casas, L. A. Suzuki, & C. M. Alexander (Eds.), *Handbook of multicultural counseling* (pp. 181–198). Thousand Oaks, CA: Sage.

Helms, J. E., & Piper, R. E. (1994). Implications of racial identity theory for vocational psychology. *Journal of Vocational Behavior, 44*, 124–136.

Phinney, J. S. (1990). Ethnic identity in adolescents and adults: Review of research. *Psychological Bulletin, 108*, 499–514.

Sue, D. W., & Sue, D. (1990). *Counseling the culturally different: Theory and practice* (2nd ed.). New York: Wiley.

Uba, L. (1994). *Asian Americans: Personality patterns, identity, and mental health*. New York: Guilford.

James Fuji Collins

CONFUCIANISM—A system of ideas founded on *Confucian* values that have, and perhaps still, influenced East Asian social, political, spiritual, and economic institutions. Although Confucian values had their origin with the Chinese philosopher Confucius (551–479 B.C.), the legacy of Confucian values has prevailed with idiosyncratic modifications in East Asian countries. Most scholars depict Confucianism as a social theory and force that molds individuals into group-oriented, or more specifically, family-oriented and socially dependent beings (Solomon, 1971). Within its fullest dimension, Confucianism is more than a code of social ethics; it is a social philosophy of practice and engagement with the moral affairs of the world (Tu, 1985). In a Confucian context, people are considered social creatures bound to others by *ren*, or human heartedness, which is only developed in relationships between people in a social context (King & Bond, 1985). In terms of social interactions, Confucianism outlines an ideal society as a complicated role system where harmonious social interactions become the highest social value, where the individual is never conceived of as an isolated, separate entity (Moore, 1967). Relationships are regulated by *li*, the term used for the set of rules, etiquette, and ritual that make relationships function smoothly.

References

King, A.Y.C., & Bond, M. H. (1985). The Confucian paradigm of man: A sociological view. In W. S. Tseng & D.Y.H. Wu (Eds.), *Chinese culture and mental health* (pp. 29–46). Orlando, FL: Academic Press.

Moore, C. A. (1967). Introduction: The humanistic Chinese mind. In C. A. Moore (Ed.), *The Chinese mind*. Honolulu: University of Hawaii Press.

Solomon, R. H. (1971). *Mao's revolution and the Chinese political culture*. Berkeley: University of California Press.

Tu, W. M. (1985). *Confucian thought: Selfhood as creative transformation*. Albany: State University of New York Press.

MaryAnna Domokos-Cheng Ham

CONNECTEDNESS—Refers to an individual's sense of relatedness and attachment to a group, usually one's community or ethnic group. Triandis (1989)
described the "collective self," which emphasizes interrelationships, cooperation, obedience, and reliability. Individuals with collectivistic perspectives view
groups, rather than individuals, as the basic units of social perception, while the
self is defined in terms of relationships with others and in-group status. Many
writers have noted the high level of connectedness among various ethnic minority groups. Fujita and O'Brien (1991) described Japanese Americans as perceiving all Japanese Americans—even those to whom they are not related—as
"quasi-kin." As a result, Japanese American-based social networks such as
voluntary organizations have developed, which enables one to become involved
in the mainstream community without sacrificing one's connection to the Japanese American community. White and Parham (1990) summarized the African
worldview, which emphasizes a holistic perspective and sense of living in a
dynamic world where everything is interrelated. This perspective also views the
tribe, not the individual, as the basic human unit, and values cooperation, concern, and responsibility toward others. White and Parham emphasized that this
perspective has persisted among African Americans today, who often refer to
each other as "brother" and "sister" even thought they might not be related.
Although American Indians are a very heterogeneous group and hundreds of
distinct tribes exist, many American Indians view the tribe as the central social
unit, and see themselves as extensions of the tribe. This provides them with a
sense of belongingness and security, where one is rewarded by engaging in
behaviors which benefit the tribe. It is suggested that Indians who leave the
reservation oftentimes lose their sense of personal identity as a result of losing
their tribal identity (Anderson & Ellis, 1988). Latinos' sense of connectedness
is based on an emphasis in family tradition and the maintenance of the extended
family, which also includes friends and godparents. Additionally, many Latinos
believe that social relations should be personal and informal (*personalismo*) and
sometimes specific relationships, such as those between godparents and god-
children, may take on an added spiritual emphasis (e.g., *comadrazco/compad-
razco*; Padilla, Ruiz, & Alvarez, 1975).

References

Anderson, M. J., & Ellis, R. (1988). On the reservation. In N. A. Vacc, J. W. Wittmer,
    & S. DeVaney (Eds.), *Experiencing and counseling multicultural and diverse
    populations* (2nd ed., pp. 107–126). Muncie, IN: Accelerated Development.
Fujita, S. S., & O'Brien, D. J. (1991). *Japanese American ethnicity: The persistence of
    a community*. Seattle: University of Washington Press.
Padilla, A. M., Ruiz, R. A., & Alvarez, R. (1975). Community health services for the
    Spanish speaking/surnamed population. *American Psychologist, 30*, 892–905.
Triandis, H. C. (1989). The self and social behavior in differing cultural contexts. *Psy-
    chological Review, 96*, 269–289.

White, J. L., & Parham, T. A. (1990). *The psychology of Blacks: An African American perspective* (2nd ed.). Englewood Cliffs, NJ: Prentice-Hall.

Gayle Y. Iwamasa

CONSULTANT—The history of *consultation* has been credited to two major sources: (1) the organizational development literature (Gallessich, 1982), and (2) the practice of mental health (Caplan, 1970). The role of consultant may be defined in several ways, depending upon the expectations of the consultation relationship. Typically, consultants offer expertise to a consultee for the purposes of improving services or products for a third party (e.g., client, customer). Although consultants offer expertise, they establish an equitable relationship with the consultee and engage as two professionals focusing on work-related issues (Brown, Kurpius, & Morris, 1988). Consultants may work with individuals, small groups, organizations, and as advocates in systems (Kurpius & Brown, 1988). Consultation is a problem-solving process which includes the following components: a professional relationship, assessment, goals and strategies, interventions, and evaluation. Consultants in multicultural work may be asked to be resources on clinical service issues or organizational development issues, such as developing a comprehensive multicultural training program (Ridley, Mendoza, & Kanitz, 1994).

References

Brown, D., Kurpius, D. J., & Morris, J. R. (1988). *Handbook of consultation with individuals and small groups.* Alexandria, VA: American Counseling Association.
Caplan, G. (1970). *The theory and practice of mental health consultation.* New York: Basic Books.
Gallessich, J. (1982). *The profession and practice of consultation.* San Francisco: Jossey-Bass.
Kurpius, D. J., & Brown, D. (Eds.). (1988). *Handbook of consultation: An intervention for advocacy and outreach.* Alexandria, VA: American Counseling Association.
Ridley, C. R., Mendoza, D. W., & Kanitz, B. E. (1994). Multicultural training: Reexamination, operationalization, and integration. *The Counseling Psychologist, 22,* 227–289.

Mary Fukuyama

CONVENTIONAL COUNSELING/WESTERN PSYCHOLOGY—The interaction between a person (client/patient) and a therapist/counselor on issues that are troubling to the client. Counseling can occur through various modes and by various professionals. The three main theoretical approaches/modes of psychotherapy are behavioristic, humanistic, and psychoanalytic (Statt, 1989). Treatment modes such as psychodynamic, cognitive-behavioral, rational emotive, nondirective and Gestalt derive from one of these three approaches. Counseling can be more ''directive,'' where the therapist plays a major role in guiding and advising the patient. ''Nondirective'' or ''client-centered'' therapy is where the counselor supports the client while they (the client) gain insight into their problem and work on finding their own solution (Stratton & Hayes, 1988). Nondirective therapy was quite innovative and originated with Carl Rogers. *Conventional therapy* can be short-term (a few sessions) or long-term (many years). Counseling can be provided by various professionals with various degrees: psychologist with a Ph.D. or Psy. D., counselor with a masters degree, psychiatrists with an M.D. Most therapists need to be licensed or certified in order to conduct therapy. *Conventional counseling* is based on White aristocratic male models. Most traditional theories were not developed using research on a diverse population (people of color, women, lower socioeconomic status, non-heterosexual, etc.). Thus, in the past 30 years, these diverse groups have developed therapeutic methods more conducive to their population (i.e., feminist and cross-cultural therapy).

References

Statt, D. (1989). *The concise dictionary of psychology.* New York: Routledge.
Stratton, P., & Hayes, N. (1988). *A student's dictionary of psychology.* New York: Edward Arnold.

Christine C. Iijima Hall

COPING—The behaviors and cognitions people use to manage a variety of problems ranging from crisis situations to daily encounters that may be perceived as stressful (Lazarus & Folkman, 1984). Earlier conceptualizations include viewing coping as merely an instinctive response to aversive stimuli in the environment. From an ego psychoanalytic approach, coping has been viewed as the use of adaptive defenses such as denial, repression, and intellectualization to deal with stressful encounters (Menninger, 1963; Vaillant, 1977). Within the last two decades, the concept of coping has emphasized the dynamic process of reciprocal interaction between the person and the environment, as well as the important role of cognitive appraisal (e.g., Lazarus & Folkman, 1984). Related concepts include *problem-solving ability* (MacNair & Elliott, 1992), *hardiness* (Kobasa, 1979), and *self-control* (Rohde, Lewinsohn, Tilson, & Seeley, 1990).

References

Kobasa, S. S. (1979). Stressful life events, personality, and health: An inquiry into hardiness. *Journal of Personality and Social Psychology, 37,* 1–11.
Lazarus, R. S., & Folkman, S. (1984). *Stress, appraisal, and coping.* New York: Springer.
MacNair, R., & Elliott, T. R. (1992). Self-perceived problem-solving ability, stress appraisal, and coping over time. *Journal of Research on Personality, 26,* 150–164.
Menninger, K. (1963). *The vital balance: The life process in mental health and illness.* New York: Viking.
Rohde, P., Lewinsohn, P., Tilson, M., & Seeley, J. R. (1990). Dimensionality of coping and its relation to depression. *Journal of Personality and Social Psychology, 58,* 499–511.
Vaillant, G. E. (1977). *Adaptation to life.* Boston: Little, Brown.

Azara L. Santiago-Rivera

COUNSELING—A professional relationship that involves an interactive process between a trained counselor and a client or clients. According to several definitions of counseling (Burks & Stefflre, 1979; Egan, 1994; George & Christiani, 1995), the counselor has several responsibilies to his/her client(s) during this process. They are: to help client(s) understand and clarify their problems, engage in the learning process, and achieve clients' treatment or counseling goals. Client's problems may involve emotional, cognitive, and/or behavioral components. These components may be reflected in the areas of personal growth, marriage, family, and other relational/interpersonal concerns. In general, the learning process includes assisting client(s) to explore ways to cope with life situations, make well-informed choices, and arrive at appropriate decisions (Patterson & Elsenberg, 1983). Furthermore, depending on the counselor's theoretical orientation and counseling approach, the learning process and counseling goals may vary to some extent (George & Christiani, 1995). For example, a cognitive-behavioral counselor's treatment goal may be concentrated on symptom reduction, whereas a psychodynamic counselor's treatment goal may be gained through insight into problems. Counseling is integrated in mental health fields of psychology, social work, school/educational guidance, and psychiatry. Psychotherapy, a term often used interchangeably with counseling, is subtly different from counseling to denote a more in-depth interactive counselor–client process that includes more severe personality or behavioral problems (Ivey, 1994).

References

Burks, H. M., & Stefflre, B. (1979). *Theories of counseling* (3rd ed.). New York: McGraw-Hill.

Egan, G. (1994). *The skilled helper: A problem-management approach to helping* (5th ed.). Pacific Grove, CA: Brooks/Cole.

George, R. L., & Christiani, T. S. (1995). *Counseling: Theory and practice* (4th ed.). Boston: Allyn & Bacon.

Ivey, A. E. (1994). *Intentional interviewing and counseling: Facilitating client development in a multicultural society* (3rd ed.). Pacific Grove, CA: Brooks/Cole.

Patterson, L. E., & Elsenberg, S. (1983). *The counseling process* (3rd ed.). Boston: Houghton Mifflin.

Randi I. Kim

COVERT INTENTIONAL RACISM—A form of racism that can occur at both an individual and institutional level. According to Ridley (1989, 1995), this form of racism is hidden from the casual observer but is a conscious process of discrimination by the perpetrator. For example, at the individual level, a high school administrator may assign African American students to the worst or most disliked teachers in the school because the administrator may not feel that African Americans can learn, anyway. At an institutional level, an exclusive private high school may set its tuition fees above the level that most African Americans in the area can afford. Covert intentional racism contrasts with *covert unintentional racism* (see entry), where the individual or institutional is unaware of the discrimination that a particular practice may produce. Covert intentional racism is a subtle, hidden equivalent to *overt intentional racism* (see entry), which is the form of racism about which most people are aware.

References

Ridley, C. R. (1989). Racism in counseling as an adverse behavioral process. In P. B. Pedersen, J. G. Draguns, W. J. Lonner, & J. E. Trimble (Eds.), *Counseling across cultures* (3rd ed., pp. 55–77). Honolulu: University of Hawaii Press.
Ridley, C. R. (1995). *Overcoming unintentional racism in counseling and therapy: A practitioner's guide to intentional intervention.* Thousand Oaks, CA: Sage.

Jeffery Scott Mio

COVERT UNINTENTIONAL RACISM—A form of racism that can occur at both an individual and institutional level. According to Ridley (1989, 1995), this form of racism is hidden from the casual observer and is an unconscious process of discrimination by the perpetrator. For example, at the individual level, a teacher may misinterpret an ethnic minority student's lack of assertiveness as a disinterest in school. At an institutional level, a graduate program may use a cutoff score on the Graduate Record Examination without recognition of personal or cultural influences that may disadvantage some ethnic minority students. Covert unintentional racism contrasts with *covert intentional racism* (see entry), where the individual or institutional is aware of the discrimination that a particular practice may produce. Covert unintentional racism is a form of racism based upon lack of knowledge about certain ethnic minority groups, as opposed to *overt intentional racism* (see entry), which is the form of racism about which most people are aware and is a disregard of knowledge of certain ethnic minority groups.

References

Ridley, C. R. (1989). Racism in counseling as an adverse behavioral process. In P. B. Pedersen, J. G. Draguns, W. J. Lonner, & J. E. Trimble (Eds.), *Counseling across cultures* (3rd ed., pp. 55–77). Honolulu: University of Hawaii Press.
Ridley, C. R. (1995). *Overcoming unintentional racism in counseling and therapy: A practitioner's guide to intentional intervention.* Thousand Oaks, CA: Sage.

Jeffery Scott Mio

LOS CRIOLLOS—American-born persons of Spanish parentage who suffered rampant social discrimination by the Spanish (Novas, 1994). They were considered second-class citizens—higher than the *mestizos* (see entry), but lower than the *peninsulares* (Spanish).

Reference

Novas, H. (1994). *Everything you need to know about Latino history*. New York: Penguin.

Cindy Yee

CROSS-CULTURAL BEHAVIOR THERAPY—*Behavior therapy*, as defined by Wolpe (1990) is ''the use of experimentally established principles and paradigms of learning to overcome maladaptive habits'' (p. 3). *Cross-cultural behavior therapy*, then, is behavior therapy used in a therapeutic context in which the therapist, client, and reference group for which assessment or treatment procedures have been validated do not share a common cultural background. Despite various distinctions, behavior therapy is often used interchangeably with cognitive therapy, cognitive-behavior therapy, and behavior modification. The habits or behaviors assessed and treated in behavior therapy may include cognitive, affective, somatic, motoric, or interpersonal responses. Cultural background, from a behavioral standpoint, refers to aspects of past learning common to members of a society or a group within a society, resulting in shared patterns of behavior that overlap to a greater or lesser extent with those of other groups. Historically, behavior therapists began to address the question of cultural differences in the 1960s (Kanfer & Saslow, 1965). Franks (1969) stressed the need to consider ''the impact of cultural and allied differences upon the behavior therapist'' (p. 21), and Skinner (1971) emphasized that culture is an integral part of the context of behavior and should be evaluated carefully through functional analysis (systematic assessment of the antecedents and consequences of behavior). Functional analysis and interview-based functional assessment have been proposed as culturally sensitive assessment modalities (Hayes & Toarmino, 1995; Tanaka-Matsumi, Seiden, & Lam, 1996), and are suitable for (a) emphasizing the client's cultural conception of problem behaviors, (b) setting specific goals in therapy, (c) arranging conditions to increase the client's expectancy of therapy success, and (d) using appropriate change agents (Tanaka-Matsumi & Higginbotham, 1996). A valuable source of information on the state of cross-cultural behavior therapy in the 1990s is a special issues of the journal *Cognitive and Behavioral Practice* which contains articles on how to conduct a cross-cultural behavioral interview, behavior therapy from the standpoint of an ethnic minority therapist, and behavior therapy with Latinos, Orthodox Jews, Japanese, African Americans, children, the elderly, gays and lesbians, and individuals affected by HIV/AIDS (Iwamasa, 1996). Persons interested in learning more about cross-cultural behavior therapy can contact the Cross-Cultural Behavior Therapy Special Interest Group of the Association for the Advancement of Behavior Therapy, as well as the more culture-specific special interest groups.

References

Franks, C. M. (Ed.). (1969). *Behavior therapy: Appraisal and status*. New York: McGraw-Hill.

Hayes, S. C., & Toarmino, D. (1995). If behavioral principles are generally applicable, why is it necessary to understand cultural diversity? *The Behavior Therapist, 18,* 21–23.

Iwamasa, G. Y. (1996). Introduction to the special series: Ethnic and cultural diversity in cognitive and behavioral practice. *Cognitive and Behavioral Practice, 3,* 209–213.

Kanfer, F. H., & Saslow, G. (1965). Behavioral analysis: An alternative to diagnostic classification. *Archive of General Psychiatry, 12,* 529–538.

Skinner, B. F. (1971). *Beyond freedom and dignity.* New York: Bantam.

Tanaka-Matsumi, J., & Higginbotham, H. N. (1996). Behavioral approaches to counseling across cultures. In P. B. Pedersen, J. G. Draguns, W. J. Lonner, & J. E. Trimble (Eds.), *Counseling across cultures* (4th ed., pp. 266–292). Thousand Oaks, CA: Sage.

Tanaka-Matsumi, J., Seiden, D. Y., & Lam, K. N. (1996). The Culturally-Informed Functional Assessment (CIFA) Interview: A strategy for cross-cultural behavioral practice. *Cognitive and Behavioral Practice, 3,* 215–233.

Wolpe, J. (1990). *The practice of behavior therapy* (4th ed.). New York: Pergamon.

Douglas Y. Seiden

CROSS-CULTURAL COUNSELING—To fully understand the concept of cross-cultural counseling, one must first have a general understanding of the terms *culture* and *counseling*. Culture consists of patterns and results of behavior transmitted by symbols to members of a particular society (Sills, 1972). It includes knowledge, beliefs, art, economics, religion, language, and social organization and can be either implicit or explicit. The term was first presented in English in an anthropological context by Edward Tyler in 1871 (Winthrop, 1991). Counseling has been described since the fourteenth century as a form of supportive psychotherapy in which the counselor empowers a client to solve his/her own problems (Simpson & Weiner, 1989). Sue and Sue (1990) described counseling as an interpersonal process of communication involving both verbal and nonverbal messages. They further stated that in the United States, counseling emphasizes verbal, emotional expressiveness, and has the goal of gaining insight. Cross-cultural counseling describes a counseling relationship involving participants who are culturally different from one another (Atkinson, Morten, & Sue, 1993). The term was often used to describe counseling relationships consisting of a White counselor and an ehtnic minority client, but is now more accurately used to describe all cross-cultural relationships, including dyads involving two or more minorities from different racial or ethnic backgrounds. Effective cross-cultural counseling occurs when verbal and nonverbal messages are effectively sent and received by the counseling dyad and when the counselor is aware of the sociopolitical realities of racial and ethnic minority clients (Sue & Sue, 1990). The term cross-cultural counseling has often been incorrectly used interchangeably with cross-cultural psychology. Cross-cultural psychology refers to the systematic study of behavior as it occurs in different cultures with the purpose of establishing which psychological laws are universal and which are culture-specific (cf. Atkinson et al., 1993; Triandis, 1980). The term multicultural counseling, however, is synonymous with cross-cultural counseling. Pedersen (1994) defined multicultural counseling as a helping relationship involving two or more persons who have different ways of perceiving their social environments. He also stated that the term multicultural referred to various groups with equal status, as opposed to cross-cultural, which implies that one culture is better than another. For this reason, he suggested that the term multicultural be used rather than cross-cultural.

References

Atkinson, D. R., Morten, G., & Sue, D. W. (1993). *Counseling American minorities: A cross-cultural perspective* (4th ed.). Madison, WI: Mark Publishers.
Pedersen, P. (1994). *A handbook for developing multicultural awareness* (2nd ed.). Alexandria, VA: American Counseling Association.
Sills, D. L. (Ed.). (1972). *International encyclopedia of the social sciences* (Vol. 3). New York: Macmillan and Free Press.
Simpson, J. A., & Weiner, E.S.C. (Eds.). (1989). *The Oxford English dictionary* (2nd ed.). Oxford: Oxford University Press.
Sue, D. W., & Sue, D. (1990). *Counseling the culturally different: Theory and practice* (2nd ed.). New York: Wiley.
Triandis, H. C. (1980). Introduction to *Handbook of cross-cultural psychology*. In H. C. Triandis & W. W. Lambert (Eds.), *Handbook of cross-cultural psychology. 1. Perspectives* (Vol. 1, pp. 1–14). Boston: Allyn & Bacon.
Winthrop, R. H. (Ed.). (1991). *Dictionary of concepts in cultural anthropology*. Westport, CT: Greenwood Press.

La Verne A. Berkel

CROSS-CULTURAL TRAINING—Refers to the preparation of mental health professionals to appropriately and effectively address the mental health needs of individuals who differ in terms of cultural background, values, and lifestyle. Also known as multicultural training, this term is most commonly understood using the narrow definition of culture, and refers to the training of mental health professionals to work with those of different racial and ethnic backgrounds. Currently, a broader definition is advocated which encompasses differences based not only on race and ethnicity, but also on other variables such as gender, age, socioeconomic status, religion, sexual orientation, physical ability, and language. Based on this broader definition, all counseling is cross-cultural (multicultural; Essandoh, 1996; Pedersen, 1991; Speight, Myers, Chikako, & Highlen, 1991; Sue et al., 1982). Such training typically focuses on increasing trainees' awareness, knowledge, sensitivity, skills, and competence in working with people who are different from themselves and involves a variety of methods such as separate specialized courses, infusion/integration into the entire training curriculum, experiential exercises, supervision, and practicum and internship experiences (Brislin, Landis, & Brandt, 1983; D'Andrea & Daniels, 1991; LaFromboise & Foster, 1992; Ridley, Mendoza, & Kanitz, 1994). Discussion of the need for cross-cultural training has taken place for over 20 years (e.g., Boxley & Wagner, 1971; Korchin, 1980; President's Commission on Mental Health, 1978) and most professional organizations and accrediting bodies specify the need for such training and provide guidelines and standards that training programs must meet to demonstrate they are addressing these issues. More recently, principles of cross-cultural training have been applied to nearly all organizations, especially those that deal directly with the public, such as police departments, fire departments, colleges and universities, and even businesses.

References

Boxley, R., & Wagner, N. (1971). Clinical psychology training programs and minority groups: A survey. *Professional Psychology, 2,* 75–81.

Brislin, R. W., Landis, D., & Brandt, M. E. (1983). Conceptualization of intercultural behavior and training. In D. Landis & R. Brislin (Eds.), *Handbook of intercultural training: Vol. 1. Issues in theory and design* (pp. 1–35). New York: Pergamon.

D'Andrea, M., & Daniels, J. (1991). Exploring the different levels of multicultural counseling training in counselor education. *Journal of Counseling and Development, 70,* 78–85.

Essandoh, P. K. (1996). Multicultural counseling as the "Fourth Force": A call to arms. *The Counseling Psychologist, 24,* 126–137.

Korchin, S. J. (1980). Clinical psychology and minority problems. *American Psychologist, 35,* 262–269.

LaFromboise, T. D., & Foster, S. L. (1992). Cross-cultural training: Scientist-practitioner model and methods. *The Counseling Psychologist, 20,* 427–489.

Pedersen, P. B. (1991). Multiculturalism as a generic approach to counseling. *Journal of Counseling & Development, 70,* 6–12.

President's Commission on Mental Health. (1978). *Report to the President of the Commission on Mental Health.* Washington, DC: U.S. Government Printing Office.

Ridley, C. R., Mendoza, D. W., & Kanitz, B. E. (1994). Multicultural training: Reexamination, operationalization, and integration. *The Counseling Psychologist, 22,* 227–289.

Speight, S. L., Myers, L. J., Chikako, I. C., & Highlen, P. S. (1991). A redefinition of multicultural counseling. *Journal of Counseling & Development, 70,* 29–36.

Sue, D. W., Bernier, J. E., Durran, A., Feinberg, L., Pedersen, P., Smith, E. J., & Vasquez-Nutall, E. (1982). Position paper: Cross-cultural counseling competencies. *The Counseling Psychologist, 10,* 45–52.

Lori Barker-Hackett

CUBAN AMERICAN—Cuban migration to the United States predates this century. By the late 1800s, there were about 100,000 Cubans concentrated mainly in New York City as well as in Tampa, Key West, and other Florida cities. People who were part of this early exodus established the tobacco industry in Southern Florida and largely remained there to become the first enclave of Cuban Americans (Diaz, 1981). Between 1959 and 1980, some 600,000 Cubans immigrated to the United States following the Castro revolution (Perez, 1985). Another 160,000 arrived between 1981 and 1990 (U.S. Census Bureau, 1992).

According to the 1990 census of the population, a total of 1,044,000 persons were identified as Cuban Americans based on the respondents who indicated that they were of Cuban origin or descent. Cuban Americans are a heterogeneous group. Because of its European, African, and Indian roots, traditional Cuban culture was described by Diaz (1981) as *ajiaco* (a typical stew of vegetables, roots, and meat). This stew has been further complicated by the pervasive influence of American institutions, language, and culture upon Cuban-American life. Most of the Cuban population in the United States are urbanites. The Cuban population surpasses the total U.S. population, as well as other Latino groups, in the proportion that reside in urban areas. The Miami–Fort Lauderdale area (Dade and Broward Counties in Florida), greater New York, and Los Angeles combined contain more than three-fourths of this population. In Miami alone, there are more than 500,000 Cubans.

References

Diaz, G. M. (1981). The changing Cuban community. In The Council on Foundations, Inc. (Ed.), *Hispanics and grantmakers: A special report of Foundation News* (pp. 18–23). Washington, DC: Council of Foundations.
Perez, L. (1985). The Cuban population of the United States: The results of the 1980 Census of the Population. *Cuban Studies, 15*, 1–16.
U.S. Census Bureau, Department of Commerce. (1992). *Statistical abstract of the United States*. Washington, DC: U.S. Government Printing Office.

Gerardo M. Gonzalez

CULTURAL ABSOLUTISM—An underlying theoretical orientation about the nature of humankind that is based upon the assumption that there are certain fundamental characteristics or traits (e.g., intelligence) that may be uniformly applied to individuals regardless of culture or experience. Central to this perspective is the belief that such characteristics are quantifiable, measurable, and may be used to explain variations in human behavior. This is the orientation that has guided much of mainstream psychology (Adamopoulos & Lonner, 1994). As a theoretical perspective guiding thinking and research in psychology, cultural absolutism is often contrasted with cultural relativism and cultural universalism (Berry, Poortinga, Segall, & Dasen, 1992). The cultural relativist believes that individuals can only be understood within the context of their culture and experience. The cultural universalist shares the belief that there are broad commonalities across human beings with that of the absolutist, but he/she differs in also believing that these characteristics are best understood within the cultural context of the individual.

References

Adamopoulos, J., & Lonner, W. J. (1994). Absolutism, relativism, and universalism in the study of human behavior. In W. J. Lonner and R. Moypass (Eds.), *Psychology and culture*. Boston: Allyn and Bacon.

Berry, J. W., Poortinga, Y. H., Segall, M. H., & Dasen, P. R. (1992). *Cross-cultural psychology: Research and applications*. New York: Cambridge University Press.

Arleen C. Lewis

CULTURAL ACCOMMODATION/CULTURAL NEGOTIATION—*Accommodation* refers to the process of adjusting to a social situation in such a way that overt conflicts between the parties involved are kept at a minimum (Zadronzy, 1959). The process involves cooperation and opposition (Reading, 1977). It can be engaged in by individuals or by groups, and is necessary for the maintenance of the social order (Gould & Kolb, 1964). The term was first used in the social science literature in 1895 and was considered the social equivalent of *biological adaptation* because both terms related to adjustment to the environment (Gould & Kolb, 1964). *Negotiation* is defined as the discussion between people in a dispute which is aimed at settling the dispute (Reading, 1977). As with accommodation, the term negotiation was first used in the late nineteenth century. Simpson and Weiner (1989) define the term as the "action of getting over or [a]round some obstacle by skillful maneuvering" (p. 303). Cultural accommodation refers to the acquisition of cultural attitudes and values by one cultural group as a result of their contact with another for the purpose of minimizing conflict between the two groups. The accommodation is affected by those individuals who are entering the new culture. Cultural accommodation has recently been studied by examining how values and attitudes associated with a particular culture are acquired along with the acquisition of the language of that culture (Ralston, Cunniff, & Gustafson, 1995). These researchers found that individuals tended to display the values and attitudes of a particular culture when responding to questions written in the language of that culture. When responding to questions in their native tongue, individuals displayed the values of their original culture.

References

Gould, J., & Kolb, W. L. (Eds.). (1964). *A dictionary of the social sciences*. Toronto: The Free Press of Glencoe.

Ralston, E. A., Cunniff, M. K., & Gustafson, D. J. (1995). Cultural accommodation: The effect of language on the responses of bilingual Hong Kong Chinese managers. *Journal of Cross-Cultural Psychology, 26*, 714–727.

Reading, H. F. (Ed.). (1977). *A dictionary of the social sciences*. London: Routledge and Kegan Paul.

Simpson, J. A., & Weiner, E.S.C. (Eds.). (1989). *The Oxford English dictionary* (2nd ed.). Oxford: Oxford University Press.

Zadronzy, J. T. (Ed.). (1959). *Dictionary of social science*. Washington, DC: Public Affairs Press.

La Verne A. Berkel

CULTURAL BIAS—Early references to *cultural bias* as a concept rather than a specific term were found in anthropological and ethnographic studies. Benedict

(1934) observed that what is judged normal in one culture may be abnormal in another. Boas (1940) recognized the relativism of cultural standards across human societies. Such commentaries may have resulted from the detailed reports of anthropologists such as Speck (1918), who studied Native American tribes in the Northeastern United States and observed differences among groups within close geographic and cultural proximity. Wolman's *Dictionary of Behavioral Science* (1973) did not list the term. However, cultural relativism, pressure, deprivation, adaptability, and related terms were listed. The term was included in the index of *The Encyclopedic Dictionary of Psychology* (Harre & Lamb, 1983) with reference to ethical problems in psychology but was not included as a specific entry. The problematic area referenced was that of cultural bias in psychological tests and assessments. Between the years 1974 and 1986, 406 journal articles that included the term cultural bias were indexed in PsycLIT Database. A major focus of the research was cross-cultural assessments and included test bias, response style variance, and levels of equivalence (Lonner, 1985). Court rulings regarding use of standardized tests to assess persons who were minimally represented in standardization samples have stimulated research on the effects of cultural or ethnic bias in testing (Anastasi, 1988; Salvia & Ysseldyke, 1995). Counseling services have been studied extensively for the effects of cultural bias in communications between counselors and clients. Sue and Sue (1990) used the term *culturocentrism* and *ethnocentric bias* to identify behaviors and environmental conditions that may contribute to the misunderstanding and oppression of persons who are not members of the dominant culture. As is the case with most complex terms, there are many possible uses and meanings of cultural bias. Language is not exact, nor are meanings consistently assigned to terms with varied social, cultural, and legal implications (Condon & Yousef, 1975).

References

Anastasi, A. (1988). *Psychological testing* (6th ed.). New York: Macmillan Publishing.

Benedict, R. (1934). *Patterns of culture*. Boston: Houghton Mifflin.

Boas, F. (1940). *Race, language and culture*. New York: The Free Press.

Condon, J. C., & Yousef, F. S. (1975). *An introduction to intercultural communication*. New York: Bobbs-Marrill.

Harre, R., & Lamb, R. (Eds.). (1983). *The encyclopedic dictionary of psychology*. Cambridge, MA: The MIT Press.

Lonner, W. J. (1985). Issues in testing and assessment in cross-cultural counseling. *The Counseling Psychologist, 13*, 599–614.

Salvia, J., & Ysseldyke, J. E. (1995). *Assessment* (6th ed.). Boston: Houghton Mifflin.

Speck, F. G. (1918). Kinship terms and the family band among the Northeastern Algonkian. *American Anthropologist, 20*, 134–161.

Sue, D. W., & Sue, D. (1990). *Counseling the culturally different: Theory and practice* (2nd ed.). New York: John Wiley & Sons.

Wolman, B. B. (1973). *Dictionary of behavioral science*. New York: Van Nostrand Reinhold.

Susanna A. Hayes

CULTURAL COMPETENCE—The knowledge and understanding of a specific culture that enables an individual to effectively communicate and function within that culture. This usually entails details regarding language and meta-language, values and customs, symbols and worldviews. The rules of social interaction are governed by assumptions and expectations regarding patterns of behaviors and their meaning. One example is that in some cultures, a person is asked if he/she wanted something (usually a food item or physical help) three times. Only after the third time could the individual politely accept. If that person had accepted the offer after the first or second time, he/she would be considered to be rude. Thus, a culturally mismatched Western individual interacting with an Eastern individual may ask the hungry Eastern individual if he/she wanted more food. The Eastern individual, displaying appropriate restraint, will decline. The Western individual, not knowing the Eastern norm of restraint before indulgement, may never offer the food again, thus leaving a hungry visitor. Depending upon the perspective one or the other individual in this interaction would be considered to be culturally *in*competent. In other cultures, there is no need for a question; the need is anticipated and the object is presented without any verbal interchange. Cultural competence is important in any social encounter (Berry, Poortinga, Segall, & Dasen, 1992; Lonner & Malpass, 1994) but is arguably an essential component for counselors and psychotherapists wishing to be effective in their work with individuals from a given culture (Sue et al., 1982). Sue et al. (1982) believe that competency entails an awareness and sensitivity to culture and institutional influences as well as a willingness to deal with diversity as it is found. There were particular skills that were called for in cross-cultural work. The more obvious skills were a broader response repertoire, so as to more effectively and appropriately communicate with clients. LaFromboise & Foster (1992) and Bernal & Castro (1994) believed that the acquisition of cultural competencies in therapists required the commitment of significant training time and effort. Both practical and ethical concerns dictate the development of culturally sensitive intervention skills to deal with a population growing in diversity.

References

Bernal, M., & Castro, F. (1994). Are clinical psychologists prepared for service and research with ethnic minorities? Report of a decade of progress. *American Psychologist, 49*, 797–805.

Berry, J., Poortinga, Y., Segall, M., & Dasen, P. (1992). *Cross-cultural psychology: Research and applications*. Cambridge: Cambridge University Press.

LaFromboise, T., & Foster, S. (1992). Cross-cultural training: Scientist–practitioner model and methods. *The Counseling Psychologist, 20*, 472–489.

Lonner, W., & Malpass, R. (1994). *Psychology and culture*. Boston: Allyn & Bacon.
Sue, D., Bernier, J., Durran, A., Feinberg, L., Pedersen, P., Smith, E., & Vasquez-Nuttall, E. (1982). Position paper: Cross-cultural counseling competencies. *The Counseling Psychologist, 10*, 45–52.

John Moritsugu

CULTURAL CONFLICT—There is tremendous variation in norms, values, and perceptions across cultures. While virtually everyone is aware of the existence of variations in culture, most people have a tendency to perceive others only through their own culture's eyes. This tendency to use one's own culture as a reference point can easily lead to misunderstandings and conflicts between individuals or groups from different cultures. Thus, it is important for people to be aware of cultural variations in order to better understand and harmonize with people from other cultures. For instance, perceptions of time can vary across cultures; while some cultures place a high value on time and view it in more precise terms, other cultures have a more loosely constructed concept of time. As such, conflict could arise if individuals with different concepts of time made a date for 2:00. One person might expect to meet within a few minutes of 2:00, while the other person might expect to meet within a few hours of that time (Sue & Sue, 1990). The former person might feel hurt or angry, which may cause the latter to feel confused and defensive. This type of conflict can be avoided by being aware of others' cultural influences, as well as our own. One's values are also strongly influenced by culture and often hold deep meaning and significance for an individual. As such, differing or contradictory values between cultures could potentially create conflict if people are not sensitive to others' individual and cultural values. For instance, some cultures value harmony with nature while other see conquest over nature as desirable. This clash in values can create antagonism between people that get along well otherwise. Cultures also hold differing expectations for personal behavior, of which other cultures may not be aware. For example, the Vietnamese culture values obedience and places an emphasis on decorum and etiquette in social interactions. As such, Americans' tendency for very casual, informal behavior might be viewed as disrespectful or rude by someone from the Vietnamese culture (Berry, Poortinga, & Pandey, 1997; Pedersen, 1994). Great differences in values exist between *individualistic* and *collectivistic cultures*. Individualistic cultures, such as the United States, place an emphasis on the individual and as such value traits like independence, competition, and self-expression. In contrast, collectivist cultures, such as Japan, place an emphasis on the collective, and thus an emphasis/value is placed upon interdependence, cooperation, and following group norms. The collective may refer to groups such as the family, the village, or the society. One is very sensitive to what the group norms expect, and when the goals of the group are in conflict with one's personal goals, individualists will usually opt for their own personal goals while collectivists tend to put aside their own goals in favor of the group's goals. Recognizing this identification and loyalty to the collective can help others understand why collectivists are humble about their own achievements but acknowledge their failures while personally identifying with and supporting the achievements of their group (Berry et al., 1997; Lonner & Malpass, 1994; Pedersen, 1994; Sue & Sue, 1990).

References

Berry, J. W., Poortinga, Y. H., & Pandey, J. (1997). *Handbook of cross-cultural psychology. 1. Theory and method.* Needham Heights, MA: Allyn & Bacon.

Lonner, W., & Malpass, R. (1994). *Psychology and culture.* Needham Heights, MA: Allyn & Bacon.

Pedersen, P. (1994). *A handbook for devloping multicultural awareness.* Alexandria, VA: American Counseling Association.

Sue, D. W., & Sue, D. (1990). *Counseling the culturally different: Theory and practice* (2nd ed.). New York: Wiley.

Lisa Frye

CULTURAL CONGRUENCE—Any thought, belief, or practice that is consistent with the traditions of a particular culture. Cultural congruence serves to help preserve a culture, which also helps the members of that culture to maintain their identity and social cohesion in a rapidly changing world (Mansperger, 1995; see CULTURAL PRESERVATION). It is further argued that culturally congruent activities can serve as an important way to promote self-understanding (McLaughlin, 1989). However, when thoughts, beliefs, or practices which conflict with those of an indigenous culture are introduced (cultural incongruence), the result is often substantial change or destruction of the minority culture (Mansperger, 1995; see CULTURAL DESTRUCTIVENESS). Change or loss of a minority culture can also occur when minority culture assimilation into the dominant culture is a goal of the dominant culture (Robinson, 1985).

References

Mansperger, M. C. (1995). Tourism and cultural change in small-scale societies. *Human Organization, 54,* 87–94.

McLaughlin, D. (1989). The sociolinguistics of Navajo literacy. *Anthropology and Education Quarterly, 20,* 275–290.

Robinson, P. (1985). Language retention among Canadian Indians: A simultaneous equations model with dichotomous endogenous variables. *American Soclological Review, 50,* 515–529.

M. D'André Wilson

CULTURAL CONTINUITY—The preservation and elaboration of an ethnic culture (Simic, 1987). It involves the conservation of traditional values, obligations, and roles, even though the means by which they are preserved may change over time (Muecke, 1992). Individuals within a culture do not acquire, accept, and internalize all the features of culture presented to them. Nor does everyone in the same social environment learn the same things or learn things in the same order. The things which are internalized and passed on account for cultural continuity (Eisenhart, 1995). As there are shifts in values or environment, aspects of the culture can change or be lost, leading to changes in cultural continuity (Winer & Boos, 1993). People who actively participate in ethnic social life and in the maintenance of ethnic institutions and culture promote cultural continuity (Simic, 1987). Within the African American community, the church has been a catalyst for change and a conduit of cultural, social, and spiritual connectedness (McAdoo & Crawford, 1991). Of course, cultures vary on a continuum of continuities and discontinuities along different dimensions in cultural conditioning (Quinn, Newfield, & Protinsky, 1985).

References

Eisenhart, M. (1995). The fax, the jazz player, and the self-story teller: How do people organize culture? *Anthropology and Education Quarterly, 26*, 3–26.

McAdoo, H., & Crawford, V. (1991). The Black church and family support programs. *Prevention in Human Services, 9*, 193–203.

Muecke, M. (1992). Mother sold food, daughter sells her body: The cultural continuity of prostitution. *Social Science and Medicine, 35*, 891–901.

Quinn, W., Newfield, N., & Protinsky, H. (1985). Rites of passage in families with adolescents. *Family Process, 24*, 101–111.

Simic, A. (1987). Ethnicity as a career for the elderly: The Serbian-American case. *The Journal of Applied Gerontology, 6*, 113–126.

Winer, L., & Boos, H.E.A. (1993). Right throughs, rings and taws: Marbles terminology in Trinidad and Tobago. *Language in Society, 22*, 41–66.

M. D'André Wilson

CULTURAL DESTRUCTIVENESS—The undermining of traditions which are indigenous to a particular culture. Cultural destruction can occur through intentional and systematic means, as demonstrated by European colonization and domination of many African and American nations since the fourteenth century (Bulhan, 1985). Or, it can occur in less overt, but perhaps more insidious ways. When minority assimilation into the dominant culture is a goal of the dominant culture, attempts to improve conditions for minorities (i.e., increasing education levels) often result in losses or destruction of the minority culture (Robinson, 1985). An example of this is the stigmatized and restricted use of the Navajo language on Navajo reservations. The thought is that "due to the *alien* nature of Christian and academic institutions in traditional Navajo society" (p. 275), these subjects are better served by English (McLaughlin, 1989). This is also the case with increased contact between tourists and peoples from small-scale societies. This increased contact often results in substantial changes or destruction of the culture of the small-scale societies (Mansperger, 1995).

References

Bulhan, H. A. (1985). *Frantz Fanon and the psychology of oppression*. New York: Plenum.

Mansperger, M. C. (1995). Tourism and cultural change in small-scale societies. *Human Organization, 54*, 87–94.

McLaughlin, D. (1989). The sociolinguistics of Navajo literacy. *Anthropology and Education Quarterly, 20*, 275–290.

Robinson, P. (1985). Language retention among Canadian Indians: A simultaneous equations model with dichotomous endogenous variables. *American Sociological Review, 50*, 515–529.

M. D'André Wilson

CULTURAL DIFFERENCE HYPOTHESIS—An explanation for observed differences among ethnic or cultural groups in their expression of presumed universal human characteristics. Such differences may be more evident in research designs which focus on individual characteristics such as personality dimensions than in designs which compare social systems characteristics such as power distance (Hofstede, 1990/1991). Another frequent usage is an explanation for consistent differences in educational achievement between White and ethnic minority children in the United States. Initially presented as an alternative to the *deficit hypothsis*, which presumes lower SES class and nonwhite children to be intellectually inferior to White middle-class children (Zigler & Trickett, 1978), this approach explains underachievement in African-American children as a result of teaching strategies and assessment techniques which do not value minority children' culture-specific knowledge. Recently, Frisby (1993) has provided a comprehensive review of the rationale for and the limitations of the "Black cultural learning styles (BCLS)" as an explanation for achievement differences between White and Black children, particularly the tendency to maximize Black–White cultural incompatibilities and to minimize within race differences.

References

Frisby, C. (1993). One giant step backward: Myths of Black cultural learning styles. *School Psychology Review, 22*, 535–557.

Hofstede, G. (1990/1991). Empirical models of cultural differences. In N. Bleichrodt & P.J.D. Drenth (Eds.), *Contemporary issues in cross-cultural psychology* (pp. 4–20). Amsterdam: Swets & Zeitlinger.

Zigler, E., & Trickett, P. (1978). I.Q., social competence, and evaluation of early childhood intervention programs. *American Psychologist, 33*, 789–798.

Deborah Kirby Forgays

CULTURAL DRIFT—Cultural evolution or change resulting from random or chance variations in the frequency or prevalence of particular cultural ideas or "traits." The following is a hypothetical example: In a small culture in which the pottery craft is transmitted from mothers to daughters, one or more families favoring a particular pottery design produce a disproportionate number of daughters due to chance fluctuations in expected sex ratios, resulting in a greater frequency in subsequent generations of the favored design idea and product

(Koerper & Stickel, 1980). In cultural evolution, *cultural drift* is the analog of *genetic drift* or "sampling error" in biological evolution. Durham (1991) describes genetic drift as arising "from the chance events of gene transmission in finite populations, particularly in small populations in which random change can have a big impact" (p. 119). This conception of cultural drift is preferred by cultural evolution theorists who draw analogies between mechanisms of biological and cultural evolution (e.g., Alexander, 1979; Boyd & Richerson, 1985; Durham, 1991), but differs from its original usage. According to Eggan (1963), the concept of cultural drift was first coined by Sapir (1921) as an analog to his more famous linguistic drift concept. Like Sapir's linguistic drift concept, cultural drift in his earlier conception was described as directional and selective rather than random or chance (e.g., Eggan, 1963; Herskovits, 1955). For example, Herskovits (1955) described cultural drift as "the piling up of minor variations that are in consonance with pre-existing tendencies . . . [and that] change is brought about by a process whereby certain deviations from established norms are taken over by a number of people, thus initiating and continuing a tendency that becomes a trend" (p. 507). As Koerper and Stickel (1980) have noted, cultural drift in this earlier conception resembles what current evolutionary theorists refer to as *cultural mutation* and *cultural selection* (e.g., Alexander, 1979; Durham, 1991). Thus, for greater clarity and differentiation of cultural evolution concepts, the current definition of cultural drift as a cultural analog of genetic drift would seem preferable.

References

Alexander, R. D. (1979). *Darwinism and human affairs*. Seattle: University of Washington Press.

Boyd, R., & Richerson, P. J. (1985). *Culture and the evolutionary process*. Chicago: University of Chicago Press.

Durham, W. H. (1991). *Coevolution: Genes, culture, and human diversity*. Stanford, CA: Stanford University Press.

Eggan, F. (1963). Cultural drift and social change. *Current Anthropology, 4*, 347–355.

Herskovits, M. J. (1955). *Cultural anthropology: An abridged revision of Man and His Works*. New York: Alfred A. Knopf.

Koerper, H. C., & Stickel, E. G. (1980). Cultural drift: A primary process of culture change. *Journal of Anthropological Research, 36*, 463–469.

Sapir, E. (1921). *Language, an introduction to the study of speech*. New York: Harcourt, Brace.

A. Timothy Church

CULTURAL ENCAPSULATION—A set manner of interpreting and relating to the world based on a need to maintain the status quo. Originally developed by Wrenn (1962) as a concept to explain the resistance to change in human beings, specifically counselors. Wrenn initially suggested that cultural encapsulation represents a cocoon which is formed in order to protect the individual from the threat of change or differing worldviews. He noted that the encapsulation can occur within an individual, a culture, or a subculture in an effort to behave as if the present will continue indefinitely. Wrenn (1985) identified two types of encapsulations which serve to deny reality: (1) *hopelessness* about the situation whereby the individual feels unable to make changes due to the vastness of the problem, its complexity, or its chronicity; and (2) a *denial* of the situation. While the term has gained acceptance in the cross-cultural literature to describe a myopic worldview and ethnocentricity (LaFromboise & Foster, 1989), there has been little advancement of the concept through theory or empirical research.

References

LaFromboise, T. D., & Foster, S. L. (1989). Ethics in multicultural counseling. In P. Pedersen, J. Draguns, W. Lonner, & J. Trimble (Eds.), *Counseling across cultures* (3rd ed.). Honolulu: University of Hawaii Press.

Wrenn, C. G. (1962). The culturally encapsulated counselor. *Harvard Educational Review, 32,* 444–449.

Wrenn, C. G. (1985). Afterword: The culturally encapsulated counselor revisited. In P. Pedersen (Ed.), *Handbook of cross-cultural counseling and therapy* (pp. 323–329). Westport, CT: Greenwood Press.

Ruben J. Echemendia

CULTURAL EQUIVALENCE—An umbrella term referring to the cross-cultural validity, utility, and fairness of a psychological construct (concept), psychological test, or single item (question) in a test or functioning at those levels. Analogous modifiers include *etic*, *culture-free*, and *invariant* (see also PSYCHOMETRIC EQUIVALENCE); common antonyms include *emic constructs*, *test bias*, and *differential item functioning* (Hui & Triandis, 1985). Although the origin of the term cultural equivalence is murky (Helms, 1992), the reasons for the term are clear. Sociologically, the term arose to describe tests and items in less polemic fashion. In some contexts, descriptors such as *fair vs. unfair* and *biased vs. unbiased* are prematurely evaluative or too political (Holland & Wainer, 1993). Statistically, the need for neutral terminology arises from the fact that a test can be nonequivalent (biased) for mean level comparisons across groups, even though that test is equally useful (fair) as a selection tool. Even without group-normed cutoff points, a test can be equally useful in predicting good candidates (for therapy, for job success, for academic success) despite its nonequivalence when making judgments about a group's average score on a construct (depression, conscientiousness, verbal ability, etc.). The converse is also true. A test can be biased as a selection tool even though it gives equal measurement of its intended construct across cultural groups (Camilli & Shepard, 1994). Distinctions regarding construct validity, predictive utility, and overall fairness are similarly important when dealing with single items or with abstract concepts (Cronbach, 1984). As such, cultural equivalency is only helpful as a general rubric. Beyond this, it is necessary to specify the context and purpose for which an item, test, or construct is allegedly equivalent or non-equivalent.

References

Camilli, G., & Shepard, L. A. (1994). *Methods for identifying biased test items*. Thousand Oaks, CA: Sage.

Cronbach, L. (1984). *Essentials of psychological testing*. New York: Harper and Row.

Helms, J. E. (1992). Why is there no study of cultural equivalency in standardized cognitive ability testing? *American Psychologist, 47*, 1083–1101.

Holland, P., & Wainer, H. (1993). *Differential item functioning*. Hillsdale, NJ: Erlbaum.

Hui, C. H., & Triandis, H. C. (1985). Measurement in cross-cultural psychology. *Journal of Cross-Cultural Psychology, 16*, 131–152.

William Peter Flannery

CULTURAL EVOLUTION—The sequence and process of cultural change over time; applied on both a general or global scale (e.g., in hypothesized universal stages of cultures or societies) and to the evolution of ideas and behaviors in specific cultural groups within and across generations. Studies of cultural evolutionary sequences have focused on the construction of stage typologies (e.g., band–tribe–chiefdom–state), the primary cause(s) of these stage sequences (e.g., technological innovation or population growth), the direction or criteria of change (e.g., greater social complexity or functional differentiation), and the limiting factors that inhibit evolutionary change (e.g., infertile soil, disease, and protein scarcity; Rambo, 1991). Studies of evolutionary process have focused on the units of selection in cultural evolution (e.g., innovation, mutation, direct transmittion, cultural drift, and cultural selection; Alexander, 1979; Boyd & Richerson, 1985; Cavalli-Sforza & Feldman, 1981). As a scientific paradigm, the perceived legitimacy of the cultural evolutionary approach has waxed and waned and the approach remains controversial. Early stage schemes in the nineteenth century were referred to as unilinear because they postulated a common trajectory or sequence of stages for all cultures (e.g., savagery–barbarism–civilization), with some cultures (e.g., Western European) having progressed further than others. By the early twentieth century these schemes were widely rejected due to their ethnocentricism, link to Social Darwinism, and limited empirical base, and because of a shift in anthropology to the detailed study of individual cultures and their unique histories and dynamics. A revival of interest in cultural evolution occurred during the 1950s and 1960s, led by White (1959), who proposed a unilinear theory of general cultural evolution based on increasing levels of energy use, and Steward (1955), who proposed a multilinear theory that focused on the local histories and ecological adaptations made by cultural groups within particular environments. In recent years a number of theories have addressed the relation between biological and cultural evolution (Boyd & Richerson, 1985; Cavalli-Sforza & Feldman, 1971; Durham, 1991).

References

Alexander, R. D. (1979). *Darwinism and human affairs*. Seattle: University of Washington Press.

Boyd, R., & Richerson, P. J. (1985). *Culture and the evolutionary process*. Chicago: University of Chicago Press.

Cavalli-Sforza, L. L., & Feldman, M. W. (1981). *Cultural transmission and evolution: A quantitative approach*. Princeton, NJ: Princeton University Press.

Durham, W. H. (1991). *Coevolution: Genes, culture, and human diversity*. Stanford, CA: Stanford University Press.

Rambo, A. T. (1991). The study of cultural evolution. In A. T. Rambo & K. Gillogly (Eds.), *Profiles in cultural evolution: Papers from a conference in honor of Elman R. Service* (Anthropological Papers No. 85, pp. 23–109). Ann Arbor: University of Michigan, Museum of Anthropology.

Steward, J. (1955). *Theory of culture change*. Urbana: University of Illinois Press.

White, L. A. (1959). *The evolution of culture: The development of civilization to the fall of Rome*. New York: McGraw-Hill.

A. Timothy Church

CULTURAL INCAPACITY—''Cultural competence is a set of congruent behaviors, attitudes and policies that come together in a (service delivery) system . . . to enable that system . . . to work effectively in cross-cultural situations'' (Cross, 1988, p. 1). The *cultural competence model*, developed by Terry L. Cross and others (1989) at the Georgetown University Child Development Center in Washington, DC, provides a framework for service delivery to children of color who have severe emotional disturbance. The model takes a developmental approach to moving the system toward providing progressively more culturally competent services (Isaacs & Benjamin, 1991). Cultural incapacity is the unintentional failure or incapacity of an agency or care delivery system to provide assistance to cultural minority clients or communities (Cross, 1988). It is one of serveral possible ways a system, agency, or professional might respond to cultural diversity. Part of a six-point continuum of cultural competence with cultural destructiveness on one end and cultural proficiency at the other end, cultural incapacity is characterized by a service delivery system that discriminates against nondominant cultures (including people of color and persons with disabilities). Although the system does not seek to deliberately destroy a culture, it is extremely biased and believes in the racial superiority of the dominant group. It supports a policy of segregation, discriminatory hiring practices, oppression through the enforcement of racist policies, stereotyping, and the uneven distribution or resources. These systems are frequently characterized by their unrealistic fear and lower expectations of cultural minority clients.

References

Cross, T. L. (1988). Cultural competence continuum. *Focal point*. Bulletin of The Research and Training Center on Family Support and Children's Mental Health, Portland State University.

Cross, T. L. (1989). *Towards a culturally competent system of care*. Monograph on effective services for minority children who are severely emotionally disturbed. Georgetown University, Washington, DC.

Isaacs, M. R., & Benjamin, M. P. (1991). *Towards a culturally competent system of care. Volume II: Programs which utilize culturally competent principles*. Monograph on effective services for minority children who are severely emotionally disturbed. Georgetown University, Washington, DC.

Monica D. Lange

CULTURAL LOSS—The literature on cross-cultural encounters (Brislin, 1981) describes the experience of both short-term and long-term cross-cultural encounters of individuals. They found that when "sojourners" returned home, the people in the "home country" made attributions regarding their behavior based on very minimal information. Often these judgments were negative and represented a belief that the culture had been lost, e.g., "they've become disrespectful" (p. 133). Nevertheless, returnees to the culture often attributed their change in behavior to situational factors. Sluzki (1979) examined immigration and family conflict and how the consequences of cultural loss "resulted in intercultural rather than intergenerational" (p. 387) clashes between second and third generation children and their parents. He stated that "the conflict between the child's dominant style of coping—congruent with the family culture—and the differently defined rules and boundaries within large sectors of the extrafamilial world results in a label of 'delinquency' for the child's behavior" (p. 387). Bulhan (1985), in discussing his stages of identity development of oppressed people, detailed the results of the imposed dominant culture on oppressed people as "less a question of overlap of cultures than the obliteration of one and the supplantation of the other" (p. 193). Bulhan discussed how the experience of cultural loss is defended against and how an oppressed person pulls together a developed self. The first stage in identity development of oppressed people is the mechanism of defense we know as *identification with the aggressor*. This "involves increased assimilation into the dominant culture while simultaneously rejecting one's own culture" (p. 193). For example, this defensive maneuver is expressed in oppressed groups by accusing educated or economically successful family members as "trying to be White." In discussing power dynamics between different groups, (Pinderhughes, 1989) explains that a shift in power from one group to another can be experienced and understood as "a psychological loss" (p. 140), including the loss in relation to one's cultural roles. Pinderhughes (1989) identified the vicious cycle of victim and aggressor by explaining the role of power in maintaining the experience of powerlessness: "the loss of that aggrandizing, gratifying role may be perceived as harmful or threatening. . . . This loss can set in motion a process whereby those who have been dominant can begin to feel themselves like victims. . . . They respond to their sense of powerlessness in all the ways we have identified to keep their sense of power" (pp. 140–141).

References

Brislin, R. W. (1981). *Cross-cultural encounters: Face-to-face interaction*. New York: Pergamon.
Bulhan, H. A. (1985). *Franz Fanon and the psychology of oppression*. New York: Plenum.
Pinderhughes, E. (1989). *Understanding race, ethnicity, & power: The key to efficacy in clinical practice*. New York: The Free Press.
Sluzki, C. E. (1979). Migration and family conflict. *Family Process, 18*, 379–390.

Leslie C. Jackson

CULTURAL MOSAIC—*Culture* is defined as the beliefs, values, attitudes, customs, experiences, and behaviors that the members of a society tend to have in common, expect of one another, and pass on to one another (Statt, 1989). *Mosaic* is defined as "decoration made by interlaying small pieces of variously colored material to form pictures or patterns" (Webster, 1989, p. 773). Thus, a cultural mosaic can be defined as a mixture of many cultures existing side-by-side that contribute to the richness of the society. The statement "The whole is greater than the sum of its parts" would describe the richness of a cultural mosaic. Another term used to define this phenomenon is *salad bowl*, where different cultures live cooperatively (like vegetables in a salad) and have a common goal (being a good salad) without each ingredient losing its own individual identity (or "vegetableness"[1]). Salad bowl and mosiac are a little different from pluralism where cultures/people live side-by-side autonomously rather than working cooperatively and interacting.

Note

1. Term coined by Christine C. Iijima Hall.

References

Statt, D. (1989). *The concise dictionary of psychology*. New York: Routledge.
Webster's Ninth New Collegiate Dictionary. (1989). Springfield, MA: Merriam-Webster.

Christine C. Iijima Hall

CULTURAL OPPRESSION—The oppression, discrimination, and racism that the culturally different experience. *Cultural oppression* involves institutional racism, which is a set of policies, priorities, and accepted normative patterns designed to subjugate, obligate, and force individuals and groups into dependence on the larger society (Sue & Sue, 1990). Radical therapists felt that emotional illness was not an intrapsychic phenomenon but was created by cultural oppression. They believed that mental illness was created by the emotional repression necessary to endure living in American society (Sayre, 1989). Traditionally, a woman's body concept and self-concept have been oppressed by the dominant, male, patriarchal culture (Dworkin, 1989). One writer has suggested that the "privileged position" enjoyed by White, middle-class men in American society oppresses the traditional oppressors by encouraging the repression of their feelings and limited emotional attachments (Schurman, 1987).

References

Dworkin, S. H. (1989). Not in man's image: Lesbians and the cultural oppression of body image. *Women and Therapy, 8,* 27–39.
Sayre, J. (1989). Radical therapy: A research note on the use of ideological work in maintaining a deviant subculture. *Deviant Behavior, 10,* 401–412.
Schurman, P. G. (1987). Male liberation. *Pastoral Psychology, 35,* 189–199.
Sue, D. W., & Sue, D. (1990). *Counseling the culturally different: Theory and practice* (2nd ed.). New York: Wiley.

M. D'André Wilson

CULTURAL PARANOIA—A hesitancy about self-disclosure based on one's concern about being misunderstood, hurt, or taken advantage of if personal information is shared. *Cultural paranoia* is often considered a healthy response to racism (Sue & Sue, 1990; see HEALTHY PARANOIA). The notion of healthy cultural paranoia was originally advanced by Grier and Cobb (1968). In this conceptualization, it is argued that for a Black man's survival in America, it is necessary to develop a cultural paranoia in which every White man is a potential enemy unless proven otherwise, and further to conceive every social system as set against him unless he personally finds out differently (Ridley, 1984). A culturally different client who is psychologically healthy but culturally guarded against racism is said to possess a healthy cultural paranoia (Ridley, 1984).

References

Grier, W. H., & Cobb, P. M. (1968). *Black rage.* New York: Bantam Books.
Ridley, C. R. (1984). Clinical treatment of the nondisclosing Black client: A therapeutic paradox. *American Psychologist, 39,* 1234–1244.
Sue, D. W., & Sue, D. (1990). *Counseling the culturally different: Theory and practice* (2nd ed.). New York: Wiley.

M. D'André Wilson

CULTURAL PLURALISM—A state of society in which members of diverse ethnic, "racial," religious, or social groups maintain an autonomous participation and development of their traditional culture, values, beliefs, and special interests within the confines of a common civilization. That means that individuals and groups enjoy mutual participation within the life of the nation with no single model or set of values, beliefs, and interests superimposed on and thus defining all life. *Cultural diversity* or *difference* exists as a matter of fact; cultural pluralism, by contrast, is a negotiated state of being wherein mutual respect for individual and group differences has been installed and serves as a social contract that ensures the right of equal participation.

Reference

Cheatham, H. E. (1991). Epilogue. In H. E. Cheatham and Associates (Eds.), *Cultural pluralism on campus* (pp. 203–205). Washington, DC: American College Personnel Association. Reprinted with permission of The American College Personnel Association.

Harold E. Cheatham

CULTURAL PRESERVATION—The maintenance of traditions which are indigenous to a particular culture. Cultural preservation can help the members of a culture maintain their identity and social cohesion in a rapidly changing world (Mansperger, 1995). Active participation in ethnic social life and maintenance of ethnic institutions help to preserve that culture and promote cultural continuity (Simic, 1987; see CULTURAL CONTINUITY). In addition to maintaining a traditional culture, it is argued that activities involved with cultural preservation can be an important way to promote self-understanding (McLaughlin, 1989). When minority assimilation into the dominant culture is a goal of the dominant culture, attempts to improve conditions for minorities (i.e., increasing education levels) often result in losses in terms of minority cultural preservation (Robinson, 1985).

References

Mansperger, M. C. (1995). Tourism and cultural change in small-scale societies. *Human Organization, 54,* 87–94.
McLaughlin, D. (1989). The sociolinguistics of Navajo literacy. *Anthropology and Education Quarterly, 20,* 275–290.
Robinson, P. (1985). Language retention among Canadian Indians: A simultaneous equations model with dichotomous endogenous variables. *American Sociological Review, 50,* 515–529.
Simic, A. (1987). Ethnicity as a career for the elderly: The Serbian-American case. *The Journal of Applied Gerontology, 6,* 113–126.

M. D'André Wilson

CULTURAL PROFICIENCY—More commonly known as *(multi-) cultural competence*, though *intercultural skill* is also a synonym, it typically refers to expertise in working effectively with a client in a human service context (historically the term has been mostly applied to counseling settings) whose cultural background differs from that of the service provider. The first use of the term is unclear, though Devereux's (1953) early study described difficulties in being culturally proficient in working with Plains Indians, while Wrenn's (1962) early paper warned of the dangers of *cultural encapsulation* against which cultural proficiency is contrasted. The Education and Training Committee of the American Psychological Asociation's (APA) Division 17 (Sue et al., 1982) proposed 11 specific cross-cultural counseling proficiencies, grouped under the three domains of (1) beliefs/attitudes, (2) knowledge, and (3) skills. In addition, APA's

Task Force on the Delivery of Services to Ethnic Minority Populations (APA, 1990) developed guidelines to providers to culturally (as well as ethnically and linguistically) diverse clients to help promote cultural proficiency. General guidebooks for cultural proficiency/multicultural competence training have been written (e.g., Pedersen, Draguns, Lonner, & Trimble, 1989; Sue & Sue, 1990), and cultural competency assessment measures have been developed (Suzuki, Meller, & Ponterotto, 1996).

References

American Psychological Association. (1990, August). *Guidelines for providers of psy-chological services to ethnic, linguistic and culturally diverse populations.* Board of Ethnic Minority Affairs Task Force on the Delivery of Services to Ethnic Minority Populations. Washington, DC: Author.

Devereux, G. (1951). Three technical problems in psychotherapy of Plains Indian pa-tients. *American Journal of Psychotherapy, 5*, 411–423.

Pedersen, P. B., Draguns, J. G., Lonner, W. J., & Trimble, J. E. (1989). *Counseling across cultures* (3rd ed.). Honolulu: University of Hawaii Press.

Suzuki, L. A., Meller, P. J., & Ponterotto, J. G. (Eds.). (1996). *Handbook of multicultural assessment: Clinical, psychological, and educational applications.* San Francisco: Jossey-Bass.

Sue, D. W., Bernier, J. E., Durran, A., Feinberg, L., Pedersen, P., Smith, E. J., & Vasques-Nuttall, E. (1982). Position paper: Cross-cultural counseling competen-cies. *The Counseling Psychologist, 10*, 45–52.

Wrenn, C. G. (1962). The culturally encapsulated counselor. *Harvard Educational Re-view, 32*, 444–449.

Fred Ninonuevo

CULTURAL RACISM—Refers to feelings, behaviors, or patterns of behavior reflecting a belief that one culture's accomplishments, acheivements, and crea-tivity are superior to other cultures' based on differences in racial composition of the groups. These cultural patterns reflect majority group dominance which lead to preconceived notions of which cultural elements (aesthetics, language, education, medicine, science, religion, standards, and norms of morality) are valued (Axelson, 1993). Cultural racism, first introduces by Jones (1972), re-flects the conscious or subconscious belief in the superiority of Euro-American cultural patterns and practices, and the inferiority of visible racial or ethnic group (i.e., Native American, Black, Hispanic, and Asian) patterns and practices (Jones & Carter, 1996). Fundamental to all forms of racism, cultural racism contains elements of both *individual racism* and *institutional racism* (see entries for those terms), and assumes superiority of one race's cultural heritage over that of an-other race (Jones, 1972). In order to avoid feelings of inferiority, minority group members may experience pressures to assimilate or acculturate to the group possessing greater prestige and power, which may create culture conflicts (Sue & Sue, 1990). Cultural racism is closely related to *ethnocentrism* (see entry).

Power is the factor that transforms ethnocentrism into cultural racism (Jones, 1972).

References

Axelson, J. A. (1993). *Counseling and development in a multicultural society* (2nd ed.). Pacific Grove, CA: Brooks/Cole.

Jones, J. M. (1972). *Prejudice and racism*. Reading, MA: Addison-Wesley.

Jones, J. M., & Carter, R. T. (1996). Racism and White racial identity. In B. P. Bowser & R. G. Hunt (Eds.), *Impacts of racism on White Americans* (pp. 1–23). Thousand Oaks, CA: Sage.

Sue, D. W., & Sue, D. (1990). *Counseling the culturally different: Theory and practice* (2nd ed.). New York: Wiley.

Saundra Tomlinson-Clarke

CULTURAL REGION—An area defined by climatic and land boundaries that must adapt to its specific resources and technological possibilities, sometimes referred to as a "culture area" or a "geocultural region." The inhabitants of these geographic regions often share the same living styles, religion, and language. They also must survive off the resources the area provides to obtain the essentials: food, clothing, tools, and shelter. Societies within each area may appear similar due to the influence they have on one another through sharing and trading technologies. These regions developed after Northern groups of North America migrated south some 20,000 years ago. However, the term's origin traces back to the first century A.D., where Tacitus tried to divide German cultures by regions (Mattingly, 1960). During the mid-1800s, Adolf Bastian utilized this concept to divide North America into five culture areas (Koepping, 1983). Meanwhile, Otis Mason applied the term to 18 Indian cultural/environmental regions within America (Mason, 1895). In the 1960s Meinig (1965) took the concept of culture area and divided it into four sections: a core, a domain, a sphere, and outliers. Today, the term is still popular in many different academic fields including economics, ethnology, anthropology, geography, and ecology.

References

Gastil, R. (1975). *Cultural regions of the U. S.* Seattle: University of Washington Press.

Koepping, K. P. (1983). *Adolf Bastian and the psychic unity of mankind*. St. Lucia, Australia: University of Queensland Press.

Mason, O. (1895). Influence of environment upon human industries or arts. *Annual Report of the Smithsonian Institution* (pp. 639–665).

Mattingly, H. (Trans.). (1960). *Cornelius Tacitus, on Britain and Germany*. Harmondsworth: Penguin Books.

Meinig, D. (1965). The Morman culture region: Strategies and patterns in the geography of the American West, 1847–1964. *Annals of the Association of American Geographers, 55*, 191–220.

Joseph E. Trimble and Heather K. Mertz

CULTURAL RELATIVISM—A theoretical construct built upon the notion that a culture can be evaluated only by its own standards (Keesing & Keesing, 1971); that no objective standards exist to evaluate culture. A relativistic perspective avoids any imposition of value judgment and seeks to understand cultural context in its own terms (Pedersen, 1995). Cultural relativism emerged at the turn of the twentieth century as part of social science's movement against evolutionist thinking or what has been termed "social Darwinism." The humanistic reaction was a call to end the speculations of the armchair anthroplogists whose writings reflected ethnocentric biases and racist implications. The works of British theorists Bronislaw Malinowski and A. R. Radcliffe-Brown, often identified functionalists, moved anthropology out of the nineteenth-century armchair perspective and into the field. Their works, while different, documented the uniqueness with which differing cultural groups problem solved, made their way, and lived in the world (Rosman & Rubel, 1981; Kaplan & Manners, 1972). There has been much debate in the anthropological and philosophical literature regarding relativism as a concept (Parsons, 1937; Herskovits, 1951, 1955). It is difficult, if not impossible, to live in and observe the world from a position that is completely nonjudgmental. One only needs to consider historical and contemporary events in the world cultures such as genocide, customs such as "genital mutilation," and cultural practices of racism and oppression to understand the complexity of a purely relativistic perspective. Herskovits (1949) described the complexity by using the example of cultural practices of monogamy versus polygamy. Both practices make sense, given their cultural backdrops, but are likely to be judged negatively by those who fail to recognize the relevant cultural rationale. If, on the other hand, one decides to judge one culture by another, or apply some set of theoretical universals, then one risks imposing values, beliefs, and ideologies at the cost of those that exist and have sustained the culture. Herskovits (1949) defines the principle of cultural relativism in the following way: "Judgments are based on experience, and experience is interpreted by each individual in terms of his own enculturation" (p. 63). Anthropologists tend to argue that cultural relativism is a position one would benefit by adopting temporarily so as to sort out meaningful actions, behaviors, customs, and traditions from the trivial (Parsons, 1937); or, as Geertz (1973) might add, to sort "winks from twitches and real winks from mimicked ones" (p. 16). Berry (1974) advocated for a position of *radical cultural relativism* in the exploration of intelligence so as to consider cultural variations and contexts in the meaning of intelligence. Intelligence was assumed to be a universal construct yet, as Berry points out, its meaning was built upon Western psychological science. Multicultural counselors can not only benefit from understanding the insider's wisdom that can be accessed through this position of cultural relativism, but are more likely to be meaningfully empathic to the culturally different client.

References

Berry, J. W. (1974). Radical cultural relativism and the concept of intelligence. In J. W. Berry & P. R. Dasen (Eds.), *Culture and cognition: Readings in cross-cultural psychology* (pp. 225–229). London: Methuen.

Geertz, C. (1973). *The interpretation of cultures*. New York: Basic Books.

Herskovits, M. (1949). *Man and his works*. New York: Alfred A. Knopf.

Herskovits, M. (1951). Tender and tough minded anthropology and the study of values in culture. *Southwestern Journal of Anthropology, 7*, 22–31.

Herskovits, M. (1955). *Cultural anthropology*. New York: Alfred A. Knopf.

Kaplan, D., & Manners, R. (1972. *Culture theory*. Englewood Cliffs, NJ: Prentice-Hall.

Keesing, R. M., & Keesing, F. M. (1971). *New perspectives in cultural anthropology*. New York: Holt, Rinehart & Winston.

Parsons, T. (1937). *The structure of social action*. New York: McGraw-Hill.

Pedersen, P. B. (1995). Culture-centered ethical guidelines for counselors. In J. G. Ponterotto, J. M. Casas, L. A. Suzuki, & C. M. Alexander (Eds.), *Handbook of multicultural counseling* (pp. 34–49). Thousand Oaks, CA: Sage.

Rosman, A., & Rubel, P. (1981). *The tapestry of culture*. Glenview, IL: Scott, Foresman.

Christopher J. Weiss

CULTURAL SYNERGY—Is the maximization of the advantages of cultural diversity without the disadvantages which accompany stereotyping (Moran & Harris, 1981). Cultural synergy within a group implies the gestalt notion that more can be accomplished by utilizing the diversity within that group than could have been produced by the summation of each subgroup's single contribution. Each subgroup must go beyond its own cultural perspective to realize the enhancement in perspectives gained from cooperatively embracing cultural pluralism and heterogeneity. That is, both differences and similarities must be recognized and respected since there are many ways to reach a final goal and each way is relevant and effective for its respective group. The culturally synergistic way for a diverse group is that which is compatible and a synthesis of perspectives of all subgroups in a way that transcends the most effective strategy for any one subgroup (Adler, 1991; Wright, 1993). For example, if all ethnic minority groups were to band together to fight racism, this would be more effective than each group fighting racism separately.

References

Adler, N. J. (1991). *International dimensions of organizational behavior*. Boston: PWS-Kent.

Moran, R. T., & Harris, P. R. (1981). *Managing cultural synergy*. Houston, TX: Gulf Publishing Company.

Wright, D. J. (1993). *Multicultural issues in organizational consultation: A conceptual model for intervention*. Paper presented at the 101st Annual Convention of the American Psychological Association, Toronto, Canada.

Yoshito Kawahara

CULTURALLY DEPRIVED—Generally used to refer to members of lower socioeconomic groups who have experienced limited access to education, and who have not benefitted from aspects of U.S. middle-class culture such as education, books, and formal language training. This term was popularized by Riessman (1962) in describing a new approach to educating "deprived" children. A large portion of the deprived co-cultures is considered to be composed of cultural and racial minority groups who were characterized as the disorganized minority element, lacking motivation, reading skills, and proper nutrition (Riessman, 1962). *Culturally deprived* is used interchangeably with *educationally disadvantaged* and *poverty-ridden*, is associated with the inner city, and although other cultural groups may be included, the term is used as a euphemism for Black people (Johnson, 1969). In challenging the genetically deficient model of behavior, social scientists used the culturally deficient model of behavior to explain the culturally different. The culturally deficient model construed environmental factors, lifestyles, and values of ethnic minorities as the basis of cultural deprivation (Katz, 1985; Sue & Sue, 1990). Culturally deprived implies an inferior culture (Ridley, 1995), or an absence of culture (Atkinson, Morten, & Sue, 1993), and assumes superiority of White middle-class values (Sue et al., 1982). The cultural deprivation model operates primarily within the U.S. education system as a reaction to the 1954 Supreme Court decision on *Brown v. Board of Education of Topeka*, and assumes that the [maladaptive] culture of Black Americans does not prepare Black children for high achievement in school (Mays, 1985) or provide opportunities for appropriate socialization, cognitive stimulation, or language development (Johnson, 1969). Baratz and Baratz (1970) presented the cultural difference model as a viable alternative to the other models of behavior that assume that the behavior of Blacks is inferior and pathological. Recent literature uses the term culturally diverse when referring to cultural differences (Sue & Sue, 1990).

References

Atkinson, D. R., Morten, G., & Sue, D. W. (1993). *Counseling American minorities: A cross-cultural perspective* (4th ed.). Madison, WI: Brown & Benchmark.

Baratz, S. S., & Baratz, J. C. (1970). Early childhood intervention: The social science base of institutional racism. *Harvard Educational Review, 40*, 29–50.

Johnson, J. L. (1969). Special education and the inner city: A challenge for the future or another means for cooling the markout? *The Journal of Special Education, 3*, 241–251.

Katz, J. H. (1985). The sociopolitical nature of counseling. *The Counseling Psychologist, 13*, 615–624.

Mays, V. M. (1985). The Black American and psychotherapy: The dilemma. *Psychotherapy, 22*, 379–388.

Ridley, C. R. (1995). *Overcoming unintentional racism in counseling and therapy: A practitioner's guide to intentional intervention.* Thousand Oaks, CA: Sage.

Riessman, F. (1962). *The culturally deprived child.* New York: Harper & Brothers.

Sue, D. W., Bernier, J. E., Durran, A., Feinberg, L., Pedersen, P., Smith, E. J., &

Vasquez-Nuttall, E. (1982). Position paper: Cross-cultural counseling competencies. *The Counseling Psychologist, 10,* 45–52.

Sue, D. W., & Sue, D. (1990). *Counseling the culturally different: Theory and practice* (2nd ed.). New York: Wiley.

Saundra Tomlinson-Clarke

CULTURALLY DISADVANTAGED—A relative term that refers to anyone who cannot participate in the dominant culture, or who is handicapped or inhibited by their background from growing up and living a competent and satisfying life in U.S. society. Low acheivement in school is associated with a culturally disadvantaged background (Johnson, 1970) The culturally disadvanteged are characterized by complex family, community, health and educational conditions, lifestyles, and values that result in the absence of basic skills, in low school achievement, and in illiteracy (Passow, 1963). Although the likelihood of being culturally disadvantaged increases if one is a member of a minority group, the terms *minority group* and *culturally disadvantaged* are not synonymous (Johnson, 1970). Associated with the deficient model of behavior (Sue et al., 1982; Sue & Sue, 1990), culturally disadvantaged is used synonymously with culturally deprived, impoverished, and culturally handicapped, and connotes inadequacy (Riessman, 1962). Related terms are educationally deprived, culturally different, and socially different (Johnson, 1969; Mays, 1985; see entries for those terms). Culturally disadvantaged was a term accepted and used by most educators in the 1960s (Johnson, 1970). The term was popularized in books such as *The Culturally Deprived Child* (Riessman, 1962), *Education in Depressed Areas* (Passow, 1963), and *Teaching the Culturally Disadvantaged: A Rational Approach* (Johnson, 1970).

References

Johnson, J. L. (1969). Special education and the inner city: A challenge for the future or another means for cooling the markout? *The Journal of Special Education, 3,* 241–251.

Johnson, K. R. (1970). *Teaching the culturally disadvantaged: A rational approach.* Palo Alto, CA: Science Research Associates, Inc.

Mays, V. M. (1985). The Black American and psychotherapy: The dilemma. *Psychotherapy, 22,* 379–388.

Passow, A. H. (Ed.). (1963). *Education in depressed areas.* New York: Teachers College Press.

Riessman, F. (1962). *The culturally deprived child.* New York: Harper & Brothers.

Sue, D. W., Bernier, J. E., Durran, A., Feinberg, L., Pedersen, P., Smith, E. J., & Vasquez-Nuttall, E. (1982). Position paper: Cross-cultural counseling competencies. *The Counseling Psychologist, 10,* 45–52.

Sue, D. W., & Sue, D. (1990). *Counseling the culturally different: Theory and practice* (2nd ed.). New York: Wiley.

Saundra Tomlinson-Clarke

CULTURALLY DISTINCT—Refers to the unique characteristics, or collection of characteristics, that typify a particular cultural or ethnic group. In describing a group as *culturally distinct*, one distinguishes that group from others on the basis of cultural traits. Triandis (1985) outlined several areas in which cultures differ, including perceptual selectivity, information-processing strategies, cognitive structures, and habits. For example, collectivistic cultures (e.g., Japan) respect the norms, rules, and hierarchy of in-groups. In contrast, people in individualistic cultures (e.g., the United States) are more concerned with personal standards and uniqueness. The ascription of people along these dimensions will form culturally distinct groups. Clinically speaking, there are a number of psychiatric disorders found in culturally distinct groups. Neurasthenia, for example, is a disorder typically found among Asians; Kleinman (1982) described the physical symptoms of weakness, headaches, and other somatic complaints as expressions of psychological distress. Somatization is often cited as a culturally acceptable expression of psychological disturbance among Asian and Asian American populations (Mollica & Lavelle, 1988; Sue & Sue, 1991). In addition, Appendix I of the *Diagnostic and Statistical Manual of Mental Disorders* (American Psychiatric Association, 1994) describes a variety of other disorders that correspond to particular cultures.

References

American Psychiatric Association. (1994). *Diagnostic and statistical manual of mental disorders* (4th ed.). Washington, DC: Author.

Kleinman, A. (1982). Neurasthenia and depression: A study of somatization and culture in China. *Culture, Medicine, and Psychiatry, 6*, 117–190.

Mollica, R. F., & Lavelle, J. (1988). Southeast Asian refugees. In L. Comas-Diaz & E.E.H. Griffith (Eds.), *Clinical guidelines in cross-cultural mental health* (pp. 262–304). New York: Wiley.

Sue, D., & Sue, D. W. (1991). Counseling strategies for Chinese Americans. In C. C. Lee & B. L. Richardson (Eds.), *Multicultural issues in counseling: New approaches to diversity* (pp. 79–90). Alexandria, VA: American Association for Counseling and Development.

Triandis, H. (1985). Some major dimensions of cultural variation in client populations. In P. Pedersen (Ed.), *Handbook of cross-cultural counseling and therapy* (pp. 21–28). Westport, CT: Greenwood Press.

Jonathan Kaplan

CULTURALLY SENSITIVE APPROACHES—Used to describe the use of techniques, tools, and mindsets that are respectful of characteristics engendered by different ethnic and cultural groups, applied in both clinical and research settings. Due to the confusion surrounding the definition and operationalization of cultural sensitivity, Ridley, Mendoza, Kanitz, Angermeier, and Zenk (1994) proposed a theoretical model of the construct. They defined *cultural sensitivity* as "the ability of counselors to acquire, develop, and actively use an accurate cultural perceptual schema in the course of multicultural counseling" (p. 130).

In the fields of counseling and clinical psychology, a culturally sensitive approach may be taken toward both assessment and treatment. For example, culture practice theory (Miller-Jones, 1989) states that skills and abilities develop in specific cultural contexts. Psychological assessments may underestimate a client's abilities when the testing environments and procedures are different from the context in which the client developed those competencies. Furthermore, culturally sensitive assessments may not only require the development of separate norms and instruments for different cultural groups, but also a psychometric reexamination of existing assessment instruments as well. For example, Chung and Singer (1995) discovered that the underlying factor structure of Western-designed questionnaire of psychiatric symptoms changed when used with Southeast Asian refugees. Concerning culturally sensitive approaches to psychotherapy, Sue and Zane (1987) warned that applying culture-specific techniques with an ethnic client in therapy may ignore ways in which that client is different from his/her ethnic group. They argue that cultural knowledge should be used to promote credibility and giving, two processes that are related to treatment outcome. Furthermore, Chin (1993) cautioned that the description of an ethnic group as having more or less of a particular trait is likely to be devalued by a therapist who examines the client from his/her own ethnocentric perspective of normality. In other words, nomothetic information about particular groups may or may not correspond to an individual client. Thus, while it is important for the therapist or counselor to have an understanding of different cultural norms, effective treatment derives from an idiographic perspective on the meanings of group membership to a particular client (Ridley et al., 1994).

References

Chin, J. L. (1993). Toward a psychology of difference: Psychotherapy for a culturally diverse population. In J. L. Chin, V. De La Cancela, & Y. M. Jenkins (Eds.), *Diversity in psychotherapy: The politics of race, ethnicity, and gender* (pp. 69–91). Westport, CT: Praeger.
Chung, R.C.-Y., & Singer, M. K. (1995). Interpretation of symptom presentation and distress: A Southeast Asian refugee example. *Journal of Nervous and Mental Disease, 183*, 639–648.
Miller-Jones, C. (1989). Culture and testing. *American Psychologist, 44*, 360–366.
Ridley, C. R., Mendoza, D. W., Kanitz, B. E., Angermeier, L., & Zenk, R. (1994). Cultural sensitivity in multicultural counseling: A perceptual schema model. *Journal of Counseling Psychology, 41*, 125–136.
Sue, S., & Zane, N. (1987). The role of culture and cultural techniques in psychotherapy: A critique and reformulation. *American Psychologist, 42*, 37–45.

Jonathan Kaplan

CULTURE—*Culture* has many definitions and conceptualizations (Kroeber & Kluckhohn, 1952). One of the earliest definitions appeared in 1891, in the book, *The Primitive Culture*. This book defined culture as the complex whole of knowledge, belief, art, law, custom, and any other capabilities and habits acquired as a member of society (Tylor, 1891). As an abstract term used to explain behavior, culture denotes habitual patterns of behavior that are characteristic of a group of people transmitted from one generation to the next through symbolic communication (Locke & Parker, 1994). Culture implies a way of life (Sundberg, 1981). Culture is learned and allows for the adaptation to natural and social settings manifested in institutions, thought patterns, and material objects; the part of the environment made by people (Herskovits, 1955). Culture represents the commonalities around which people develop norms, family life-styles, social roles, and behaviors in response to historical, political, economic, and social realities (Christensen, 1989). Persons in a specific culture share a common history, common experience, common language or dialect, and live in an identifiable geographical area. Culture is subjective and dynamic (Locke, 1990). Culture consists of all that people have learned to do, believe, and enjoy in their history (Sue & Sue, 1990), and may be described as *emic* (culturally specific, culturally localized; see entry) or *etic* (culturally generalized or universal; see entry) in perspective (Johnson, 1990; Pedersen, 1994; Sue & Sue, 1990). Culture is often confused with *race* and *ethnicity* (Johnson, 1990; Ponterotto & Casas, 1991; see entries for those terms) and is often used synonymously with *social race* (Johnson, 1990).

References

Christensen, C. P. (1989). Cross-cultural awareness development: A conceptual model. *Counselor Education and Supervision, 22,* 270–289.

Herskovits, M. J. (1955). *Cultural dynamics.* New York: Alfred A. Knopf.

Johnson, S. D., Jr. (1990). Toward clarifying culture, race and ethnicity in the context of multicultural counseling. *Journal of Multicultural Counseling and Development, 18,* 41–50.

Kroeber, A. L., & Kluckhohn, C. (1952). *Culture: A critical review of concepts and definitions.* New York: Vintage Books.

Locke, D. C. (1990). A not so provincial view of multicultural counseling. *Counselor Education and Supervision, 30,* 18–25.

Locke, D. C., & Parker, L. D. (1994). Improving the multicultural competence of educators. In P. Pedersen & J. C. Carey (Eds.), *Multicultural counseling in schools* (pp. 39–58). Needham Heights, MA: Allyn & Bacon.

Pedersen, P. (1994). *A handbook for developing multicultural awareness* (2nd ed.). Alexandria, VA: American Counseling Association.

Ponterotto, J. G., & Casas, J. M. (1991). *Handbook of racial/ethnic minority counseling research.* Springfield, IL: Charles C. Thomas.

Sue, D. W., & Sue, D. (1990). *Counseling the culturally different: Theory and practice* (2nd ed.). New York: Wiley.

Sundberg, N. (1981). Cross-cultural counseling and psychotherapy: A research overview. In A. Marsella & P. Pedersen (Eds.), *Cross-cultural counseling and psychotherapy* (pp. 28–63). Elmsford, NY: Pergamon.

Tylor, E. (1891). *The primitive culture.* New York: John Murray.

Saundra Tomlinson-Clarke

CULTURE-BLINDNESS—A failure to acknowledge the cultural realities and experiences of their clients (Pedersen, 1994). The term was adapted from *color-blindness* which was investigated as a physiological defect in humans. It was investigated as a way to explain evolution patterns; humans who did not have the capability to perceive color were not naturally selected to migrate to certain regions of the earth (Thompson, 1980). More recently, it has been used in the social science literature to refer to the failure of people to see a person's color as a salient part of his or her existence. People who exhibit culture-blindness often do so out of a need to feel impartial. These individuals are often uneasy discussing racial issues and are insecure about their own feelings about race (Pedersen, 1994). Research examining the perceived competence of culture-blind or culture-sensitive counselors revealed that Asian Americans and Blacks perceived culturally blind counselors as being less competent (Gim, Atkinson, & Kim, 1991; Pomales, Claiborn, & LaFromboise, 1986). When counselors are culturally sensitive and recognize the influence of ethnic and cultural realities on their clients, more effective cross-cultural counseling can occur.

References

Gim, R. H., Atkinson, D. R., & Kim, S. J. (1991). Asian American acculturation, counselor ethnicity and cultural sensitivity, and ratings of counselors. *Journal of Counseling Psychology, 38*, 57–62.

Pedersen, P. (1994). *A handbook for developing multicultural awareness* (2nd ed.). Alexandria, VA: American Counseling Association.

Pomales, J., Claiborn, C. D., & LaFromboise, T. D. (1986). Effects of Black students' racial identity on perceptions of White counselors varying in cultural sensitivity. *Journal of Counseling Psychology, 33*, 57–61.

Thompson, W. R. (1980). Cross-cultural uses of biological data and perspectives. In H. C. Triandis & W. W. Lambert (Eds.), *Handbook of cross-cultural psychology: Perspectives* (Vol. 1, pp. 205–252). Boston: Allyn & Bacon.

La Verne A. Berkel

CULTURE-BOUND—The extent to which specific characteristics of a person or group (e.g., ideas, values, attitudes, beliefs, norms, practices, behaviors) are believed to be inherently linked or "bound" to a particular culture or subculture. This term was first used to describe the culture-specific norms and behaviors of non-Western groups in sociology and anthropology (Marsella, 1993; Wittkower & Dubreuil, 1973). In every society, it is anticipated that there are culturally constructed patterns of behaviors or practices whose origins and expressions are traceable to particular values and normative emphases including Western cultures; however, characteristics often referred to as *culture-bound* are labelled as such because the cultures they are bound to are usually foreign to the ordinary cultural expectations of Western observers (Simon & Hughes, 1993). In recent years, the term culture-bound has been used in psychiatry and psychology to describe a broad category of mental disorders with "recurrent, locality-specific patterns of aberrant behavior and troubling experience" which are now included in the *Diagnostic and Statistical Manual of Mental Disorders* (American Psychiatric Association, 1994, p. 844). The existence of culture-bound syndromes (see entry) dates back to the 1770s when the Malaysian syndrome *amok* was first reported (Gaw & Berstein, 1992). While initially assigned a variety of labels such as *exotic psychoses* (Arieti & Meth, 1959), *ethnic psychoses and neuroses* (Devereux, 1956), *psychogenic psychoses* (Faergeman, 1963), and *hysterical psychoses* (Langness, 1967), Yap (1967) was the first to use the terms *culture-bound reactive syndromes* or *culture-bound syndromes* to describe these mental health problems. Most recently, social scientists have proposed the use of even more precise terms such as *syndromes not seen in Western cultures* (Favazza, 1985), *culture-specific disorders* (Berstein & Gaw, 1990; Kaplan & Sadock, 1991), and *folk diagnostic categories* (Simon & Hughes, 1993). Despite considerable criticism, the common term culture-bound syndromes has remained the best recognized description for these phenomena (Levine & Gaw, 1995).

References

American Psychiatric Association. (1994). *Diagnostic and statistical manual of mental disorders* (4th ed.). Washington, DC: Author.

Arieti, S. M., & Meth, J. M. (1959). Rare, unclassifiable, collective, and exotic psychotic syndromes. In S. M. Arieti (Ed.), *American handbook of psychiatry, Vol. I* (pp. 546–553). New York: Basic Books.

Bernstein, R. L., & Gaw, A. C. (1990). Koro: Proposed classification for the *DSM-IV*. *American Journal of Psychiatry, 147*, 1690–1674.

Devereux, G. (1956). Normal and abnormal: The key problem of psychiatric anthropology. In J. B. Casagrande & T. Galdwin (Eds.), *Some uses of anthropology: Theoretical and applied* (pp. 30–48). Washington, DC: Anthropological Society of Washington.

Faergeman, P. (1963). *Psychogenic psychoses*. London: Butterworth.

Favazza, A. R. (1985). Anthropology and psychiatry. In H. I. Kaplan & B. Saddock (Eds.), *Comprehensive textbook of psychiatry* (4th ed., pp. 247–264). Baltimore, MD: Williams and Wilkins.

Kaplan, H. I., & Sadock, B. J. (1991). *Comprehensive glossary of psychiatry and psychology*. Baltimore, MD: Williams and Wilkins.

Langness, L. L. (1967). Hysterical psychosis: the cross-cultural evidence. *American Journal of Psychiatry, 124*, 143–152.

Levine, R. E., & Gaw, A. C. (1995). Culture-bound syndromes. *The Psychiatric Clinics of North America, 8*, 523–536.

Marsella, A. J. (1993). Sociocultural foundations of psychopathology: An historical overview of concepts, events and pioneers prior to 1970. *Transcultural Psychiatric Research Review, 30*, 97–142.

Simon, R. C., & Hughes, C. C. (1993). Culture-bound syndromes. In A. C. Gaw (Ed.), *Culture, ethnicity, and mental illness* (pp. 75–99). Washington, DC: American Psychiatric Press.

Wittkower, E. D., & Dubreuil, G. (1973). Psychocultural stress in relation to mental illness. *Social Science & Medicine, 7*, 691–704.

Yap, P. M. (1969). The culture-bound reactive syndromes. In W. Caudill & T. Y. Lin

(Eds.), *Mental health research in Asia and the Pacific* (pp. 33–53). Honolulu, HI: East–West Center Press.

Phillip D. Akutsu

CULTURE-BOUND SYNDROME—A unique psychosis found within specific cultures, sometimes referred to as *ethnic psychosis* or *cultural-specific syndrome*. These syndromes include reactions that are perceived as abnormal and are produced by shock, trauma, or stress (Landy, 1977). Each syndrome has its own set of distinguishable symptoms, treatment, interpretation, and cause of the illness. Emil Kraeplin who studied various Indonesian populations in the early 1900s found that there were cultural differences in the amount, manifestation, and cause of disorders or illnesses (Marsella, Tharp, & Ciborowski, 1979). Shortly thereafter, many more culture-specific or culture-bound syndromes were being reported such as *latah*, *amok*, *pibloktoq*, and *windigo psychosis* (see entries). Cultural psychiatric research has suggested that these reported illnesses are similar to illnesses in other cultures, although identified differently. In addition, these syndromes were found to be equivalent to Western psychiatric disorders (Honigmann, 1973).

References

Honigmann, J. (1973). *Handbook of social and cultural anthropology*. Chicago: Rand McNally and Company.
Landy, D. (1977). *Culture, disease and healing*. New York: Macmillan Publishing Co.
Marsella, A., Tharp, R., & Ciborowski, T. (1979). *Perspectives on cross-cultural psychology*. New York: Academic Press.

Joseph E. Trimble and Heather K. Mertz

CULTURE BROKER—A person specifically selected to play critical roles in transitioning monocultural Western-Anglo institutions to multiculturalism. The concept of *culture broker* is based on the assumption that U.S. institutions are rooted in Eurocentric cultural norms that generated institutional racism, or instituional standards and practices which resulted in inequalities among racial and ethnic groups (Jones, 1994). Since the culture brokers' critical roles are to shape the institution to become multicultural, they must adopt a perspective that accepts cultural differences as well as truly understand various cultural viewpoints, including the Eurocentric view (Weinrach, 1987). They can then bridge the cultural gap by actively integrating other cultural viewpoints and conditions into the existing system. The challenge for culture brokers in this process is to promote *cultural pluralism*, as defined by Triandis (1988) as, "the development of interdependence, appreciation and the skills for interacting intimately with persons from other cultures" (p. 48). Such practices can empower culturally different people within that institution to reach their full potential and succeed. As an example, a specific cultural broker model has been developed to create a multicultural college campus (Stage & Manning, 1992). Based on this model, an effective culture broker, whether that person be an administrator or a student, participates in the areas that include (a) self-examination of one's own underlying cultural assumptions, (b) studying culture-specific knowledge, (c) engaging in cross-cultural interactions to the extent of acculturating oneself to different cultures, and (d) promoting activity to maintain a multicultural campus. Historically, culture broker is related to W.E.B. Du Bois' (1986) notion of *cultural translator*, a term used to describe those African Americans ("the talented tenth") familiar with both Black and White cultures who could translate concepts between the two cultures.

References

Du Bois, W.E.B. (1986). The souls of Black folk. In N. Huggins (Ed.), *W.E.B. Du Bois: Writings* (pp. 357–547). New York: Library of America. (Original work published in 1903)
Jones, J. M. (1994). The African American: A duality dilemma? In W. J. Lonner & R. Malpass (Eds.), *Psychology and culture* (pp. 17–21). Boston: Allyn & Bacon.
Stage, F. K., & Manning, K. (1992). *Enhancing the multicultural campus environment: A cultural brokering approach.* San Francisco: Jossey-Bass.
Triandis, H. C. (1988). The future of pluralism revisited. In P. Katz & D. Taylor (Eds.), *Eliminating racism: Profiles in controversy* (pp. 31–50). New York: Plenum.
Weinrach, S. G. (1987). Microcounseling and beyond: A dialogue with Allen Ivey. *Journal of Counseling and Development, 65,* 532–537.

Randi I. Kim

CULTURE-CENTERED—An adjective attached to a noun or verb indicating a special emphasis in the use of the word on the cultural patterns and context which are central to the meaning of the word, as in "culture-centered counseling" or "an interpretation of the process which is culture-centered." *Culture* is central and not marginal or peripheral to the meaning of the term, suggesting the generic application of a *culture-centered interpretation* throughout the social sciences. The term recognizes that all behaviors are learned and displayed in a cultural context. Accurate assessment, meaningful understanding, and appropriate intervention require that the cultural context be kept central to our interpretation of the social science terms (Beardsley & Pedersen, 1997). The term culture-centered was modeled after Carl Rogers' notion of client-centered or person-centered and Kelly's personal construct theory. Culture-centered counseling skills focus on the culturally defined assumptions that shape and direct behaviors and the context in which identity is constructed. According to Pedersen and Ivey (1993), the term was developed as an alternative to multicultural (which has become politically controversial), cross-cultural (which suggests a comparative approach where one culture is better than another), transcultural (which is an abstraction), and intercultural (which minimizes the complexity of culture).

References

Beardsley, L., & Pedersen, P. (1997). Health and culture-centered intervention. In J. Berry, M. Segall, & C. Kagitcibasi (Eds.), *Handbook of cross-cultural psychology. Vol. 3: Social behavior and applications* (pp. 413–448). Needham Heights, MA: Allyn & Bacon.
Pedersen, P. B., & Ivey, A. E. (1993). *Culture-centered counseling and interview skills.* Westport, CT: Praeger.

Paul Pedersen

CULTURE CONTACT—Refers to the exposure of two different cultures to one another (Jones, 1972). Contact begins with the encounter of images or real people of visibly distinct groups (Jones & Carter, 1996). Prejudice may be reduced by equal status contact between majority and minority groups in pursuit of common goals, sanctioned by institutional supports (Allport, 1954). The use of the term culture contact appeared in anthropology literature as early as 1934, when a series of articles was published on the methods of study of culture contact (Fortes, 1936; Hunter, 1934; Mair, 1934). Culture contact was the focus of several cultural anthropology books and articles such as *Culture-contact as a Dynamic Process* (Fortes, 1936), *Acculturation: The Study of Culture Contact* (Herskovits, 1938), and *An Example of Culture-contact without Conflict: Reindeer Tungus and Cossacks of Northwestern Manchuria* (Lindgren, 1938).

References

Allport, G. W. (1954). *The nature of prejudice.* Reading, MA: Addison-Wesley.
Fortes, M. (1936). Culture-contact as a dynamic process. An investigation in the northern territories of the Gold Coast. *Africa, 9,* 24–55.
Herskovits, M. J. (1938). *Acculturation: The study of culture contact.* New York: Augustin.
Hunter, M. (1934). Methods of study of culture contact. *Africa, 7,* 335–350.
Jones, J. M. (1972). *Prejudice and racism.* Reading, MA: Addison-Wesley.
Jones, J. M., & Carter, R. T. (1996). Racism and White racial identity. In B. P. Bowser & R. G. Hunt (Eds.), *Impacts of racism on White Americans* (pp. 1–23). Thousand Oaks, CA: Sage.
Lindgren, E. J. (1938). An example of culture-contact without conflict: Reindeer Tungus and Cossacks of Northwestern Manchuria. *American Anthropologist, 40,* 605–621.
Mair, L. P. (1934). The study of culture contact as a practical problem. *Africa, 7,* 415–422.

Saundra Tomlinson-Clarke

CULTURE-FREE TESTING—Refers to the creating, administering, and scoring of culturally unbiased tests, especially intelligence, achievement, and aptitude tests (see TEST BIAS). Since the 1920s, *culture-free testing* (or *culture-fair testing*, as it was later called) was a recognizable movement among test makers for over 50 years (Anastasi, 1954/1976). The goal of the movement was to measure intelligence with drawings of geometric figures, blocks, matrices, and mazes. For example, participants were asked to imagine what a piece of paper would look like after it was folded over twice, and then cut on the lower, left-hand corner. Such questions, along with their potential answers, were presented solely in terms of pictures and arrows. Although there were some promising results with Raven's Progressive Matrices and Cattell's Culture Free Intelligence Test (Cattell, 1940), the movement encountered two major obstacles. First, the tests were criticized for only measuring a subfacet of intelligence (inductive, spatial reasoning) instead of measuring general intelligence. Second, cultural groups with less exposure to paper drawings (and to geometric shapes) still performed below average on the tests. Today, most experts agree that culture-free testing is impossible. Even if minority culture experts review and revise a given test, that test will still contain some cultural content. Thus, test developers can only attempt to make culturally "fairer" tests. Not surprisingly, policy makers disagree on the use of these supposedly "fairer yet still flawed" tests. Given such tests, policy makers can only speculate as to whether the standardized testing of eighth graders, for example, produces more harm than good, or whether college applicants would be treated more fairly if SAT scores were banned from the application process. Occasionally, such issues are played out in civil courts. In *Allan v. the Alabama Board of Education* (Drasgow, 1987), the defendants agreed to use only those achievement questions for which the proportion of correct answers for Blacks and Whites differed by less than 5 percent. Elsewhere, in the famed Golden Rule settlement, Educational Testing Service (ETS) and the Illinois Department of Insurance agreed to make insurance licensing exams with questions in which the answers of Blacks and Whites differed by less than 15 percent (*Golden Rule Insurance Company v. Washburn et al.*, 1985). Many have questioned these settlements on the grounds that if there are real group differences on academic achievement (or professional licensing knowledge), the above settlements will undermine test validity. In contrast, most hold the view that fairness in testing requires equal test scores, and thus equal opportunity, for all cultural groups.

References

Anastasi, A. (1954/1976). *Psychological testing*. New York: MacMillan.

Cattell, R. B. (1940). A culture free intelligence test: Part I. *Journal of Educational Psychology, 31*, 161–179.

Drasgow, F. (1987). Study of the measurement bias of two standardized psychological tests. *Journal of Applied Psychology, 19*, 19–29.

Golden Rule Insurance Company v. Washburn et al., No. 419–76 (stipulation for dismissal and order dismissing cause, Circuit Court of the Seventh Judicial Circuit, Sangamon County, IL, 1984).

William Peter Flannery

CULTURE SHOCK—The difficulties associated with adaptation to a new culture (Oberg, 1960). Feelings of anxiety, depression, loss, and helplessness accompany one's transition to a new cultural environment (Church, 1982). Other terms have also been used to describe this process, including *sojourner adjustment, cross-cultural adaptation or adjustment,* and *acculturative stress.* In practice, the phrase *culture shock* is typically assigned to short-term sojourners. Church (1982) provided a thorough summary and critique of the culture shock literature. He determined that most studies relied on cross-sectional, questionnaire-based data. Accordingly, he urged for the adoption of longitudinal designs and other data collection methods. In order to disentangle the cultural transition process, Searle and Ward (1990) made a distinction between *psychological* and *sociocultural adjustment.* Psychological adjustment is based on stress and coping processes. In contrast, *sociocultural adjustment* is based on a social cognition framework. Empirical evidence suggests that psychological and sociocultural adjustment are associated with different predictors (Searle & Ward, 1990; Ward & Kennedy, 1993). A recent study (Cross, 1995) lends support for the *cultural fit hypothesis* of adjustment. This hypothesis proposes that one who has a similar orientation to the surrounding culture will be better adjusted than someone who has different cultural values. In a comparison of visiting Asian students, Cross (1995) discovered that students who were more individualistic and used direct coping styles reported less stress than students who were more group-oriented and used indirect coping responses.

References

Church, A. T. (1982). Sojourner adjustment. *Psychological Bulletin, 91,* 540–572.

Cross, S. E. (1995). Self-construals, coping, and stress in cross-cultural adaptation. *Journal of Cross-Cultural Psychology, 26,* 673–697.

Oberg, K. (1960). Culture shock: Adjustment to new cultural environments. *Practical Anthroplogy, 7,* 177–182.

Searle, W., & Ward, C. (1990). The prediction of psychological and sociocultural adjustment during cross-cultural transitions. *International Journal of Intercultural Relations, 14,* 449–464.

Ward, C., & Kennedy, A. (1993). Where's the "culture" in cross-cultural transition? Comparative studies of sojourner adjustment. *Journal of Cross-Cultural Psychology, 24,* 221–249.

                                                            Jonathan Kaplan

D

DEAF CULTURE—This term represents a recognition that Deaf groups are different from those of hearing people. While *culture* is a complex construct, it typically encompasses "the customary beliefs, social forms, and material traits of a racial, religious, or social group" (*Merriam-Webster's Collegiate Dictionary*, 1996). *Deaf Culture* in the United States represents a social group that values the use of American Sign Language (Lane, Hoffmeister, & Bahan, 1996; Padden & Humphries, 1988). Members of this culture have established unique interactive social connections and shared perspectives of life based on this value identification. They do not view being deaf as a pathological, medically based hearing loss construct that focuses on a deficiency to be corrected. Rather, *Deaf* is a way of life to which Deaf people adhere. For the sake of clarification, "deaf" refers to those with significant hearing loss, while "Deaf" reflects cultural membership (Woodward, 1972). Even though Deaf persons have coalesced into groups for at least the past three centuries (Van Cleve & Crouch, 1993), the recent validation of American Sign Language as a formal language made it possible to acknowledge that a Deaf Culture existed (Parasnis, 1996). Since roughly 95 percent of deaf children are born to hearing parents with no exposure to Deaf Culture (Moores, 1996), the transmission of Deaf Culture typically takes place within school systems and Deaf social organizations where deaf individuals are exposed to members of Deaf Culture, including Deaf offspring or Deaf parents (Lane, Hoffmeister, & Bahan, 1996; Padden & Humphries, 1988).

References

Lane, H., Hoffmeister, R., & Bahan, B. (1996). *A journey into the Deaf-World.* San Diego: DawnSign Press.

Merriam-Webster's Collegiate Dictionary (10th ed.). (1997). Springfield, MA: Merriam-
    Webster, Inc.
Moores, D. F. (1996). *Educating the deaf: Psychology, principles, and practices.* Boston:
    Houghton Mifflin.
Padden, C., & Humphries, T. (1988). *Deaf in America: Voices from a culture.* Cam-
    bridge, MA: Harvard University Press.
Parasnis, I. (1996). On interpreting the Deaf experience within the context of cultural
    and language diversity. In I. Parasnis (Ed.), *Cultural and language diversity and
    the Deaf experience* (pp. 3–19). New York: Cambridge University Press.
Van Cleve, J., & Crouch, B. (1993). *Deaf history unveiled: Interpretations from the new
    scholarship.* Washington, DC: Gallaudet University Press.
Woodward, J. (1972). Implications for sociolinguistics research among the Deaf. *Sign
    Language Studies, 1*, 1–7.

                                          Irene W. Leigh and Arlene B. Kelly

DEVIANCE—Any thought, feeling, or action which moves away from the
norm or which societal/social groups view as a violation of the rules (Douglas
& Waksler, 1992). The American Psychiatric Association (1994) acknowledges
that deviance can vary from one culture or time period to another, depending
upon what is considered acceptable by a society. It is in the best interest of the
individual to remain within the norm (nondeviant) in order to maintain interpersonal relationships and "fit in" with society and thereby avoid stigma, stereotypes, and prejudice (Levinson & Ember, 1996). Edgerton (1973) points out
that different cultures view various behaviors differently; what is troublesome
behavior in one culture may be acceptable in another. With reference to theft,
suicide, violence, and sexuality across culture, Edgerton points out that issues
are complex. In fact, in some cultures the lack of an action considered deviant
in one culture may be an *expectation* in another. Kohn (1969) and Chesebro
(1981) concur with the notion that any behavior which does not "conform" to
the rules of a particular society will be defined as deviant by that society. Stafford and Scott (1986) suggested that the norm was once defined as the typical
features of society (e.g., White, Protestant, heterosexual, etc.). To stray from the
norm (i.e., to deviate) often incurred sanctions for the individual. These sanctions elicited conformity, thus maintaining social order. Sanctions could be both
formal (e.g., legal) and informal (e.g., relationships), but usually focused on the
negative and emphasized reintegration into the "norm" (Levinson & Ember,
1986).

References

American Psychiatric Association. (1994). *Diagnostic and statistical manual of mental
    disorders* (4th ed.). Washington, DC: Author.
Chesebro, J. (1981). *Gayspeak.* New York: Pilgrim.
Douglas, D. D., & Waksler, F. C. (1982). *The sociology of deviance: An introduction.*
    Toronto: Little, Brown.

Edgerton, R. (1976). *Deviance: A cross-cultural perspective.* Menlo Park, CA: Cummings.

Kohn, M. (1969). *Class conformity: A study in values.* Homewood, IL: Dorsey.

Levinson, D., & Ember, M. (Eds.). (1986). *Encyclopedia of cultural anthropology.* New York: Holt.

Stafford, M. C., & Scott, R. R. (1986). Stigma, deviance, and social control: Some conceptual issues. In S. C. Ainlay, G. Becker, & L. M. Coleman (Eds.), *The dilemma of difference* (pp. 77–91). New York: Plenum.

Raechele L. Pope

DIA DE LA RAZA—Columbus Day. Literally translated, it means "Day of the Races," or the coming together of two races or ethnic groups (i.e., Spanish and Amerindian). This is an official holiday throughout Latin America, and celebrated by Hispanic/Mexican Americans to mark the event of culture contact (Henderson & Thompson, 1997; Milne, 1965).

References

Henderson, H., & Thompson, S. E. (Eds.). (1997). *Holidays, festivals, and celebrations of the world dictionary* (2nd ed.). Detroit: Omnigraphics.

Milne, J. (1965). *Fiesta time in Latin America.* Los Angeles: Ward Ritchie Press.

Cindy Yee

DIGNIDAD: RESPETO Y RELAJO—A key aspect of Puerto Rican culture which has direct roots to Puerto Rico's Hispanic heritage (Wagenheim, 1970). *Dignidad* is a quality of self that is important, presented in interpersonal relationships and expressed in idioms such as *hay que darse a respetar* (one must have self-respect and earn the respect of others) and formalities such as greetings and handshaking. It is believed that anyone, regardless of his/her status in life, is thought to be worthy of *respeto* (respect). The opposite of *respeto* is *relajo.* *Relajo* is a kind of joking that is engaged in when there is *confianza* (a sense of trust in the other person), otherwise it could be interpreted as *una falta de respeto* (lack of respect). *Relajo* is usually not considered appropriate between acquaintances. Any *falta de respeto* toward a person violates their *dignidad.* Puerto Ricans will usually not openly ridicule another to the point where it strips them of their *dignidad.* To lack moral standards or *dignidad* is to be called a *sinverguenza* (a person without shame) and is considered a major insult to a Puerto Rican who holds traditional values. These values continue to be emphasized by Puerto Ricans on the Island and in the United States, although they are being challenged by new generations and modified by forces such as urbanization, industrialization, and American influence on Puerto Rico. (Editor's note: These terms are also used in Mexican culture and, perhaps other Latin American cultures, given its Spanish roots. See Falicov, 1982, 1996.)

References

Falicov, C. J. (1982). Mexican families. In M. McGoldrick, J. K. Pearce, & J. Giordano (Eds.), *Ethnicity and family therapy* (pp. 134–163). New York: Guilford.
Falicov, C. J. (1996). Mexican families. In M. McGoldrick, J. Giordano, & J. K. Pearce (Eds.), *Ethnicity and family therapy* (2nd ed., pp. 169–182). New York: Guilford.
Wagenheim, K. (1970). *Puerto Rico: A profile.* New York: Praeger.

Maria Rodriguez

DISADVANTAGED—Describes individuals, groups, and institutions which are lacking in the basic resources or conditions necessary for an equal position in society. *Disadvantaged* is a term rooted in social theory. According to Merton (1968), there are two major types of reference groups, "the normative type which sets and maintains standards for the individual and comparison type which provides a frame of comparison relative to which the individual evaluates himself and others" (p. 337). The term results from social comparisons of various attributes such as values, beliefs, abilities, and experiences. Characteristics which fall outside of accepted standards are attributed to groups or individuals who are then deemed to be disadvantaged (Arroyo & Zigler, 1995). Social, material, and educational inequalities among groups or individuals also signal a disadvantaged condition (Taylor, Moghaddam, Gamble, & Zeller, 1987). Disadvantaged describes a temporary condition since it is assumed that an individual or group can transcend disadvantaged status. Taylor et al. (1987) describe three responses that disadvantaged group members make in response to inequalities, "Acceptance of one's disadvantaged position, attempts at individual upward mobility, and the instigation of collective action" (p. 260). Disadvantaged as a descriptive term dates back to the 1960s with the advent of great society programs designed to assist people in moving toward the normative reference group. Disadvantaged individuals are also referred to as *low-income, low-achieving, at-risk, neglected, delinquent,* or *minority.* Disadvantaged is frequently used as a modifier for such descriptive terms as *economically, socially,* and *culturally.* However, it is generally agreed that because culture is immutable, no one can actually be culturally disadvantaged even while holding value and function outside of the dominant culture.

References

Arroyo, C. C., & Zigler, E. (1995). Racial identity, academic achievement, and the psychological well-being of economically disadvantaged adolescents. *Journal of Personality and Social Psychology, 69,* 903–914.
Merton, R. K. (1968). *Social theory and social structure.* New York: The Free Press.
Taylor, D. M., Moghaddam, F. M., Gamble, I., & Zeller, E. (1987). Disadvantaged group responses to percieved inequality: From passive acceptance to collective action. *Journal of Social Psychology, 127,* 259–272.

Raechele L. Pope

DISCRIMINATION—In psychological terms, the ability to discriminate is "the ability to perceive and respond to differences among stimuli" (Britannica Online, 1996). It is a neutral term, describing the act of discerning difference. However, in more common usage, discrimination occurs when a dominant group or one of its members acts in a detrimental way against another group of people based on a perceived difference between the two groups. In other words, two people or groups of people are treated in different ways based on some variation in their physical appearance or beliefs. This term carries a negative connotation, as denoted in racial, gender, size, and age discrimination. Discrimination requires external action or behavior, but may be intentional or unintentional, conscious or unconscious (Marger, 1997). It may be motivated by one person's prejudice, or on a larger scale, by an institution's policies or social customs (Simpson & Yinger, 1985). The practice of racial segregation is one example of large-scale institutional discrimination. Discrimination occurs in employment, education, housing, etc., but always results as the lack of equal opportunity due to some intrinsic characteristic of a subordinate group and its members (Allport, 1979; Marger, 1997). The United States federal government has made attempts to meliorate past discrimination and to prevent future discrimination through several Civil Rights Acts, dating to the Civil Rights Act of 1875 (Brigham, 1984). Laws which attempt to correct past discriminatory practices, such as affirmative action laws, have been controversial, with people in majority groups accusing the government of practicing "reverse discrimination" (Cheatham, 1991). However, by definition, discrimination is practiced individually and institutionally by dominant groups in society (Marger, 1997).

References

Allport, G. W. (1979). *The nature of prejudice* (25th anniversary ed.). Reading, MA: Addison-Wesley.

Brigham, J. (1984). *Civil liberties and American democracy*. Washington, DC: CQ Press.

Britannica Online. (1996). *Discrimination*. Available: http://www.eb.com:180/cgibin/g?keywords=discrimination & DBase=Articles&hits=10&context=all.

Cheatham, H. (1991). Affirming affirmative action. In H. Cheatham (Ed.), *Cultural pluralism on campus* (pp. 9–21). Lanham, MD: ACPA.

Marger, M. N. (1997). *Race and ethnic relations: American and global perspectives* (4th ed.). Belmont, CA: Wadsworth.

Simpson, G. E., & Yinger, J. M. (1985). *Racial and cultural minorities: An analysis of prejudice and discrimination* (5th ed.). New York: Harper and Brothers.

Raechele L. Pope

DISEASE—Most commonly understood from the molecular level perspective, defined as "a condition that may result from infection, metabolic imbalances, traumatic injury, or other etiology commonly referred to as active pathology" (Nagi, 1965, p. 101). A definition of disease is advanced by classifying diseases into physical diseases, mental diseases, and emotional diseases in which the latter two often (but not always) involve some type of organic damage to the brain (Livneh, 1987). Lewis (1991) suggests that although definitions of disease can lead to a broad range of conditions called diseases, a stricter definition of disease as applied to psychiatric and addictive disorders includes the following criteria: a clear biological origin, the presence of discrete entities, and predictable signs, symptoms, and courses. While biologically based conditions can be described in terms of specific physical characteristics (e.g., tissue damage), mental and affective disorders often require inferences from observations of behavior and are therefore of a more generalized nature (Halpern, 1984). Mental diseases are short-term conditions that affect thought and memory processes (e.g., delirium states, organic hallucinosis), while affective diseases affect emotional response appropriateness (e.g., schizophrenic reactions, manic disorders; Livneh, 1987). Several scholars (Caplan, Englehardt, & McCartney, 1981; Neuhaus, 1993; Rosenberg, 1989) suggest that the concept of disease and diagnosis of disease do not exist in a social vacuum and are closely tied to the values and judgments of society. For example, Rosenberg (1989) indicated, "it is fair to say that in our culture, a disease does not exist as a social phenomenon until we agree that it does" (p. 2). Within a multicultural context and as it relates to issues of race, gender, and sexual orientation, for example, what is considered a disease varies. Caplan, Englehardt, and McCartney (1981) noted that the field of medicine has regarded certain sexual activities, habits, and ethnic differences as diseases leading to tragic outcomes for certain social groups. On the other hand, when discussing racism, Katz (1978) cites a number of authors (e.g., Berry, 1970; Clark, 1963; Comer, 1972; Delaney, 1972; Katz, 1978; Thomas & Sillen, 1972) who have offered theories that view racism as a disease: a "pervasive and critical form of a mental illness" (Katz, 1978, p. 12).

References

Berry, W. (1970). *The hidden wound.* Boston: Houghton-Mifflin.
Caplan, A. L., Engelhardt, H. T., Jr., & McCartney, J. J. (Eds.). (1981). *Concepts of health and disease: Interdisciplinary perspectives.* Reading, MA: Addison-Wesley.
Clark, K. (1963). *Prejudice and your child.* Boston: American.
Comer, J. P. (1972). White racism: Its root, form, and function. In R. L. Jones (Ed.), *Black psychology* (pp. 311–317). New York: Harper and Row.
Delaney, L. T. (1972). The other bodies in the river. In R. L Jones (Ed.), *Black psychology* (pp. 335–343). New York: Harper and Row.
Halpern, A. S. (1984). Functional assessment and mental retardation. In A. S. Halpern & M. J. Fuhrer (Eds.), *Functional assessment and rehabilitation* (pp. 61–78). Baltimore, MD: Brooks.
Katz, J. H. (1978). *White awareness: Handbook for anti-racism training.* Norman: University of Oklahoma Press.
Lewis, D. C. (1991). Comparison of alcoholism and other medical diseases: An internist's view. *Psychiatric Annals, 21,* 256–265.
Livneh, C. (1987). Person–environment congruence: A rehabilitation perspective. *International Journal of Rehabilitation Research, 10,* 3–19.

Nagi, S. Z. (1965). Some conceptual issues in disability and rehabilitation. In M. B. Sussman (Ed.), *Sociology and rehabilitation* (pp. 100–113). Washington, DC: American Sociological Association.

Neuhaus, C. (1993). The disease controversy revisited: An ontologic perspective. *The Journal of Drug Issues, 23*, 463–478.

Rosenberg, C. E. (1989). Disease in history: Frames and framers. *The Milbank Quarterly, 67*, 1–15.

Thomas, A., & Sillen, S. (1972). *Racism and psychiatry*. New York: Brunner/Mazel.

Raechele L. Pope

DISSONANCE STAGE—Stage two of a five-stage identity model of the *Minority Identity Development* (MID) model which provides a developmental, process-oriented perspective (Atkinson, Morten, & Sue, 1989). Later refined and renamed the *Racial/Cultural Identity Development* (R/CID) model (Sue & Sue, 1990), the *Dissonance Stage* suggests that minorities have ambivalent feelings about both the dominant culture and their own minority culture, because they have encountered information and/or experiences inconsistent with their culturally held beliefs, attitudes, and values. Movement from the *Conformity Stage* (see entry) into this stage is thought to be a gradual process. Individuals in the Dissonance Stage are in conflict with discordant information which causes questioning of their self-concept. According to Sue and Sue (1990), one begins to have conflicts: conflict between self-depreciating and self-appreciating attitudes and beliefs; conflict between group-depreciating and group-appreciating attitudes and beliefs; conflict between dominant-held views of minority hierarchy and feelings of shared experiences; and conflict between group-appreciating and group-depreciating attitude. This stage is a period when an individual begins to question and challenge the attitudes and convictions of the Conformity Stage. The Dissonance Stage is similar to the *moratorium status* described by Marcia (1980), *encounter* by Cross (1978), *awareness of differentness and dissonance* by Kich (1982, 1992), *dissonance (encounter) status* by Helms (1995), *refusal/ suppression phase* by Collins (1996), *dissonance phase* by Myers et al. (1991), and *awakening* by Kim (1981).

References

Atkinson, D., Morten, G., & Sue, D. W. (1989). *Counseling American minorities: A cross-cultural perspective* (3rd ed.). Dubuque, IA: W. C. Brown.

Collins, J.L.F. (1996). *Biracial Japanese American identity: Hapa, double, or somewhere in between*. Unpublished doctoral dissertation, The Fielding Institute, Santa Barbara, CA.

Cross, W. E. (1978). The Thomas and Cross models of psychological nigrescence: A literature review. *Journal of Black Psychology, 4*, 12–31.

Helms, J. E. (1995). An update of Helm's White and people of color racial identity models. In J. G. Ponterotto, J. M. Casas, L. A. Suzuki, & C. M. Alexander (Eds.), *Handbook of multicultural counseling* (pp. 181–198). Thousand Oaks, CA: Sage.

Kich, G. K. (1982). *Eurasians: Ethnic/racial identity development of biracial Japanese/*

White adults. Unpublished doctoral dissertation, Wright Institute Graduate School of Psychology, Berkeley, CA.

Kich, G. K. (1992). The developmental process of asserting a biracial, bicultural identity. In M.P.P. Root (Ed.), *Racially mixed people in America* (pp. 304–317). Newbury Park, CA: Sage.

Kim, J. (1981). *The process of Asian-American identity development: A study of Japanese American women's perceptions of their struggle to achieve positive identities.* Unpublished doctoral dissertation, University of Massachusetts, Amherst, MA.

Marcia, J. (1980). Identity in adolescence. In J. Adelson (Ed.), *Handbook of adolescent psychology* (pp. 159–187). New York: Wiley.

Myers, L. J., Speight, S. L., Highlen, P. S., Cox, C. I., Reynolds, A. L., Adams, E. M., & Hanley, C. P. (1991). Identity development and worldview: Toward an optimal conceptualization. *Journal of Counseling and Development, 70*, 54–63.

Sue, D. W., & Sue, D. (1990). *Counseling the culturally different: Theory and practice* (2nd ed.). New York: Wiley.

James Fuji Collins

DIVERSIFICATION—The cultural, racial, and ethnic changes that are occurring in society. This increased diversity along multiple dimensions in the composition of the population leads to challenges of the professional counseling community to address this ongoing change. Diversification means that the competence of mental health professionals needs to incorporate working with different norms, values, and worldviews (Ponterotto, Casas, Suzuki, & Alexander, 1995). During the early part of the twentieth century, dialogue relating to diversity often meant a view from the norm, or even inferiority. In the 1960s, voices of more multicultural groups such as the Association of Black Psychologists, which exerted pressure on the American Psychological Association, opened the doors for the affirmation of diversification. Going beyond a deficit model, diversification, along with *multiculturalism*, may now represent *cultural pluralism* and an affirmation of *cultural identity* in all of its multiple uses and meanings (Trickett, Watts, & Birman, 1994).

References

Ponterotto, J. G., Casas, J. M., Suzuki, L. A., & Alexander, C. M. (1995). *Handbook of multicultural counseling.* Thousand Oaks, CA: Sage.

Trickett, E. J., Watts, R., & Birman, D. (1994). *Human diversity: Perspectives on people in context.* San Francisco: Jossey-Bass.

Matthew R. Mock

DIVERSITY—A "difference" or "variety" (Guralnik, 1982) as applied to any and/or every existing variable (e.g., types of services, ideas, style, color, theories, etc.). In the psychological and educational realm, the term *diversity* may be used to describe the cultural differences existing among those whose experiences are unlike those of the dominant group (Katz, 1989; Sedlacek, 1994). Additionally, diversity may be used to describe those experiences which are not only different from those of the dominant group, but those cultural differences which exist within groups (Reynolds & Pope, 1991). The cultural traits which the term has come to encompass may include race, gender, sexual orientation, physical ability, nationality, age, and religion (Katz, 1989; Reynolds & Pope, 1991). Any one, or all, or a selected combination of these cultural traits, may be referred to by the term diversity. Diversity may also be referred to within culturally similar groups. In this case, the term diversity is more closely associated, in the human context, to *difference* or *variety*. It refers to those qualities—other than cultural traits—which make people from the same cultural perspective different from each other. Diversity, then, refers to "the multiplicity of ways in which we can be 'human' '' (Sue, 1991).

References

Guralnik, D. B. (Ed.). (1982). *Webster's new world dictionary of the American language* (7th ed.). New York: Warner.
Katz, J. H. (1989). The challenge of diversity. In Woolbright (Ed.), *Valuing diversity on campus* (pp. 1–21). Bloomington, IN: Association of College Unions–International.
Reynolds, A. L., & Pope, R. L. (1991). The complexities of diversity: Exploring multiple oppressions. *Journal of Counseling and Development, 70*, 174–180.
Sue, D. W. (1991). A diversity perspective on contextualism. *Journal of Counseling and Development, 70*, 300–301.

Raechele L. Pope

DIVINATION—Derived from the Latin root *divinatus*, meaning *faculty* (i.e., capacity) or foretelling (Guralnik, 1982). *Divination* is used in respect to traditional physical and mental healing in an individual's culture (Leff, 1981). The importance of divination to the individual depends on the influence of his/her society and his/her relationship with the community. The diviner, who diagnoses and guides the individual through the individual's trouble, acts as a therapist. The divination procedure can include key people in the person's life by involving them in the therapy sessions or the individual can be given traditional therapeutic prescriptions such as amulets or potions. The individual is either put in a trance state or stays in a clear mind when interacting with the diviner for healing (Leff, 1981; Pugh, 1983). The application of divination in a nontrance state is often used with devices such as horoscopes, palms, fortune sticks, dice, or cards (Pugh, 1983). The language used between the diviner and the individual is a standard language practiced in that culture. The significance of the communication is often equivocal but directed to a particular dilemma of the individual (Leff, 1981; Pugh, 1983). The term divination is applied to both psychology and sociology since its use is in both domains of problem solving and medical anthropology (Nuckolls, 1991). Although used principally with reference to cultural methods of healing in non-Western society, it can apply across cultures.

References

Guralnik, D. B. (Ed.). (1982). *Webster's new world dictionary of the American language* (7th ed.). New York: Warner.

Leff, J. (1981). *Psychiatry around the globe: A transcultural view*. New York: Marcel Dekker.

Nuckolls, C. W. (1991). Deciding how to decide: Possession mediumship on Jarari divination. *Medical Anthropology, 13*, 52–82.

Pugh, J. F. (1983). Astrological counseling in contemporary India. *Culture, Medicine, and Psychiatry, 7*, 279–299.

Amy L. Reynolds

E

EDUCATIONALLY DISADVANTAGED—Used to describe the population of students entering special admissions programs established in colleges and universities in the United States during the late 1960s. These programs were established by law to provide access to higher education for students who do not meet the regular admissions criteria and may have a greater financial aid need. In an effort to achieve the goal of equality of educational opportunity, special admissions programs such as SEEK (Search for Education, Elevation, and Knowledge in New York City, 1966), EOP (Educational Opportunity Programs) in state university systems, and HEOP (Higher Educational Opportunity Programs) in private colleges and universities were created. These programs typically provide one or more of the following service components: recruitment, tutoring, financial aid, course load reduction, counseling, and remedial, developmental, and/or compensatory instruction which are in addition to the regular programs and services offered by colleges and universities. Another term for educationally disadvantaged has been *academically and economically disadvantaged*. The term academically and economically disadvantaged is preferred because the nature of the so-called "disadvantage" is defined (Gordon, 1975).

Reference

Gordon, E. W. (1975). *Opportunity programs for the disadvantaged in higher education.* ERIC/Higher Education Research Report No. 6, Washington, DC (ERIC Document Reproduction Service No. ED 114 028).

Maria Rodriguez

EIDOS—A standardization of the cognitive aspects of the personality of individuals and its expression in cultural specific behavior. Also, the term applies to the process by which individuals are molded to resemble each other in their behavior by the ideas, values, beliefs, and assumptions of their respective cultural groups. The term was first used by Gregory Bateson in his partial ethnographic study of the Iatmul of Papua, New Guinea (Bateson, 1958). Although the term means "knowledge and understanding" in Greek, Bateson expanded its meaning by applying it to ethnographic studies. To study *eidos*, Bateson maintained that one must identify the structure of a cultural group and from this eidos is deduced; piece-by-piece the underlying system is deduced from the resulting description (Bateson, 1958, 1972). Colby's (1966) review of ethnographic semantics includes eidos with cognitive map, mazeway, and model; these terms are taken to refer to a mental image that includes all of the important aspects of one's surroundings.

References

Bateson, G. (1958). *Naven* (2nd ed.). Palo Alto, CA: Stanford University Press. (First edition published in 1936.)
Bateson, G. (1972). *Steps to an ecology of mind*. New York: Ballantine Books.
Colby, B. N. (1966). Ethnographic semantics: A preliminary study. *Current Anthropology, 7*, 3–28.

Joseph E. Trimble

EMIC—See ETIC/EMIC.

EMPOWERMENT—A process of personal development and change that involves: self-assessment, goal setting, and operationalization of goals. *Empowerment* involves a balance of thinking, feelings, and actions that impacts self-esteem and a sense of personal power (Arredondo, 1997, personal communication). With regard to the workplace, it is defined as a process that enables and motivates subordinates through an increase in their personal efficacy (Conger & Kanungo, 1989). For example, a person may believe that she is powerless to change jobs. An empowerment process would engage this person in examining thinking and feelings about change, her current work, and the possibility of new work.

Reference

Conger, J. A., & Kanungo, R. N. (1988). The empowerment process: Integrating theory and practice. *Academy of Management Review, 13*, 471–482.

Melissa Lamson

ENCOMIENDAS—Grants given to early Spanish settlers to own and control Native American land, labor, and produce. This was, in actuality, the first codification of slavery (Keith, 1971; Lockhart, 1969). *Encomiendas* were granted to the initial conquerors (*conquistadors*) and their descendants by the Spanish crown. "It placed hundreds and sometimes thousands of Indians under the control of individual Spaniards at a time when a bureaucracy had not yet been established'' (Ramirez, 1996, p. 492). Indians were forced to work gold and silver mines, build houses, build churches, cultivate crops, herd animals, and so forth, under the opression of encomiendas.

References

Keith, R. G. (1971). *Encomienda, hacienda, corregimiento* in Spanish America: A structural analysis. *Hispanic American Historical Review, 51,* 431–446.

Lockhart, J. (1969). *Encomienda* and *hacienda*: The evolution of the great estate in the Spanish Indies. *Hispanic American Historical Review, 49,* 411–429.

Ramirez, S. E. (1996). Encomienda. In B. A. Tenenbaum, G. M. Magassy, M. Karasch, J. J. TePaske, & R. L. Woodward, Jr. (Eds.), *Encyclopedia of Latin American history and culture* (Vol. 2, pp. 492–493). New York: Charles Scribner's Sons.

Cindy Yee and Jeffery Scott Mio

ENCULTURATION—The process whereby individuals learn about their culture including its beliefs, values, and customs. While the term is most often applied to development during childhood, *enculturation* is considered to be a lifelong process. The term is often used interchangeably with *socialization.* However, some authors make a distinction between the two, using the term socialization to describe the general process of learning about social norms while enculturation is used to described the process of learning about one's personal culture (Hunter & Whitten, 1976). Historically, enculturation has been an important focus of study within cultural anthropology. It is through enculturation that individuals acquire the knowledge and skills necessary to achieve competence within individuals cultures. This includes learning to anticipate the responses of others and to satisfy the role expectations associated with one's status and position (Goodenough, 1980). Enculturation is assumed to involve both conscious and unconscious processes, with knowledge about culture being transmitted both through direct instruction and imitation (Crapo, 1993).

References

Crapo, R. H. (1993). *Cultural anthropology: Understanding ourselves and others* (3rd ed.). Guilford, CT: Duskin Publishing Group.

Goodenough, W. H. (1980). Ethnographic field techniques. In H. C. Triandis & J. W. Berry (Eds.), *Handbook of cross-cultural psychology (Vol. 2). Methodology* (pp. 29–55). Boston: Allyn & Bacon.

Hunter, D. E., & Whitten, P. (1976). *The study of anthropology.* New York: Harper & Row.

Arleen C. Lewis

EQUAL EMPLOYMENT OPPORTUNITY (EEO)—A concept of nondiscrimination in labor practices that became codified into law by Title VII of the Civil Rights Act of 1964 (Burstein, 1991, 1992). Precursors to Title VII were the Equal Pay Act of 1963 (29 U.S.C. sec. 206[d]), the Civil Rights Acts of 1866 and 1871 (42 U.S.C. sec. 1981 and 42 U.S.C. sec. 1983, respectively), the

Railway Labor Act of 1926 (45 U.S.C. secs. 151–88), and the Labor Management Relations Act of 1947 (29 U.S.C. sec. 151), all of which banned forms of discrimination against women and/or ethnic minority groups (Burstein, 1991). "Title VII thus gave women and a variety of minorities, not just [B]lacks, a resource to use in their struggle for EEO. In fact, the law made them allies, in that usually a victory for one group was a victory for all" (p. 1205). In recent years, opponents of affirmative action have attacked the notion of equal employment opportunity, at least as it has been practiced through court decisions. For example, Belz (1991) has asserted that EEO was transformed from a prohibition of race-based policies to an imposition of race in the selection of workers. Nieli (1991) has warned that such practices will ultimately lead to civil war. However, in defending EEO, Burstein (1992) concluded that although there have been abuses in the past when employing EEO principles, "it is important to maintain some perspective. The adoption of EEO legislation was a critical step in the United States's attempt to end employment discrimination" (p. 919).

References

Belz, H. (1991). *Equality transformed: A quarter-century of affirmative action.* New Brunswick, NJ: Transaction.

Burstein, P. (1991). Legal mobilizatin as a social movement tactic: The struggle for equal employment opportunity. *American Journal of Sociology, 96,* 1201–1225.

Burstein, P. (1992). Affirmative action, jobs, and American democracy: What has happened to the quest for equal opportunity? *Law and Society Review, 26,* 901–922.

Nieli, R. (Ed.). (1991). *Racial preference and racial justice: The new affirmative action controversy.* Washington, DC: Ethics & Public Policy Center.

Jeffery Scott Mio

EQUALITY/INEQUALITY—*Equality* is defined as the respect and dignity which is owed to every person as a function of their humanness rather than their social standing (Simpson & Weiner, 1989; Williams, 1962). *Inequality*, then, is the unequal according of that respect based on one's social position (Engel, 1971; Simpson & Weiner, 1989). Temkin (1993), however, has suggested that equality is promoted simply to reduce inequality. Modern philosophical theories of equality and inequality have been postulated in the writings of such authors as Burke, Marx, Tocqueville, and Weber (Fallers, 1973). Equality is intrinsically tied to our beliefs about morality, fairness, and justice (Messick & Sentis, 1983; Rawls, 1971). According to this belief, people who have a sense of morality and justice and who are prepared to act on those beliefs automatically, deserve equality. Rawls (1971) noted that the difficulty with this notion is that "the criteria for equality are subjective, psychological dimensions" (p. 69). It is questionable that since inequality exists, those who lack power will never have an opportunity to determine if they have that sense of morality and justice thus perpetuating their unequal state. Equality is generally measured in terms of equality of outcome and opportunity (Messick & Sentis, 1983); race and class are among the factors which contribute to one's acquisition of equality (Ogbu, 1994).

References

Engel, M. (1971). *Inequality in America: A sociological perspective*. New York: Thomas Crowell.

Fallers, L. A. (1973). *Inequality: Social stratification revisited*. Chicago: University of Chicago Press.

Messick, D. M., & Sentis, K. (1983). Fairness, preference and fairness biases. In D. M. Messick & K. S. Cook (Eds.), *Equity theory: Psychological and sociological perspectives* (pp. 61–94). New York: Praeger.

Ogbu, J. W. (1994). Social stratification and education in the United States: Why inequality persists. *Teachers College Record, 96*, 264–298.

Rawls, J. (1971). *A theory of justice*. Cambridge, MA: Belknap Press.

Simpson, J. A., & Weiner, E.S.C. (Eds.). (1989). *The Oxford English dictionary* (2nd ed.). Oxford: Oxford University Press.

Temkin, L. S. (1993). *Inequality*. New York: Oxford University Press.

Williams, B. (1962). The idea of equality. In P. Laslett & W. G. Runciman (Eds.), *Philosophy, politics, and society* (pp. 110–131). New York: Barnes and Noble.

Amy L. Reynolds

ETHNIC CLEANSING—The systematic, purposeful elimination of one group of persons identified by heritage or race by another ethnic group living in geographical proximity. Historically, this practice has been justified as equitable retribution for previous human atrocities committed by the group targeted for elimination, or as a necessary method for protection of homogeneity or purity of a race. This importance of racial purity has been publicly endorsed by such notable historical figures as Comte de Gobineau, composer Richard Wagner, and anatomist Retzius. But it was the Nazi regime that provided the world with a procedural blueprint for assuring the racial purity of the *Herrenwolk* (master race; Gutman, 1990; Safire, 1993). During this time, the term *racial hygiene* was introduced in proposals for the "final solution" and is the likely derivative for the current phrase of ethnic cleansing. The recent conflict in the former Yugoslavia provided an *in vivo* example of ethnic cleansing practices among the Serbs, Croats, and Muslims which could be viewed as the logical reaction to General Tito's failed attempts to resolve the "Macedonian Question" and create a homogeneous population, devoid of ethnic ties. Jean-William Lapierre suggests that nations often create laws and citizen protections presuming a homogeneous populace, and this faulty reasoning promotes ethnic conflict (Lapierre, 1993). Others discussing this topic are Danforth (1993) and Thompson (1989).

References

Danforth, L. (1993). Claims to Macedonian identity. *Anthropology Today, 9*, 3–10.

Gutmann, I. (1990). *The encyclopedia of the Holocaust. Vol. 1*. New York: Macmillan.

Lapierre, J.-W. (1993). Ethnies et territories. *Peuples Mediterraneens, 64–65*, 87–94.
Safire, W. (1993). Ethnic cleansing. *The definitive guide to the new language of politics* (pp. 246–247). New York: Random House.
Thompson, R. (1989). *Theories of ethnicity.* Westport, CT: Greenwood Press.

Deborah Kirby Forgays

ETHNIC GLOSS—An overgeneralization or simplistic categorical label of ethnic groups such as American Indians, Hispanics, and Blacks that neglect the unique differences found among individuals in various cultures or groups (Trimble, 1995). For example, using the label American Indian ignores the special distinction of behaviors and traditions among the 500 or more tribes in the United States (Collins, 1995). The use of ethnic gloss in research contributes to problems of validity and generalizability and misrepresents the sample population. Researchers can avoid or minimize the use of ethnic gloss by elaborating on the population descriptives through administering detailed demographic or ethnic identification measures. Elimination of ethnic glosses will assist in the establishment of proper treatment and prevention programs (e.g., substance abuse) necessary for various ethnic groups (Trimble, 1990–91).

References

Collins, R. L. (1995). Issues of ethnicity in research on the prevention of substance abuse. In G. Botvin, S. Schinke, & M. A. Orlandi (Eds.), *Drug abuse prevention with multiethnic youth* (pp. 28–45). Thousand Oaks, CA: Sage.
Trimble, J. E. (1990–91). Ethnic specification, validation prospects, and the future of drug use research. *The International Journal of the Addictions, 25 (2A)*, 149–170.
Trimble, J. E. (1995). Toward an understanding of ethnicity and ethnic identity, and their relationship with drug use research. In G. Botvin, S. Schinke, & M. A. Orlandi (Eds.), *Drug abuse prevention with multiethnic youth* (pp. 3–27). Thousand Oaks, CA: Sage.

Joseph E. Trimble and Heather K. Mertz

ETHNIC IDENTITY—Within the social sciences (i.e., sociology, anthropology, and psychology), *ethnic identity* has been defined in a variety of different ways. An oft-cited definition stemming from the "social" identity perspective is offered by Tajfel (1981) as an awareness of one's membership in a particular social group. It has also been defined from a cultural perspective as an individual's perceptions of the behaviors, beliefs, values, and norms characteristic of the ethnic group to which one is a member (Ferdman, 1990). Others have described ethnic identity as multidimensional, consisting of (a) self-identification or the label individuals give thmselves, (b) knowledge about the culture including language, customs, values, beliefs, and traits, and (c) the feelings and attitudes individuals have about their group membership (e.g., Bernal & Knight, 1993; Parham & Helms, 1981). It has been suggested that ethnic identity is a complex dynamic process that changes over time (see ETHNIC IDENTITY DEVELOPMENT). Within the psychological literature, various racial identity models have been proposed for adults centered on the type and quality of contact with American dominant society (e.g., Cross, 1971; Helms, 1990; Sue & Sue, 1990). In recent years, the ethnic identity development of adolescents and young adults has received more attention in the literature (e.g., Phinney, 1990, 1993; Rotheram-Borus, 1989).

References

Bernal, M. E., & Knight, G. P. (Eds.). (1993). *Ethnic identity: Formation and transmission among Hispanics and other minorities.* Albany: State University of New York Press.

Cross, W. E. (1971). Negro-to-Black conversion experience: Toward a psychology of Black liberation. *Black World, 20,* 13–27.

Ferdman, B. M. (1990). Literacy and cultural identity. *Harvard Educational Review, 60,* 181–204.

Helms, J. E. (1990). *Black and White racial identity: Theory, research and practice.* Westport, CT: Greenwood Press.

Parham, T. A., & Helms, J. E. (1981). The influence of Black students' racial identity attitudes on preference for counselor's race. *Journal of Counseling Psychology, 28,* 250–257.

Phinney, J. S. (1990). Ethnic identity in adolescents and adults: Review of research. *Psychological Bulletin, 108,* 499–514.

Phinney, J. S. (1993). A three-stage model of ethnic identity development in adolescence. In M. E. Bernal & G. P. Knight (Eds.). *Ethnic identity: Formation and transmission among Hispanics and other minorities* (pp. 61–79). Albany: State University of New York Press.

Rotheram-Borus, M. (1989). Ethnic differences in adolescents' identity status and associated behavior problems. *Journal of Adolescence, 12,* 361–374.

Sue, D. W., & Sue, D. (1990). *Counseling the culturally different: Theory and practice* (2nd ed.). New York: Wiley.

Tajfel, H. (1981). *Human groups and social categories.* Cambridge: Cambridge University Press.

Azara L. Santiago-Rivera

ETHNIC IDENTITY DEVELOPMENT—The development of ethnic identity is a human necessity that offers a sense of belonging to self and culture (see ETHNIC SELF-IDENTIFICATION). Ethnic identity development is acknowledgment of one's ethnicity and is ''a process of differentiation and integration'' (Smith, 1991). Ethnic identity develops at different ages among children. Children between the ages of three and four years old are able to recognize differences in ethnicity, such as color. Children four to eight years old begin to affiliate ethnic groups with certain beliefs and preferences. Children between the ages of eight and ten years old begin to concentrate on their own ethnic group and exploring other ethnic cultures (Goodman, 1964). Erickson (1963) believes acquiring a sense of identity during adolescence is a key factor in one's ethnic identity development. Compliance to both social and personal factors must agree for a healthy identity to develop. However, cultural dissonance arises when there is a discrepancy between one's ethnic identity and the ethnic identity one wants to be associated with. This cultural dissonance may then emerge into a defensive identity or an identity change. For example, some adolescent Spanish-Americans do not want to be associated with Spanish ethnicity. Therefore, they learn to speak and dress like Americans, which they believe will help them achieve higher status and acceptance as Americans (Romanucci-Ross & DeVos, 1995).

References

Erickson, E. (1963). *Childhood and society*. New York: W. W. Norton
Goodman, M. (1964). *Race awareness in young children* (rev. ed.). New York: Collier.
Romanucci-Ross, L., & DeVos, G. (1995). *Ethnic identity: Creation, conflict, and accommodation* (3rd ed.). Walnut Creek, CA: Altamira Press.
Smith, E. J. (1991). Ethnic identity development: Toward the development of a theory within the context of majority/minority status. *Journal of Counseling and Development, 70*, 181–188.

Joseph E. Trimble and Heather K. Mertz

ETHNIC REFERENCE GROUP—The term *reference group* is borrowed from social psychology and is used to indicate an individual's psychological relatedness to a group (Sherif, 1964; Merton, 1968). However, Elsie Smith used the term *ethnic reference group* in about 1985 with respect to ethnic identity development (Smith, 1985). A reference group may be defined in three ways (Shibutani, 1955). First, it may point to a group which serves as the individual's point of comparison for evaluating one's status or self-image. Second, it may indicate the group whose acceptance an individual desires to gain or to maintain. Third, it may suggest that group whose perspectives function as social frames of reference for structuring a person's perceptual field. An ethnic reference group is a group to which an individual commits his/her identity. It refers to the group into which one wants to be counted as a member and the group whose opinions, standards, and goals are prized (Smith, 1989). Initially, an individual does not choose an ethnic reference group. One's parents, friends, and society may impose an ethnic reference group on one. However, at some point in one's life, one consciously chooses to identify with one ethnic group rather than another. An individual's ethnic identification can be measured by assessing the degree to which he/she uses the signs, symbols, and language of the culture associated with the ethnic group in question. Ethnic identification may vary from little or no identification to high identification with one's ethnic membership group, and the same situation may exist with respect to ethnic nonmembership groups (Smith, 1991).

References

Merton, R. K. (1968). *Social theory and social structure*. New York: The Free Press.
Sherif, M. (1964). Reference groups in human relations. In M. Sherif & M. O. Wilson

(Eds.), *Group relations at the crossroads* (pp. 203–231). New York: Harper & Row.

Shibutani, T. (1955). Reference groups as perspectives. *American Journal of Sociology, 60,* 562–569.

Smith, E. J. (1985). Ethnic minorities: Life stress, social support and mental health issues. *The Counseling Psychologist, 13,* 537–579.

Smith, E. J. (1989). Black racial identity development: Issues and concerns. *The Counseling Psychologist, 17,* 277–288.

Smith, E. J. (1991). Ethnic identity development: Toward the development of a theory within the context of majority/minority status. *Journal of Counseling and Development, 70,* 181–188.

Elsie J. Smith

ETHNIC SELF-IDENTIFICATION—An individual's sense of belonging or identification associated with membership in an ethnic group. From a social-psychological perspective, it answers the question: Who am I? One's identity includes personal, social, and cultural components as related to ethnicity. However, it is the intrinsic motivation to maintain a positive self-concept that is the decisive determinant of how one expresses who he or she is. One's identity represents one's past, present, and future self (Romanucci-Ross & DeVos, 1995). It can encompass the way one talks, the way one dresses, and one's beliefs, attitudes, and behaviors, which then can become symbols used to identify a specific ethnic group. Recognition of these symbols will, therefore, assist in identifying one's ethnicity and facilitating the appropriate interaction necessary (Levinson, 1994). "Social Identity Theory" (Tajfel, 1982) states that one's self-concept is composed of one's understanding of his or her ethnic membership and the importance of its value. Through this understanding, an individual compares himself or herself to others within the same group distinguishing the similarities and differences. Most theorists believe that a person chooses his or her own identity; although, among collectivistic-oriented populations such as Asian-Americans, identity is not freely chosen. Furthermore, in South Africa, one's ethnic identity includes not only the personal, social, and cultural features, but also political and economic features. These features of one's ethnic identity then control whether they will be included or excluded from various social domains (Roosens, 1989). However, in other areas of the world, ethnic identity is unimportant to culture.

References

Levinson, D. (1994). *Ethnic relations: A cross-cultural encyclopedia.* Santa Barbara, CA: ABC-CLIO.

Romanucci-Ross, L. & DeVos, G. (1995). *Ethnic identity: Creation, conflict, and accommodation* (3rd ed.). Walnut Creek, CA: Altamira Press.

Roosens, E. (1989). *Creating ethnicity: The process of ethnogenesis.* Newbury Park, CA: Sage.

Tajfel, H. (1982). *Social identity and intergroup relations*. Cambridge: Cambridge University Press.

Joseph E. Trimble and Heather K. Mertz

ETHNICITY—Derived from the ancient Greek word *ethnos*, which referred to a range of situations in which a group of people lived and acted together (Jenkins, 1997). *Ethnicity* more specifically refers to one's values and general lifestyle that is shared with a particular ethnic group. One does not necessarily have to live within the same geographical area as the ethnic group with which one identifies, nor does one need to be of the same race as the majority of the ethnic group. Thus, ethnicity is a fluid concept, while race is static (Jenkins, 1997; Paniagua, 1994; Pope-Davis & Coleman, 1997). Although the definitions/meanings of race and ethnicity differ considerably, confusion can arise concerning the difference between the two terms. This results in the terms being sometimes used interchangeably despite significant differences. While *race* refers to a person's genetic heritage, ethnicity refers to the cultural values, beliefs, and norms that a person ascribes to and identifies with. It is therefore possible to belong to a certain race without necessarily sharing the same ethnicity, and vice versa (Jenkins, 1997; Paniagua, 1994; Pope-Davis & Coleman, 1997; Rex, 1986). While most researchers agree on the distinction between ethnicity and race, there are those who feel that the distinction is unimportant or does not even exist. Several researchers have suggested that race is simply one of the ways in which ethnic boundaries are constructed, while others argue that the boundaries overlap considerably (Jenkins, 1997; Weber, 1978). Overall, however, most agree that race, unlike ethnicity, seems to be more of a matter of social categorization rather than of group identification. That is, while people may choose to share certain characteristics with an ethnic group, certain physical characteristics of their race are imposed upon them. As such, some perceive those of the same race as belonging to the same group and treat them according to a preconceived social category (Jenkins, 1997).

References

Jenkins, R. (1997). *Rethinking ethnicity*. Thousand Oaks, CA: Sage.
Marshall, G., & Barthel, D. (1994). *The concise Oxford dictionary of sociology*. New York: Oxford University Press.
Paniagua, F. (1994). *Assessing and treating culturally diverse clients*. Thousand Oaks, CA: Sage.
Pope-Davis, D. B., & Coleman, H.L.K. (1997). *Multicultural counseling competencies: Assessment, education and training, and supervision*. Thousand Oaks, CA: Sage.
Rex, J. (1986). *Race and ethnicity*. Houston, TX: Open University Press.
Weber, M. (1978). *Economy and society*. Berkeley: University of California Press.

Lisa Frye

ETHNOCARING—Pertains to "cognitive, assistive, facilitative or enabling acts or decisions that are valued and practiced" in a particular culture to assist the functioning of individuals, families, or groups (Leininger, 1985, p. 196). The behaviors and methods of ethnocaring portrayed and accepted by culture can take a form of folk medicine, and verbal and nonverbal interaction (Bailey, 1991; Leininger, 1978; Leininger, 1985). The term has been used respecting transcultural nursing in qualitative research through observation of culture (Leininger, 1978). Madeline Leininger, founder of the transcultural nursing field (Gaut & Leininger, 1991), first used the term in 1966 in her research conceptual model to illustrate transcultural nursing care constructs (Leininger, 1978). Some of the taxonomic caring constructs used by Leininger's model are compassion, emphathy, nurturance, protective behaviors, and health instruction (Leininger, 1978).

References

Bailey, E. J. (1991). *Urban African American health care.* Lanham, MD: University Press of America.

Gaut, D. A., & Leininger, M. M. (Eds.). (1991). *Caring: The compassionate healer.* New York: National League for Nursing Press.

Leininger, M. M. (1978). *Transcultural nursing: Concepts, theories, and practices.* New York: Wiley.

Leininger, M. M. (1985). Southern rural Black and White American lifeways with focus on care and health phenomena. In M. M. Leininger (Ed.), *Qualitative research methods in nursing* (pp. 195–210). Orlando, FL: Grune and Stratton.

Amy L. Reynolds

ETHNOCENTRISM—As it pertains to counseling and therapy, *ethnocentrism* refers to (1) devaluation of or discriminatory behavior towards a client on the basis of ethnicity, or (2) failure to include in the clinical decision-making process the possible impact of ethnocultural variables on the accuracy of assessment and effectiveness of potential interventions. The term was coined by Sumner (1906/ 1940), who defined it as "this view of things in which one's own group is the center of everything, and all others are scaled and rated with reference to it" (p. 13). Adorno, Frenkel-Brunswik, Levinson, and Sanford (1950/1982) created an Ethnocentrism Scale, and characterized the construct as "stereotyped negative imagery and hostile attitudes regarding outgroups, stereotyped positive imagery and submissive attitudes regarding ingroups, and a hierarchical, authoritarian view of group interaction in which ingroups are rightly dominant, outgroups subordinate" (p. 150). LeVine and Campbell (1972) discussed ethnocentrism as a possible universal aspect of group relations (Berry, Poortinga, Segall, & Dasen, 1992, p. 8). Though at an attitudinal level ethnocentrism is a form of prejudice, when it involves behaviors that lead to systematic victimization, it becomes racism (Ridley, 1995). Ridley distinguished between *intentional* (overt or covert) and *unintentional racism*, each of which may be individual or institutional. Lòpez (1989) similarly proposed that bias due to prejudiced (or ethnocentric) attitudes is different from clinical judgment errors due to faulty information processing. Errors in adjusting norms or failure to adjust norms to correspond with those of the client's culture may lead to over-pathologization or minimization of symptom severity, and to overdiagnosis or underdiagnosis (Lòpez, 1989). Consequences of intentional or unintentional ethnocentrism could range from failure to provide services, client attrition, and selection of inappropriate treatment modalities (Ridley, 1995) to involuntary hospitalization and increased use of medication and restraints (Flaherty & Meahger, 1980; Homma-True, Greene, Lòpez, & Trimble, 1993). Another term for this is *ethnocentric monoculturalism*, and a related term is *racial superiority* (Sue & Sue, 1999).

References

Adorno, T. W., Frenkel-Brunswik, E., Levinson, D. J., & Sanford, R. N. (Eds.). (1982). *The authoritarian personality* (Abridged ed.). New York: Norton. (Original work published in 1950.)

Berry, J. W., Poortinga, Y. H., Segall, M. H., & Dasen, P. R. (1992). *Cross-cultural psychology: Research and applications.* New York: Cambridge University Press.

Flaherty, J., & Meagher, R. (1980). Measuring racial bias in inpatient treatment. *American Journal of Psychiatry, 137,* 679–682.

Homma-True, R., Greene, B., Lòpez, S. R., & Trimble, J. E. (1993). Ethnocultural diversity in clinical psychology. *The Clinical Psychologist, 46,* 50–63.

LeVine, R. A., & Campbell, D. T. (1972). *Ethnocentrism.* New York: Wiley.

Levinson, D. J. (1982). The study of ethnocentric ideology. In T. W. Adorno, E. Frenkel-Brunswik, D. J. Levinson, & R. N. Sanford (Eds.), *The authoritarian personality* (Abridged ed., pp. 102–150). New York: Norton. (Original work published in 1950.)

Lòpez, S. R. (1989). Patient variable biases in clinical judgment: Conceptual overview and methodological considerations. *Psychological Bulletin, 106,* 184–203.

Ridley, C. R. (1995). *Overcoming unintentional racism in counseling and psychotherapy: A practitioner's guide to intentional intervention.* Thousand Oaks, CA: Sage.

Sue, D. W., & Sue, D. (1999). *Counseling the culturally different: Theory and practice* (3rd ed.). New York: Wiley.

Sumner, W. G. (1940). *Folkways: A study of the sociological importance of usages, manners, customs, mores, and morals.* New York: Ginn. (Original work published in 1906.)

Douglas Y. Seiden

ETHNOGRAPHY—The observation of human cultures, points of difference, and customs collected over time as they occur within the subject's environment (Gay, 1987; Simpson & Weiner, 1989). The word origins of *ethnography* are divided into two parts: *ethno* from the Greek meaning race or people, and *graphia* meaning writing (Barnhart, 1995; Berube, 1992). Literally translated, ethnography is writing about a race or people. Evidence shows that ethnography is a borrowed derivation of the German word *ethnographie*, meaning the ''geographical distribution of humans,'' and is synonymous with the American term *anthropography*, the study of the characteristics and customs of humankind

(Barnhart, 1995; Guralnik, 1982). Ethnography as a practice of observation began as missionaries and explorers during the late fifteenth century began to encounter cultures which were different from their own. Their efforts to chronicle what they saw and experienced during their travels were considered some of the earliest attempts to conduct ethnographic research. During the nineteenth century, as professional historians, museum collectors, and experienced travelers became more involved in the ethnographic process, it evolved into a more academic practice. Sills (1968) noted that after 1950, "ethnography began to attract more theoretical and methodological attention" (p. 174) with a greater emphasis placed on having researchers systematically consider the effects of cultural and personal differences on observations, the creation of models to study culture, and an overall increase in the study of cultures. With the professionalization of the field of ethnography, researchers began to use tools to document their observations to assist them in making future analysis. Ethnographic tools included photography, audio recording, video taping, and in some cases aerial mapping (Sills, 1968). Currently, professionals who utilize ethnography are described as anthropologists who attempt to "record and describe the culturally significant behaviors of a particular society" (Sills, 1968, p. 172). With increased technology, exposure, and research, the ethnographic process has evolved from an event of happenstance to a technical, analytical discipline of reporting, evaluating, and documenting cultural observations and artifacts.

References

Barnhart, R. (Ed.). (1995). *The Barnhart concise dictionary of etymology*. New York: H. W. Wilson.

Berube, M. S. (Ed.). (1992). *The American heritage dictionary of the English language* (3rd ed.). Boston: Houghton Mifflin.

Gay, L. R. (Ed.). (1987). *Educational research: Competencies for analysis and application*. Columbus, OH: Merrill.

Guralnik, D. B. (Ed.). (1982). *Webster's new world dictionary of the American language* (7th ed.). New York: Warner.

Sills, D. (Ed.). (1968). *International encyclopedia of the social sciences* (Vol. 5). New York: Macmillan.

Simpson, J. A., & Weiner, E.S.C. (Eds.). (1989). *The Oxford English dictionary* (2nd ed.). Oxford: Oxford University Press.

Amy L. Reynolds

ETHNOMETHODOLOGY—The process of determining the methods or relationships individuals use and sustain in understanding and organizing the world. *Ethno* refers to one's common knowledge within his or her society and *methodology* refers to the manner in which individuals deal with such knowledge (Turner, 1974). Harold Garfinkel (1967) coined the term in the mid-1950s while researching jurors and the methods they used to organize and communicate knowledge. Ethnomethodology is a combination of phenomenology and sociology. Ethnomethodologists study a wide range of social phenomena ranging from how people in different cultures communicate, to how people continue conversation after interruption. One of the most common methods of study utilized is how people use language to categorize behavior or individuals and the decision-making process involved with those categorizations. Ethnomethodology is concerned with the process of how social structures work, including how it originates and is maintained. Ethnomethodology is the common sense people use to determine what is appropriate, logical, and expected (Rogers, 1983).

References

Garfinkel, H. (1967). *Studies in ethnomethodology*. Englewood Cliffs, NJ: Prentice-Hall. Republished in 1984, Cambridge: Polity Press.
Rogers, M. (1983). *Sociology, ethnomethodology, and experiences*. Cambridge: Cambridge University Press.
Turner, R. (1974). *Ethnomethodology*. Harmondsworth, England: Penguin Books.

Joseph E. Trimble and Heather K. Mertz

ETHNONATIONALISM—Refers to the extreme internalization of national values and policies. Ethnonationalism is the result of emphasis being placed on national sentiment and identity. It often manifests as intense tension between and violence directed towards other national identities (Connor, 1994; Group for the Advancement of Psychiatry, 1987). Ethnonationalism has recently received increased attention due to the ethnic and religious wars between nations located in Eastern Europe, Africa, and the Middle East. KecManovic (1996) defined ethnonationalism as ''a set of ideas and prejudices partly grounded in one's group mentality and reinforced by the themes and other characteristics of nationalist ideology'' (p. 26). KecManovic identified five central tenets of ethnonationalism: (1) group and ethnic mentality—members share group characteristics, interests, and goals; (2) self-assertive and integrative tendency—members can maintain their individuality while conforming to the group norms; (3) group cohesion—internal cohesion is increased by maintaining in-group interaction, and rejecting out-group interaction decreases external cohesion; (4) nationalism—nationalistic status is chosen by an individual, not ascribed; and (5) ethnonational prejudices—prejudices towards other people are determined through socialization, not through personal experience. There are common characteristics that occur among ethnonational groups. Each characteristic may vary somewhat between groups, but some combination of these characteristics is present in all ethnonational groups. The characteristics include: oversimplification of social reality, dichotomization, demarcation of group needs, traditionalism, biologism (perceived biological determination of the group), and extremism. These characteristics are the most common and do not represent an exhaustive list. It must be noted that the literature on ethnonationalism tends to use the terms *nationalism* and *ethnonationalism* interchangeably, but only after defining nationalism by the same criteria listed above.

References

Connor, W. (1994). *Ethnonationalism: The quest for understanding*. Princeton, NJ: Princeton University Press.
Group for the Advancement of Psychiatry. (1987). *Us and them: The psychology of ethnonationalism*. New York: Brunner/Mazel.
KecManovic, D. (1996). *The mass psychology of ethnonationalism*. New York: Plenum Press.

John Johnson

ETHOS—The expression of spirit and emotions found among an organized society. This Greek term in its original form means "character or custom." Ethos is the recurrent morals and standards of human behavior that individuals abide by that distinguishes each group from the other. Ethos as a concept traces back to the early sixth century B.C. Greek philosophers began studying society's morals which later evolved into the study of ethics and philosophy. In the late 1800s W. G. Sumner, a sociologist, reinvented the concept which was later repopularized by Ruth Benedict's research on national character. The concept also can be applied when studying the various emotional or personality-related components tied to the different behaviors within each culture. Bateson (1972), commenting on the relation between ethos and culture, stated that "ethos molds the banks and the banks guide the river" (p. 83).

References

Bateson, G. (1972). *Steps to an ecology of mind*. New York: Ballantine Books.
Benedict, R. (1989). *Patterns of culture*. Boston: Houghton Mifflin.
Sumner, W. (1914). *Advancing social and political organization in the United States*. New Haven, CT: Yale University Press.

Joseph E. Trimble and Heather K. Mertz

ETIC/EMIC—The distinction between *etic* and *emic* was first made by Kenneth Pike (1967). These concepts were taken from the linguistic terms *phonemic* and *phonetic* (Jahoda, 1982; Mestenhauser, 1983; Pike, 1967). Both terms provide a model for the way we examine and observe the cultural norms of different groups. The emic approach observes the behavior of only one culture from within that culture, thus taking into account only what the group members assign importance (Brislin, 1980). The etic approach is referenced when a culture is studied from the outside of that particular group or system so that only universal aspects of behavior are considered (Berry, Poortinga, Segall, & Dasen, 1992). The distinction between the two approaches raises an important philosophical question: Can effective generalizations be made across cultures? Ideally, the etic/emic process begins when the researcher postulates an etic behavioral variable and attempts to validate its existence by searching for the appropriate and corresponding emic variable (Berry et al., 1992). If successful, a cross-cultural norm is identified. Triandis (1978) suggested using a "combined etic/emic" approach.

Such a model would allow us to take a more general etic approach and to find a more appropriate emic tool with which to measure a particular construct (Berry et al., 1992). Very few studies have identified a "derived" etic, which suggests that psychologists are primarily concerned with the "inner" rather than the "outer" qualities of a cultural group (Ongel & Smith, 1994).

References

Berry, J. W., Poortinga, Y. H., Segall, M. H., & Dasen, P. R. (1992). *Cross-cultural psychology: Research and applications.* Cambridge: Cambridge University Press.

Brislin, R. W. (1980). Translation and content analysis of oral and written materials. In H. C. Triandis & J. W. Berry (Eds.), *Handbook of cross-cultural psychology: Vol. 2. Methodology* (pp. 389–444). Boston: Allyn and Bacon.

Jahoda, G. (1982). *Psychology and anthropology: A psychological perspective.* London: Academic Press.

Mestenhauser, J. A. (1983). Learning from sojourners. In D. Landis & R. W. Brislin (Eds.), *Handbook of intercultural training: Vol. 11. Issues in training and methodology* (pp. 153–185). New York: Pergamon.

Ongel, U., & Smith, P. B. (1994). Who are we and where are we going? *JCCP* approaches its 100th issues. *Journal of Cross-Cultural Psychology, 25,* 25–53.

Pike, K. L. (1967). *Language in relation to a unified theory of the structure of human behavior.* The Hague: Mouton.

Triandis, H. C. (1978). Some universals of social behavior? *Personality and Social Psychology, 4,* 1–16.

                                                                    Amy L. Reynolds

EURO-AMERICAN—The prefix *Euro* pertains to "European: of western European communities" (Mish, 1993, p. 400). The term *Euro-American* was first used in 1941 to describe those who were "common to Europe and America" (Mish, 1993, p. 400) as a way of describing the increasing numbers of Europeans immigrating to the United States. There is further distinction made among those considered to be Euro-American. There are also those who immigrated to the United States from Southern and Eastern Europe and consider themselves Southern and Eastern Euro-Americans (Markus & Kitayama, 1991; Triandis, 1989). Included within this specific subgroup of Euro-Americans are Jewish, Greek, Italian, and Russian peoples. There are several terms which are often used interchangeably throughout the research literature to mean Euro-American, including *European Americans, Anglo-Saxons, Whites,* and the broader classification of *Caucasians.* Helms (1992) provided a differing perspective in suggesting that Whites are those who bear physical resemblance to "White Europeans" (p. ii) in American society. Some of these values include the nuclear configuration of the family, individualistic concept of self, scarcity of resources mode, and a European standard of beauty (Helms, 1984). Euro-Americans are often defined in terms of their relationships with other ethnic groups. Triandis (1993) defined Euro-Americans in the context of their relationships with Hispanics and African Americans. He explained the dynamics that develop as a result of joint relationships between ethnic groups "tends to result in a culture of its own which he explained has its own institutionalized way of thinking and acting derived from historical/experiential events involving that particular relationship" (p. 218). Throughout the literature, Euro-Americans also have been defined based on their chronicled relationship and interactions with Native Americans.

References

Helms, J. E. (1984). Toward a theoretical explanation of the effects of race on counseling: A Black and White model. *The Counseling Psychologist, 12,* 153–165.

Helms, J. E. (1992). *A race is a nice thing to have: A guide to being a White person or understanding the White persons in your life.* Topeka, KS: Content Communications.

Markus, H. R., & Kitayama, S. (1991). Culture and the self: Implications for cognition, emotion, and motivation. *Psychological Review, 98,* 224–253.

Mish, F. C. (Ed.). (1993). *Merriam-Webster's collegiate dictionary* (10th ed.). Springfield, MA: Merriam-Webster, Inc.

Triandis, H. C. (1989). The self and social behavior in differing cultural contexts. *Psychological Review, 96,* 506–520.

Triandis, H. C. (1993). Extracting the emic of diversity. *International Journal of Intercultural Relations, 17,* 217–234.

Amy L. Reynolds

EUROCENTRIC—Denotes one's point of origin and worldview; as well, it identifies an orientation of one's cultural values and attitudes. In the United States, it is presumed that Eurocentrism is based on the White Anglo-Saxon Protestant value system, which reflects an aggregation of values and beliefs of diverse ethnic groups (e.g., German, French, English, Scandinavian, etc.) whose origins are Northern and Western Europe and who immigrated to the United States between the eras of colonization and the early 1900s. The amalgamation of European cultures in American society led to the formation of an implicit White value system of which most people of European origin are unaware due to their dissolution of ties to the old country and need to identify as being a citizen of a new nation (Banks, 1991). Characteristics considered to be the basis of the American White value system include individualism, time-consciousness, a future-oriented perspective, competitiveness, and action orientation, and objective and linear thinking (Katz, 1985). More complex definitions of Eurocentric require comprehension of *ethnocentrism, racism,* and their related political dynamics. Sumner (1960) defined ethnocentrism (sometimes termed *culturocentrism;* Jones, 1981) as the "view of things in which one's own group is the center of everything and all others are scaled and rated with reference to it" (pp. 27–28). Based on this definition, Eurocentrism is a specific form of ethnocentrism. Like ethnocentrism, Eurocentrism has positive and negative connotations. In its positive form, the term Eurocentrism denotes pride in one's heritage as evidenced in a pro-European (pro-White) attitude, loyalty to the values, beliefs, and members of a European background. As human nature goes, it is considered a universal trait to value one's own culture more highly than the cultures of others. This kind of ethnocentrism—in this case, positive Eurocentrism—is often associated with a negative view of other cultural groups. Such negative views, manifested in prejudices and stereotypes, grow out of the constant evaluation of other groups based on the values of one's own group. Both variants of ethnocentrism are intricately embedded in the social, economic, and political institutions and interactions among groups. As a result, ethnocentrism can evolve into a special form of racism—cultural racism—which is the promotion of a societal belief that everything of the dominant culture (e.g., language, dress, traditions, etc.) is superior to other cultures (Atkinson, Morten, & Sue, 1993; Feagin, 1989; Jones, 1981; see CULTURAL RACISM). "Eurocentrism is the single global term that encompasses the totality of oppressive experiences that racial and ethnic groups share collectively because of a history that fell outside of European definitions of civilization, culture, and humanity" (Lowry, 1995, p. 714). This macroview of Eurocentrism can be observed at a micro-level in the everyday life of Americans. Specifically, the development of Western psychology has been based on a Eurocentric perspective and has been perpetuated in all spheres of theory, research, and practice. Wrenn (1962) underscored the presence of ethnocentrism in counselors when coining the term *culturally encapsulated* to describe counselors' unawareness of the cultural values of their clients and of their own cultural perspective. A growing number of writers (Atkinson et al., 1993; Speight, Meyers, Cox, & Highlen, 1991; Sue & Sue, 1990) have noted that many problems in counseling have occurred directly from the utilization of a Eurocentric perspective to view culturally diverse populations. As these problems are recognized, more culturally diverse worldviews are being incorporated into the theory and practice of counseling. Since the 1990s the hegemony of Eurocentrism has been challenged by other ethnocentric worldviews, the most prominent being *Afrocentrism* (Asante, 1988).

References

Asante, M. K. (1988). *Afrocentricity*. Trenton, NJ: Africa World Press.

Atkinson, D. R., Morten, G., & Sue, D. W. (1993). *Counseling American minorities: A cross-cultural perspective* (4th ed.). Madison, WI: Brown & Benchmark.

Banks, J. A. (1991). *Teaching strategies for ethnic studies* (5th ed.). Boston: Allyn & Bacon.

Feagin, J. R. (1989). *Racial & ethnic relations* (3rd ed.). Englewood Cliffs, NJ: Prentice-Hall.

Jones, J. M. (1981). The concept of racism and its changing reality. In B. P. Bowser & R. G. Hunt (Eds.), *Impacts of racism on White Americans* (pp. 27–49). Beverly Hills, CA: Sage.

Katz, J. H. (1985). The sociopolitical nature of counseling. *The Counseling Psychologist, 13*, 615–624.

Lowy, R. F. (1995). Eurocentrism, ethnic studies, and the new world order: Toward a critical paradigm. *Journal of Black Studies, 25*, 712–736.

Speight, S. L., Meyers, L. J., Cox, C. I., & Highlen, P. S. (1991). A redefinition of counseling. *Journal of Counseling and Development, 70*, 29–36.

Sue, D. W., & Sue, D. (1990). *Counseling the culturally different: Theory and practice* (2nd ed.). New York: Wiley.

Sumner, W. G. (1960). *Folkways.* New York: Mentor Books.

Wrenn, C. G. (1962). The culturally encapsulated counselor. *Harvard Educational Review, 32*, 444–449.

Beverly J. Vandiver

EXORCISM—Typically defined as the method or cure for ridding a person of unclean, malevolent, controlling, and unwanted spirits (Ward, 1989). Many cultures throughout history have conceptualized any form of abnormal behavior or mental illness in terms of demonic or spirit possession, for which the appropriate treatment is *exorcism*. Exorcism in principle is often very similar in varying cultures: the exorcist either attempts to enlist the aid of a supernatural power that is thought to be willing to participate in the exorcism, or he/she attempts to make the evil spirit too uncomfortable or displeased to stay in the possessed person's body (Hall, LeCann, & Gardner, 1982). Exorcisms are typically practiced only by experts who have received training in specific methods of exorcism and/or who are thought to have special spiritual powers. Evidence of the earliest attempts at exorcism have been found in the perforated skulls of ancient corpses, a technique referred to as *trephining* (the hole in the head was thought to have provided an exit for the possessing spirit). Other methods of exorcism range from the use of holy symbols or objects, dances, prayers and incantations, to the severe beating of the possessed person (Suwanlert, 1976; Ward, 1989). This view has been contrasted with those of cultures that see mental illness as being caused by malfunction of the body (Kemp, 1989), the treatment for which would fall under the domain of medical doctors. The ancient Greeks and Romans believed mental illness was caused by an imbalance of the bodily humors. Most modern Western perspectives propose it is due to imbalances of neurotransmitters, faulty genes, or maladaptive patterns of behavior and thinking. On the other hand, some have attempted to integrate the two models to better reflect the beliefs of people in general. Pfeifer (1994) has noted that even in Western cultures when lay persons are given symptom descriptions that match various *DSM-IV* psychotic disorders, they will attribute supernatural causes as often as natural causes for the illness. Osterreich (1930) made an early attempt at integration, suggesting that the diagnostic category of "possession syndrome" may be helpful. Psychoanalytically oriented psychologists have often compared exorcism to the process of psychotherapy, noting that therapeutically helpful elements such as emotional arousal and suggestibility, social support, hope, expectancy of cure, faith, and the use of symbols are present in many forms of helping, including exorcism (Hall et al., 1982). Some have suggested that the aid of exorcists may be helpful when such an approach matches a client's worldview (Ward, 1989).

References

Hall, R., LeCann, A., & Gardner, E. (1982). Demonic possession: A therapist's dilemma. *Journal of Psychiatric Treatment and Evaluation, 4,* 517–523.

Kemp, S. (1989). "Ravished or a fiend": Demonology and Medieval madness. In C. Ward (Ed.), *Altered states of consciousness and mental health: A cross-cultural perspective. Cross-cultural research and methodology series, Vol. 12* (pp. 67–78). Newbury Park, CA: Sage.

Osterreich, T. (1930). *Possession, demoniacal and other among primitive races, in antiquity, the middle ages, and modern times.* New York: Wendt & Klauwell.

Pfeifer, S. (1994). Belief in demons and exorcism in psychiatric patients in Switzerland. *British Journal of Medical Psychology, 67,* 247–258.

Suwanlert, S. (1976). Neurotic and psychotic states attributed to Thai "Phii Pob" spirit possession. *Australian and New Zeland Journal of Psychiatry, 10,* 119–123.

Ward, C. A. (1989). Possession and exorcism: Psychopathology and psychotherapy in a magico-religious context. In C. Ward (Ed.), *Altered states of consciousness and mental health: A cross-cultural perspective. Cross-cultural research and methodology series, Vol. 12* (pp. 125–144). Newbury Park, CA: Sage.

Devin Marsh

EXTERNAL LOCUS OF CONTROL–EXTERNAL LOCUS OF RESPONSIBILITY (EC–ER) AND EXTERNAL LOCUS OF CONTROL–INTERNAL LOCUS OF RESPONSIBILITY (EC–IR)—Terms that Sue (1978, 1981) used to describe two quadrants in his conception of worldviews (the other two quadrants involving *internal locus of control*; for definitions of *internal locus of control–internal locus of responsibility* and *internal locus of control–external locus of responsibility*, see entries for those terms). In this conceptualization, Sue combined the internal–external locus of control distinction made by Rotter (1954, 1966) with the internal–external locus of responsibility distinction made in attribution theory (Jones, Kanouse, Kelley, Nisbett, Valins, & Weiner, 1972). The locus of control distinction identified outcomes of life as being under our own personal influence or as being controlled by external factors such as fate. Sue (1981) put this distinction in behavioral terms: " 'Internal control' (IC) refers to people's belief that reinforcements are contingent on their own actions and that people can shape their own fate. 'External control' (EC) refers to people's belief that reinforcing events occur independently of their actions and that the future is determined more by chance and luck" (p. 74). The locus of responsibility distinction identified outcomes of life events as being either internal to or external from the individual. For example, if one were to have a successful career, one might attribute this positive outcome to one's own hard work or one's own abilities. These would be *internal* locus of responsibility (IR) attributions. Alternatively, one might attribute one's successful career to luck, being at the right place at the right time, others' efforts on one's behalf, and so on. These would be *external* locus of responsibility attributions. Similarly, an unsuccessful career can be attributed to internal (poor ability, poor effort) or external (bad luck, others' interference) locus of responsibility (ER) factors. When the dimensions of locus of control and locus of responsibility are crossed, it yields four quadrants: IC–IR, IC–ER, EC–ER, and EC–IR. IC–IR is the dominant cultural view here in the United States, but many ethnic minorities may have worldviews in the other three quadrants. As this definition is only concerned with the EC–ER and EC–IR quadrants, the reader is referred to the entries for the IC–IR and IC–ER terms to gain a more complete understanding of the collection of terms. In *external locus of control–external locus of responsibility* (EC–ER), the worldview is bleak. One sees one's poor conditions of living as being due to a system that does not care or is exploitative, and that there is very little one can do about these conditions. Sue (1981; Sue & Sue, 1999) likens this condition to Seligman's (1975) *learned helplessness* frame of mind. Even if one might be able to make more tolerable one's condition, one has given up trying to make such changes. Alternatively, some EC–ER individuals may adopt what Sue calls a "placater" attitude. Here one views social forces as too powerful to challenge, and one goes along with systemic inequities so as to avoid reprisals from the system. Sue (1981; Sue & Sue, 1999) recommends that culturally sensitive counselors seeing clients with EC–ER worldviews attempt to teach new coping strategies, assist the clients in experiencing successes, and validate the clients and what they represent. In *external locus of control–internal locus of responsibility* (EC–IR), one accepts the view that one is responsible for one's conditions, yet one feels helpless in actually effecting change. Sue (1981; Sue & Sue) likens this condition to Stonequist's (1935) *marginal man (marginal person)* discussion. Here, one feels marginalized, not feeling part of either culture to which one might belong. These feelings of marginalization can lead to self-hatred, as one hates being in an inferior status from the majority population, yet one accepts the responsibility for being in the inferior position. Sue (1981; Sue & Sue, 1999) recommends that culturally sensitive counselors help clients having EC–IR worldviews understand the superior–inferior political forces that perpetuate feelings of marginalization and to help clients make a distinction between positive attempts of acculturation versus rejection of one's culture of origin.

References

Jones, E. E., Kanouse, D. E., Kelley, H. H., Nisbett, R. E., Valins, S., & Weiner, B. (Eds.) (1972). *Attribution: Perceiving the causes of behavior.* Morristown, NJ: General Learning Press.

Rotter, J. B. (1954). *Social learning and clinical psychology.* New York: Prentice-Hall.

Rotter, J. B. (1966). Generalized expectancies for internal versus external control of reinforcement. *Psychological Monographs, 80* (Whole No. 609).

Seligman, M.E.P. (1975). *Helplessness: On depression, development and death.* San Francisco: Freeman.

Stonequist, E. (1935). The problem of the marginal man. *American Journal of Sociology, 41*, 1–12.

Sue, D. W. (1978). Eliminating cultural oppression in counseling: Toward a general theory. *Journal of Counseling Psychology, 25,* 419–428.

Sue, D. W. (1981). *Counseling the culturally different: Theory and practice.* New York: Wiley.

Sue, D. W., & Sue, D. (1999). *Counseling the culturally different: Theory and practice* (3rd ed.). New York: Wiley.

Jeffery Scott Mio

EXTERNALIZE—A term used in three different ways within the psychology literature. It first describes the process of bringing forth thoughts or emotions. This first usage is similar to *catharsis* without the explicit theoretical implications or narrow definitional confines of psychoanalysis. To have ideas or feelings externalized means to have them expressed. Ball, Piercy, and Bischof (1993) described cartoons as a novel way of externalizing the problem at hand. The second use of the term externalize relates to Rotter's (1966) attributional style. Individuals acquire an internal or external locus of control regarding their world. Internal control denotes a sense of personal influence on the environment; what one does has an impact on the setting. External control fatalistically suggests that the environment is determined by forces beyond the person's domain. Therefore, individuals have no influence on the world around them. The concept of internal and external locus of control has provoked a great amount of research. There are over 10,000 journal references to locus of control between 1967 and 1996. Recent research has differentiated between situations where control can realistically be expected and where control is not really possible (Zuckerman, Knee, Kieffer, & Rawsthorne, 1996). The ability to distinguish between what can be controlled and what cannot be controlled is important. The third form of externalize deals with a variant on this distinction between internal and external attribution. In the literature on oppression and on abuse, the term externalize describes an individual's discovery that they are not to be blamed for their vicitimization and a resulting behavior pattern. Social, environmental, or family contexts impose circumstances which then produce particular actions. The feedback cycle within the environment maintains and encourages certain conduct and discourages other ways of behaving. Weitz's (1982) work on feminist therapy techniques described the value of externalizing the blame for certain problem behaviors. Hoagwood (1990) found victims of abuse to benefit from externalizing the blame for their victimization. Externalization allows individuals to realistically examine the circumstances for their oppression and victimization as well as the actions that this engendered. The externalization depathologizes individuals and focuses attention to others' (or the environment's) contributions to the problem situations.

References

Ball, E., Piercy, F., & Bischof, G. (1993). Externalizing the problem through cartoons: A case example. *Journal of Systemic Therapies, 12,* 19–21B.

Hoagwood, K. (1990). Blame and adjustment among women sexually abused as children. *Women and Therapy, 9,* 89–110.

Rotter, J. (1966). Generalized expectancies for internal versus external control of reinforcement. *Psychological Monographs, 80* (Whole No. 609).

Weitz, R. (1982). Feminist consciousness raising, self concept and depression. *Sex Roles, 8,* 231–241.

Zucherman, M., Knee, C. R., Kieffer, S., & Rawstherne, L. (1996). Beliefs in realistic and unrealistic control: Assessment and implications. *Journal of Personality, 64,* 435–464.

John Moritsugu

F

FACE—Refers to a claimed sense of favorable social self-worth that a person wants others to have of her/him (Ting-Toomey, 1988). It is a vulnerable identity-based resource, because this resource can be enhanced or threatened in any uncertain social situation. Situations such as conflict management, business transactions, and diplomatic negotiation entail active facework management. Additionally, the term *facework* refers to a set of communicative behaviors that people use to regulate their estimated social self-worth and to support or challenge others' social self-worth. *Face* and *facework* are about interpersonal self-worth issues and mutual respectability issues. The study of facework has been linked to complimenting, compliance-gaining, politeness, requesting, embarrassment, apology, shaming (see SHAME), decision-making, and conflict behavior (see Ting-Toomey, 1994; Ting-Toomey & Kurogi, 1998). According to Hu (1944), Goffman (1959), Ho (1976), and Bond (1991), the concept of face originated with the Chinese. Hu describes two Chinese conceptualizations of face: *lien* and *mien-tzu*. *Lien* is the underlying moral face that involves a person's internalized notions or standards of shame, integrity, debasement, and honor issues. *Mien-tzu* is the external social face that involves social recognition, position, authority, influence, and power. *Lien* and *mien-tzu* reciprocally influence one another. They are two interdependent constructs—with *lien* as the internalized moral compass and *mien-tzu* as the externalized social image. *Mien-tzu* (which corresponds more closely to the term *face* found in both past and current psychology, sociology, sociolinguistics, and communication literature) can be further understood on two levels: subjective and objective (Cheng, 1986). The subjective level of *mien-tzu* emphasizes a person's subjective estimation of one's self-value and self-worth with regard to social relationships and society at large. It is an identity respectability quotient to which one believes one is entitled (e.g., by virtue of social position, reputation, rank, expertise, etc.). This respectability quotient is commensurate with the level one expects to command in the community. The objective level of *mien-tzu*, on the other hand, emphasizes the social position or value of a person as recognized by others in the community or by a network of individuals (or a specific person) in a particular situation. The historical roots of *lien* and *mien-tzu* can be traced back to the philosophical principles of Confucious (circa 500 B.C.). Confucianism advocates that a "civilized" person should always be a responsive, connected individual, aware of his/her hierarchical role or position in society, and perform his/her duty accordingly. In Chinese culture, to be aware of one's social relation with others at all times and to engage in appropriate facework negotiation with others is an integral part of being a competent, "civilized" individual (Gao & Ting-Toomey, 1998). In everyday encounters, when our social poise is attacked or teased, we feel the need to restore or save face. When we are being complimented or given credit for a job well done, we feel our social self-worth is enhanced and stroked. *Face saving* refers to the communication behaviors in which we engage to circumvent or recoup face loss. When one's face is being threatened (or in anticipation of being threatened), the typical face saving strategies are preventive face-saving strategies and restorative face-saving strategies. *Preventive facework strategies* (e.g., disclaimers and hedges) refer to actions designed to "hide, soften, ward off, prevent, or block . . . and to control the occurrence of future events that one expects will foster an appearance of weakness or vulnerability, particularly when it is presumed that such events will impair one's image or the image of those whom one represents" (Brown, 1977, pp. 278–279). *Restorative facework strategies* refer to verbal and nonverbal actions (e.g., justifications and excuses) designed to "repair damaged or lost face [and are] occurring in response to events that have already transpired. Thus, it is past-oriented and defensive. It reflects actions designed to reestablish or reassert one's capability and/or strength after one feels they have been damaged" (Brown, 1977, p. 281). *Face giving* refers to the communication behaviors (e.g., compliments and honorifics) that we engage in to upgrade someone's social self-worth or social standing. It also means not humiliating or embarrassing one another in the public arena in a confrontative manner. It means leaving room enough for the other to retrieve his/her social dignity without total demolition of the other person's public image. The conceptualization of self, and hence, face is the generative mechanism for all communicative behaviors. While face and facework are universal phenomenon, how we "frame" the situated meaning of face, and how we enact facework behaviors, differ from one culture to another. Using a cultural variability approach of individualism–collectivism to the study of face and facework, Ting-Toomey and Kurogi (1998; Ting-Toomey, 1988) propose a theoretical model, the *face-negotiation theory* (with 7 assumptions and 32 propositions). The dimension of individualism–collectivism serves as a conceptual grid in explaining why the meaning of self (face) varies across cultures.

References

Bond, M. (1991). *Beyond the Chinese face*. Hong Kong: Oxford University Press.

Brown, B. (1977). Face-saving and face-restoration in negotiation. In D. Druckman (Ed.), *Negotiations: Social-psychological perspectives* (pp. 275–299). Beverly Hills, CA: Sage.

Cheng, C.-Y. (1986). The concept of face and its Confucian roots. *Journal of Chinese Philosophy, 13*, 329–348.

Gao, G., & Ting-Toomey, S. (1998). *Communicating effectively with the Chinese*. Thousand Oaks, CA: Sage.

Goffman, E. (1959). *The presentation of self in everyday life*. Garden City, NY: Doubleday.

Ho, D. (1976). On the concept of face. *American Journal of Sociology, 81*, 867–884.

Hu, H.-C. (1944). The Chinese concept of "face." *American Anthropologist, 46*, 45–64.

Ting-Toomey, S. (1988). Intercultural conflict styles: A face-negotiation theory. In Y. Y. Kim & W. Gudynkunst (Eds.), *Theories of intercultural communication* (pp. 213–238). Newbury Park, CA: Sage.

Ting-Toomey, S. (Ed.). (1994). *The challenge of facework*. Albany: State University of New York Press.

Ting-Toomey, S., & Kurogi, A. (1998). Facework competence in intercultural conflict: An updated face-negotiation theory. *International Journal of Intercultural Relations, 22*, 187–225.

Stella Ting-Toomey

FAMILY—Traditionally, family has been known to be a mother, a father, and their offspring. However, the definition of *family* has been called into question as human relationships have reconfigured in recent decades. Yet, throughout these changes, myths of the *traditional family* have persisted, lagging behind emerging social realities (Walsh, 1993). In spite of evidence to the contrary, the following myths continue to exert a powerful influence on expectations for families: (a) that multigenerational family solidarity exists, (b) that the nuclear family is ideal and essential, (c) that one norm fits all families, and (d) that family members maintain specific gender roles determined by society (Walsh, 1993). A useful perspective that can be used for defining family while incorporating the rapid changes occurring in Western societies is to consider families not as static institutions, but as organisms continually engaged in a process and evolving from their experiences in the society in which they exist (Henslin, 1989). In order to develop a fresh conceptualization of empirical reality accumulated by the massive evidence for the breadth and depth of ongoing behavioral variation (Bumpass, 1990), some family researchers have suggested a "new action theory" that is responsive to persons' circumstances and choices instead of being limited *a priori* to ties of blood and marriage (Scanzoni & Marsiglio, 1993). The contention of these researchers is that *postmodern families* reflect diversity, rather than uniformity in living arrangements. This diversity results from a response to ever-shifting situations, some of a family's choosing and others imposed on them (Cheal, 1991).

References

Bumpass, L. L. (1990). What's happening to the family? Interactions between demographic and institutional change. *Demography, 27,* 483–498.

Cheal, D. (1991). *Family and the state of theory.* Toronto: University of Toronto Press.

Henslin, J. M. (1989). The social and historical context of marriage and family in American society. In J. M. Henslin (Ed.), *Marriage and family in a changing society* (3rd ed., pp. 3–14). New York: The Free Press.

Scanzoni, J., & Marsiglio, W. (1993). New action theory and contemporary families. *Journal of Family Issues, 14,* 105–132.

Walsh, F. (1993). Conceptualization of normal family process. In F. Walsh (Ed.), *Normal family processes* (2nd ed.). New York: Guilford.

MaryAnna Domokos-Cheng Ham

FATALISMO—A belief seen in some Hispanic/Latino populations (and other minority groups) that life's events are inevitable and usually attributed to "God's will" as evidenced in the phrase *que sea lo que Dios quiera* (Sandoval & De la Roza, 1986). Individuals feel at the mercy of natural and supernatural forces which they cannot control thus, they must resign themselves to their fate. *Fatalismo* accompanies an attitude of powerlessness immersed in passive resignation and subjugation. Since the universe is controlled by exterior forces, so is destiny, and the best approach to life is to take it "as it comes." *Fatalismo* can be interpreted as a potentially adaptive response to uncontrollable life situations often experienced by minorities. A fatalistic orientation is hypothesized to be maladaptive in more individualistic cultures, whereas fatalism may be considered more adaptive in less individualistic cultures.

Reference

Sandoval, M. C., & De la Roza, M. C. (1986). A cultural perspective for serving the Hispanic client. In H. P. Lefley & P. B. Pedersen (Eds.), *Cross-cultural training for mental health professionals* (pp. 151–181). Springfield, IL: Charles C. Thomas.

Sandra I. Lopez-Baez

FEMINISM—A term that has been defined differently by various groups across time, the most widely accepted current definition involves the belief in and action towards the social, political, and economic equality between the sexes (e.g., Hyde, 1991; *Merriam-Webster's Collegiate Dictionary*, 1993). Thus, *feminism* has both a worldview or perspective component, as well as reference to a form of activism or political movement. Feminism has at various times also been referred to as "the feminist movement," "the women's movement," and "women's liberation." This is ironic, given that the word initially was coined in the 1850s and referred to the "state of being feminine" (Barnhart, 1988, p. 375). It was not until 1895 that the definition changed to refer to issues regarding women's rights (Barnhart, 1988). As a social and political movement, Ruth

(1990) suggests that we should not attempt to limit our understanding of feminism to a single or even a series of activist periods. Rather, we should see feminism as a continuing effort to move women forward regarding their own personal awareness, as well as in the sociopolitical arena. These efforts may take shape differently in various cultures across different historical periods. In addition, a number of feminist researchers have pointed out that feminism means different things to different people. It has often been conceptualized as "liberal," "cultural," or "radical," depending on its focus (e.g., Unger & Crawford, 1996; Worrell, 1996). Doyle and Paludi (1991) note that the current feminist movement in the United States sprung from the early abolition movement. The 1848 Women's Rights Convention held in Seneca Falls, New York, is often seen as the formal beginning of the modern U.S. women's movement. This was followed by organized activities in the early 1900s aimed at acquiring equal rights for women, culminating in 1920 with the passage of the Nineteenth Amendment giving women the right to vote. The 1960s saw another resurgence of activism focused on educational, workplace and pay equity, expanded personal and social roles, and contraceptive and reproductive rights. Current feminist goals include maintaining and furthering these goals, with an increased focus on women's rights globally. The specific nature of these activities varies depending on the country, but all efforts focus on improving women's lives individually and collectively (Matlin, 1996).

References

Barnhart, R. K. (Ed.). (1988). *The Barnhart dictionary of etymology*. New York: Wilson.
Doyle, J., & Paludi, M. (1991). *Sex and gender* (2nd ed.). Dubuque, IA: Brown.
Hyde, J. S. (1991). *Half the human experience: The psychology of women* (4th ed.). Lexington, MA: D.C. Health.
Matlin, M. (1996). *The psychology of women* (3rd ed.). New York: Harcourt Brace.
Merriam-Webster's collegiate dictionary (10th ed.). (1993). Springfield, MA: Merriam-Webster.
Ruth, S. (1990). *Issues in feminism* (2nd ed.). Mountain View, CA: Mayfield.
Unger, R., & Crawford, M. (1996). *Women and gender: A feminist psychology*. New York: McGraw-Hill.
Worrell, J. (1996). Feminist identity in a gendered world. In J. C. Chrisler, C. Golden, & P. D. Rozee (Eds.), *Lectures on the psychology of women* (pp. 359–370). New York: McGraw-Hill.

Laurie A. Roades

FETAL ALCOHOL SYNDROME—*Fetal Alcohol Syndrome* (FAS) is a totally preventable birth defect caused by prenatal alcohol exposure (Dorris, 1989; Streissguth, 1994). It is most frequently diagnosed in the children of mothers who consumed large amounts of alcohol while pregnant, although the exact amount of alcohol which can be drunk during pregnancy is still unknown. Some of the other variables which appear to influence the risk for FAS in children are: when the mother used alcohol during the pregnancy, other drug usage, and smoking. FAS is a medical diagnosis and is made on the basis of a clinical examination by a birth defects' specialist. It is defined by the presence of low birthweight, physical anomalies of the face, and signs of mental retardation. Some of the physical anomalies of the face include both discriminating features and associated features. The discriminating features can include small head circumference, large distance between eyes, a flat midface, short nose, and a thin upper lip. The associated features can include low nasal bridge and minor ear anomalies. Other children who are exposed to alcohol before birth may have some of the features previously mentioned, but not all of them. These children are described as possible Fetal Alcohol Effects (FAE) children, which is not a medical diagnosis (Streissguth, 1994; Streissguth, LaDue, & Randels, 1987). It is beneficial for children to be screened at birth and diagnosed early so that appropriate treatment for both the mother and child can begin quickly. Effective prenatal screening, screening at birth, and accurate diagnosis can assist communities in the development of treatment programs which address both the child's developmental needs and the mothers' alcoholism which can further reduce the risk for producing more children with FAS or FAE (May & Hymbaugh, 1982; Plaisier, 1989).

References

Doris, M. (1989). *The broken cord.* New York: HarperCollins.

May, P. A., & Hymbaugh, K. J. (1982). A pilot project on fetal alcohol syndrome among American Indians. *Alcohol Health and Research World, 7*, 3–9.

Plaisier, K. J. (1989). Fetal alcohol syndrome prevention in American Indian communities of Michigan's upper peninsula. *American Indian & Alaska Native Mental Health Research—Journal of the National Center, 3*, 16–33.

Streissguth, A. P. (1994). Fetal alcohol syndrome: Understanding the problem; understanding the solution; what Indian communities can do. *American Indian Culture and Research Journal, 18*, 45–83

Streissguth, A. P., LaDue, R. A., & Randels, S. P. (1987). Indian adolescents and adults with fetal alcohol syndrome: Findings and recommendations. *The Primary Care Provider, 12*, 89–91.

Grace Powless Sage

FIELD DEPENDENCE/INDEPENDENCE—A cognitive style based on the relative influence of environmental or contextual factors in an individual's perceptual functioning. Generally assessed as a perceptual task where the subject is required to differentiate an object from its contextual background (e.g., The Rod-and-Frame Test, embedded figures), *field dependence/independence* (FD/I) has been associated with a variety of individual and group differences. Originally developed by Herman Witkin (Goodenough, 1989), a continuum of personality and perceptual characteristics has been found with field dependent individuals having greater difficulty differentiating an item from its background. Field dependent individuals tend to be strongly influenced by their environment, are generally interpersonally skilled, tend to rely on others, are generally dependent on those around them for self-identity, and tend to use integrative approaches to problems solving and learning. Individuals who are field independent have greater facility solving perceptual problems, since they more easily discount interference from the perceptual background. They tend to be self-reliant, competitive, and generally function without being highly influenced by the environment or the context in which they function. The concepts of FD/I have enjoyed considerable popularity in psychology and have generated sizeable literature which has been compiled into a series of publications (e.g., Cox, 1980, 1981; Cox & Witkin, 1978). Developmental trends have been demonstrated in FD/I from childhood through adulthood (towards greater independence), and cross-cultural research has demonstrated relations between FD/I and the type of society and home in which a child was raised. Authoritarian or agrarian societies tend to have individuals who are more field dependent, where individuals from democratic, industrialized societies tend to be more field independent (Berry, 1976; Witkin & Goodenough, 1981).

References

Berry, J. W. (1976). *Human ecology and cognitive style: Comparative studies in cultural and psychological adaptation.* New York: Wiley.

Cox, P. W. (1980). *Field dependence–independence and psychological differentiation* (Supplement No. 4 ETS RR-80–20). Princeton, NJ: Educational Testing Service.

Cox, P. W. (1981). *Field dependence–independence and psychological differentiation* (Supplement No. 5 ETS RR-80–29). Princeton, NJ: Educational Testing Service.

Cox, P. W., & Witkin, H. A. (1978). *Field dependence–independence and psychological differentiation* (Supplement No. 5 ETS RR-80–29). Princeton, NJ: Educational Testing Service.

Goodenough, D. R. (1989). History of the field dependence construct. In M. Bertini, L. Pizzamiglio, & S. Wapner (Eds.), *Field dependence in psychological theory, research, and application* (pp. 5–13). Hillsdale, NJ: Erlbaum.

Ruben J. Echemendia

G

GENERIC CHARACTERISTICS OF COUNSELING—Counseling and psychotherapy in the United States reflect the traditional cultural values of Western society. Irrespective of theoretical basis (psychodynamic, behavioral, client-centered, etc.), common components of White cultural values and beliefs are present. Katz (1985) and Sue and Sue (1990) identify many of the values of Western Cultures: individualism, competition, openness and expressiveness, action orientation, Protestant work ethic, emphasis on scientific method, clear distinction between physical and mental well-being, and nuclear family structure. Clearly, the above beliefs and values have influenced the practice of counseling and psychotherapy (Sue & Sue, 1990). These values and expectations are likely to be different for people from other cultural and/or ethnic heritage. For example, some American Indian characteristics are: present-time orientation, cooperation, noncompetitive individualism, folk or supernatural explanations, extended family orientation, short-range goals, and concrete and tangible approach to dealing with one's problems (Sue & Sue, 1990). Clearly, American Indians' values and approaches are different from White cultural values. Such differences can also be seen with other ethnic minority groups. According to Sue and Sue (1990), there are three major characteristics of counseling that may put ethnic minority groups at a disadvantage. The first characteristic is the expectation that the client will exhibit openness and be psychologically minded in his/her insight seeking. The second characteristic is the expectation that the client will discuss intimate facts of his/her life with a counselor. Finally, the third characteristic is the ambiguous nature of therapy that relies on the active participation of the client. For a counselor who is working with an ethnic minority client, the above characteristics may likely be a barrier and a source of incorrect assumptions. For an effective therapeutic relationship, counselors should be aware of the cultural and the class-bound values as well as language variables that are the foundation of psychotherapy and counseling. What they have been trained to believe is generic aspects of counseling are really culturally determined qualities.

References

Katz, J. (1985). The sociopolitical nature of counseling. *The Counseling Psychologist, 13*, 615–624.
Sue, D. W., & Sue, D. (1990). *Counseling the culturally different: Theory and practice* (2nd ed.). New York: Wiley.

Rakefet Richmond

GENOGRAM—A type of family tree that records information about family members and their relationships over at least three generations. Genograms are frequently associated with Bowen's family system theory (Bowen, 1978) but their use is not restricted to clinicians with this theoretical orientation, and they are in fact used by clinicians with a wide variety of orientations. The conceptual framework that underlays the interpretation of genograms is based on Bowen's work. There are five basic Bowenian beliefs which relate to the use of genograms. These include: (1) people are organized within family systems and functioning can be affected by where the individual fits within the family structure; (2) what happens in one generation in the family is likely to repeat itself in other generations (multigenerational transmission); (3) events occurring in different parts of the family are interconnected in a systematic way; (4) genograms can map relationship patterns within families; and (5) the members of a system fit together as a functional whole (McGoldrick & Gerson, 1985). Many modifications of the original genogram have been developed. These include: the use of genograms combined with Transactional Analysis script matrices (Massey, Comey, & Just, 1988), cultural genograms (Hardy & Laszloffy, 1995), solution-oriented genograms (Koehl, 1995), genograms used with eco-maps (Hartman, 1995), genograms with occupations for career counseling (Heppner, O'Brien, Hinkelman, & Humphrey, 1994), and placement genograms in child welfare (McMillen & Grore, 1994). Boyd-Franklin (1989) and others caution against using genograms with certain ethnic groups prior to having properly joined with the clients. Hines and Boyd-Franklin (1996) and Brice-Baker (1996) also indicate that with African Americans and Jamaican families extended kinship networks are important to explore rather than restricting the genogram to blood lines. Other families (e.g., adoptive families, gay and lesbian families) may also require modifications in the administration of the genogram so as to encompass the family structure and relationships that these families comprise.

References

Bowen, M. (1978). *Family therapy in clinical practice*. New York: Jason Aronson.
Boyd-Franklin, N. (1989). *Black families in therapy: A multisystems approach*. New York: Guilford.

Brice-Baker, J. (1996). Jamaican families. In M. McGoldrick, J. K. Pearce, & J. Giordano (Eds.), *Ethnicity and family therapy* (pp. 85–95). New York: Guilford.

Hardy, K. V., & Laszloffy, T. A. (1995). The cultural genogram: Key to training culturally competent family therapists. *Journal of Marital and Family Therapy, 21,* 227–238.

Hartman, A. (1995). Diagrammatic assessment of family relationships. *Families in Society, 76,* 111–122.

Heppner, M. J., O'Brien, K. M., Hinkelman, J. M., & Humphrey, C. F. (1994). Shifting the paradigm: The use of creativity in career counseling. *Journal of Career Development, 21,* 77–86.

Hines, P. M., & Boyd-Franklin, N. (1996). African American families. In M. McGoldrick, J. K. Pearce, & J. Giordano (Eds.), *Ethnicity and family therapy* (pp. 66–84). New York: Guilford.

Koehl, B. P. (1995). The solution-oriented genogram: A collaborative approach. *Journal of Marital and Family Therapy, 21,* 239–250.

Massey, R. F., Comey, S., & Just, R. L. (1988). Integrating genograms and script matrices. *Transactional Analysis Journal, 18,* 325–335.

McGoldrick, M., & Gerson, R. (1985). *Genograms in family assessment.* New York: W. W. Norton.

McMillen, J. C., & Groze, V. (1994). Using placement genograms in child welfare practice. *Child Welfare, 73,* 307–318.

Michele Harway

GHOST SICKNESS—An illness believed to be brought on by ghosts. A belief in ghost sickness is common among more traditional members of the Navajo Indian nation. Symptoms of ghost sickness include nightmares, confusion, loss of appetite, anxiety, fear of danger, loss of breath, paralysis, hallucinations and hopelessness. These symptoms and associations may vary depending upon the culture. For instance, the Mohave *ghost weylak* is associated with soul loss. Similar American Indian cultures have associated death with this sickness, including the Lipan, Chiricahua, Kiowa Apache, Jicarilla, and the Mescalero (Opler & Bittle, 1961). If someone has been attacked or "ghosted," a ghost has stolen their breath. The Paiute believed that after one's death, his or her breath journeys to the sky where it becomes a ghost. The ghost, separated from its loved ones, will then try to catch the breath of its relatives to join him or her. If a relative thinks about the deceased, the ghost believes it is a call to come and capture the relative's breath. If the ghost is successful, the relative will lose consciousness or become delirious and eventually die. However, one can recapture his or her breath with the assistance of a doctor or healer. The elderly and sick are most vulnerable to ghost sickness because it is believed that their breath is the easiest to steal (Landy, 1977). This is only one interpretation, and ghost sickness may manifest differently in other cultures.

References

Landy, D. (1977). *Culture, disease, and healing.* New York: Macmillan Publishing Co.

Opler, M., & Bittle, W. (1961). The death practices and eschatology of Kiowa Apache. *Southwestern Journal of Anthropology, 17,* 383–394.

Joseph E. Trimble and Heather K. Mertz

GLASS CEILING—A specific form of discrimination in the workplace which occurs when White women and ethnic minorities seek promotions into primarily upper management positions in corporations. *Glass ceiling* was popularized in the 1980s, but it is unknown who introduced the concept and when. Morrison and her colleagues' (1987) work is frequently cited as providing an initial definition, but other writings prior to their work reference the term. Individual and organizations have provided various definitions of the term restricting its use to either a particular group or a particular level of promotion. Most of the definitions specify either White women or ethnic minorities as the primary target group, while some definitions specify both groups. Some restrict use of the term to discussions of career opportunities of the upper levels of management, while some use it at all levels of career mobility. Regardless of the specificity of the definition, each refers symbolically to invisible barriers which restrict upward mobility by those groups typically underrepresented in high status positions in all work environments. The invisible barriers are reflected in the attitudes and practices of those in power, who are typically White males (Hymowitz & Schellhardt, 1986; Morrison & Von Gilnow, 1990; Scandura, 1992; U.S. Department of Labor, 1991). The two most commonly cited definitions are: (1) "glass ceiling describes a barrier so subtle that it is transparent, yet so strong that it prevents women and ethnic minorities from moving up in the management hierarchy" (Morrison & Von Gilnow, 1990, p. 200); and (2) glass ceilings are artificial barriers based on attitudinal or organizational bias that prevent qualified individuals' upward mobility into management-level positions (U.S. Department of Labor, 1991, p. 1). Scandura (1992), for example, has emphasized the statistical fact that White women and minorities are not represented at top levels in U.S. organizations. The concept is not typically applied solely to the promotion barriers of a single individual but describes the systematic discrimination of a group to which the individual belongs. Korn/Ferry International (1982) and the U.S. Department of Labor (1991) have illustrated that the glass ceiling phenomenon not only exists for women and ethnic minorities at the upper-management level, but also occurs at lower levels of employment status; that ethnic minorities experience it earlier in their career than do women; and that the cause for the discrimination varies from company to company (U.S. Department of Labor, 1991). Since the late 1980s, this form of discrimination has received increased attention at the federal level and across various workplaces and industries, resulting in an increase in research of it and the number of solutions or recommendations offered. A future trend in addressing its effect appears to be its influence on other groups such as new immigrants and the disabled, who have typically faced workplace discrimination as well. Also, the current conceptualization of the glass ceiling has been challenged as too unidimensional and simplistic. Other reconceptualizations (e.g., *process and structural interaction* and *social constructivism*) of the concept have been recommended with the belief that a more complex understanding of the phenomenon will lead to more effective ways of ameliorating such career promotion barriers (Buzzanell, 1995; Heward, 1994).

References

Buzzanell, P. M. (1995). Reframing the glass ceiling as a socially constructed process: Implications for understanding and change. *Communication Monographs, 62,* 327–354.

Heward, C. (1994). Academic snakes and merit ladders: Reconceptualizing the "glass ceiling." *Gender and Education, 6,* 249–262.

Hymowitz, C., & Schellhardt, T. D. (1986, March 24). The glass ceiling: Why women can't seem to break the invisible barriers that block them from the top jobs. *Wall Street Journal,* 1D, 4D–5D.

Korn/Ferry International. (1982). *Profile of women senior executives.* New York: Author.

Morrison, A. M., & Von Glinow, M. A. (1990). Women and minorities in management. *American Psychologist, 45,* 200–208.

Morrison, A. M., White, R. P., Van Velsor, E., & The Center for Creative Leadership. (1987). *Breaking the glass ceiling: Can women reach the top of America's largest corporations?* Reading, MA: Addison-Wesley.

Scandura, T. A. (1992). *Breaking the glass ceiling in the 1990s* (Doc U.S. L 36.102:G 46). Washington, DC: Government Printing Office.

U.S. Department of Labor. (1991). *A report on the glass ceiling initiative.* Washington, DC: Author.

Beverly J. Vandiver

GO FOR BROKE—A gambling term, meaning "go for it," "shoot the works," or "place all of your money on this one bet." *Nisei* soldiers (see *NISEI*) adopted this *pidgin* (i.e., a simplified speech used for communication between people with different languages) Hawaiian slang expression as their batallion motto in World War II and for their "battle cry for life" (Tanaka, 1982, p. iii). Regarding *Go for Broke*, Senator Daniel K. Inouye stated, "I don't know how it got started, but pretty soon our pidgin-English expression 'Go for Broke!' became the Combat Team (the 442nd Regimental Combat Team) motto. What did it mean? To give everything we did, everything we had, to jab every bayonet dummy as though our lives depended on it; to march 'quick-time' until we were ready to drop, and then to break into a trot. The words were to become part of the language, but in those spring and summer days of 1943, if a newcomer to Shelby (Camp Shelby, Mississippi) asked what 'Go for Broke' meant, chances are he'd be told it was that crazy *Nisei* outfit that fought every tactical problem as though it was the Battle of Bataan" (Inouye & Elliott, 1967, p. 99).

References

Inouye, D. K., & Elliott, L. (1967). *Journey to Washington.* New York: Prentice-Hall.

Tanaka, C. (1982). *Go for broke: A pictorial history of the 100th/442nd regimental combat team.* Richmond, CA: Go For Broke, Inc.

Patricia J. Matsumoto

H
─────────

HEALTHY PARANOIA—Better known as *healthy cultural paranoia*, the term was coined by Grier and Cobbs in *Black Rage* (1968). They noted that Blacks exhibit far more paranoid symptoms, such as being suspicious and mistrustful, than do their White counterparts. To identify accurately those Blacks who actually suffered from clinical paranoid disorders, Grier and Cobbs provided the term healthy cultural paranoia to describe a normal state of being for Blacks living in America. This distinction has been supported by others in the field (Jones, 1985; Jones & Seagull, 1977; May, 1985). As a result of Blacks' history of oppression (slavery and history of discrimination) against them, being mistrustful of Whites had proven to be important for survival in a racist society. Thus, a healthy state of paranoia is considered to be an adaptive behavior. The implication of this perspective is that Blacks and other nondominant groups must be viewed from a broader sociopolitical reality than that typically used in the dominant society or discourse when addressing Blacks' mental functioning. The criteria for constituting normality and abnormality need to be flexible based on the cultural values and norms of the specific cultural group instead of the assessment and treatment of all people based on Western criteria and values (Sue & Sue, 1990). The term healthy cultural paranoia is now used to heighten counselors' awareness of the need to understand the behavioral stance some African Americans might have when entering counseling with a White counselor and to take this into account when assessing and devising treatment for African Americans in particular, but also being mindful of the general principle for other diverse groups (Atkinson, Morten, & Sue, 1993).

References

Atkinson, D. R., Morten, G., & Sue, D. W. (1993). *Counseling American minorities: A cross-cultural perspective* (4th ed.). Madison, WI: Brown & Benchmark.

Grier, W. H., & Cobbs, P. M. (1968). *Black rage*. New York: Basic Books.

Jones, A. C. (1985). Psychological functioning in Black Americans: A conceptual guide for use in psychotherapy. *Psychotherapy: Theory, Research, Practice, Training, 22*, 363–369.

Jones, A. C., & Seagull, A. A. (1977). Dimensions of the relationship between the Black client and the White therapist: A theoretical overview. *American Psychologist, 32*, 850–855.

Mays, V. M. (1985). The Black American and psychotherapy. *Psychotherapy: Theory, Research, Practice, Training, 22*, 379–389.

Sue, D. W., & Sue, D. (1990). *Counseling the culturally different: Theory and practice* (2nd ed.). New York: Wiley.

Beverly J. Vandiver

HIGH–LOW CONTEXT COMMUNICATION—Contrasts the degree to which communication relies on implicit, contextual cues (*high context*) versus the stated content of the communication (*low context*). The concept originated with Hall (1976): "A high context (HC) communication or message is one in which most of the information is either in the physical context or internalized in the person while very little is in the coded, explicit, transmitted part of the message. A low context (LC) communication is just the opposite: i.e. the mass of information is vested in the explicit code" (p. 79). HC is faster, more economical, more efficient, and more satisfying than LC due to the different characteristics associated with each type of culture. HC cultures are characterized by collectivism, spiral logic, and an overall emphasis on more positive, relaxed individual relationships, while LC cultures are characterized by individualism, cause–effect logic, and an emphasis on task completion (Ting-Toomey, 1989). African Americans, Asian Americans, Latinos, and Native Americans utilize and value HC communications, whereas individuals from the United States, Switzerland, Scandinavia, and Germany utilize and value LC communications (Hall, 1976). When two individuals from different cultural contexts engage in a therapeutic relationship, miscommunication may occur. For instance, African Americans, due to their use of HC communication, may wrongly be characterized as nonverbal, inarticulate, and unintelligent (Sue, 1990). LC individuals may see HC individuals as missing points or not communicating well; HC individuals may see LC individuals as rude, blunt, or lacking subtlety. HC or LC orientation will also likely affect how clients and therapists approach therapy and their expectations of interactional patterns. Gudykunst and Nashida (1984) found that HC and LC individuals varied in the strategies they used for uncertainty reduction: HC individuals showed higher levels of attributional confidence about strangers' behavior, and lower levels of interrogation and self-disclosure, whereas LC engage in more verbal communication, including interrogation and self-disclosure.

References

Hall, E. T. (1976). *Beyond culture*. Garden City, NY: Anchor Press.

Gudykunst, W. B., & Nishida, T. (1984). Individual and cultural influences on uncertainty reduction. *Communication Monographs, 51*, 23–36.

Sue, D. W. (1990). Culture-specific strategies in counseling: A conceptual framework. *Professional Psychology: Research and Practice, 21*, 424–433.

Ting-Toomey, S. (1989). Intergroup communication and simulation in low- and high-context cultures. In D. Crockall & D. Saunders (Eds.), *Communication and simulation: From two fields to one theme* (pp. 169–176). Philadelphia: Multilingual Matters, Ltd.

Karen L. Suyemoto and Honora Kwon Batelka

HISPANIC/LATINO—*Hispanic* is an ethnic label given in 1978 by the Office of Management and Budget to describe a person of Mexican, Puerto Rican, Cuban, Central or South American, or other Spanish culture or origin, regardless of race (Marin & Van Oss Marin, 1991). The term Hispanic identifies those individuals who trace their ancestral backgrounds to one of those countries in the Americas. The label Latino is perceived by some individuals as accurately reflecting the political, geographical, and historical links present among Latin American nations. The term Latino preserves the national origin of the referents (regardless of languages spoken) as a significant characteristic, it is also culturally and racially neutral. The Hispanic/Latino population will use either term as an ethnic descriptor. A more precise self-descriptor is the country of origin with which the individual identifies.

Reference

Marin, G., & Van Oss Marin, B. (1991). *Research with Hispanic populations*. Newbury Park, CA: Sage.

Sandra I. Lopez-Baez

HOLOCULTURAL METHOD—A statistical procedure primarily intended to test theories about generalities of phenomena across cultures or differences among cultures through massive correlational procedures. Units of analysis are whole societies or cultures. The preferred term appears to be *hologeistic*, meaning "whole world." Naroll, Michik, and Naroll (1980) identified three kinds of hologeistic studies: (1) *holonational*—a sample from the population of all nation states; (2) *holocultural*—a sample from the population of all primitive cultures; and (3) *holohistorical*—a sample from the population of all historically known cultures. Kobben (1952) examined the history of this term while also assessing the usefulness of such studies. The term hologeistic appears to have been first used by T. S. van der Bij (1929, cited in Kobben, 1952). Van der Bij advocated statistical methods together with inductive reasoning to distill the differences among cultures. Such attempts had been made at least as far back as S. R. Steinmetz's (1898–1899, cited in Kobben, 1952) work, but Kobben criticized attempts by early researchers, as they often came up with contradictory conclusions. However, he was impressed with work coming out of the Yale University Human Relations Area Files (HRAF). The HRAF project was designed to catalog every known culture in the history of the world. This catalog has allowed researchers in the field to compare any subset of cultures using standard data sets. Naroll and Michik (1975) developed a computer program to calculate data derived from HRAF files. Rohner et al. (1978) warn that holocultural procedures be conducted with caution since the data consist of broad generalizations of cultures. They identified two methods of holocultural research: a quick method and a safe method. Quick methods are cost-effective but open to criticism because they necessarily leave out important and time-consuming procedures to ensure generalizations of the conclusions. Safe methods address the problems raised by critics of holocultural methods in general. These criticism were identified as 11 problem areas by Campbell and Naroll (1972): (1) sampling; (2) societal unit definition; (3) data accuracy; (4) conceptualization, classification, and coding; (5) Galton's problem; (6) causal analysis of correlations; (7) paucity of relevant data; (8) the "combing," "dredging," or "mudsticking" problem (renamed "group significance" by Naroll, Michik, & Naroll, 1980); (9) the general problem of statistical significance; (10) regional variation; and (11) deviant case analysis. If researchers take care in addressing these problem areas, conclusions will be more accepted as generalizable.

References

Campbell, D. T., & Naroll, R. (1972). The mutual methological relevance of anthropology and psychology. In F.L.K Hsu (Ed.), *Psychological anthropology* (pp. 435–463). Cambridge, MA: Schenkman.

Kobben, A.J.F. (1952). New ways of presenting an old idea: The statistical method of social anthropology. *Journal of the Royal Anthropological Institute of Great Britain and Ireland, 82*, 129–146. Reprinted in F. Moore (Ed.), *Readings in cross-cultural methodology* (pp. 175–192). New Haven, CT: HRAF Press.

Naroll, R., & Michik, G. L. (1975). HRAFLIB: A computer program library for hologeistic research. *Behavioral Sciences Research, 10*, 283–296.

Naroll, R., Michik, G. L., & Naroll, F. (1980). Holocultural research methods. In H. C. Triandis & J. W. Berry (Eds.), *Handbook of cross-cultural psychology (Vol. 2). Methodology* (pp. 479–521). Boston: Allyn & Bacon.

Rohner, R. P., Naroll, R., Barry, H., III, Divale, W. T., Erickson, E. E., Schaefer, J. M., & Sipes, R. G. (1978). Guidelines for holocultural research. *Current Anthropology, 19*, 128–129.

Jeffery Scott Mio

HOMELESS—The Stewart B. McKinney Homeless Assistance Act of 1987 (Public Law 100–77) was a comprehensive federal legislation developed to address the emergency needs of homeless individuals. The Act defines a homeless person as: (1) an individual who lacks a fixed, regular, and adequate nighttime residence; and (2) an individual who has a primary nighttime residence that is (a) a supervised publicly or privately operated shelter designed to provide temporary living accommodations (including welfare hotels, congregate shelters, and transitional housing for the mentally ill); (b) an institution that provides a temporary residence for individuals intended to be institutionalized; or (c) a public or private place not designed for, or ordinarily used as, a regular sleeping accommodation for human beings (Alker, 1992). In the last decade, the homeless population has grown in numbers. Current estimates suggest the homeless population exceeds 2.5 million people in the United States. In 1988, The U.S. Department of Housing and Urban Development found the following characteristics of the homeless population: single men—45 percent; single women—14 percent; families—40 percent; children under 18 years of age—26 percent; persons with mental illness—34 percent; physically disabled persons—11 percent; and victims of domestic violence—21 percent. Schutt and Garrett (1992) described the problems that face the homeless as: poverty, limited social ties or support, mental illness, alcoholism, physical illness, victimization, and past criminal involvement. Diblasio and Belcher (1993) describe the homeless as suffering from a sense of worthlessness, low self-esteem, isolation, alienation, deprivation, and fatigue.

References

Alker, J. (1992). Modern American homelessness. In C. Solomon & P. Jackson-Jobe (Eds.), *Helping homeless people: Unique challenges and solution* (pp. 7–14). Alexandria, VA: American Association for Counseling and Development.

Schutt, R. K., & Garrett, G. R. (1992). *Responding to the homeless: Policy and practice.* New York: Plenum.

Diblasio, F. A., & Belcher, J. R. (1993). Social work outreach to homeless people and the need to address issues of self-esteem. *Health & Social Work, 18,* 281–287.

U.S. Department of Housing and Urban Development. (1988). *National survey of shelters for the homeless.* Washington, DC: Author.

Patricia Taimanglo Pier

HO'OPONOPONO—One of the most powerful methods of family and group therapy in Hawaii. *Ho'oponopono*, or ''setting to right,'' is a practice for maintaining harmonious relationships and resolving conflicts within the extended family system (Shook, 1985). Troubled social relationships are repaired through the process of talking out and sharing negative feelings (no matter how painful) and conflicts (Marsella, Oliveira, Plummer, & Crabbe, 1995). According to Marsella et al. (1995), ''*ho'oponopono* is derived from the words *ho'o*, meaning 'to cause' and *pono*, meaning 'proper, balanced, moral, and righteous.' Through a combination of prayer, discussion, confession, repentance, and forgiveness, and good family, community relationships could be restored and *lokahi* or harmony could be achieved'' (p. 106). *Ho'oponopono* is usually led by an elder (*kapuna*) or healer (*kahuna*), who facilitates and directs the family members in the group process to tell the truth. It is essentially a family matter, involving all the nuclear family or only those most concerned with the problem (Pukui, Haertig, & Lee, 1972).

References

Marsella, A. J., Oliveira, J. M., Plummer, C. M., & Crabbe, K. M. (1995). Native Hawaiian (Kanaka Maoli) culture, mind, and well-being. In H. I. McCubbin, E. A.

Thompson, A. I. Thompson, & J. E. Fromer (Eds.), *Resiliency in ethnic minority families. Vol. I: Native and immigrant American families* (pp. 93–113). Madison: University of Wisconsin System.

Pukui, M. K., Haertig, E. W., & Lee, C. A. (1972). *Nana I Ke Kumu: Look to the source* (Vol. I). Honolulu, HI: Hui Hanai.

Shook, E. V. (1985). *Ho'oponopono: Contemporary uses of a Hawaiian problem-solving process*. Honolulu: University of Hawaii Press.

Patricia Taimanglo Pier

I

IBERIANS—The name preferred by the Basque people, who have long sought independence from the rest of Spain. Spain occupies five-sixths of the Iberian Peninsula in southwestern Europe, and the Basque people live in one of these regions (Douglass & Bilbao, 1975; Gallop, 1970).

References

Douglass, W. A., & Bilbao, J. (1975). *Amerikanuak: Basques in the new world.* Reno: University of Nevada Press.
Gallop, R. (1970). *A book of the Basques.* Reno: University of Nevada Press.

Cindy Yee

IDENTITY—The concept of *identity* has been in existence since the fourteenth century. Derived from the Latin root *idem* meaning "sameness," it is used in various fields, from psychology to mathematics and physics, to explain the properties of entities (Simpson & Weiner, 1989). In psychology, and particularly the subspecialties of personality and individual psychology, identity is defined as the essence or sameness of a person throughout the phases or stages of existence: "the continuity of the personality" (Simpson & Weiner, 1989, p. 620). As a result of the writings of philosophers such as Locke in the 1600s and Hume in the 1700s, the term was intimately linked to the concept of *individualism*. This linkage of terms has continued in modern times and is one of the reasons that the concept of identity has gained in popularity since the 1950s. As Western societies shifted from an agrarian life to an industrial one, there was an increasing erosion of the meaning of a mass society. Individuals began a subsequent search for their identity. A most poignant moment in the history of the United States, which highlights the American people in search of their identites was during the 1960s, the beginning of the Civil Rights Movement, anti-war and social justice movements, and the women's movement. The concept of identity was played out at two levels—individual and group (Marshall, 1994). In the social sciences, a parallel process of understanding identity was also occurring from two major perspectives, psychodynamic and sociological. Undergirding the psychodynamic perspective was Freud's theory of *identification and psycho-sexual development*, which emphasized the existence of an inner core of psychic structure (identity). From a psychodynamic perspective, the concept of identity was further developed by Erik Erickson, who theorized that identity was a process located both within the core of an individual and within the core of a community. Thus, identity was conceived to exist at two levels, individually and group (or internally and externally). During World War II, Erikson coined the term *identity crisis* to explain those soldiers who had lost a sense of identity. In addition, he defined identity as it evolved over a lifespan. Identity from a sociological perspective has been linked to the concept of *symbolic interactionism* and developed from the work of William James and George Herbert Mead. Again, their concepts of identity take into account its development at individual and group levels (Marshall, 1994). The modern view of identity is undergoing tremendous shifts in meaning, becoming increasingly individualistic while at the same time giving rise to a distinctive form of politics and psychology. As we move into the postmodern era, the concept of *identity politics*, sometimes called *cultural politics*, has gained in prominence from the movements which occurred in the 1960s. Identity politics has been associated with ethnic and religious minorities, feminists, gay and lesbian movements, and possibly may be reflected in the increasing number of hate and anti-government groups (Marshall, 1994). In the area of psychology, identity politics is evidenced in the emergence of *ethnicity/racial identity models* (Ponterotto, Casas, Suzuki, & Alexander, 1995), *gender identity models* (Gilligan, 1982; Levant & Pollack, 1995), and *gay/lesbian identity models* (Cass, 1979).

References

Cass, V. (1979). Homosexual identity formation: A theoretical model. *Journal of Homosexuality, 4*, 219–235.

Erikson, E. H. (1950). *Childhood and society*. New York: Norton.

Freud, S. (1964). *The standard edition of the complete psychological works of Sigmund Freud* (Vols. I–XXIV). (J. Strachey, Trans.) London: Hogarth.

Gilligan, C. (1982). *In a different voice: Psychological theory and women's development*. Cambridge, MA: Harvard University Press.

Levant, R. F., & Pollack, W. S. (Eds.). (1995). *A new psychology of men*. New York: Basic Books.

Marshall, G. (Ed.). (1994). *The concise Oxford dictionary of sociology*. Oxford: Oxford University Press.

Ponterotto, J. G., Casas, J. M., Suzuki, L. A., & Alexander, C. M. (Eds.). (1995). *Handbook of multicultural counseling*. Thousand Oaks, CA: Sage.

Simpson, J. A., & Weiner, E.S.C. (Eds.). (1989). *The Oxford English dictionary* (2nd ed.). Oxford: Oxford University Press.

Beverly J. Vandiver

IDENTITY STRUCTURE ANALYSIS—A metatheoretical framework developed by Paul Weinreich (1986, 1988) that relies heavily upon Kelly's (1955) personal construct theory to understand how personal identity develops. At its core, it describes how individuals undergo identity transformations throughout their lifetimes while keeping an essence of past identities. However, it borrows from social anthropology, sociological symbolic interactionism, psychoanalysis, cognitive-affective consistency theory, and Kelly's personal construct theory to apply identity development to issues involving ethnic identity. Weinreich (1988) asserted that there cannot be universal conceptions of ethnic identity development. This is because each ethnic group is also subject to cultural influences such as gender identity and regional differences. Thus, ethnic identity development is a result of shared sociocultural experiences. Moreover, identity is not an end state; rather, it is a process that evolves throughout one's lifetime, changing as one encounters new people and situations. "One's identity is defined as the totality of one's self-construal, in which how one construes oneself in the present expresses the continuity between how one construes oneself as one was in the past and how one construes oneself as one aspires to be in the future" (Weinreich, 1988, p. 154). Weinreich uses Kelly's (1955) personal construct theory which uses important polarities of constructs (e.g., "good–bad," "intelligent–unintelligent," "moral–immoral"). These polarities are individually developed throughout one's lifetime, and individuals seek role models who epitomize these polarities. When an individual observes these role models contradict the individual's past conceptions of the role models (e.g., a good person doing bad things), the individual encounters psychological discomfort. This discomfort motivates the individual to seek a resolution of the conflict through a process of redefining the role model, seeking new role models, or reexamining one's own personal constructs and perhaps rearranging the centrality of some constructs or redefining them. Weinreich and his colleagues (Weinreich & Gault, 1984; Weinreich, Wilson, Matthews, & Asquith, 1985) developed a computer program to calculate momentary identity structures.

References

Kelly, G. A. (1955). *The psychology of personal constructs*. New York: Norton.

Weinreich, P. (1986). The operationalisation of identity theory in racial and ethnic relations. In J. Rex & D. Mason (Eds.), *Theories of race and ethnic relations* (pp. 299–320). Cambridge: Cambridge University Press.

Weinreich, P. (1988). The operationalization of ethnic identity. In J. W. Berry & R. C. Annis (Eds.), *Ethnic psychology: Research and practice with immigrants, refugees, native peoples, ethnic groups and sojourners* (pp. 149–168). Amsterdam: Swets & Zeitlinger.

Weinreich, P., & Gault, D. (1984). *IDEX–IDIO (Identity Exploration–Idiographic) computer program userguide.* Jordanstown, Ireland: University of Ulster at Jordanstown.

Weinreich, P., Wilson, N., Matthews, D., & Asquith, L. (1985). *IDEX–NOMO (Identity Exploration–Nomothetic) computer program and userguide.* Jordanstown, Ireland: University of Ulster at Jordanstown.

Jeffery Scott Mio

IDIOCENTRISM—The tendency for individuals to place their own needs over the needs of the collective. According to Triandis (1989), *"individualism* and *collectivism* should be used to characterize cultures and societies, the terms *idiocentric* and *allocentric* should be used to characterize individuals" (p. 509; see ALLOCENTRISM). Thus, *idiocentrism* is the conceptual equivalent to *individualism* at the individual—as opposed to societal—level, and can be construed as a personality trait as opposed to a societal norm. Idiocentric individuals living in individualistic societies know what cultural/societal expectations are of them. Since most people in such societies are idiocentric, competitive interpersonal relations are expected. However, idiocentric individuals living in collectivistic societies can experience a great deal of stress as a result of their own behaviors tending to violate societal norms and such individuals being treated as outcasts. While idiocentric individuals report concerns with achievement, they are often lonelier than their allocentric counterparts. Triandis and his colleagues (Bontempo, Lobel, & Triandis, 1990; Triandis, 1989, 1995; Triandis, Bontempo, Villareal, Asai, & Lucca, 1988; Triandis, Leung, Villareal, & Clack, 1985) have discussed such mismatches of cooperative styles. However, most researchers do not use the term idiocentrism, applying instead the term individualism to both individuals and societies.

References

Bontempo, R., Lobel, S., & Triandis, H. (1990). Compliance and value internalization in Brazil and the U.S. *Journal of Cross-Cultural Psychology, 21,* 200–213.

Triandis, H. C. (1989). The self and social behavior in differing cultural contexts. *Psychological Review, 96,* 506–520.

Triandis, H. C. (1995). *Individualism and collectivism.* Boulder, CO: Westview.

Triandis, H. C., Bontempo, R., Villareal, M. J., Asai, M., & Lucca, N. (1988). Individualism and collectivism: Cross-cultural perspectives on self–ingroup relationships. *Journal of Personality and Social Psychology, 54,* 323–338.

Triandis, H. C., Leung, K., Villareal, M. J., & Clack, F. L. (1985). Allocentric versus idiocentric tendencies: Convergent and discriminant validation. *Journal of Research in Personality, 19,* 395–415.

Jeffery Scott Mio

ILLNESS—According to Simpson and Weiner (1989), *illness* has been in existence since the 1500s. Three primary definitions are listed: (1) bad moral quality, condition, or character; (2) unpleasantness, disagreeableness, or troublesomeness; and (3) bad or unhealthy condition of the body, ailment, or malady. The history of various societies reveals the use of all three definitions in describing or explaining a person's mental and physical conditions. In some eras, physical and/or mental illnesses were thought to be due to gods or demons afflicting persons with malicious and capricious spirits for failure to adhere to the standards of acceptable attitudes and behaviors or due to bodily imbalances or imbalance of natural processes (Ducey & Simon, 1975; Ng, 1990; Rosen, 1968). During the seventeenth, eighteenth, and nineteenth centuries in European societies, the demonic and religious conceptualizations of mental and physical illnesses were gradually replaced with medical and scientific knowledge. As a result, mental illnesses were treated as physical illnesses, as is evidenced by Hippocrates' and Galen's view of mental illnesses. Although Freud pioneered the view that psychological bases could explain physical as well as mental illnesses, the psychodynamic perspective still was steeped in the traditions of the medical profession. The medical model of mental illness persists today in explaining such mental disorders as schizophrenia and bipolar disorders (Sills, 1972). Yet, in non-Western societies, despite Western influence, illness is defined and treated not only as biological and metaphysical conditions but also as a sociocultural one. Not until the mid-nineteenth century in European and American societies was the role of social and cultural factors in health and illness recognized as salient. In the mid-twentieth century, a scientific subfield was organized called the *sociology of illness*, a collaborative interdisciplinary effort of physicians, psychologists, psychiatrists, sociologists, and cultural anthropologists. In particular, Talcott Parson, recognized for his contribution to this new subfield, conceived of illness as a social role which is shaped by the society in which the sick person belongs (Sills, 1972). Szasz (1960) agreed with Parson, as he contended that mental illness is a myth based on the cultural and social context of the prevailing society. In general, Western culture has attempted to control the definitions of illness and the roles played by the patient and medical agents. Restricted or monocultural views of illness have led to misdiagnoses and limited treatment options. *Restricted* or *monocultural views* of illness have led to misdiagnoses and limited treatment options. In particular, in the treatment of mental health disorders, patients from nondominant and non-Western cultures have been diagnosed with more severe mental disorders which has led to more restrictive and invasive treatment (Pavkov, Lewis, & Lyons, 1989). Yet research findings (e.g., Kleinman, 1991; Snowden & Cheung, 1990; Tavris, 1992) indicate that the incident and expression of and biases about physical and mental illnesses are also a reflection of sociocultural factors, lifestyle, and environment. As non-Western views of illness have been accepted, more homeopathic treatment methods for mental and physical illnesses are being offered by Western society to members of dominant and nondominant cultures.

References

Ducey, C., & Simon, B. (1975). Ancient Greece and Rome. In J. G. Howells (Ed.), *World history of psychiatry*. New York: Brunner/Mazel.

Kleinman, A. (1991, April). *Culture and DSM-IV: Recommendations for the introduction and for the overall structure.* Paper presented at the National Institute of Mental Health-sponsored Conference on Culture and Diagnosis, Pittsburgh, PA.

Ng, V. W. (1990). *Madness in late imperial China: From illness to deviance.* Oklahoma City: University of Oklahoma Press.

Pavkov, T. W., Lewis, D. A., & Lyons, J. S. (1989). Psychiatric diagnoses and racial bias: An empirical investigation. *Professional Psychology: Research and Practice, 19,* 364–368.

Rosen, G. (1968). *Madness in society: Chapters in the historical sociology of mental illness.* Chicago: University of Chicago Press.

Sills, D. L. (Ed.). (1972). *International Encyclopedia of the Social Sciences* (Vol. 7). New York: The Macmillan Company and the Free Press.

Simpson, J. A., & Weiner, E.S.C. (Eds.). (1989). *The Oxford English dictionary* (2nd ed.). Oxford: Oxford University Press.

Snowden, L. R., & Cheung, F. K. (1990). Use of inpatient mental health services by ethnic minority groups. *American Psychologist, 45,* 347–355.

Szasz, T. S. (1960). The myth of mental illness. *American Psychologist, 15,* 113–118.

Tavris, C. (1992). *The mismeasure of woman.* New York: Simon & Schuster.

Beverly J. Vandiver

INCLUSIVITY—Refers to that which is broad in orientation or scope, that which takes in parts of a larger aggregate or principle (Woolf, 1974). In multicultural terms, *inclusivity* is used to describe something or some process which recognizes subgroups and individuals as essential components of a larger whole. It becomes imperative to consider aspects of human diversity such as race, ethnicity, and gender—among many others—in order to accurately portray a complete picture of humanity. An inclusive psychology would attempt to correct the "White, middle-class, heterosexual, able-bodied male norm" (Yoder & Kahn, 1993, p. 846) which has historically been accepted as accurate and adequate for all people. White male experience has been used as the basis for determining wellness vs. illness, diagnosis and prognosis, psychometric and research norms. The specific as well as the more general experiences of nondominant groups and individuals has not been viewed as relevant or important (Guthrie, 1976) until recent work by culturally sensitive psychologists has helped to create multiculturalism as a "fourth force" (Pedersen, 1990) in counseling theory and practice. As we struggle to incorporate multicultural inclusion in all aspects of counseling, we begin to discard old images like the American "melting pot" in which all differences disappear, in favor of more helpful images like the vision of America as a "tossed salad" in which individuals maintain their separate integrity while their differences complement one another (Sue, 1987). As the field of psychology begins to recognize that a multiculturally inclusive perspective simply enhances all aspects of our work as clinicians, teachers, and researchers, attention to human differences has become embedded in our practice, training, and literature. The recent revision of the Ethics Code (American Psychological Association, 1992) holds psychologists responsible for respect, awareness, nondiscrimination, and competent work with the range of human differences represented by our clients, students, colleagues, and community members. Psychologists striving for an ethical, accurate perspective on human experience must remain open to learning, teaching, and practice which is inclusive of "cultural, individual, and role differences, including those due to age, gender, race, ethnicity, national origin, religion, sexual orientation, disability, languages, and socioeconomic status (Ethical Code of Psychologists, Preamble—Principle D).

References

American Psychological Association (1992). *Ethical principles of psychologists and code of conduct*. Washington, DC: Author.

Guthrie, R. V. (1976). *Even the rat was white: A historical view of psychology*. New York: Harper.

Pedersen, P. (1990). The multicultural perspective as a fourth force in counseling. *Journal of Mental Health Counseling, 12*, 93–95.

Sue, S. (1987). *Academic achievement among ethnic minorities*. Invited address presented at the 67th Annual Meeting of the Western Psychological Association, Long Beach, CA.

Woolf, H. B. (Ed.). (1974). *Webster's new collegiate dictionary*. Springfield, MA: G. & C. Merriam.

Yoder, J. D., & Kahn, A. S. (1993). Working toward an inclusive psychology of women. *American Psychologist, 48*, 846–850.

Kelly L. Willson

INDIAN HEALTH SERVICE—In 1824, the United States government created the Bureau of Indian Affairs (BIA) in an attempt to bring a halt to the wars between the American Indian and the European settlers. In addition to other responsibilities, the BIA was mandated to provide quality health care as part of the treaty agreements signed by the tribes and the United States government (Deloria & Lytle, 1983). The office of Commissioner of Indian Affairs was created in 1932 to handle all matters concerning American Indians, including health care promises made in the treaty agreements. In 1849, the Bureau of Indian Affairs office was transferred from the War Department to the Department of the Interior. Multiple policy changes were made and, finally, the goals of the department to eliminate corruptness in the Bureau and to provide support, protection, and the assimilation of the Native American were sought. Despite these efforts, Indian wars continued to erupt in the 1860s, 1870s, and 1880s. John Collier became the Commissioner of Indian Affairs in 1933, and in addition to major relief measures and educational reform, Collier tried to improve health conditions which had always been under the management of the Bureau of Indian Affairs. Collier recognized how inadequate the government health programs were on the reservations, despite treaty promises, and demanded increased government appropriations for the Indian Medical Service. Conditions did not change and finally resulted in the Act of August 5, 1954, which transferred the facilities, property, personnel, and budget of the Indian Health Service (formerly the Indian Medical Service) of the Bureau of Indian Affairs to the U.S. Public Health Service (P.H.S.). Originally, the transfer was a step by the United States government to bring Native Americans under programs open to all citizens of the United States. What made the Indian Health Service programs different and problematic from other programs administered by the P.H.S. was the alarmingly high numbers of Indians with tuberculosis, other communicable diseases, and diabetes; the isolated and rural regions and reservations where American Indians lived; and the vastly diverse, cultural differences, both tribally and regionally, among American Indians. This specially designed program, Indian Health Service specifically for Native Americans, has established medical facilities and services on a number of reservations and has contract services in nearby urban areas for other kinds of health and mental health care provisions. As the United States government has changed its policy and relationship with American Indians, so has the direction and the accessibility of governmental programs and services to the Indian tribes and communities. Despite gains and advances since Collier first attempted to improve health care to American Indians in 1933, the overall approach has been somewhat sporadic and piecemeal, and a more carefully planned and comprehensive approach to Native American health and mental health care affairs still needs to be developed (Olson & Wilson, 1984).

References

Deloria, V., Jr., & Lytle, C. M. (1983). *American Indians, American justice*. Austin: University of Texas Press.
Olson, J. S., & Wilson, R. (1984). *Native Americans in the twentieth century*. Champaign: University of Illinois Press.

                                                              Grace Powless Sage

INDIVIDUAL RACISM—One form of racism and, like the term *racism*, is defined multidimensionally. Carmichael and Hamilton (1967) are credited with first using the terms *individual racism* and *institutional racism* as a way to distinguish between the two forms of racism and understand the dynamics of each (Feagin, 1989). They defined individual racism as overt acts, which can be observed in the process of commission, by individual Whites against individual Blacks and can lead to harmful consequences such as death, injury, or the violent destruction of property. The most poignant example that Carmichael and Hamilton used, White terrorists bombing a Black church, is salient even today as an example of individual racism. Institutional racism (see entry) are institutional practices that systematically advantage Whites over Blacks (or other groups on the downside of power). The most commonly used definition of individual racism has been that of Jones (1972, 1981), in which a person's prejudice is based on biological considerations of a racial/ethnic group and is exhibited in actual behavior that is discriminatory in nature. Building on the work of Jones, Ridley (1989) has proposed a behavioral model of racism which can be utilized in counseling settings. He defines individual racism as ''the adverse behavior of one person or small group of people'' (p. 35). Unlike the earlier definition introduced by Jones, prejudice is not considered a required component of racism. A racist person may or may not have a prejudiced attitude towards an ethnic group. However, as in institutional racism, individual racism is composed of more specific units of behavior: *overt, covert intentional,* and *covert unintentional* (see entries for those terms). Intentionality of the perpetrator is implied in overt individual racism; the motive of the racist is obvious. Covert individual racism implies subtlety; racism is reflected in the behavior of the individual but the underlying motives for the behavior is not clear but hidden, leaving others to infer the actual reason for the racist's action. Intentional covert racism (e.g., to avoid serving a person of color, a White sales clerk pretends to be preoccupied with an important task) involves malicious intent, whereas unintentional covert racism involves no expectation or intent to harm. In fact, the consequences are incongruent with the motives of the person. For example, a White person greets every Asian American with a bow, believing it will reflect a sign of respect and cultural understanding. As noted by the above example, individual racism is no longer defined as only a Black–White interaction, that individual racism is no longer viewed as unidirectional, and that only Whites can be discriminatory against other ethnic groups (Ridley, 1995).

References

Carmichael, S., & Hamilton, C. V. (1967). *Black power: The politics of liberation in America.* New York: Random House.
Feagin, J. R. (1989). *Racial & ethnic relations* (3rd ed.). Englewood Cliffs, NJ: Prentice-Hall.
Jones, J. M. (1972). *Prejudice and racism.* Reading, MA: Addison Wesley.
Jones, J. M. (1981). The concept of racism and its changing reality. In B. J. Bowser & R. G. Hunt (Eds.), *Impacts of racism on White Americans* (pp. 27–49). Beverly Hills, CA: Sage.
Ponterotto, J. G., & Pedersen, P. B. (1993). *Preventing prejudice: A guide for counselors and educators.* Newbury Park, CA: Sage.
Ridley, C. R. (1989). Racism in counseling as an aversive behavioral process. In P. B. Pedersen, J. G. Draguns, W. J. Lonner, & J. E. Trimble (Eds.), *Counseling across cultures* (3rd ed., pp. 55–77). Honolulu: University of Hawaii Press.
Ridley, C. R. (1995). *Overcoming unintentional racism in counseling and therapy: A practitioner's guide to intentional intervention.* Thousand Oaks, CA: Sage.

Beverly J. Vandiver

INDOCHINESE REFUGEES—According to the 1951 United Nations Convention Relating to the Status of Refugees and the 1967 Protocol Relating to the Status of Refugees, a refugee is defined as one who is unable or unwilling to return to his/her country due to well-founded fears of persecution or death due to factors such as race, religion, or political opinion (Wain, 1981). Indochinese refugees are persons from Vietnam, Laos, and Cambodia who fled their countries in the aftermath of the end of the Vietnam Conflict in 1975, resettling primarily in the United States but also in other countries such as Australia, Canada, China, and France. According to Takaki (1989), the initial Vietnamese refugees were military personnel and their families fleeing the North Vietnamese troops in the wake of the collapse of the South Vietnamese government in 1975. A second wave fled Vietnam a few years later, primarily by boat (sometimes referred to as *boat people*), and frequently faced threats from Thai pirates. Ethnic Laotian and Hmong refugees from Laos who had supported the United States left Laos starting in 1975, after the *Pathet Lao*, who had been supported by North Vietnam, took power and began a campaign of bloody repression (Takaki, 1989). Finally, the Cambodian exodus occurred after 1975, when the *Khmer Rouge* forces led by Pol Pot came to power, renamed the country Kampuchea, and began systematic killing of Cambodians associated with the prior, American-supported, Lon Nol government. When Pol Pot was overthrown in early 1979, hundreds of thousands of Cambodians fled to Thailand and became refugees. By 1980, over 1 million Indochinese had fled the region (United States Department of State, Bureau of Public Affairs, 1980). An annotated bibliography on Indochinese refugees who resettled in the United States is offered by Ashmun (1983).

References

Ashmun, L. F. (1983). *Resettlement of Indochinese refugees in the United States: A selective and annotated bibliography*. DeKalb, IL: Northern Illinois University, Center for Southeast Asian Studies.

Takaki, R. (1989). *Strangers from a different shore: A history of Asian Americans*. Boston: Little, Brown.

United States Department of State, Bureau of Public Affairs. (1980, February). *Refugee fact sheet: Indochinese resettlement in the United States*. Washington, DC: Author.

Wain, B. (1981). *The refused: The agony of the Indochina refugees*. New York: Simon & Schuster.

Fred Ninonuevo

INSTITUTIONAL RACISM—Refers to the rules, regulations, and practices of an institution that are intended to be race-neutral, but that still have an unfair impact on members of racial and ethnic minority groups (Cashmore, 1994; Kammeyer, Ritzer, & Yetman, 1994. (*Editor's note: Institutional racism* can also be *overtly* racist policies, although such policies are generally not publically sanctioned.) One of the less obvious manifestations of racism, institutional racism is not the intentional consequence of prejudicial or stereotypical thinking. Rather, it stems from unspoken assumptions made by the dominant group about the abilities of racial or ethnic minority groups (Parillo, Stimson, & Stimson, 1985). Whatever the intention, the demonstration of these assumptions and beliefs often supports and protects the status of the privileged at the expense of racial and ethnic minorities (Giddens, 1991). In 1967, Black activists Stokely Carmichael and Charles V. Hamilton first used the term in the book *Black Power: The Politics of Liberation in America* (Cashmore, 1994). During this era, although existing Civil Rights legislation outlawed overt racial discrimination, Black Americans were still considered to be at a disadvantage in occupational and educational opportunities, access to housing, and the legal justice system. Institutional racism results from policies that are based upon seemingly rational thought, although these policies are often influenced by the unconscious presence of derogatory stereotypes that prevent racial and ethnic minorities from achieving truly equal opportunities. As a result, African Americans and other minorities may experience discriminatory or exclusionary treatment by the societal institutions and policies that were intended to support them. Rex (1986) examined the link between *disadvantage* and *discrimination*, and concluded that disadvantage per se resulted from a capitalistic society where the poor find themselves with fewer opportunities rather than from specific discrimination of ethnic groups. Although it is true that many U.S. racial and ethnic minorities are represented in this category, this theory does not explain how these individuals "land" there. Rex stated that if systematic disadvantage is caused by discrimination, then it can be corrected. It is this logic that underlies affirmative action laws and policies, which represent conscious and direct efforts to combat institutional racism. It is often difficult to identify the specific causes of institutional racism. The difficulty in eliminating institutional racism is two-fold: (1) many people are unaware that the attitudes they hold are inherently disadvantageous to others; and (2) the blame for institutional racism cannot be placed upon any one individual.

References

Cashmore, E. (1994). Institutional racism. *Dictionary of race and ethnic relations* (3rd ed., pp. 145–148). London: Routledge.
Giddens, A. (1991). *Introduction to sociology*. New York: Norton.
Kammeyer, K., Ritzer, G., & Yetman, N. R. (1994). *Sociology: Experiencing changing societies* (6th ed.). Boston: Allyn and Bacon.
Parillo, V. N., Stimson, J., & Stimson, A. (1985). *Contemporary social problems*. New York: Wiley.
Rex, J. (1986). *Race and ethnicity*. Milton Keynes, England: Open University Press.

Madonna G. Constantine

INSTITUTIONS—Collections of organizations and formal structures established to address the basic human needs or activities of a society (Kammeyer, Ritzer, & Yetman, 1994). Institutions tend to be organized around the common values of their constituents, and they help to provide order to modern societies. Primary examples of institutions include the family, the government, education, religion, and the economic system, all of which seem to be present in most cultures (Cargan & Ballantine, 1991). The major institutions of a society, when examined together, may provide a picture of the nature and functions of that society (Kammeyer et al., 1994). Although institutions attempt to meet the needs of societies, their forms may vary. For example, although families are viewed as universal institutions, their compositions and definitions may change across cultures or societies. Family units may consist only of parents and siblings, or they may also include cousins, grandparents, grandchildren, or even friends. Once formed, institutions become a part of the normative expectations of societies (Cargan & Ballantine, 1991). When societal institutions become ineffective or fail to support portions of the populations they were intended to serve, the balance and well-being of the societies may be compromised (Parillo, Stimson, & Stimson, 1985). For example, a government that is formed to represent an entire society, but that does not support the needs of its racial and ethnic minority constituents, is not a successful institution (see INSTITUTIONAL RACISM).

References

Cargan, K., & Ballantine, J. H. (1991). *Sociological footprints: Introductory readings in sociology* (5th ed.). Belmont, CA: Wadsworth.
Kammeyer, K., Ritzer, G., & Yetman, N. R. (1994). *Sociology: Experiencing changing societies* (6th ed.). Boston: Allyn and Bacon.
Parillo, V. N., Stimson, J., & Stimson, A. (1985). *Contemporary social problems*. New York: Wiley.

Madonna G. Constantine

INTEGRATIVE AWARENESS STAGE OF IDENTITY—Developmental models of ethnic identity posit a stagewise progression of identity change, from a *diffuse, unexplored identity* to an *achieved, committed identity* (Helms, 1990; Phinney, 1990). The *integrative awareness stage* refers to the final level of ethnic identity development, in which the individual fully incorporates ethnicity into the self-concept. Theoretical models suggest that the process leading to integrative awareness is often a difficult and conflicted one. Several of these models derive from Erikson's (1963) general model of ego development, focusing explicitly on his discussion of adolescent identity development. Low ethnic identification, referred to by theorists as the pre-encounter, conformity, unexamined, diffuse, or forclosed stage, is accompanied by preference for the majority group, negative evaluation of one's ethnic group, little involvement or interest in one's ethnic group, and little commitment or sense of ethnic-group belonging. Situational cues or internal motives impel a need for greater cultural awareness and ethnic self-acceptance, leading to the process of identity conversion (Cross, 1971). The *Nigrescence model* calls this the *Negro-to-Black conversion process*. This process culminates in the integration of one's ethnic self into the overall self-concept, referred to by theorists as the *internalized, incorporated*, or *achieved stage*. This fully realized level of ethnic identity is characterized by strong identification as an ethnic group member, positive evaluation of the group, high involvement and interest in one's group, and a sense of commitment and group belonging. Some psychologists suggest that ethnic identity development continues throughout the life-span, proceeding beyond adolescence and into adulthood (Parham, 1989). In a process termed *recycling*, individuals who achieve the integrated awareness stage of identity often repeat the developmental process (Cross, 1971), characterized by new conflicts and resolutions. Thus, an integrated ethnic identity is not a fixed, stable property but a firm yet constantly evolving and dynamic foundation for the ethnic self-concept.

References

Cross, W. E., Jr. (1971). The Negro-to-Black conversion experience: Toward a psychology of Black liberation. *Black World, 20,* 13–26.

Erikson, E. H. (1963). *Childhood and society* (2nd ed.). New York: Norton.

Helms, J. E. (1990). *Black and White racial identity: Theory, research, and practice.* Westport, CT: Greenwood Press.

Parham, T. A. (1989). Cycles of psychological Nigrescence. *The Counseling Psychologist, 17,* 187–226.

Phinney, J. S. (1990). Ethnic identity in adolescents and adults: Review of research. *Psychological Bulletin, 108,* 499–514.

Don Operario

INTERACTIVE DECISION MODEL—Refers to a process or schema that individuals use to make "on the spot" decisions in an interactive situation (e.g., counseling, teaching; also known as *interactive decision making*), and that results in a conscious choice to implement a specific action (Clark & Peterson, 1986). Much of the research on interactive decision making has focused on teachers and the cognitive processes and behaviors they employ while instructing students (Borko & Shavelson, 1990). However, interactive decision models are often used by counselors when, for example, they consider a number of possible treatment interventions during a specific counseling session, and then select the best alternative based on phenomena present in the therapeutic context or relationship. Because counselors frequently engage in interactive decision making during a counseling session, this somewhat spontaneous behavior should be distinguished from pre-planned interventions they have developed prior to the session for use with a client. For example, counselors may consider alternative treatment options during a session, if they decide it is not going well. They may gauge the efficacy of their interventions by a client's level of interest and involvement in the session. In making decisions in this context, counselors may be willing to be slightly flexible with a client's treatment plan when necessary, rather than to deviate from it in a significant way. Multiculturally competent counselors may frequently use interactive decision models in working with cultural and ethnic minority clients in order to reflect their openness to and flexibility in providing culturally sensitive interventions.

References

Borko, H., & Shavelson, R. J. (1990). Teacher decision making. In B. Jones & L. Idol (Eds.), *Dimensions of thinking and cognitive instruction* (pp. 311–346). Hillsdale, NJ: Erlbaum.
Clark, C. M., & Peterson, P. L. (1986). Teachers' thought processes. In M. C. Wittrock (Ed.), *Handbook of research on teaching* (3rd ed., pp. 255–296). New York: Macmillan.

Madonna G. Constantine

INTERCULTURAL SENSITIVITY—Refers to an individual's willingness to search for possible cultural differences as an explanation for behavior that is not understood. One of the main issues pertaining to *intercultural sensitivity* involves the ability to be aware of the differences in appropriate behaviors between individualistic and collectivistic cultures. Individuals with high levels of intercultural sensitivity are high in flexibility, can quickly assess the cultural environment (e.g., assess if the culture tends to be more individualistic versus collectivistic), and then adjust their behaviors accordingly such that their own behaviors are culturally appropriate. Individuals high in intercultural sensitivity are likely to be effective in interactions requiring extensive intercultural interaction, enjoy intercultural activities, and often have lived in other cultures for extended periods of time (Bhawuk & Brislin, 1992). Other related characteristics of individuals who are successful in intercultural interactions include cultural flexibility (ability to substitute one's own culture-valued activities with activities appropriate to the host culture), skills in conflict resolution, patience, tolerance for, and interest in, differences among people, and a sense of humor (Martin, 1989). Triandis (1994) described Intercultural Sensitivity Training, also known as the Cultural Assimilator, as being very effective. In this program, trainees are presented with a set of 100–200 scenarios where people from two cultures interact with one another. Each episode concludes with four or five explanations for why the member of the other culture behaved in a certain way. The trainee selects the explanation which he or she believes best explains the person's behavior and then receives feedback regarding the explanation that was chosen. Construction of assimilator training is culture specific and often requires the use of samples of people from the two cultures being presented. In this way, the training is validated as it is being used. Topics included in the Cultural Assimilator include differences in: norms, roles, how behaviors are used to express emotions, self-concept, valued behaviors, the determinants of behavior, and the kinds of reinforcements that people expect for certain behaviors. A journal devoted to presenting research on intercultural relations is the *International Journal of Intercultural Relations*.

References

Bhawuk, D. P., & Brislin, R. (1992). The measurement of intercultural sensitivity using the concepts of individualism and collectivism. *International Journal of Intercultural Relations, 16,* 413–436.

Martin, J. N. (1989). Intercultural communication competence. *International Journal of Intercultural Relations, 13*, 227–328.

Triandis, H. C. (1994). *Culture and social behavior.* New York: McGraw-Hill.

Gayle Y. Iwamasa

INTERGROUP MARRIAGE—*Intergroup marriage* or *intermarriage*, the more common term, refers to the legal union between two members of different cultural, ethnic, racial, religious or social groupings (Smith, 1996). Most marriages are *homogeneous* (Smith, 1996). That is, most people, for personal as well as social reasons, select mates within their racial, ethnic, and/or religious group. However, intermarriage is increasing throughout the world (Barron, 1971). In 1941, Merton suggested that although any marriage is, literally, intermarriage when it occurs between two people of different family groups, certain types of marriage are considered distinctive from the rest. These types include *intercultural, interethnic, interfaith, interracial,* and *interreligious marriages* (Gordon, 1964; Smith, 1996). Intercultural marriages occur between members of different cultural groups who may or may not share race, ethnicity, and/or religion. Married individuals who come from and identify with different ancestries, religious or racial groups have an interethnic marriage. When individuals from two broad religious divisions such as Judaism and Christianity marry, they are identified as an interfaith couple. Couples in an interreligious marriage belong to different denominations within a particular faith such as Christianity. Also referred to as mixed marriage, the regulation of intermarriage has been described since Biblical times and varies from country to country and culture to culture. Worldwide, societal reactions to intermarriage, especially interracial marriage, range from mild support to open hostility and deadly social control (Johnson & Warren, 1994).

References

Barron, M. L. (1971). Intergroup aspects of choosing a mate. In M. Fishbein & J. Fishbein (Eds.), *Successful marriage* (pp. 132–141). Garden City, NY: Doubleday & Doubleday.

Gordon, A. I. (1964). *Intermarriage: Interfaith, interracial, interethnic* (pp. 1–5). Boston: Beacon Press.

Johnson, W. R., & Warren, D. M. (Eds.). (1994). *Inside the mixed marriage* (pp. 1–13). Lanham, MD: University Press of America.

Merton, R. K. (1941). Intermarriage and the social structure: Fact and theory. *Psychiatry, 4*, 361–374.

Smith, R. C. (1996). *Two cultures, one marriage: Premarital counseling for mixed marriages.* Berrien Springs: Andrews University Press.

Monica D. Lange

INTERNAL LOCUS OF CONTROL–INTERNAL LOCUS OF RESPONSIBILITY (IC–IR) AND INTERNAL LOCUS OF CONTROL–EXTERNAL LOCUS OF RESPONSIBILITY (IC–ER)—The background of the dimensions discussed here is contained in the definitions of *external locus of* *control–external locus of responsibility* and *external locus of control–internal locus of responsibility* entries. In *internal locus of control–internal locus of responsibility*, people see themselves as personally powerful and attribute success in the world to their own efforts. The IC–IR orientation typifies middle-class White American cultural values which emphasize individualism, self-reliance, and control. Mainstream counseling tends to reinforce these values, and counselors need to be aware that clients from other cultural backgrounds and/or ethnic minority group experiences may view themselves quite differently (Katz, 1985). For instance, clients with a more externally based worldview may define their problems differently from an internally based counselor, and therefore see solutions differently as well (Sue & Sue, 1990). Worldview orientation may also influence preferences for counseling style, types of therapeutic interventions, and client retention in counseling (Ibrahim, 1985). In *internal locus of control–external locus of responsibility*, individuals have self-efficacy (they believe in their personal power and capabilities) and also perceive that obstacles for change exist outside of themselves (e.g., in the system). People with an IC–ER worldview are likely to be upset with society and distrust counselors and/or be social activists who reinforce personal empowerment and challenge systemic issues such as racism and other forms of oppression.

References

Ibrahim, F. A. (1985). Effective cross-cultural counseling and psychotherapy: A framework. *The Counseling Psychologist, 13*, 625–638.

Katz, J. (1985). The sociopolitical nature of counseling. *The Counseling Psychologist, 13*, 615–624.

Sue, D. W., & Sue, D. (1990). *Counseling the culturally different: Theory and practice* (2nd ed.). New York: Wiley.

Mary Fukuyama

INTERRACIAL—Used to describe couples, married or not, where each partner is of a different racial background. This term may also be used to describe a family whose composition is made up of persons of different racial backgrounds, as when parents of one racial background adopt children of different racial backgrounds (Root, 1992; Spickard, 1989). According to the U.S. Bureau of the Census (1993), there were 1,161,000 interracial married couples in the United States. Other related terms are *miscegenation, mixed marriage, biracial,* and *multiracial* (see entries for these terms).

References

Root, M.P.P. (1992). *Racially mixed people in America.* Newbury Park, CA: Sage.

Spickard, P. R. (1989). *Mixed blood: Intermarriage and ethnic identity in twentieth-century America.* Madison: University of Wisconsin Press.

U.S. Bureau of the Census. (1993). *Statistical abstract of the United States* (113th ed.). Washington, DC: U.S. Government Printing Office.

Kelley R. Kenney

INTROSPECTION STAGE—Refers to a stage in the *Minority Identity Development* (*MID*) model proposed by Atkinson, Morten, and Sue (1979). This model was based upon similar models (e.g., Cross, 1971, Sue & Sue, 1971). The Atkinson et al. (1979) model was a five-stage model, with the first stage being *conformity*, the second stage being *dissonance*, the third stage being *resistance and immersion*, the fourth stage being *introspection*, and the fifth stage being *synergetic* (see entries for these terms). These stages describe the process by which ethnic minorities form their respective ethnic/racial identities within the context of a dominant, larger society. Briefly, the conformity stage is where ethnic minority individuals adhere to the values and traditions of the majority society. In the dissonance stage, there is a challenge to this view of adherence. In the resistance and immersion stage, these individuals reject the majority society completely and immerse themselves into their own ethnic/racial group. In the introspection stage, these individuals come to recognize that the rejection of the majority of society is unsatisfying and that the complete immersion into their own ethnic/racial group is too rigid and confining. Therefore, they reexamine their overly strong views of the resistance and immersion stage and begin to integrate their feelings and values of their own ethnic/racial group with those of the majority group. Finally, in the synergetic stage (more fully, the *synergetic articulation and awareness stage*), the integration of ethnic/racial and majority group values is complete. Individuals have a secure sense of their own ethnic/racial identity and oppose oppression of all forms. All of these stages also have implications for attitudes and behaviors towards individuals of other ethnic minority groups. In the introspection stage, individuals resolve their conflicts from the previous stage of feeling empathy toward other groups while trying to experience the world in a culturally immersed manner. Instead, they view or judge those of other ethnicities according to their own ethnocentric bias.

References

Atkinson, D. R., Morten, G., & Sue, D. W. (1979). Proposed minority identity development model. In D. R. Atkinson, G. Morten, & D. W. Sue (Eds.), *Counseling American minorities: A cross-cultural perspective* (pp. 191–200). Dubuque, IA: Brown.

Cross, W. E. (1971). The Negro-to-Black conversion experience. *Black World, 20,* 13–27.

Sue, S., & Sue, D. W. (1971). Chinese-American personality and mental health. *Amerasia Journal, 1,* 36–49.

Jeffery Scott Mio

ISSEI—The first generation Japanese who emigrated to the United States beginning in 1868 (Parillo, 1985). Due to the Oriental Exclusion Proclamation of 1907, *Issei* were ineligible for U.S. citizenship until 1952 (Guralnik, 1988).

References

Guralnik, D. B. (Ed.). (1988). *Webster's new world dictionary* (3rd ed.). New York: Simon & Schuster.

Parillo, V. (1985). *Strangers to these shores: Race and ethnic relations in the United States*. New York: Wiley.

Patricia J. Matsumoto

ITALIAN AMERICAN—Those of Italian ancestry born in the United States or immigrants who become American citizens. *Italian Americans* became an accepted form of self-identification as immigrants became more settled after World War I. Mass migrations from Italy, which began in 1880 and ended in 1924, brought the realization that the United States would be their permanent home (Glazer & Moynihan, 1970). The ascendance of the second generation, who had no contact with Italy, and the emergence of mutual support organizations that were not tied to a particular region of Italy and increased relations across provincial lines, further contributed to the use of this identifier. Initially, immigrants from Italy identified themselves as residents of a particular village or geographic region in Italy and not as "Italians." Currently, the term *Italians* is generally used to refer to recent immigrants. Occasionally, the term Italians may also be used interchangeably with Italian Americans. Outside of large urban centers, the terms Americans of Italian descent and American Italians may be used particularly by third and fourth generations who want to emphasize their identification with the United States (Alba, 1985).

References

Alba, R. (1985). *Italian Americans: Into the twilight of ethnicity*. Englewood Cliffs, NJ: Prentice-Hall.

Glazer, N., & Moynihan, D. P. (1970). *Beyond the melting pot: The Negroes, Puerto Ricans, Jews, Italians, and Irish of New York City*. Cambridge, MA: M.I.T. Press.

Maria Rodriguez

J

JAPANESE AMERICANS—United States citizens who have Japanese ancestry. The history of *Japanese Americans* dates back to the late 1800s, when Japanese male laborers were recruited to Hawaii and the West Coast to work mainly in agriculture. First generation Japanese Americans are known as *Issei*, while their children, second generation Japanese Americans, are known as *Nisei*. Third generation Japanese Americans are known as *Sansei*, and fourth generation as *Yonsei* (see entries for these terms, and *KIBEI*). According to the way in which Japanese Americans count, the "first generation" are the ones who immigrated to the United States, and the first generation born in the United States are considered to be "second generation" Japanese Americans. This contrasts with the way European immigrants counted their generational roots, where the first generation born in the United States were considered to be the "first generation" Americans. The life experiences of Japanese Americans are very diverse, in large part due to where one's family lived during World War II. During World War II, as a result of Executive Order 9066, all Japanese Americans on the West Coast were evacuated from their homes and businesses, and placed in internment camps for the duration of the war. While this caused irreparable damage to these individuals, including the loss of homes, property, and businesses, many Japanese American men from the camps volunteered to serve in the U.S. military in order to prove their loyalty to the United States. The all-Japanese-American 442nd Regimental Combat Team was the most highly decorated battalion from World War II. Incarcerated Japanese Americans were mainly *Issei* and *Nisei*. The *Nisei* began the Redress and Reparations movement, which in the late 1980s culminated in payments to all of the survivors of the internment camps. These life experiences are very different from the experiences of Japanese Americans who lived in Hawaii during World War II.

Japanese Americans were one of the largest ethnic groups in Hawaii, and thus, during the war did not experience racism to the extent as did those who lived on the West Coast. Japanese Americans who lived in inland U.S. territories also were not incarcerated during the war. In addition to differences from Asians from other ethnic groups, there are many differences among Japanese Americans. For example, Japanese Americans are very diverse in their level of acculturation, ethnic identity, adherence to traditional Japanese traditions and values, ability to speak Japanese, and generational status. Additionally, there can be great differences among newer, younger, first generation Japanese Americans (also considered to be *Issei)* and the original, now elderly, group of *Issei.*

References

Chan, S. (1991). *Asian Americans: An interpretative history.* Boston: Twayne Publishers.
Fujita, S. S., & O'Brien, D. J. (1991). *Japanese American ethnicity: The persistence of a community.* Seattle: University of Washington Press.
Hosokawa, B. (1992). *Nisei: The quiet Americans.* Niwot, CO: University Press of Colorado.
Kitano, H.H.L. (1969). *Japanese Americans: The evolution of a subculture.* Englewood Cliffs, NJ: Prentice-Hall.
Uba, L. (1994). *Asian Americans: Personality patterns, identity, and mental health.* New York: Guilford.

Gayle Y. Iwamasa

K

KIBEI—Second generation Japanese Americans who were born in the United States but educated in Japan, returning to the United States shortly before World War II (Glen, 1986). These individuals are the same generation as the *Nisei* (see entry). According to the Japanese language, individuals who immigrated to the United States are called *Issei*, or "first generation." The children of the *Issei* were referred to as *Nisei*, which means "second generation," but the *Nisei* who were sent back to Japan to be educated were referred to as *Kibei*. American and European languages would typically refer to the *Nisei* and *Kibei* generation as "first generation of Americans," because this generation was the first to be born in the United States. Some *Issei* parents sent their children back to Japan for economic reasons. The children were raised by relatives in Japan, thus freeing the parents to work and make enough money to raise a family here in the United States. Besides economic reasons, Glen (1986) stated, "Parents were also motivated by a desire for their children to receive a proper Japanese upbringing so that they would not be overly Americanized. They wanted their children to be inculcated with traditional virtues, such as respect for elders, discipline, and appreciation of the arts" (p. 53). About nine percent of the children in internment camps during World War II were *Kibei* (Glen, 1986).

Reference

Glen, E. N. (1986). *Issei, Nisei war bride: Three generations of Japanese American women in domestic service*. Philadelphia: Temple University Press.

Jeffery Scott Mio

KINESICS—The study of body movements, including posture, facial expression, eye behavior, and other characteristics of movement (Marshall & Barthel,

1994; Paniagua, 1994; Sue & Sue, 1990). Particular bodily movements can be consciously performed, and convey meanings whether intentional or unintentional. The form, meaning, and subsequent interpretation of such movements is strongly influenced by culture. However, it is important to recognize that while many bodily gestures are universal, their meanings might not be (Pantiagua, 1994; Pope-Davis & Coleman, 1997; Sue & Sue, 1990). For instance, the act of smiling is perceived by most Americans to convey happiness or other positive feelings, but when Japanese smile, they may be conveying other meanings besides happiness, such as embarrassment, discomfort, or shyness (Sue & Sue, 1990). Still other cultures use the act of smiling to indicate dominance, which could lead to serious misunderstanding between cultures. While faces may offer/ give out strong signals in most cultures, Japanese cultures value emotional control, and as such it is much more difficult to read Japanese faces. In fact, while the Japanese calligraphic character *kao* is more commonly used for the word "face," another pronunciation of the written character is *men*, which can mean either "face" or "mask" (Sue & Sue, 1990; Wolfgang, 1984). Another example of cultural differences in kinesics is eye contact. While White individuals regard eye contact while listening as an important indication of attentiveness, African Americans do not see this behavior as necessary to indicate attention; in fact, when being reprimanded, an African American norm of showing respect is to hang one's head while being corrected or scolded. In the past, this had often been interpreted as showing disinterest or avoidance by White teachers (Sue & Sue, 1990). Thus, simply because a person does not exhibit obvious signs of emotion does not mean that there is nothing to be expressed; some cultures and individuals are simply aware of the meanings of some body language and attempt to control it on a conscious level. Kinesics are a subset of the broader category of nonverbal communication, which includes factors such as silence, avoidance, body proximity, and vocal intonation.

References

Knapp, M. L. (1972). *Nonverbal communication in human interaction.* New York: Holt, Rinehart & Winston.

Marshall, G., & Barthel, D. (1994). *The concise Oxford dictionary of sociology.* New York: Oxford University Press.

Paniagua, F. (1994). *Assessing and treating culturally diverse clients.* Thousand Oaks, CA: Sage.

Pope-Davis, D. P., & Coleman, H. (1997). *Multicultural counseling competencies.* Thousand Oaks, CA: Sage.

Sue, D. W., & Sue, D. (1990). *Counseling the culturally different: Theory and practice* (2nd ed.). New York: Wiley.

Wolfgang, A. (1984). *Nonverbal behavior, perspectives, applications, intercultural insights.* Lewiston, NY: C. J. Hogrefe.

Lisa Frye

KOREAN AMERICAN—A person of Korean descent who is also a resident and citizen of the United States. Korean immigration to the United States is a relatively recent occurrence/development, with the first few Koreans arriving near the end of the nineteenth century (Collier, 1993). The majority of these first immigrants were students that were encouraged by American missionaries to pursue further education in the United States. The next influx of Korean immigrants a few years later was also encouraged by a missionary, Horace N. Allen (Auerbach, 1994). He was interested in finding ways to involve the United States in Korea in order to counter Japanese influence and reassert Korean independence. Towards this end, Allen heavily recruited Koreans to work as laborers on the Hawaiian sugar plantations. He was successful in his recruiting, and more than 7,200 Koreans immigrated to Hawaii between 1903 and 1905 to work for the Hawaiian Sugar Planters' Association. This occurrence apparently had little or no effect on reducing Japan's influence, as Korea soon came under tighter Japanese control. In 1905, Japan effectively stopped Korean immigration to the United States by closing the Korean immigration office and forbidding anyone to leave Korea. In addition, the United States determined that its "Gentleman's Agreement" with Japan that severely restricted Japanese immigration also applied to Korean immigration. The only exceptions to this restriction applied to wives of already resident Korean aliens and "picture brides" (women who contracted marriages on the basis of an exchange of photographs); this practice was banned in 1924. Korean emigration began to rise after World War II with the surrender of Japan and the U.S. occupation of Korea. Emigration increased even more after the Korean War (1950–1953), and surged after the Immigration Law of 1965 repealed the old restrictions (Themstrom, 1980). More than 175,000 Koreans were admitted into the United States between 1965 and 1976. A significant number of these immigrants were wives of American servicemen. These women were often looked down upon by other members of the Korean community, who considered the women to be of a lower social class, uneducated, and socially unacceptable. Although there was no basis for this judgment, this stereotype persisted for many years within the Korean community. Discrimination by Americans directed towards the Korean community as a whole had occurred ever since the Koreans' arrival in the United States. Most of the earlier immigrants worked as laborers on the sugar plantations of Hawaii or in rice fields on the mainland. This work involved working long hours under harsh conditions for low wages, but it was all that was available for the immigrants, as they were "aliens ineligible for citizenship" under prevailing law. Thus, for many years Koreans were exploited as workers in the United States. They also encountered intense hostility when they attempted to find better economic opportunities as White laborers had formed the Japanese and Korean Exclusion League in 1905 to keep Asians from taking jobs. By the 1930s, however, doors had opened a bit wider to Koreans and they were able to establish modest businesses, such as fruit stands, restaurants, and small stores. While many past and present Koreans came to the U.S. as well-educated professionals, they were/are often forced to take menial labor-type jobs while they learn English or make arrangements to reenter their profession. Currently, there are over one million Korean Americans living in the United States.

References

Auerbach, S. (1994). *Encyclopedia of multiculturalism*. North Bellmore, NY: Marshall Cavendish Corp.

Colier, P. F. (1993). *Collier encyclopedia*. New York: Author.

Themstrom, S. (1980). *Harvard encyclopedia of ethnic groups*. Cambridge, MA: President and Fellows of Harvard College.

Lisa Frye

KWANZAA—A cultural celebration from December 26 through January 1 that was created in 1966 by Maulana Ron Karenga (Karenga, 1972). *Kwanzaa*, a Swahili word, means first fruits. The first fruits concept is directly related to the agricultural tradition of celebrating and giving thanks for the bounty of crops and harvests tended throughout the year. Karenga's intent was to minimize the commercialization and economic pressures of overspending in preparation for Christmas. Kwanzaa has African roots as a base although the holiday was created and first celebrated in the United States. Kwanzaa has created a viable component of the African American's need for ownership of a celebration/holiday that is based on properties void of other culture's influence. Kwanzaa is replete with symbols and symbolism: the *mkeka* (straw mat) for African tradition and history, the *kinara* (candle holder) representing parents and ancestors, the *mshumaa* (seven candles) representing the seven principles of Kwanzaa, the *muhindi* (ears of corn) representing children of the home or the potential for children, the *zawadi* (gifts) used as rewards and recognition, the *mazao* (the harvest) which is the fruits of our labors, and the *kikombe* (unity cup) showing oneness of purpose. The seven days of Kwanzaa also have meaning: *umoja* means unity, *kujichagulia* means self-determination, *ujima* means collective work and responsibility, *ujamaa* means cooperative economics, *nia* means purpose, *kuumba* means creativity, and *imani* means faith. It is a holiday that connects peoples of African descent worldwide by observing a common holiday (plumpp, 1976). Kwanzaa is a direct result of ethnic pride that has established collective values and racial/ethnic pride.

References

Karenga, R. M. (1972). *Kwanzaa*. Chicago: Institute of Positive Education.

plumpp, s. d. (1976). *black rituals*. Chicago: Third World Press.

Tengemana Mapule Thumbutu

L

LABELING THEORY—Refers to the social process by which some people in society label other people as deviant (Kammeyer, Ritzer, & Yetman, 1994). This theory, proposed by Becker (1963), was developed to understand and explain an individual's or a group's deviance from the norms of a society. *Deviance*, as Becker defines it, is a socially constructed phenomenon whereby members of a dominant group create rules of interaction. Any person who breaks these rules is labeled *deviant* or *abnormal*. No specific behavior is labeled as deviant. Instead, behavior becomes deviant only when others define it that way (Bryjak & Soroka, 1992). Labeling theorists believe that often, the process of being labeled negatively affects an individual. For example, if a person commits an illegal act, he/she may be labeled as dishonest and untrustworthy, and as a criminal. However, if this person were unable to rent an apartment, find a job, or obtain social acceptance, she or he may find it easier to commit further crimes because there may be few "socially acceptable" avenues available to her or him, and because society may expect further criminal behavior. This behavior serves to further intensify society's views of the individual, and an escalating cycle is created (Becker, 1963). That is, a behavior results in a consequence that begets (or again elicits) the behavior as the individual is unable independently to eradicate or modify the behavior. Typically, labels are created from within the power structure of a society. As such, labeling theorists suggest that the rules of behavior to be followed are constructed by the wealthy for the poor, by the majority culture for minority cultures, and so on (Giddens, 1991). Labeling theory may also contribute to the perpetuation of poverty. For example, if poor people are blamed for their condition and told that they are lazy and apathetic, they may begin to believe these stereotypes (Parillo, Stimson, & Stimson, 1985). Such stereotypes often have a significant impact on the self-efficacy and self-esteem of these individuals.

References

Becker, H. S. (1963). *Outsiders: Studies in the sociology of deviance*. New York: Free Press.
Bryjak, G. J., & Soroka, M. P. (1992). *Sociology: Cultural diversity in a changing world*. Boston: Allyn and Bacon.
Giddens, A. (1991). *Introduction to sociology*. New York: Norton.
Kammeyer, K., Ritzer, G., & Yetman, N. R. (1994). *Sociology: Experiencing changing societies* (6th ed.). Boston: Allyn and Bacon.
Parillo, V. N., Stimson, J., & Stimson, A. (1985). *Contemporary social problems*. New York: Wiley.

Madonna G. Constantine

LAOTIAN—A person of or from the country of Laos (the Lao People's Democratic Republic, a single party socialist state since 1975). Laos is a landlocked nation in Southeast Asia, bounded by Thailand, Vietnam, Myanmar (formerly Burma), China, and Kampuchea (formerly Cambodia). It is ethnically diverse, with 65 ethnic groups officially identified; however, the government has classified them into four groups, the *Lao Lum* (or *Lao Loum*), the *Lao Thai*, the *Lao Theung*, and the *Lao Soung* (Cordell, 1991). The Lao Lum, or lowland Lao, are ethnically related to the Lao Thai; they live in the lowland areas in small villages and have traditionally been the dominant group politically and numerically. The Lao Thai, or Upland Thai or Tribal Thai, live higher up in the valleys. The Lao Theung live on lower mountain slopes; they consist of several ethnic groups who speak a Mon-Khmer language and in the past were referred to as *Kha*, a derogatory term meaning "slave." The fourth group, the Lao Soung, live on the higher slopes of the mountains; they are descendents of the *Miao-Yao* tribes who migrated south from China in the nineteenth century. The largest group of Lao Soung are the Hmong, formerly called Miao or Meo, a derogatory term meaning "barbarian." The Hmong were recruited by the Central Intelligence Agency to fight the Pathet Lao during the Vietnam War. This resulted in a mass exodus of the Hmong after the end of the war in 1975 (Eliot, Bickersteth, & Colet, 1996). In all, about 10 percent of the people left Laos during this period. When the term Laotian is used to refer to Indochinese refugees, it typically does not include the Hmong, who are usually placed in their own separate category. Cordell (1991) provides an annotated bibliography of Laos and cites the systematic treatment of its ethnography in Lebar, Hickey, and Musgrave (1964).

References

Cordell, H. (1991). *Laos. World bibliographic series* (Vol. 133). Oxford: Clio Press.
Eliot, J., Bickersteth, J., & Colet, J. (Eds.). (1996). *1996 Vietnam, Laos & Cambodia handbook* (2nd ed.). Bath, England: Trade and Travel.

Lebar, F. M., Hickey, G. C., & Musgrave, J. K. (1964). *Ethnic groups of mainland Southeast Asia.* New Haven, CT: Human Relations Area Files Press.

Fred Ninonuevo

LATAH—A state of uncontrollable behavior that includes imitation of movement and speech, automatic obedience, sexual delusions, and extreme suggestibility. It is brought on by a frightful, startling experience or stress that can be very ordinary in nature, but failure to cope with this fear or stress leads to anxiety. Latah in its original form means "ticklish" from the Malay language. Latah is often found among women in lower social classes, in countries such as Malaysia, the Philippines, and Indonesia. It is common to find women suffering from latah shouting obscenities, behaving in ways they would not normally behave or causing self-harm. Yap (1952) discovered that cultures within Japan, Siberia, the Philippines, and the United States also displayed the same behavior but categorized it under different names. In addition, it has been suggested that both latah and *Arctic hysteria* (see entry) are identical (Aberle, 1952). After studying cultural groups in Peninsular Malaysia and Borneo, Winzler (1995) concluded that latah is related to neurobiological factors. Latah also has been related to psychological factors that are explained by impairment in one's consciousness (Landy, 1977). Other Westerners have concluded that latah is a hysteria or psychosis among defenseless women who live in societies with limited social or technological development (Honigmann, 1973).

References

Aberle, D. (1952). Arctic hysteria and latah in Mongolia. *Transactions of the New York Academy of Sciences, 22*, 291–297.
Honigmann, J. (1973). *Handbook of social and cultural anthropology.* Chicago: Rand McNally.
Landy, D. (1977). *Culture, disease, and healing.* New York: Macmillan Publishing.
Winzler, R. (1995). *Latah in South-East Asia: The history and ethnography of a culture-bound syndrome.* Cambridge: University Press.
Yap, P. (1952). The latah reactions: Its pathodynamics and nosological position. *Journal of Mental Science, 98*, 515–564.

Joseph E. Trimble and Heather K. Mertz

LEARNED HELPLESSNESS—The phenomenon whereby an experience with uncontrollable events leads one to conclude that future events will also elude one's control. Seligman and Maier (1967) and Overmier and Seligman (1967) first used this phrase to explain dogs' responses to uncontrollable shocks administered in an experimental laboratory. These dogs, initially exposed to shocks from which they could not escape, gave up all of their avoidance behaviors such as barking, running, and jumping. When subsequently placed in an environment where they could simply jump over a low barrier to escape further shocks, these dogs remained passive and accepted the shocks. Seligman and his colleagues theorized that these dogs learned they were unable to effect change on their environment and, consequently, had abandoned their efforts to do so (Seligman, 1991). The original theory of learned helplessness was published by Seligman (1975), and was revised three years later by Abramson, Seligman, and Teasdale (1978) to include more cognitive elements. Since the initial publications of learned helplessness theory, there has been extensive research identifying learned helplessness in humans. Studies of learned helplessness in people suggest that when humans are exposed to situations in which their actions have no impact on the outcomes, they often experience feelings of depression, anxiety, anger, and decreased aggressiveness. Continued exposure to these uncontrollable events may lead to motivational, cognitive, and emotional deficits (Abramson, Garber, & Seligman, 1980). However, not all humans engage in passive or helpless behavior when confronted with unmanageable circumstances (Silver & Wortman, 1980). Abramson et al. (1978) proposed that the nature of the helplessness effect on individuals is governed by the causal attributions these individuals devise in response to an uncontrollable situation. That is, individuals may ascribe the cause of their helplessness to either internal or external, stable or unstable, and global or specific factors. Generally, individuals who explain their helplessness with an internal, stable, and global attributional style are prone to suffer from depression and lack of self-esteem (Garber, Miller, & Abramson, 1980). Silver and Wortman (1980) indicated that chronic stressors in peoples' lives may deplete their coping resources, leaving them vulnerable to experiencing feelings of helplessness. The learned helplessness phenomenon may help to explain why some people feel entrapped in a cycle of poverty from which they cannot seem to free themselves, or why cultural and ethnic minorities report "racist" experiences that others label "exaggerated" or worse, "paranoid."

References

Abramson, L. Y., Garber, J., & Seligman, M.E.P. (1980). Learned helplessness in humans: An attributional analysis. In J. Garber & M.E.P. Seligman (Eds.), *Human helplessness: Theory and applications* (pp. 3–34). New York: Academic Press.

Abramson, L. Y., Seligman, M.E.P., & Teasdale, J. (1978). Learned helplessness in humans: Critique and reformulation. *Journal of Abnormal Psychology, 87,* 49–74.

Garber, J., Miller, S. M., & Abramson, L. Y. (1980). On the distinction between anxiety and depression: Perceived control, certainty, and probability of goal attainment. In J. Garber & M.E.P. Seligman (Eds.), *Human helplessness: Theory and applications* (pp. 197–221). New York: Academic Press.

Overmier, J. B., & Seligman, M.E.P. (1967). Effects of inescapable shock upon subsequent escape and avoidance learning. *Journal of Comparative and Physiological Psychology, 63,* 28–33.

Seligman, M.E.P. (1975). *Helplessness: On depression, development and death.* San Francisco: Freeman.

Seligman, M.E.P. (1991). *Learned optimism.* New York: Alfred A. Knopf.

Seligman, M.E.P., & Maier, S. F. (1967). Failure to escape traumatic shock. *Journal of Experimental Psychology, 74,* 1–9.

Silver, R. L., & Wortman, C. B. (1980). Coping with undesirable life events. In J. Garber & M.E.P. Seligman (Eds.), *Human helplessness: Theory and applications* (pp. 279–340). New York: Academic Press.

Madonna G. Constantine

M

MACHISMO—Similar to "sexism." The belief in Latin American countries in the superiority of males over females in a patriarchal culture, valuing dominant qualities like physical strength, virility, bravery, power, domination, and aggressiveness (Torres, 1998; Zambrana, 1995).

References

Torres, J. B. (1998). Masculinity and gender roles among Puerto Rican men: Machismo on the U.S. mainland. *American Journal of Orthopsychiatry, 68,* 16–26.
Zambrana, R. E. (Ed.). (1995). *Understanding Latino families: Scholarship, policy and practice.* Thousand Oaks, CA: Sage.

Cindy Yee

MACROCULTURE—Refers to the national or shared culture of a society or nation state which includes the national overarching values, symbols, and ideations shared to some degree by all smaller cultures (i.e., *microcultures*—see entry; Banks, 1994). Values such as justice, equality, and human dignity are overarching values in the United States (Myrdal, 1944), although these values, while internalized, are violated daily. In the United States, *macroculture* is synonymous with the American society; it is often a preferred term to *majority* or *dominant culture.*

References

Banks, J. R. (1994). *Multiethnic education: Theory and practice.* Needham Heights, MA: Allyn & Bacon.

Myrdal, G. (1944). *An American dilemma: The Negro problem and modern democracy.*
New York: Harper & Row.

Adelaida Santana Pellicier

MAGIC—An attempt to control supernatural forces through the use of specific practices such as potions, chants, or ritual practices (Giddens, 1991; Nanda, 1980). To gain the desired outcome, magicians often rely on a set of clear-cut ritual procedures designed to lead to a predictable end (Spradley & McCurdy, 1980). Human beings who perform magic may believe that their actions can have a direct effect, both good and bad, on the lives of other people and on the natural world (Nanda, 1980). Some individuals resort to magic during times of vulnerability, uncertainty, trouble, misfortune, or danger (Giddens, 1991). Magic and religion share a common belief in the supernatural, and neither can be verified using scientific or rational means (Ferraro, 1992). Magic, however, can be differentiated from religion in its attitudes and ultimate goals. Magic assumes that individuals have a certain level of control as they work toward immediate goals (Bates & Julian, 1975). In religion, gods are asked (rather than manipulated) to bring about a particular outcome (Nanda, 1980); religion also seeks to inspire deep emotions and reverence as it examines the more supreme issues of human existence, salvation, and the soul (Ferraro, 1992). Religion is generally practiced by a community, while magic may be performed by an individual or a small group (Giddens, 1991). Two different types of magic have been identified: *contagious* and *imitative*. Contagious magic is seen as an attempt to manipulate or treat an object in order to influence a person or object closely associated with it. For example, a magician may perform a ceremony using an individual's hair strand, believing that the spell will influence the person to whom it belongs. Imitative magic, on the other hand, relies on the belief that imitating a desired outcome through a specific procedure will cause it to occur (Beals & Hoijer, 1971). For example, an individual who engages in imitative magic may construct a clay model of his/her enemy and then destroy it, hoping that this enemy will be injured or killed. The power of magic continues to be felt in modern society, as seen in the continued existence of superstitions such as avoiding cracks on the sidewalk and the efficacy of lucky charms. Magic may be expressed in various ways across cultures, and is believed by some individuals to influence phenomena such as infertility, illness, famine, drought, and even unrequited love.

References

Bates, A. P., & Julian, J. (1975). *Sociology: Understanding social behavior.* Boston: Houghton Mifflin.
Beals, R. L., & Hoijer, H. *An introduction to anthropology* (4th ed.). New York: Macmillan.
Ferraro, G. (1992). *Cultural anthropology: An applied perspective.* St. Paul, MN: West.
Giddens, A. (1991). *Introduction to sociology.* New York: Norton.

Nanda, S. (1980). *Cultural anthropology*. New York: Van Nostrand.
Spradley, J. P., & McCurdy, D. W. (1980). *Anthropology: The cultural perspective* (2nd ed.). New York: Wiley.

Madonna G. Constantine

MAINSTREAM CULTURE—A contextually oriented membership, affiliation, or a sharing of some element within the prevailing current trend, or direction of a particular culture or society (Greenhill, personal correspondence, 1996). The term has roots in the mid-1800s in reference to literary trends and music, such as "Byron and Shelly will be long remembered . . . for their . . . titanic effort to flow in the main stream of modern literature" or "mainstream jazz, typified by musicians like Basie, Ellington, Armstrong" (*Oxford English Dictionary*, 2nd edition, on compact disc, 1992). The *mainstream culture* assumes a position of centrality within a given social system. Language, practices, and beliefs, for example, identified as fitting "the norm" or "the standard" within a society are representative of mainstream culture. "Many people . . . who are referred to as 'minority group members' in their countries do not want to lose valued parts of their cultures. . . . [R]ather than disappearing on the fringes of society, they want to take respected places within the mainstream of their cultures" (Brislin & Yoshida, 1994, p. 2; Bachtold & Eckvall, 1978). Indicating how "mythical ideals" within various social contexts have created "pressures to conform," Ramirez (1991) advances examples of mainstream American mythical ideals based on qualitative comparisons of human characteristics ranging among skin color, gender, intelligence, physical stature, and even competence in the arts as opposed to the sciences. The notion of mainstream culture may or may not imply a racist or exclusivist character; rather, the context and "mainstream attitudes" determine this. Pauline Greenhill sees mainstream life as more unexamined than the Ramirez quote implies; she suggests that "Mainstream-ness assumes everybody is like us; if by chance, they're not, then they must want to be" (personal correspondence, October 1996). Understanding the ethos—and the impact—of the mainstream culture is crucial to counselors working with diverse clients. A central theme within the multicultural counseling literature is the notion that traditional counseling techniques are likely to be ineffective with non-mainstream clients (McFadden, 1993; Atkinson, Morten, & Sue, 1989; Ponterotto & Casas, 1987). The multicultural field has acknowledged that counseling practices grounded in Western world, middle-class, White male values and the use of "mainstream definitions" have supported the oppression of minority groups and neglected their needs (Sue & Sue, 1990; Wehrly, 1995). The term has also been used by scholars in the disability field, or special education, who refer to the process of including students with disabilities in "regular education" classrooms as *mainstreaming* (Biklen, 1987, 1992; Knoblock, 1982). The term was formally used in this sense by psychologists who referred to returning patients to society from institutions as mainstreaming. Some terms often associated with the construct mainstream culture include *majority culture*, *dominant culture*, *general culture*, and *cultural norm*.

References

Atkinson, D. R., Morten, G., & Sue, D. W. (1989). A minority identity development model. In D. R. Atkinson, G. Morten, & D. W. Sue (Eds.), *Counseling American minorities* (3rd ed., pp. 35–45). Dubuque, IA: Brown.

Bachtold, L. M., & Eckvall, K. L. (1978). Current value orientations of American Indians in Northern California: The Hupa. *Journal of Cross-Cultural Psychology, 9*, 367–375.

Biklen, D. (1992). *Schooling without labels*. Philadelphia: Temple University Press.

Biklen, D. (1987). In pursuit of education. In M. S. Berres & P. Knoblock (Eds.), *Program models for mainstreaming: Integrating students with moderate to severe disabilities* (pp. 19–40). Rockville, MD: Aspen.

Brislin, R. W., & Yoshida, T. (1994). The content of cross-cultural training: An introduction. In R. W. Brislin & T. Yoshida (Eds.), *Improving intercultural interactions* (pp. 1–14). Thousand Oaks, CA: Sage.

Greenhill, P. (1994). *Ethnicity in the mainstream*. Montreal: McGill–Queen's University Press.

Knoblock, P. (1982). *Teaching and mainstreaming autistic children*. Denver, CO: Love.

McFadden, J. (1993). Introduction. In J. McFadden (Ed.), *Transcultural counseling* (pp. xiii–xxii). Alexandria, VA: American Counseling Association.

Oxford English Dictionary (2nd ed.). (1992). *The Oxford English dictionary [computer file]: On compact disk*. New York: Oxford University Press.

Ponterotto, J. G., & Casas, J. M. (1987). In search of multicultural competence within counselor education programs. *Journal of Multicultural Counseling and Development, 64*, 432–434.

Ramirez, M. (1991). *Psychotherapy and counseling with minorities*. New York: Pergamon.

Sue, D. W., & Sue, D. (1990). *Counseling the culturally different: Theory and practice* (2nd ed.). New York: Wiley.

Wehrly, B. (1995). *Pathways to multicultural counseling and competence: A developmental journey*. Pacific Grove, CA: Brooks/Cole.

Christopher J. Weiss

MAJORITY—Generally divided into two definitions: (1) numerical; and (2) political. In its numerical sense, *majority* is understood as greater than half of the total number of a given population (Morris, 1973). Taken in the political sense, majority is understood in relation to power and qualitatively occupying a position of superior power over those considered members of minority groups (see MAJORITY STATUS). *Minority* has been defined as "a group of people who, because of physical or cultural characteristics, are singled out from the others in society in which they live for differential and unequal treatment, and who therefore regard themselves as objects of collective discrimination" (Wirth, 1945, p. 347; see MINORITY). Inherent in this political context is the power relationship of majority to minority, those not subjected to oppression versus those who are and/or have been subjected to oppression (Atkinson, Morten, & Sue, 1993; Sue & Sue, 1990). Multicultural counseling often involves the facilitation of the client's awareness of their level of affiliation or identification with majority and minority groups. Acknowledging the salient political contexts of the term majority and its relevance to minority group members is a critical component of the knowledge, awareness, and skills the multicultural practitioner brings to the intervention.

References

Atkinson, D. R., Morten, G., & Sue, D. W. (1993). *Counseling American minorities: A cross-cultural perspective* (4th ed.). Madison, WI: Brown & Benchmark.

Morris, W. (Ed.). (1973). *The American heritage dictionary of the English language.* Boston: American Heritage Publishing.

Sue, D. W., & Sue, D. (1990). *Counseling the culturally different: Theory and practice* (2nd ed.). New York: Wiley.

Wirth, L. (1945). The problem of minority groups. In R. Linton (Ed.), *The science of man in the world crisis* (pp. 347–372). New York: Columbia University Press.

Christopher J. Weiss

MAJORITY STATUS—Smith (1991) writes, "Majority status is defined primarily in terms of a group's superior numerical representation within a given society; however, it may also be defined on the basis of a group's position of power within a society" (p. 182; see MAJORITY). An individual's status as a "minority" or "majority" member must be understood in relation to the dominant group. Members of the dominant group are, by this definition, individuals with majority status. Members of "oppressed groups," or individuals not of the dominant group, are generally characterized as members with minority status. Thus, numerical superiority is not necessarily the criterion used to define *majority status*. For example, women are often thought to have *minority status* in the United States, despite the fact that they are the numerical superiority in the country. Similarly, Pinderhughes (1989) emphasizes the importance of power in relation to majority/minority status. The notion of *power* here is understood in relation to privilege and access to resources. Pinderhughes points out that stereotypes not only impact the relationships between the culturally different, but "can also influence which differences determine minority or majority status" (p. 8). She refers to "social structures" as maintaining status affiliation and "cultural background" as embracing "racial categorization, ethnic belonging, social class, and minority–majority group status" (p. 10). Related terms include *dominant majority*, *mainstream culture*, and *majority group*.

References

Pinderhughes, E. (1989). *Understanding race, ethnicity, and power: The key to efficacy in clinical practice.* New York: The Free Press.

Smith, E. J. (1991). Ethnic identity development: Toward the development of a theory within the context of majority/minority status. *Journal of Counseling and Development, 70,* 181–188.

Christopher J. Weiss

MANAGING DIVERSITY—Frequently identified as a "strategy" popularized in the early 1990s to address an increasingly diversifying workforce (Rodgers, 1995). The concept of managing diversity emerged from, and is most prominent in, the organizational management and training literature. Cox (1993) describes it as "organizational systems and practices" of managing people who strive to maximize the "potential advantages of diversity" while minimizing the "potential disadvantages." Also, Cox views managing diversity "as maximizing the ability of all employees to contribute to organizational goals and to achieve their full potential unhindered by group identities such as gender, race, nationality, age, and departmental affiliation" (p. 11). He articulates "three types of organizational goals facilitated by managing diversity . . . (1) moral, ethical, and social responsibility goals; (2) legal obligations; and (3) economic performance goals" (p. 11). Thomas (Gordon, 1992) stated, "Managing diversity is about coping with 'unassimilated differences' . . . [it is] about managing people who aren't like you and who don't necessarily aspire to be like you . . . [it also has to do with] human performance . . . making a profit . . . [and] remaining competitive" (pp. 23–24). He also indicates that one of the central goals of managing diversity is to "learn to look at people as individuals, and to see individual strengths and weaknesses instead of merely registering bothersome variances from arbitrary corporate norms" (p. 29). If we take diversity as having to do with differing worldviews and/or paradigms, then the management of these differences has to do with creating a work place wherein these views can contribute equally to an organization's common goals (Rodgers, 1995). Trainers developing and presenting workshops on the management of diversity focus not only upon individual differences and similarities but "organizational cultures" as well. Fernandez (1991) summarizes the importance of managing a diverse work force by making the prediction that "those companies . . . unwilling to take into account their employees' differences will be unable to attract a sufficient number of workers to fill their needs, because workers will gravitate by preference to organizations where they are fully appreciated" (p. 2). Terms such as *work force diversity, diversity training, organizational culture,* and *inclusion* are related concepts.

References

Cox, T. (1993). *Cultural diversity in organizations.* San Francisco: Berrett-Koehler.
Fernandez, J. (1991). *Managing a diverse work force: Regaining the competitive edge.* Lexington, MA: D.C. Heath.
Gordon, J. (1992, January). Rethinking diversity. *Training Magazine,* 23–30.
Rodgers, J. (1995). Winning with diversity: The next phase. *Managing Diversity, 5,* 1–4.

Christopher J. Weiss

MARGINAL MAN (PERSON)—A person of minority group or multiracial status who is living on the borders or margins of two separate cultures (majority versus minority) because he/she is not fully accepted by either culture (Gordon, 1964; Sue, 1981). This concept was first introduced by Park (1928) and further developed by Stonequist (1935, 1937) in sociology and anthropology. Although a "cosmopolitan" or "racial hybrid" of these two cultures may positively benefit from this status (e.g., greater insight and creativity; Riesman, 1954), the *marginal person* is more likely to develop negative identity or personality traits or characteristics (e.g., insecurity, self-loathing) because of a growing frustration with the majority culture, ambivalence and discontent with the more restrictive minority culture, and unresolved conflicts in trying to negotiate these two worlds (Antonovsky, 1956; Golovensky, 1952; Gordon, 1964; Green, 1947; Hughes, 1949; Stonequist, 1935, 1937). In the past, social scientists have often argued this negative state is reflective of the internal conflicts arising in the marginal person with little consideration of the hostile social climate (Sue, 1981). Despite these claims of a flawed personality or character (Stonequist, 1935), recent studies suggest these observations may not accurately reflect the current experiences of minority or multiracial people (Hall, 1992; LaFromboise, Coleman, & Gerton, 1993; Nakashima, 1992; Root, 1990, 1996). Researchers now believe the negative aspects of marginality may only develop within a person or group that internalizes the conflicts and tensions that are created by the majority or host culture's oppression of racial and ethnic minority groups and refusal to view races and cultures as equal (Hall, 1992; Root, 1990). According to Freire (1970), once the structure of this dominant–subordinate power relationship between the majority and minority cultures can be reduced or eliminated in the larger society, the possible negative aspects of marginality will dissipate and no longer present possible conflicts for a person or group of minority or racial status individuals. (See MARGINALITY; EXTERNAL LOCUS OF CONTROL–INTERNAL LOCUS OF RESPONSIBILITY.)

References

Antonovsky, A. (1956). Toward a refinement of the "marginal man" concept. *Social Forces, 35,* 57–62.

Freire, P. (1970). *Cultural action for freedom.* Cambridge, MA: Harvard Educational Review Press.

Golovensky, D. I. (1952). The marginal man concept: An analysis and critique. *Social Forces, 30,* 333–339.

Gordon, M. M. (1964). *Assimilation in American life.* New York: Oxford University Press.

Green, A. W. (1947). A re-examination of the marginal man concept. *Social Forces, 26,* 167–171.

Hall, C. (1992). Please choose one: Ethnic identity choices for biracial individuals. In M.P.P. Root (Ed.), *Racially mixed people in America* (pp. 162–178). Newbury Park, CA: Sage.

Hughes, E. C. (1949). Social change and status protest: An essay on the marginal man. *Phylon, 10,* 58–65.

LaFromboise, T. D., Coleman, H., & Gerton, J. (1993). Psychological impact of biculturalism: Evidence and theory. *Psychololgical Bulletin, 114,* 395–412.

Nakashima, C. L. (1992). An invisible monster: The creation and denial of mixed-race people in America. In M.P.P. Root (Ed.), *Racially mixed people in America* (pp. 162–178). Newbury Park, CA: Sage.

Park, R. E. (1928). Human migration and the marginal man. *American Journal of Sociology, 33,* 881–893.

Riesman, D. (1954). *Individualism reconsidered.* Glencoe, IL: The Free Press.

Root, M.P.P. (1990). Resolving "other" status: Identity development of biracial individuals. In L. Brown & M.P.P. Root (Eds.), *Complexity and diversity in feminist theory and therapy* (pp. 185–205). New York: Haworth.

Root, M.P.P. (1996). *The multiracial experience: Racial borders as the new frontier* (pp. xiii–xxviii). Newbury Park, CA: Sage.

Stonequist, E. V. (1935). The problem of the marginal man. *American Journal of Sociology, 41,* 1–12.

Stonequist, E. V. (1937). *The marginal man.* New York: Charles Scribner's Sons.

Sue, D. W. (1981). *Counseling the culturally different: Theory and practice.* New York: Wiley.

Phillip D. Akutsu

MARGINALITY—A condition of psychosocial turmoil or tension experienced by a person who mainly belongs to two different and conflicting cultures (Stonequist, 1961). It is also defined as having no strong intragroup and intergroup identifications to either culture (Pettigrew, 1988). Of the two cultures, one represents the White/Anglo majority culture, and the other, native minority culture. Cultural identification depends on many factors including family, language proficiency, socioeconomic status, friendships, place of residence, religion, and other cultural variables (Lee & Hall, 1994). A person's experience of *marginality* depends on the interplay between his/her perception and acceptance of oneself in relation to others, and others' perceptions and acceptance of that person. *Others*, in this case, are members of two cultures to which he/she belongs. Based on skin color and physical and ethnic differences, a person with two cultures may be perceived differently by others and, therefore, not be fully accepted by either culture. "Marginal" people respond to this cultural tension in several ways. For example, they might rebel against their native culture and exist as a White/Anglo American (or majority group member). Or they might continue their struggles by vacillating between the two cultures. Marginality cannot take place without examining others' racist and ethnocentric attitudes because they directly influence marginal people's struggles with their own racial and cultural identity (Atkinson, Morten, & Sue, 1989; Lee & Hall, 1994). (See MARGINAL MAN and EXTERNAL LOCUS OF CONTROL–INTERNAL LOCUS OF RESPONSIBILITY.)

References

Atkinson, D. R., Morten, G., & Sue, D. W. (1989). A minority identity development model. In D. R. Atkinson, G. Morten, & D. W. Sue (Eds.), *Counseling American minorities* (3rd ed., pp. 35–52). Dubuque, IA: W. C. Brown.

Lee, D. J., & Hall, C.C.I. (1994). Being Asian in North America. In W. J. Lonner & R. Malpass (Eds.), *Psychology and culture* (pp. 29–34). Boston, MA: Allyn & Bacon.

Pettigrew, T. F. (1988). Integration and pluralism. In P. Katz and D. Taylor (Eds.), *Eliminating racism: Profiles in controversy* (pp. 19–30). New York: Plenum.

Stonequist, E. V. (1961). *The marginal man.* New York: Russell & Russell.

Randi I. Kim

MARIANISMO—Used to describe the cult of feminine spiritual superiority which teaches that women are semidivine, morally superior to, and spiritually stronger than men (Stevens, 1973). *Marianismo* is a New World phenomenon with ancient roots in Old World cultures. Many of the contributing elements can be found even today in Italy and Spain, but the fully developed syndrome occurs only in Latin American countries, particularly the Caribbean, Central America, and South America. *Marianismo* reinforces the stereotype of the ideal woman which encourages the emulation of the Virgin Mary's virtues, in particular her pain and suffering (these are the test of true womanhood). Among the characteristics of the ideal woman are: semidivinity, moral superiority, and spiritual strength. Such characteristics engender an infinite capacity for humility and sacrifice. Hispanic/Latina women must bear the indignities inflicted by men in order to attain a higher spiritual stature.

Reference

Stevens, E. P. (1973). *Marianismo*: The other face of *machismo* in Latin America. In A. Pescatello (Ed.), *Female and male in Latin America* (pp. 89–101). Pittsburgh, PA: University of Pittsburgh Press.

Sandra I. Lopez-Baez

MARIELITO—In the summer of 1980, 125,000 Cubans migrated to Key West, Florida, from the port of Mariel near Havana, Cuba. In May 1980 alone, more Cuban refugees arrived in the United States than in all of 1962, the previous record year for Cuban immigration (Bach, Bach, & Triplete, 1981–1982). The large influx of Cuban immigrants who arrived in the Mariel "Freedom Flotilla" as well as the estimated 7,000 criminals Castro sent to the United States with this group as a result of the post-Mariel prison riots and other events, gave rise for the first time to widespread anti-Cuban sentiment in the United States (Cuban American National Council, 1989). Although this group was not significantly different in terms of socioeconomic status from the Cuban immigrants who had arrived since the early 1970s, the image of a Cuban exodus composed of professionals, businessmen, and middle-class families was tarnished by the negative publicity as well as the perception of this group as another burden on an economy already beseiged by high unemployment, inflation, and recession. As a result, the 125,000 Cubans who arrived as part of the Mariel boatlift were labeled *Marielitos*. As a group, *Marielitos* were often perceived as culturally, educationally, and socioeconomically inferior to the Cuban professionals, landowners, and businessmen who had arrived during the earlier Cuban immigration waves. In fact, however, most of the *Marielitos* have been integrated into the U.S. economy and have achieved a standard of living that is comparable to the general Cuban American population.

References

Bach, R. L., Bach,. J. B., & Triplete, T. (1981–1982). Flotilla "entrants": Latest and most controversial. *Cuban Studies, 11 & 12*, 29–48.
Cuban American National Council. (1989). *The elusive decade of Hispanics*. Miami, FL: Author.

Gerardo M. Gonzalez

MENTAL ILLNESS—Can be described as a person's experience of behavioral, psychological, or biological dysfunction, associated with harm to that person's well-being as determined by universal or local values and meanings. This definition recognizes that *mental illness* "lies on the boundary between the given natural world and the constructed social world . . . simultaneously biological and social" (Wakenfield, 1992, p. 373). The description above blends the definitions offered by the committee that revised the fourth edition of the *Diagnostic and Statistical Manual of Mental Disorders* (American Psychiatric Association, 1994; Wakefield, 1992). Both sources acknowledge the cultural, racial, gender, and sexual identity biases possible when psychologists use traditional definitions of mental illness or inappropriately classify individuals through psychodiagnosis. Among the criteria traditionally used to define mental illness are (1) statistical abnormality, (2) presence of extreme socially disruptive behavior, and (3) absence of ideal mental health consisting of acceptable characteristics, adaptability, and adequate personal functioning. Problems have been identified with all of these criteria when they are used within a multicultural context. Sue and Sue (1990) dispute the reliance upon statistical concepts when this inevitably establishes the dominant, numerical majority as "normal" and subcultural differences in values, behaviors, and adaptation (healthy or not) as "abnormal." Using universally disruptive behaviors to define mental illness is insufficient for explaining internal or less visible dysfunction as well as culture-specific problems (Draguns, 1982). When different cultures have different interpretations of what comprises healthy, positive behavior, it also seems inaccurate to select one universal standard for optimal personal functioning without regard for contextual factors such as culture, oppression, and even the concept of change over time (Sue & Sue, 1990). Researchers sensitive to the potential for bias in the conceptualization of mental health and mental illness also have addressed historical and current misapplication of mental illness terminology in multicultural contexts. Psychodiagnostic errors and abuses range from the mere existence of historical diagnoses such as "drapetomania"—the "disorder" afflicting slaves who ran away from their masters (Szasz, 1971)—and "lack of vaginal orgasm" (Kaplan, 1983) to the current disproportionately high rates in diagnosis of severe psychopathology (schizophrenia, paranoia) in ethnic minority populations (Sue & Sue, 1990; Willie, Kramer, & Brown, 1973). The work to eliminate references to homosexuality as a mental disorder (and the "treatment" of homosexuality by so-called "change therapies") represents both a historical and present struggle (Bayer & Spitzer, 1982; Garnets, Hancock, Cochran, Goodchilds, & Peplau, 1991). When mental illness terminology can so easily be used as a means of oppression and social control, it is particularly imperative to seek definitions and diagnoses that attempt to balance biology and behavior with context and culture. It becomes possible to acknowledge individual and cultural differences, as well as variability in context and time, when mental illness is viewed as specific behavioral, cognitive, emotional, or biological dysfunction *in the context of* socially constructed norms and values which identify this dysfunction as harmful to the individual in terms of personal distress, individual or interpersonal disability, or increased risk of greater harm or death.

References

American Psychiatric Association. (1994). *Diagnostic and statistical manual of mental disorders* (4th ed.). Washington, DC: Author.

Bayer, R., & Spitzer, R. L. (1982). Edited correspondence on the status of homosexuality in *DSM-III*. *Journal of the History of the Behavioral Sciences, 18*, 32–52.

Draguns, J. G. (1982). Methodology in cross-cultural psychopathology. In I. Al-Issa (Ed.), *Culture and psychopathology*. Baltimore, MD: University Park Press.

Garnets, L., Hancock, K. A., Cochran, S. D., Goodchilds, J., & Peplau, L. A. (1991). Psychotherapy with lesbians and gay men: Survey of psychologists. *American Psychologist, 46*, 964–972.

Kaplan, M. (1983). A woman's view of *DSM-III*. *American Psychologist, 38*, 786–792.

Sue, D. W., & Sue, D. (1990). *Counseling the culturally different: Theory and practice* (2nd ed.). New York: Wiley.

Szasz, T. S. (1971). The sane slave. *American Journal of Psychotherapy, 25*, 228–239.

Wakefield, J. C. (1992). The concept of mental disorder: On the boundary between biological facts and social values. *American Psychologist, 47*, 373–388.

Willie, C. V., Kramer, B. M., & Brown, B. S. (Eds.). (1973). *Racism and mental health*. Pittsburgh, PA: University of Pittsburgh Press.

Kelly L. Willson

MESTIZO—The term used to describe the mixed Native American (Maya, Aztec, Hopi) and Spanish or Caucasian heritage of most Mexican Americans/ Chicanos (Bean & Tienda, 1987; Zack, 1993). These individuals, while being accorded higher status than indigenous peoples (Hernandez, 1996), were still oppressed by the White European settlers who owned the land (Garcia-Preto, 1996). According to Hernandez (1996), "Today, there are still clear racial divisions where non-White people are socially, politically, and racially discriminated against" (p. 215). Some estimate that 85–90 percent of all those in Mexico are of mestizo heritage (Fernandez, 1992; Morner, 1970), although many Indians speak Spanish language, so these may be erroneously counted as mestizos.

References

Bean, F. D., & Tienda, M. (1987). *The Hispanic population of the United States*. New York: Russell Sage Foundation.
Fernandez, C. A. (1992). La raza and the melting pot: A comparative look at multiethnicity. In M.P.P. Root (Ed.), *Racially mixed people in America* (pp. 126–143). Newbury Park, CA: Sage.
Garcia-Preto, N. (1996). Latino families: An overview. In M. McGoldrick, J. Giordano, & J. K. Pearce (Eds.), *Ethnicity and family therapy* (2nd ed., pp. 141–154). New York: Guilford.
Hernandez, M. (1996). Central American families. In M. McGoldrick, J. Giordano, & J. K. Pearce (Eds.), *Ethnicity and family therapy* (2nd ed., pp. 214–224). New York: Guilford.
Morner, M. (Ed.). (1970). *Race and class in Latin America*. Boston: Little, Brown.
Zack, N. (1993). *Race and mixed race*. Philadelphia: Temple University Press.

Cindy Yee and Jeffery Scott Mio

MICROCULTURE—Refers to the concept of smaller cultures which may constitute a society. Thus, *Amerindians* (*Native Americans*), *Amerilatins* (*Hispanics*), *Amerasians* (*Asian Americans*), *Amerafricans* (*African Americans*), *Women*, *Gays*, *Lesbians*, *Bisexuals*, *The Physically Challenged*, *Men*, *Class*, *Religious Affiliations*, and *Geographical Regions* may all be considered *microcultures* within the American *macroculture* (see MACROCULTURE). Microculture is often used as a more empowering term in lieu of *subculture* or *minority*. Individuals belong to many microcultures and are influenced in a variety of ways by the interrelationships of these cultures, interacting to influence individual behavior (Banks, 1994). Thus, a Puerto Rican woman living in the Southwest may be influenced by her ethnicity as well as her gender to be less oriented toward individuation than an *Amerianglo* woman, as both ethnicity and gender influence individuation.

Reference

Banks, J. R. (1994). *Multiethnic education: Theory and practice*. Needham Heights, MA: Allyn & Bacon.

Adelaida Santana Pellicier

LA MIGRA—The Spanish term for the Immigration and Naturalization Service (INS). *La Migra* is particularly an issue with Mexican American individuals. Mexican Americans tend to have darker skin than most other Latinos. Consequently, they suffer discrimination of all sorts, including housing, education, and jobs. Discrimination is no more evident than in the attention they receive from the INS (Falicov, 1996). According to Bustamante (1995), while Mexicans comprise only about 18 percent of the entire undocumented immigrant population in the United States, they represent 86 percent of all detentions by the INS. Consequently, many Mexican nationals and Mexican Americans both fear and loathe La Migra for their discriminatory practices.

References

Bustamante, J. (1995). *The socioeconomics of undocumented migration flood.* Presentation at the Center for U.S.–Mexican Studies, University of California, San Diego.
Falicov, C. J. (1996). Mexican families. In M. McGoldrick, J. Giordano, & J. K. Pearce (Eds.), *Ethnicity & family therapy* (2nd ed., pp. 169–182). New York: Guilford.

Jeffery Scott Mio

MINORITY—Not of the majority or not of the dominant group, referring not necessarily to the lack of numerical dominance, but rather to the lack of dominance in terms of power and status. The term with this definition originated with Wirth (1945): "We may define a minority group as a group of people who, because of their physical or cultural characteristics, are singled out from the others in the society in which they live for differential and unequal treatment, and who therefore regard themselves as objects of collective discrimination" (p. 345). Experiences unifying diverse minority groups (*ethnic minorities, the disabled, gays, lesbians, bisexuals,* and *women*) include: (a) stigma; (b) issues of segregation and social distance; (c) lack of social acceptance; (d) role strain when attempting to join the dominant group; (e) lack of respect and being viewed as inferior; and (f) the existence and negative effects of stereotypes, prejudice, and discrimination (Wertlieb, 1985). *Minority status* may also be viewed as an aspect of *ethnicity* (Phinney, 1996): coming to terms with oppression (both internally in terms of identification and externally in terms of behavior) may be a primary part of identification with the ethnic group. This view requires that when examining the impact of minority status, one must also examine other aspects of ethnicity, including ethnic identity and culture (see ETHNIC IDENTITY; CULTURE). Minority status may affect mental health and psychological treatment in a variety of ways, although it is extremely difficult to separate the effects of minority status (i.e., the lack of power and experience of personal and collective oppression) from the effects of other aspects of culture and ethnicity (such as cultural values, communication styles, identity). Empirical studies investigating differences between minority groups and majorities (ethnic minority groups and Whites in the United States) in prevalence of psychopathology, expression of psychopathology, diagnostic assessment, and treatment offerings have shown mixed results (Sue, 1991). While it is uncertain how minority status affects general issues of mental health and treatment, it is likely that minority status will affect the process and individual interactions of cross-cultural therapy. Pinderhughes (1989) presents an analysis of race, ethnicity, and power in clinical practice, exploring how power and the lack of power affects individuals and the clinical process.

References

Phinney, J. S. (1996). When we talk about American ethnic groups, what do we mean? *American Psychologist, 51,* 918–927.
Pinderhughes, E. (1989). *Understanding race, ethnicity, and power: The key to efficacy in clinical practice.* New York: The Free Press.
Sue, S. (1991). Ethnicity and culture in psychological research and practice. In J. Goodchilds (Ed.), *Psychological perspectives on human diversity in America* (pp. 51–85). Washington, DC: American Psychological Association.
Wertlieb, E. C. (1985). Minority group status of the disabled. *Human Relations, 38,* 1047–1063.
Wirth, L. (1945). The problem of minority groups. In R. Linton (Ed.), *The science of man in the world crisis.* New York: Columbia University.

Karen L. Suyemoto

MINORITY GROUP COUNSELING—Any counseling relationship in which the client identifies as a member of a minority group regardless of the status of the counselor. That is, the counselor may be a member of the same minority group, a different minority group, or identify with the majority group. The majority of the literature has focused on racial or ethnic minority groups, especially the majority identified counselor and minority client relationship. Not only have other relationships from other groups been examined, but the focus on *minority group counseling* has been criticized for implying a minority pathology especially when viewed from different norms (Atkinson, Morten, & Sue, 1993). In order to move away from the term minority often synonymously implying inferiority, *multicultural* or *diverse group counseling* may be more appropriate (Paniagua, 1994).

References

Atkinson, D. R., Morten, G., & Sue, D. W. (1993). *Counseling American minorities: A cross-cultural perspective* (4th ed.). Dubuque, IA: W. C. Brown.
Paniagua, F. (1994). *Assessing and treating culturally diverse clients: A practical guide.* Thousand Oaks, CA: Sage.

Matthew R. Mock

MINORITY IDENTITY MOVEMENT—Subsequent to the Civil Rights and Black Power movements of the 1960s, research addressing minority and ethnic identity flourished, both in number and in theoretical complexity. Prior to this period, early work addressing ethnic issues postulated that societal prejudice and racial hostility lead to poor psychological functioning for all members of minority groups (Karniner & Ovesey, 1951; Pettigrew, 1964). Framed thus, studies examining minority mental health in general, and the Black self-concept in particular, assumed psychological debilitation and inadequacy. But impelled by a changing political and cultural milieu, researchers advanced new models of ethnic psychology: Black Power contributed to the development of *Black identity and militancy models*, the Watts riots contributed to the development of *relative deprivation models*, and increasing immigration contributed to the development of *acculturation models* (Cross, 1991). These emerging theories of *minority identity* questioned the simplistic "self-hate" paradigms that predominated earlier thinking. Hence, an intellectual transformation accompanied social-political movements, which together advanced collective consciousness regarding the minority experience. Common theme bridged emerging models of minority identity (Phinney, 1990; Spencer & Markstrom-Adams, 1990). First, many models adopted a developmental or life-span approach, arguing that the self-concept undergoes constant evolution. Second, models posited individual differences among group members, which derive from differences in self-identification, sense of belonging, evaluations of one's group, ethnic involvement, social support, and contextual variables. Third, individuals' overall psychological well-being emerges from multidimensional sources, typically involving the additive contributions of (a) personal identity and (b) reference group orientation (Cross, 1991). The minority identity movement in psychology has yielded manifold social ramifications. By depicting the complexity within minority individuals, contemporary research discredits the simplistic idea of psychological inferiority associated with minority status. This intellectual and scientific movement reinforces the growing sense of political empowerment throughout the larger society, as minorities themselves contribute knowledge and insight to the field. Thus, self-definition replaces imposed categorization in academic psychology. Empirical findings from theoretical advances in minority identity research also carry strong implications for public policy and psychological intervention, thereby increasing the sociopolitical value of this social and academic movement.

References

Cross, W. E., Jr. (1991). *Shades of Black: Diversity in African-American identity*. Philadelphia: Temple University Press.
Kardiner, A., & Ovesey, L. (1951). *The mark of oppression*. New York: Norton.
Pettigrew, T. (1964). *A profile of the American Negro*. New York: Van Nostrand Reinhold.
Phinney, J. S. (1990). Ethnic identity in adolescents and adults: Review of research. *Psychological Bulletin, 108*, 499–514.
Spencer, M. B., & Markstrom-Adams, C. (1990). Identity processes among racial and ethnic minority children in America. *Child Development, 61*, 290–310.

Don Operario

MINORITY STANDARD TIME (ETHNIC STANDARD TIME)—Refers to differing time orientations of different cultural groups. People from traditional communities may have a stronger past and present time orientation while groups from more modernistic perspectives may sometimes be more oriented toward the future. As such, this may have an impact on an individual's importance and use of time. Some have written on the past and present time orientation of Asian American or Hispanic clients, and the more present time orientation of African American or Native American clients. These perceptions and use of time may contrast with a White middle-class orientation that may be heavily influenced by a more future time orientation (Sue & Sue, 1990). Because of this future orientation, "time is money" is the result, so punctuality is demanded. Often, because of the present and/or past orientation of many ethnic minority groups, punctuality is not the highest of priorities. Consequently, many ethnic minorities are late to events such as meetings or, more clinically relevant, therapy sessions. It should be noted that when used, sometimes through majority viewpoints *minority* or *ethnic standard time* can be used negatively or even with derogatory reference.

Reference

Sue, D. W., & Sue, D. (1990). *Counseling the culturally different: Theory and practice* (2nd ed.). New York: Wiley.

Matthew R. Mock

MISCEGENATION—The sexual union of persons from two distinct racial backgrounds occurring within or without the context of marriage (see INTER-RACIAL; MIXED MARRIAGE). As early as 1661, laws existed in the United States that prohibited *miscegenation*. These laws were regionally based and for the most part specified those racial groups which were forbidden to marry or form unions with Caucasians. In a few states, *antimiscegenation laws* also existed forbidding marriages or unions between Indians and African Americans (Davis, 1991; Funderburg, 1994). In 1958, a White man named Richard Loving and a Black woman named Mildred Jeter were married in Washington, DC. Upon their return to their hometown in the Commonwealth of Virginia, the couple was rousted out of bed in the middle of the night by a local sheriff, arrested, tried, and sentenced to one year in prison. Their sentences were suspended on the condition that they leave Virginia for a period of 25 years. The Lovings appealed the ruling, taking it all the way to the United States Supreme Court. Hence, in 1967, the Court overturned the antimiscegenation laws which remained on the books of approximately 16 states (Spickard, 1989).

References

Davis, F. J. (1991). *Who is Black? One nation's definition*. University Park: The Pennsylvania State University Press.
Funderburg, L. (1994). *Black, White, other: Biracial Americans talk about race and identity*. New York: William Morrow.

Spickard, P. R. (1989). *Mixed blood: Intermarriage and ethnic identity in twentieth-century America.* Madison: University of Wisconsin Press.

Kelley R. Kenney

MIXED MARRIAGE—A synonym for *intermarriage.* This term describes a marriage between persons of distinctly different religious backgrounds or a marriage between persons of distinctly different racial or ethnic backgrounds. A marriage, for example, between Jews and non-Jews who do not convert to Judaism is considered a mixed marriage. Similarly, marriages between persons of Irish and Italian ethnicities and between persons of Asian and Latino racial backgrounds are considered mixed marriages (Spickard, 1989; see INTERGROUP MARRIAGE and MISCEGENATION).

Reference

Spickard, P. R. (1989). *Mixed blood: Intermarriage and ethnic identity in twentieth-century America.* Madison: University of Wisconsin Press.

Kelley R. Kenney

MOJADOS—The Spanish name for "wetbacks." It is offensive slang, used as a disparaging term for a Mexican, especially a laborer, who crosses the United States–Mexican border illegally (Novas, 1994). Translated literally, this term means "the wet ones," and originated from the fact that the Rio Grande was a common point of entry.

Reference

Novas, H. (1994). *Everything you need to know about Latino history.* New York: Penguin.

Cindy Yee

MONOCULTURAL—Having familiarity with only one culture or sharing a common culture, usually to the exclusion of others. Initially, the word referred to the cultivation of a single crop (Simpson & Weiner, 1989). People who are *monocultural* may mistakenly apply their culture's values and norms to all individuals, regardless of their culture(s). This may lead to misunderstandings in therapy if the client or the therapist takes a monocultural approach, and the cultures of the client and the therapist are not the same. The therapist who takes a monocultural approach with a client from a different culture may encounter problems with diagnosis (over- or under-diagnosing disorders), assessment, interpretation of symptoms, and chosen treatment methods (Fabrega, 1995). To overcome *monoculturalism*, therapists must become aware of their own cultural heritage, recognize the generic characteristics of counseling and how they are culturally embedded, familiarize themselves with the culture(s) of their clients, and assess the appropriateness of theory and approach (Sue & Sue, 1990). The culture of counseling and therapy is often viewed as being monocultural itself, emphasizing a European-American cultural tradition, including emphases on the individual, verbal expression, insight, self-disclosure, a cause-and-effect approach, the separation of mental and physical health, and a lack of structure (Sue & Sue, 1990). Some researchers disagree, and state that counseling is inherently multicultural, as all people are cultural and no two are exactly the same (Patterson, 1996). Patterson argues for a universal approach, emphasizing necessary counselor characteristics including respect, genuineness, empathy, and structure. Most researchers in the field of multicultural counseling and psychotherapy believe that while there are some generic characteristics in counseling which may be generalized across cultures, the recognition and respect of different values, patterns of behavior, and norms that characterize different cultures is necessary for effective treatment (McFadden, 1996). Recent recommendations attempt to examine specific cultural effects on more basic, generic characteristics, addressing the conflict above; Sue and Zane (1987) focus on how culture affects the clients view of therapist credibility and the client's experience of direct benefit from therapy.

References

Fabrega, H. (1995). Hispanic mental health research: A case for cultural psychiatry. In A. Padilla (Ed.), *Hispanic psychology: Critical issues in theory and research* (pp. 107–130). Thousand Oaks, CA: Sage.

McFadden, J. (1996). A transcultural perspective: Reaction to C. H. Patterson's "Multicultural counseling: From diversity to universality." *Journal of Counseling & Development, 74,* 231–235.

Patterson, C. H. (1996). Multicultural counseling: From diversity to universality. *Journal of Counseling & Development, 74,* 227–231.

Simpson, J. A., & Weiner, E.S.C. (Eds.). (1989). *The Oxford English dictionary* (2nd ed.). Oxford: Oxford University Press.

Sue, D. W., & Sue, D. (1990). *Counseling the culturally different: Theory and practice* (2nd ed.). New York: Wiley.

Sue, S., & Zane, N. (1987). The role of cultural techniques in psychotherapy. *American Psychologist, 42,* 37–45.

Karen L. Suyemoto and Honora Kwon Batelka

MONOCULTURAL ORGANIZATION—One in which uniformity is emphasized. The notion is very similar to that of *organizational culture*, which can be defined as the shared values, beliefs, and assumptions of behavior within an organization (Ott, 1989). The idea of a culture within an organization grew out of observations in the early 1980s that the most successful American companies tend to be quite similar to each other in many ways (Peters & Waterman, 1982). Companies can be classified by the strength of their culture. A company with a strong, dominant organizational culture is one in which patterns of behavior change little over time, primarily because little deviation from company norms is tolerated, whereas a weak organizational culture is one for which there are few clear standards for behavior (O'Reilly, 1989). A moncultural organization is thus one in which the culture is strong and dominant. Many theorists believe that a strong culture is essential for success in business, because the strong culture clearly conveys to customers what the company stands for (Barney, 1986). However, it has also been argued that strong cultures are more likely to foster interpersonal problems than are weak cultures, if those strong cultures contain dysfunctional norms. For example, Sheridan (1992) demonstrated that companies within which the cultural emphasis is on rules and procedures have greater rates of turnover than do companies that emphasize cooperation and interpersonal respect; Gutek (1985) presented evidence that companies with strong cultures in which women are seen as subordinates have more sexual harassment charges filed against them than do any other type of company; and Ott (1989) showed that workers in strong cultures who resolve role conflicts by adhering to personal, rather than organizational, standards can experience considerable ostracism and conformity pressure. These studies seem to suggest an obvious solution whenever cultural clashes arise: Change the organization's culture so that respect is emphasized. However, attempts to do just this have shown that changing organizational culture is extremely difficult (Dipboye, Smith, & Howell, 1996). Many industrial/organizational psychologists are skeptical of the notions of organizational culture and monocultural organizations. It is not clear, for example, that organizational culture is conceptually distinct from the more general, and very well-established, construct of *job satisfaction*. Many of the problems that stem from dysfunctional cultures have also been shown to result from an individual's dissatisfaction with his/her job (Glick, 1985), and it is known that individuals who positively perceive their organization's culture are typically very satisfied workers (Meglino, Ravlin, & Adkins, 1989). Hence, what we have been calling a monocultural organization may really just be a company with low levels of worker satisfaction. Research is needed that truly establishes organizational culture as a distinct phenomenon before it will gain widespread acceptance among psychologists.

References

Barney, J. B. (1986). Organizational culture: Can it be a source of sustained competitive advantage? *Academy of Management Review, 11*, 656–665.

Dipboye, R. L., Smith, C. S., & Howell, W. C. (1996). *Understanding industrial and organizational psychology*. Fort Worth, TX: Harcourt Brace.

Glick, W. H. (1985). Conceptualizing and measuring organizational and psychological climate: Pitfalls in multilevel research. *Academy of Management Review, 10*, 601–616.

Gutek, B. A. (1985). *Sex and the workplace*. San Francisco: Jossey-Bass.

Meglino, B. M., Ravlin, E. C., & Adkins, C. L. (1989). A work values approach to corporate culture: A field test of the value congruence process and its relationship to individual outcomes. *Journal of Applied Psychology, 74*, 424–432.

O'Reilly, C. A. (1989). Corporations, culture, and commitment: Motivation and social control in organizations. *California Management Review, 31*, 9–25.

Ott, J. S. (1989). *The organizational culture perspective.* Pacific Grove, CA: Brooks/
     Cole.
Peters, T. J., & Waterman, R. H., Jr. (1982). *In search of excellence.* New York: Warner
     Books.
Sheridan, J. E. (1992). Organizational culture and employee retention. *Academy of Man-
     agement Journal, 35,* 1036–1056.

Craig D. Parks

MONOLINGUAL—Speaking only one language. In relation to multicultural
counseling and psychotherapy, *monolingualism* is a problem when the therapist
is monolingual and the client is bilingual or when both therapist and client are
monolingual but in different languages. Sue and Sue (1990) stated that therapy
overall has a monolingual orientation (standard English) which can act as a
barrier to providing adequate services for multilingual populations. When clients
are bilingual and therapists are monolingual, a monolingual therapy (reliance on
the shared language only) may adversely affect the client's progress. Some evidence for language independence suggests that bilingual individuals may use
different languages to discuss different experiences and emotions; monolingual
therapy may, therefore, lead to some areas of the intrapsychic world being una-
vailable or discussion of some experiences being avoided through association
with the language that is not being used in therapy (Marcos & Alpert, 1976).
When clients and therapists are both monolingual in different languages, an
interpreter is commonly used. Issues related to interpretation in psychotherapy
include: (a) difficulties with translating (exchanging words from one language
to another), versus interpreting (translating meaning, with a focus on connotative
as well as denotative meaning); (b) difficulties finding interpreters familiar with
psychological language, techniques, and attitudes; (c) difficulties related to including a third person in the therapy (transference, countertransference, general
relational issues); and (d) difficulties with ethical issues of confidentiality and
responsibility (Westermeyer, 1990). Finally, monolingualism versus bilingualism is commonly used as a measure of ethnicity and cultural identity (Phinney,
1990). For example, research supports that language proficiency and preference
are part of cultural identity and reliably differentiate between cultural identity
groups (e.g., Latino/a-identified vs. high and low bicultural vs. American-
identified; Felix-Ortiz de la Garza, Newcomb, & Myers, 1995).

References

Felix-Ortiz de la Garza, M., Newcomb, M. D., & Myers, H. F. (1995). A multidimen-
     sional measure of cultural identity for Latino and Latina adolescents. In A. M.
     Padilla (Ed.), *Hispanic psychology: Critical issues in theory and research* (pp.
     26–42). Thousand Oaks, CA: Sage.
Marcos, L. R., & Alpert, M. (1976). Strategies and risks in psychotherapy with bilingual
     patients: The phenomenon of language independence. *American Journal of Psy-
     chiatry, 33,* 1275–1278.

Phinney, J. S. (1990). Ethnic identity in adolescents and adults: Review of research. *Psychological Bulletin, 108*, 499–514.

Sue, D. W., & Sue, D. (1990). *Counseling the culturally different: Theory and practice* (2nd ed.). New York: Wiley.

Westermeyer, J. (1990). Working with an interpreter in psychiatric assessment and treatment. *Journal of Nervous and Mental Disease, 178*, 745–749.

Karen L. Suyemoto

MULTICULTURAL COUNSELING—A counseling situation where a client and a therapist are of different ethnicities, races, cultures, etc. More recently, *multicultural counseling* (MCC) has been broadened to a general theory of counseling, generic to all counseling. As such, it applies to all counseling relationships, complementing psychodynamic, behavioral, and humanistic scientific theories to explain human behavior (Pedersen, 1991). *Multicultural counseling* suggests both a conceptual framework of and a tool for a process concerned with culturally appropriate attitudes, strategies, and skills that consider how individuals are influenced by their particular culture, the interlockings and interrelationships among the many microcultures to which they belong and the many social forces that impact on their position, and situations at any given moment such as the political, economic, social, and legal systems (Sue & Sue, 1990). Thus, it is a perspective that combines universalism and relativism, "common ground universals and within-group differences that are shared across cultures" (Pedersen, 1991, p. 6). Pedersen (1991) has referred to this as *The Fourth Force* in counseling, referring to the impact it has had and may continue to have on the counseling profession, similar to behaviorism, psychodynamics, and humanism. In addition, MCC suggests a prototype to counseling which considers a wide range of microcultures without rank-ordering the importance of the microcultures. The foundation of MCC proposes that human behavior is symbiotically connected to the sociocultural context in which an individual lives. (See CROSS-CULTURAL COUNSELING; MACROCULTURE; MICROCULTURE.)

References

Pedersen, P. (1991). Multiculturalism as a generic approach to counseling. *Journal of Counseling and Development, 70*, 6–12.

Sue, D. W., & Sue, D. (1990). *Counseling the culturally different: Theory and practice* (2nd ed.). New York: Wiley.

Adelaida Santana Pellicier

MULTICULTURAL ORGANIZATION—A company that supports workers who wish to behave in a manner consistent with the dictates of their respective cultural backgrounds. The term seems to have originated in the popular press, as researchers tend to favor the more unwieldy "company engaged in diversity management" (Greenberg, 1996), so as to avoid confusion with the concepts of *organizational culture* and *multinational organization.* Traditionally, culture has referred explicitly to ethnicity, but some theorists have begun including gender, sexual orientation, age, body shape, and physical disability status as valid types of culture (Carr-Ruffino, 1996). The notion of *diversity management* has recently come to prominence in the popular press, but in fact diversity management programs have been in place in American industry for over 30 years. An increasing number of corporations are designing and implementing diversity management programs (also called multicultural awareness programs) that are aimed at modifying the corporate culture so that workers from different backgrounds can make substantial contributions to the organization (Alderfer, 1992; Ferdman, 1992; Kossek & Zonia, 1993). However, these programs have been sharply criticized for the negative assumptions that they make regarding the workplace experiences of cultural minorities (Nkomo, 1992). Further, it is known that White males tend to feel highly threatened by notions of a diverse workplace (Tsui, Egan, & O'Reilly, 1992), and it is not clear that multicultural awareness programs are effective at changing attitudes towards cultural minorities (Greenberg, 1996). Despite the rather long history of interest in diversity, researchers have only recently begun to ask how cultural differences influence workplace behavior and experiences. What little research has been conducted suggests that support of diversity is desirable. For example, multicultural organizations seem to have fewer problems with worker conflict, and higher rates of interworker cooperation, than do companies that ignore or suppress cultural differences (Cox, Lobel, & McLeod, 1991; Jackson, 1993).

References

Alderfer, C. P. (1992). Changing race relations embedded in organizations: Report on a long-term project with the XYZ corporation. In S. E. Jackson & Associates (Eds.), *Diversity in the workplace* (pp. 138–166). New York: Guilford.

Carr-Ruffino, N. (1996). *Managing diversity.* Belmont, CA: Thomson Executive Press.

Cox, T. H., Lobel, S. A., & McLeod, P. I. (1991). Effects of ethnic group cultural differences on cooperative and competitive behavior on a group task. *Academy of Management Journal, 34,* 827–847.

Ferdman, B. (1992). The dynamics of ethnic diversity in organizations: Toward integrative models. In K. Kelly (Ed.), *Issues, theory and research in industrial/organizational psychology* (pp. 339–383). Amsterdam: North Holland.

Greenberg, J. (1996). *Managing behavior in organizations.* Upper Saddle River, NJ: Prentice-Hall.

Jackson, S. E. (1993). Participation in decision making as a strategy for reducing job-related strain. *Journal of Applied Psychology, 68,* 3–19.

Kossek, E. E., & Zonia, S. C. (1993). Assessing diversity climate: A field study of reactions to employer efforts to promote diversity. *Journal of Organizational Behavior, 14,* 61–81.

Nkomo, S. M. (1992). The emperor has no clothes: Rewriting "race in organizations." *Academy of Management Review, 17,* 487–513.

Tsui, A. S., Egan, T. D., & O'Reilly, C. A., III. (1992). Being different: Relational demography and organizational attachment. *Administrative Science Quarterly, 37*, 549–579.

Craig D. Parks

MULTIPLE PERSPECTIVES—Many points of view, ways of seeing, studying, knowing, and/or understanding a phenomenon or phenomena. Accepting the existence and validity of multiple perspectives is a relativistic position. Anthropological ethnography, in seeking to understand and present subjects' perspectives, uses the term *native views*, which is likely the origin of the *multiple perspectives* construct (Gregory, 1983; Malinowski, 1922; Spradley, 1979). Within-group and between group differences can both be expressed with this term. Ivey (1995), in his work on racial and ethnic identity development, uses the phrase *multiperspective integration* to denote a stage wherein an individual is able "to see many points of view and take action, as appropriate to the situation" (p. 69). Oetting and Beauvais' (1991) theory of "orthogonal" cultural identity articulates that individuals belong to multiple cultures simultaneously and successfully—or unsuccessfully—negotiate the complexity of cultural interactions relative to their awareness and acceptance of multiple perspectives.

References

Gregory, K. (1983). Native-view paradigms: Multiple cultures and culture conflicts in organizations. *Administrative Science Quarterly, 28*, 359–376.

Ivey, A. (1995). Psychology as liberation: Toward specific skills and strategies in multicultural counseling and therapy. In J. G. Ponterotto, J. M. Casas, L. A. Suzuki, & C. M. Alexander (Eds.), *Handbook of multicultural counseling* (pp. 53–72). Thousand Oaks, CA: Sage.

Oetting, E. R., & Beauvais, F. (1991). Orthogonal cultural identification theory: The cultural identification of minority adolescents. *International Journal of the Addictions, 25*, 655–685.

Malinowski, B. (1922). *Argonauts of the Western Pacific*. London: Routledge.

Spradley, J. (1979). *The ethnographic interview*. New York: Holt, Rinehart and Winston.

Christopher J. Weiss

MULTIRACIAL—Used synonymously with *biracial* and therefore refers to persons whose parents are of two different racial backgrounds (see BIRACIAL). It is also used to refer to families that consist of parents of one racial or ethnic background who adopt children of different racial or ethnic backgrounds. Finally, it is used to refer to persons whose lineage encompasses two or more distinctly diverse racial backgrounds, such as persons who have one or both biological parents who are of biracial heritage or persons who, for example, have a combination of European, Indian, and African roots or ancestries (Funderburg, 1994; Gibbs, 1989; Root, 1992).

References

Funderburg, L. (1994). *Black, White, other: Biracial Americans talk about race and identity*. New York: William Morrow.

Gibbs, J. T. (1989). Biracial adolescents. In J. T. Gibbs & L. N. Huang (Eds.), *Children of color: Psychological interventions with minority youth* (pp. 322–350). San Francisco: Jossey-Bass.
Root, M.P.P. (1992). *Racially mixed people in America.* Newbury Park, CA: Sage.

Kelley R. Kenney

MUY MACHA—The Spanish term used to describe females that are brave, strong, or resolute in their beliefs (see MACHISMO). More recently, this expression has taken on the connotation of Latinas being more sexually aggressive (Castillo, 1994).

Reference

Castillo, A. (1994). *Massacre of the dreamers: Essays on Xicanisma.* Albuquerque: University of New Mexico Press.

Cindy Yee

N

NISEI—Second generation Japanese American. According to the Japanese language, individuals who immigrated to the United States are called *Issei*, or "first generation." The children of the *Issei* were referred to as *Nisei*, which means "second generation." The *Nisei* were born and educated in the United States (Mish, 1994). American and European languages would typically refer to the *Nisei* generation as "first generation of Americans," because this generation was the first to be born in the United States.

Reference

Mish, F. C. (Ed.). (1994). *Merriam-Webster's collegiate dictionary* (10th ed.). Springfield, MA: Merriam-Webster.

Patricia J. Matsumoto

NON-STANDARD ENGLISH—Any variant of the English language spoken by a distinct cultural, social, or regional group, incorporating slang or modified syntax and not resulting from fusion with other standard languages. A form of the English language that is not conforming in grammatical construction, pronunciation, idiom, or word selection to the usage typically characteristic of standard, educated English. This definition should not be interpreted as meaning *substandard* or in any way *inferior* to the English language, although in its original usage, Bloomfield (1933) used the term to mean "bad" or "vulgar" English. However, linguists have since discarded the value-laden nature of the original definition and now refer to it primarily as *non-standard*. Research on non-standard English covers a variety of areas in psychology, education, linguistics, and sociology, including the relation between non-standard English and job discrimination (Atkins, 1993), teacher instruction (Washington & Miller-

Jones, 1989), learning disabilities (Cartledge, Stupay, & Kaczala, 1988), school entry (Craig & Washington, 1994), and the therapeutic relationship in counseling (Beaman, 1989).

References

Atkins, C. P. (1993). Do employment recruiters discriminate on the basis of non-standard dialect? *Journal of Employment Counseling, 30*, 108–118.

Beaman, D. (1994). Black English and the therapeutic relationship. *Journal of Mental Health Counseling, 16*, 379–386.

Bloomfield, L. (1933). *Language.* New York: Holt.

Cartledge, G., Stupay, D., & Kaczala, C. (1988). Testing language in learning disabled and non-learning disabled Black children: What makes the difference? *Learning Disabilities Research, 3*, 101–106.

Craig, H. K., & Washington, J. A. (1994). The complex syntax skills of poor, urban African-American preschoolers at school entry. *Language, Speech and Hearing Services in Schools, 25*, 181–190.

Washington, V. M., & Miller-Jones, D. (1989). Teacher interactions with non-standard English speakers during reading instruction. *Contemporary Educational Psychology, 14*, 280–312.

Christine Yeh

NONVERBAL COMMUNICATION—Expressing messages without using linguistic means, or the communication that is transmitted in conjunction with the strictly verbal part of a message. A communication that is nonverbal is not necessarily one that is unspoken, as is commonly thought; written words are not considered *nonverbal communication*, while certain aspects of the voice (e.g., sighs, laughs, inflections) can be. Most communication scholars/researchers do not define sign language as nonverbal communication, because sign language uses words to communicate (Adler, 1993; Marshall & Barthel, 1994; Sue & Sue, 1990; Wolfgang, 1984). However, these scholars do contend that most communication occurs at a nonverbal level, apart from the words used in the communication. Nonverbal communication is not always intentional; people often send messages about themselves without intending to do so, such as when they blush, stammer, or sweat. In fact, most nonverbal behavior is performed on an unconscious level, and people often respond on an unconscious and culturally defined level (Adler, 1993; Paniagua, 1994; Pope-Davis & Coleman, 1997; Wolfgang, 1984). For example, when talking with someone who suddenly crossed his/her arms across his/her chest, many in the United States may suddenly start speaking defensively and even copy the arm-crossing action without being aware of it. This response may not necessarily be the one with which someone from another culture responds. A related term is *paralanguage*, which refers to vocal cues such as loudness, rate, inflection, pauses, or silences. The meanings of such sounds vary widely across cultures. One such example is the reaction to silence. Most people in the United States feel that a long silence is awkward and feel a need to fill it with talk. Other cultures, however, view silence differently. Many Chinese and Japanese are momentarily silent after making a particular point, but may intend to continue speaking after offering a respectful silence. To the English and Arabs, silence is used for privacy, while in the Asian culture, silence is a sign of respect for elders. Still other cultures, such as Russian, French, and Spanish, perceive silence as an agreement among those present (Sue & Sue, 1990).

References

Adler, T. (1993). *Looking in/looking out*. Orlando, FL: Harcourt Brace.

Knapp, M. L. (1972). *Nonverbal communication in human interaction*. New York: Holt, Rinehart & Winston.

Marshall, G., & Barthel, D. (1994). *The concise Oxford dictionary of sociology*. New York: Oxford University Press.

Paniagua, F. (1994). *Assessing and treating culturally diverse clients*. Thousand Oaks, CA: Sage.

Pope-Davis, D. P., & Coleman, H. (1997). *Multicultural counseling competencies*. Thousand Oaks, CA: Sage.

Sue, D. W., & Sue, D. (1990). *Counseling the culturally different: Theory and practice* (2nd ed.). New York: Wiley.

Wolfgang, A. (1984). *Nonverbal behavior: Perspectives, applications, intercultural insights*. Lewiston, NY: C. J. Hogrefe.

Lisa Frye

NUYORICAN—A term referring to the Puerto Rican experience in the United States, which became the subject of Puerto Rican literature, primarily poetry, produced in the United States during the late 1960s. The following terms are variations of *Nuyorican*: *Neorican*, *New Rican*, and *nuevayorquino puertorriqueño* (Algarin & Pinero, 1975). This literature was characterized by the switching from Spanish to English and bilingual writing. In addition, the literature is an attempt to affirm the struggles faced by Puerto Ricans in urban environments. The term has also been used to refer to Puerto Ricans in the United States who are predominantly English language speakers and to distinguish them from Puerto Ricans who never lived away from the island. The use of the term in this latter manner has not been favorably viewed by some who have returned to live in Puerto Rico (Esteves, 1987).

References

Algarin, M., & Pinero, M. (Eds.). (1975). *Nuyorican poetry: An anthology of Puerto Rican words and feelings*. New York: William Morrow.

Esteves, S. M. (1987). Ambivalence or activism from the *Nuyorican* perspective in poetry. In A. Rodriguez de Laguna (Ed.), *Images and identities: The Puerto Rican in two world contexts* (pp. 164–170). New Brunswick, NJ: Transaction Books.

Maria Rodriguez

O

ONTOGENETIC THEORY OF CULTURE—Researchers have long sought to determine how cultures are formed, maintained, and transmitted. That is, how do groups of people come to have shared ways of understanding the world, public customs, and symbolic systems (Strauss & Quinn, 1992)? One of the early theories of *culture acquisition* was postulated by an Austrian psychoanalyst, Géza Róeheim. Róheim began his fieldwork in 1928 and spent the next several decades attempting to evaluate Freud's (1918) hypotheses about the universality of developmental stages, cultural evolution, and the relation between primitives and neurotics (Bourguignon, 1971). As a result of his field observations, Róheim (1943) developed his *ontogenetic theory of culture*, which proposes that all aspects of culture are a result of *delayed infancy*. The theory rests on the fact that humans, when compared to other organisms, spend an extremely long time developing from infancy into mature adulthood. It is during this time Róeheim argued that variations in the way parents raise their children lead to a self-perpetuating pattern called *culture*. Each culture varies in the *ontogenetic trauma* it imparts to its children, thus accounting for variations in cultural characteristics. In fact, Róheim argued that the specific ontogenetic trauma of a culture is more important than "real" experiences like the availability of food or shelter. For example, Róheim (1932) noted that while aborigines live in a harsh climate with few available resources, it is unheard of for them to worry about their next meal. While the so-called realities of life would suggest anxiety about food, Róheim argued that because aborigines' mothers never refuse them milk, even the harshest of environments cannot break their faith that they will always be provided for. Thus, the theory argues that the pattern of culture is determined in infancy and that *"all adult activities are seen as derivative*, involving sublimation or acting out on the level of reality (as in economic activities) or on the level of fantasy (as in rituals)'' (Bourguignon, 1971, p. 89). While Róeheim's ideas were fairly well-accepted at the time, among those trained in the psychoanalytic tradition, his psychoanalytic reductionism never became popular among anthropologists or psychologists (Bourguignon, 1971). He has been criticized for minimizing the importance of adult experiences, for not acknowledging the possibility of cultural change (the cycle of parenting repeats itself indefinitely), and for leaving his case examples open to alternative interpretations (Bourguignon, 1971; McGregor, 1987).

References

Bourguignon, E. (1971). *Psychological anthropology: An introduction to human nature and cultural differences.* New York: Holt, Rinehart, & Winston.

Freud, S. (1918). *Totem and taboo: Resemblances between the psychic lives of savages and neurotics.* New York: Random House.

McGregor, G. (1987). The "primal scene" as a culture-specific phenomenon: A speculative rereading of Freudian—or Freud's—psychology. *Journal of Mind and Behavior, 8,* 133–152.

Róheim, G. (1932). Psychoanalysis of primitive cultural types. *International Journal of Psychoanalysis, 13,* 224.

Róheim, G. (1943). *The origin and function of culture. Nervous and Mental Disease Monographs.* New York: Johnson Reprint Co.

Strauss, C., & Quinn, N. (1992). Preliminaries to a theory of culture acquisition. In H. Pick, Jr., P. W. van den Broek, & D. Knill (Eds.), *Cognition: Conceptual and methodological issues* (pp. 267–294). Washington, DC: American Psychological Association.

Devin Marsh

OPPRESSION—Used by Hampole in 1340 to describe the "wretched" conditions of the world (Simpson & Weiner, 1989). In a similar manner, the word is used currently in reference to sociopolitical forces that perpetuate discriminatory practices. These practices are woven into the fabric of American institutions, and they operate in favor of culturally, socially, and economically dominant groups (e.g., White Americans, men, heterosexuals, etc.). Such favoritism is gleaned from the systematic abuse, exploitation, and injustice directed toward culturally subordinate groups. More specifically, it involves "the sanctioning of selective enforcement of laws, the blocking of economic opportunities and outcomes, and the imposition of forced assimilation/acculturation on the culturally different" (Sue & Sue, 1990, p. 78). Collectively, these tactics comprise the phenomena commonly known as the use of denial, projection, and transference of blame. The culturally different have devised a variety of strategies for coping with the reality of oppression. Typical strategies utilize covert as opposed to overt methods of resistance and are engendered by mistrust of members of the dominant culture. "Cool pose" or appearing calm when threatened (Majors & Billson, 1992) and "The Uncle Tom Syndrome," (Sue & Sue, 1990) in which aggressive feelings are suppressed and identification with the oppressor is portrayed, are examples of defense mechanisms used historically by individuals of African descent. On the one hand, these response sets serve as a means of protection against physical and psychological harm. On the other hand, they promote the behaviors against which they are protecting via the suppression of natural inclinations. According to Majors and Billson (1992), interpersonal strain, trouble with authorities, and self-deception are potential consequences of suppressive behavior. These consequences serve as barriers to help seeking and engagement in the therapeutic alliance in counseling and psychotherapy.

References

Majors, R., & Billson, J. M. (1992). *Cool pose: The dilemmas of Black manhood in America*. New York: The Free Press.
Simpson, J. A., & Weiner, E.S.C. (Eds.). (1989). *The Oxford English dictionary* (2nd ed.). Oxford: Oxford University Press.
Sue, D. W., & Sue, D. (1990). *Counseling the culturally different: Theory and practice* (2nd ed.). New York: Wiley.

Angela M. White

ORIENTAL—Literally, "to the east," thus referring to Asia's location in reference to Europe and America (*The American Heritage Dictionary of the English Language*, 1996). As an adjective, the common use of Oriental pertains to something or someone that is characteristically Eastern or Asiatic. As a noun, the common use of Oriental refers to a person who has been raised in one of the civilizations of Asia (Middle East, South Asia, Southeast Asia, or East Asia). The term *Asian* is currently the preferred term, as it indicates the geographic place of origin as opposed to the Western-centric term Oriental implies. Said (1979), a Palestinian, in his theory of *Orientalism*, brought to the attention of the academic community an understanding of how images of Asians are constructed by the Western world. Said asserted that the *Occidental* or Western perceptions of the Orient were founded upon the power that Western imperialism and colonialism imposed upon the Middle East, East Asia, Southeast Asia, and South Asia during the eighteenth and nineteenth centuries (Chan, 1981). The Western body of knowledge about Asians, their traditions and philosophy, as depicted in theories, novels, social description, and political accounts was a Western pattern for dominating, restructuring, and having authority over the Orient (Said, 1979). Said's impact has been incorporated by responses from cultural anthropologists who are concerned with the description and analysis of non-Western cultures (Marcus & Fischer, 1986). In Israel, the word Orientals often refers to *Sephardis*, or *Oriental Jews* who are from the countries of North Africa and the Middle East. About half the population of Israel is divided between Oriental Jews and Jews originating from Europe, the *Ashkenazis*, who are generally compared to Western populations (Stahl, 1993a, 1993b).

References

The American heritage dictionary of the English language (3rd ed.). (1996). Boston: Houghton Mifflin.

Chan, A. B. (1981). "Orientalism" and image making: The sojourner in Canadian history. *The Journal of Ethnic Studies, 9,* 37–46.

Marcus, G. E., & Fischer, M.M.J. (1986). *Anthropology as cultural critique: An experimental moment in the human sciences.* Chicago: University of Chicago Press.

Said, E. (1979). *Orientalism.* New York: Random House.

Stahl, A. (1993a). Changing attitudes toward the old in Oriental families in Israel. *International Journal of Aging and Human Development, 37,* 261–269.

Stahl, A. (1993b). Educating for change in attitudes toward nature and environment among Oriental Jews in Israel. *Environment and Behavior, 25,* 3–21.

MaryAnna Domokos-Cheng Ham

ORTHOGONAL CULTURAL IDENTIFICATION THEORY—The conceptualization of personal cultural identification based on the proposition that an individual may identify with two or more cultures and that each culture exists in an independent dimension (i.e., they are "orthogonal" to each other). The most critical aspect of the theory is that cultures do not necessarily compete for allegiance within the individual. A person may participate fully in one culture and still have the capacity to incorporate the values, beliefs, and behaviors of another culture without any detriment to or loss from the original culture. The person may also be anomic, with a weak identification with any of the cultures within his/her environment. The theory was first applied by Oetting and Beauvais (1991) in examining the psychosocial characteristics related to the use of drugs by minority youth. Elements of the theory were later expanded by Oetting (1993). Central to the theory is the notion that cultural identification is a personal trait that emerges from the interaction of the individual with the cultural environment. The person whose beliefs, values and behaviors are congruent with the environment is rewarded by that environment and consequently has a "stake" (Ferguson, 1976) in that culture. Conversely, if the environment is not rewarding, no stake develops and the individual will not acquire a sense of identification with the culture, will not be involved in cultural activities, and will not feel a sense of future success in that culture. Most importantly, there is no barrier to multiple sets of beliefs, values, and behaviors that interact with and are rewarded by matching environments, thus the possibility of multicultural individuals. This differs from other past and current models of cultural identification that are linear and implicitly contain the notion that bicultural or multicultural identification involve acculturation stress—that is, as an individual moves from one culture to another, he/she will inevitably encounter loss and conflict in the process. *Orthogonal Cultural Identification Theory* indicates that there are many possible paths for changing cultural identification, and that stress occurs only when the individual fails to meet cultural requirements or the relevant culture fails to meet that person's needs.

References

Ferguson, F. (1976). Stake theory as an explanatory device in Navajo alcoholism treatment response. *Human Organization, 35*, 65–78.

Oetting, E. (1993). The theoretical links between cultural identification and substance use. In M. De La Rosa (Ed.), *Drug abuse among minority youth: Methodological issues and recent research advances* (pp. 32–56). Rockville, MD: National Institute on Drug Abuse (Research Monograph #30, NIH Pub. #93–3479).

Oetting, E., & Beauvais, F. (1991). Orthogonal cultural identification theory: The cultural identification of minority adolescents. *The International Journal of the Addictions, 25*, p. 655–685.

Fred Beauvais

OVERT INTENTIONAL RACISM—A form of racism that can occur at both the individual and institutional levels. According to Ridley (1989, 1995), this form of racism is the type about which most people are aware and is a conscious process of discrimination by the perpetrator. For example, at the individual level, a teacher who openly believes that ethnic minority students are less motivated than their White counterparts may assign these ethnic minority students to less desirable educational experiences. At an institutional level, administrators at an exclusive private college may believe that ethnic minority students will detract from the school's prestige, so they may instruct college recruiters not to visit high schools of predominately ethnic minority student bodies. *Overt intentional racism* contrasts with *covert intentional racism* (see COVERT INTENTIONAL RACISM), where the individual or institution is more subtle in discriminatory practices.

References

Ridley, C. R. (1989). Racism in counseling as an adverse behavioral process. In P. B. Pedersen, J. G. Draguns, W. J. Lonner, & J. E. Trimble (Eds.), *Counseling across cultures* (3rd ed., pp. 55–77). Honolulu: University of Hawaii Press.

Ridley, C. R. (1995). *Overcoming unintentional racism in counseling and therapy: A practitioner's guide to intentional intervention.* Thousand Oaks, CA: Sage.

Jeffery Scott Mio

P

PACIFIC ISLANDERS—Natives, inhabitants, or descendents of an island in the Pacific Ocean. There are over 25,000 islands in the Pacific. These island are identified by three geographic areas: Polynesia (many islands), Micronesia (tiny islands), and Melanesia (black islands; Barringer, Gardner, & Levin, 1993). Polynesia is the largest in area, spanning approximately 39 million square kilometers. It covers a large triangle with the three points formed by Hawaii, New Zealand, and Pitcairn Islands. Polynesia includes American Samoa (a territory of the United States), Cook Islands, Easter Island, French Polynesia, Niue, Norfalk Islands, Tonga, Tokelau, Tuvalu, Wallis and Fatuna, and Western Samoa. Most Fijians are primarily of Melanesian racial stock but have more in common with Polynesians (Barringer et al., 1993; Howe, Kiste, & Lal, 1994). Micronesia is a large oval at the equator, consisting of the U.S. Territory of Guam, the Commonwealth of the Northern Marianas, the Federated States of Micronesia, the Republic of the Marshall Islands, the Republic of Palau, Nauru, and Kiribati. Melanesia, the largest in population, is south of Micronesia and to the west of Polynesia. Melanesia includes Paupua New Guinea, Solomon Islands, Vanuatu, and New Caledonia. According to Barringer et al. (1993), the 1990 U.S. Census recorded over 365,000 Pacific Islanders living in the United States. The largest groups were Hawaiians (221,014), Samoans (62,964), Guamanians (49,345), Tongans (17,606), and Fijians (7,036).

References

Barringer, H. R., Gardner, R. W., & Levin, M. J. (1993). *Asian and Pacific Islanders in the United States*. New York: Russell Sage.

Howe, K. R., Kiste, R. C., & Lal, B. V. (Eds.). (1994). *Tides of history: The Pacific Islands in the Twentieth Century*. Honolulu: University of Hawaii Press.

Patricia Taimanglo Pier

PARALANGUAGE—Refers to the system of non-phonemic but vocal patterns and cues in speech that are used in communication. It includes tone and loudness of voice, silences, tempo of speech, inflections, pauses, and hesitations. *Paralanguage* is embedded in daily communication such as in the ways we greet or take turns in speaking. The rules of paralanguage are particularly complex in communication between people of different cultures (Jensen, 1985). Hall (1976) illustrates this complexity with the perception of silence. While White Americans try to avoid silence, Japanese and Chinese individuals may see silence as a sign of respect and politeness. A cross-cultural appreciation of the different meanings that silence may have is critical; filling the gaps of silence with talking may not be welcomed with individuals of other cultural groups. In the counseling realm, a Western oriented counselor who may be uncomfortable with silence may try to verbally process the information just discussed. This may prevent the client from elaborating further (Sue & Sue, 1990). The client's silence may also be interpreted as a form of resistance or unwillingness to cooperate with the counselor. Volume and intensity are also viewed differently from culture to culture. Whereas in some countries loud speech and music is acceptable, these may be viewed as lack of respect and invasion of one's privacy in another culture. Some may also automatically interpret a louder volume of speech as a sign of anger and a softer volume of speech as a sign of weakness or depression, although just the opposite may be true in another culture or under different circumstances.

References

Hall, E. T. (1976). *Beyond culture*. New York: Anchor Press.
Jensen, J. V. (1985). Perspective on nonverbal intercultural communication. In L. A. Samovar & R. E. Porter (Eds.), *Intercultural communication: A reader*. Belmont, CA: Wadsworth.
Sue, D. W., & Sue, D. (1990). *Counseling the culturally different: Theory and practice* (2nd ed.). New York: Wiley.

Rakefet Richmond

PATERNALISTIC RACISM—*Paternalism* is manifested in the systemic contention that those in authority have a responsibility to ensure the well-being of others. In doing so, the authority figures draw upon their own cultural framework to determine the attitudes, behaviors, values, and beliefs that will be both positively and negatively reinforced. Both forms of reinforcement promote and inculcate the indoctrination of the authority's worldview at the expense of alternative and equally valid perspectives. In addition, those being controlled eventually learn to rely on the authority for guidance. The manifestation of this phenomenon in general, and within cross-cultural counseling dyads in particular, has been identified as a threat to psychological assessment and subsequent treatment (Sue & Sue, 1990). Racism is manifested in the justification that those assuming the position of authority are entitled to their status by virtue of perceived and asserted superiority. Despite evidence to the contrary, persons in authority uphold their perceptions (and the privilege associated with them) at all costs. Comer (1991) characterized such behavior as "a low level defense and adjustment mechanism utilized by groups to deal with psychological and social insecurities" (p. 591). These defenses, in turn, foster pathology in the form of acting out, denial of reality, projection, transference of blame, dissociation, and justification (Delaney, 1991). Within the social science literature, paternalism has been identified as a theory as opposed to a type of racism. This theory was examined in ESSED's (1991) comparative analysis of Black women representing the U.S. and the Netherlands. In sharing their experiences with and interpretations of racism, it was noted that the Black women of the U.S. adopted a conflict orientation while the Dutch subscribed to a paternalistic view (see OPPRESSION). The conflict model of racism operates on the premise that racism is unjustifiable, and it seeks to challenge the distribution of societal power with the objective of replacing it with equality at the forefront. Conversely, acceptance of the status quo and feelings of powerlessness reflect the paternalistic paradigm.

References

Comer, J. P. (1991). White racism: Its root, form, and function. In R. L. Jones (Ed.), *Black psychology* (pp. 591–596). San Francisco: Cobb and Henry.

Delaney, L. T. (1991). The other bodies in the river. In R. L. Jones (Ed.), *Black psychology* (pp. 597–607). San Francisco: Cobb and Henry.

ESSED, P. (1991). Knowledge and resistance: Black women talk about racism in the Netherlands and the USA. *Feminism & Psychology, 1,* 201–219.

Sue, D. W., & Sue, D. (1990). *Counseling the culturally different: Theory and practice* (2nd ed.). New York: Wiley.

Angela M. White

PEER CLUSTER THEORY—The developmental process that describes how adolescents aggregate into small clusters of peers (or dyads) and how attitudes, beliefs, values, and behaviors are shaped by the interactions that occur within these groups. Early socialization processes (primarily within the family), school adjustment, and emotional characteristics are the bases upon which peer group associations develop. Youth who have had similar family experiences and who share common psychological characteristics are more likely to select each other as friends and form compatible peer clusters. *Peer Cluster Theory* places a strong emphasis on the norming that occurs within the group where each member contributes significantly to the dynamics of the group. In this sense, the theory differs from the commonly attributed process of "peer pressure" or from the theory of "differential association" (Sutherland & Cressey, 1970). The theory was first proposed by Oetting and Beauvais (1986) in describing the development of drug use patterns among adolescents and was later extended by Oetting (1992) to describe a wider range of deviant behaviors. The theory has been tested in a number of contexts, and it has been demonstrated that the variables specified by the theory account for the largest proportion of variance in the prediction of drug use (Swaim, Oetting, Edwards, & Beauvais, 1989; Swaim, Oetting, Thurman, Beauvais, & Edwards, 1993). While Peer Cluster Theory has been tested and validated on a number of ethnic minority populations, it is important to note that the relative influence of peer clusters, compared to other socialization factors such as family influence, may vary by culture. It should be recognized that Peer Cluster Theory, while its original application was to the problem of deviance, it is a more general theory of adolescent development and is essential in describing the adolescent socialization process. Peer clusters operate equally effectively in the promotion of deviance and positive and prosocial behavior. From this perspective, intervention approaches to the prevention or treatment of deviance must address the issues of reforming the peer environment of individuals, preventing the formation of deviant peer clusters, breaking up of negative peer clusters, and the formation of positive peer clusters.

References

Oetting, E. (1992). Planning programs for prevention of deviant behavior: A psychosocial model. In J. Trimble, C. Bolek, & S. Niemcryk (Eds.), *Ethnic and multicultural drug abuse* (pp. 313–334). Binghamton, NY: Haworth Press.

Oetting, E., & Beauvais, F. (1986). Peer cluster theory: Drugs and the adolescent. *Journal of Counseling and Development, 65*, 17–22.

Oetting, E., & Beauvais, F. (1987). Peer cluster theory, socialization characteristics and adolescent drug use: A path analysis. *Journal of Counseling Psychology, 34*, 205–213.

Sutherland, E., & Cressey, D. (1970). *Criminology.* Philadelphia: Lippincott.

Swaim, R., Oetting, E., Edwards, R., and Beauvais, F. (1989). The links from emotional distress to adolescent drug use: A path model. *Journal of Consulting and Clinical Psychology, 57*, 227–231.

Swaim, R., Oetting, E., Thurman, P., Beauvais, F., & Edwards, R. (1993). American Indian adolescent drug use and socialization characteristics: A cross-cultural comparison. *Journal of Cross-Cultural Psychology, 24*, 53–70.

Fred Beauvais

PERSONALISMO—A cultural trait typical of many Latino groups (e.g., Cubans, Mexicans, and Puerto Ricans) in which high importance is given to the qualities of positive interpersonal and social skills and trust (Comaz-Diaz, 1985). An individual who demonstrates this cultural trait often takes a leadership role and is characterized as being charismatic (Hauberg, 1974).

References

Comas-Diaz, L. (1985). Effects of cognitive and behavioral group therapy with Puerto Rican women: A comparison of content themes. *Hispanic Journal of Behavioral Sciences, 7,* 273–282.
Hauberg, C. A. (1974). *Puerto Rico and the Puerto Ricans.* New York: Twayne.

Azara L. Santiago-Rivera

PLURALISM—Popularized in the late nineteenth century after having been introduced in response to the industrialization of Europe (Sills, 1968). At that time, *pluralism* was considered to be a mechanism for fostering a sense of community despite economic trends to the contrary (e.g., the technological replacement of individuals in the workplace). It involved the creation of alternative environments designed to promote personal development via human connection. This view of pluralism is grounded in the ecclesiastical and philosophical principles advanced in the *Oxford English Dictionary* (Simpson & Weiner, 1989). As a whole, these principles set forth the notion that more than one ultimate reality exists (see MULTIPLE PERSPECTIVES). Given the notion of multiple realities, cultural diversity as well as human commonalities are respected and provided an opportunity for full expression (Bernstein, 1987; Bolin, 1996). With the context of multiculturalism, pluralism transcends the mere acknowledgment of diverse realities. Instead, it seeks to incorporate these realities into existing institutional structures. In doing so, those representing various worldviews have access to a number of tools required for success in a given environment. Success is gauged by the extent to which the vision that is upheld by an institution is actualized by its members (Cheatham, 1991).

References

Bernstein, R. J. (1987). The varieties of pluralism. *American Journal of Education, 95,* 509–525.
Bolin, B. (1996). Pluralism: Coming to terms. *English Journal, 85,* 101–102.
Cheatham, H. E. (1991). *Cultural pluralism on campus.* Alexandria, VA: American College Personnel Association.
Sills, D. L. (1968). *International encyclopedia of the social sciences.* New York: MacMillan and The Free Press.
Simpson, J. A., & Weiner, E.S.C. (Eds.). (1989). *The Oxford English dictionary* (2nd ed.). Oxford: Oxford University Press.

Angela M. White

POLITICALLY CORRECT—Coined originally to render support for multiculturalism by addressing the power that language has to oppress. Language is oppressive when it is used intentionally or unintentionally in ways that threaten the human rights of others in general and of cultural minorities particularly. The nature of the threat posed is contingent upon the subjective experience of the individual(s) at whom it was directed. The threat can have intellectual, emotional, spiritual, social, and/or physical ramifications. With that in mind, the selection of word choices that minimize the ramifications advanced exemplify political correctness (Pedersen, 1991; Ridley, Mendoza, & Kanitz, 1994). Such words reflect cultural sensitivity, respect for individual differences, and the acknowledgement that the salience of word usage has the potential to change over time (e.g., the evolution of reference made to *African Americans* from *Negro* to *Colored* to *Black*). Although the adherence to a politically correct style of language has been identified as a step towards multiculturalism, the strategies employed have become quite controversial. One issue raised involves the extent to which the constitutional right of freedom of speech can be compromised in service of equal protection under the law. A second issue that has emerged confronts the purpose of adopting a politically correct ideology. Specifically, it is argued that changes in verbalizations do not ensure attitudinal reform. Instead, it requires that individuals become savvy at saying the "right" things to the "right" people under the "right" circumstances. It should be noted that the original intent of this term has been muted and countered as the political right purloined it and employed it as negative in intent; that is to "police" the speech of those opposing such liberal thought and doctrine as multiculturalism.

References

Pedersen, P. B. (1991). Multiculturalism as a generic approach to counseling. *Journal of Counseling and Development, 70*, 6–12.
Ridley, C., Mendoza, D., & Kanitz, B. (1994). Multicultural training: Reexamination, operationalization, and integration. *Counseling Psychology, 22*, 227–289.

Angela M. White

POPOL VUH—The most important surviving work of Maya literature in the Latin alphabet, written by a young nobleman from Quiche. According to Edmonson (1996), the *Popol Vuh* is "the most impressive work of literature written to date by a native American author. Often called the 'American Bible,' it is a Mayan description of the creation and evolution of the world" (p. 431).

Reference

Edmonson, M. S. (1996). In B. A. Tenenbaum, G. M. Magassy, M. Karasch, J. J. TePaske, & R. L. Woodward, Jr. (Eds.), *Encyclopedia of Latin American history and culture* (Vol. 4, pp. 431–432). New York: Charles Scribner's Sons.

Cindy Yee and Jeffery Scott Mio

POWER—The concept of power should not be limited to the idea that it is the ability to use force or coercion on other persons or groups. Domhoff (1998) proposed *class-domination* theory and defined power as "the capacity of some persons to produce intended and foreseen effects on others" (p. 18). There are four indicators of power: (1) Who benefits? (2) Who governs? (3) Who wins? (4) Who shines? According to Domhoff, all four of these indicators point toward the "power elite" in America, which consists of the corporate community, social upper class, and the policy-formation organization. The corporate community earns much of the nation's large income. This community naturally forms the social upper class, and it feeds into policy-formation organizations. In America, this class generally consists of White males. Although there are ethnic minorities and women in government and top executive positions, most of them are from the social upper class similar in thought and opinions to White males in the corporate community. Alternative theories to power are *pluralism* and *state-centered theory*. The idea behind pluralism is that power is dispersed among groups and classes and no one dominant group holds the power. In general, this theory holds that the general public has the power through pressuring elected officials for whom they voted into office. Another version of pluralism is that power is rooted in the interest groups that are working for certain organizations such as bankers, labor unions, and environmentalists. Proponents of this theory hold that businesses are too fragmented to form one cohesive group. Domhoff (1998) argues, however, that business interest groups are part of a corporate community that is "able to develop class-wide cohesion on the issues of greatest concern to it: Opposition to unions, high taxes, and government regulation" (p. 10). State-centered theory recognizes the government's potential to dominate and shape private groups. It holds that the government has "autonomy" over states with its power to tax, and its power to protect the country from foreign attacks. Again, however, Domhoff argues that because most government officials are greatly influenced by big corporations in order to win elections, the state-centered theory of power is merely a version of his class-domination theory.

Reference

Domhoff, G. W. (1998). *Who rules America?* Mountain View, CA: Mayfield.

Gangaw Zaw

PREJUDICE—Used as early as 1290 by Becton (although not as it is currently construed; Simpson & Weiner, 1989) and was elaborated in the social science literature by Otto Klineberg (1968). Cognitive, affective, and behavioral components comprise prejudice. Cognitively, prejudice involves the formation of preconceived judgments or opinions occurring in the absence of relevant information lending support for them. As a result, the information processed is based on either inadequate or imaginary evidence (see STEREOTYPE). Affectively, the stereotypes comprising the cognitive aspect of prejudice provide the rationalization for attitudes regarding the ascription of positive or negative valence. Behaviorally, prejudice consists of a readiness to express, through one's actions, the judgments and feelings one experiences (although the behavioral component is typically reserved for *discrimination* as opposed to *prejudice*; see DISCRIMINATION). Alternatively, prejudice has been defined as *social discrimination of the invalid type* (Klineberg, 1968). Social discrimination includes the persistent application of criteria that are arbitrary, irrelevant, or unfair by dominant standards, with the result that some persons receive undue advantage and others, although equally qualified, suffer an unjust penalty ("unequal treatment of equals" or "equal treatment of unequals"). The preferred definition of *prejudice* is Klineberg's (1968) conceptualization with modifications. Utilizing Klineberg's framework, prejudices can be positive or negative, and they can be directed toward objects and people alike. Currently, the word has been used primarily to describe negative aspects of people distinct from oneself (Jones, 1972). These negative judgments are a function of ethnocentrism (McGoldrick, Pearce, & Giordano, 1982; see ETHNOCENTRISM) and are perpetuated as a means of securing self-esteem. According to social identity theory, the in-group is almost always favored over the out-group. When threats to in-group membership are posed, the need for in-group favoritism is increased (Tajfel, 1982).

References

Jones, R. L. (1972). Labeling children culturally deprived and culturally disadvantaged. In R. L. Jones (Ed.), *Black psychology* (pp. 285–294). New York: Harper & Row.

Klineberg, O. (1968). Prejudice: The concept. In D. L. Sills (Ed.), *International encyclopedia of the social sciences* (Vol. 12, pp. 439–448). New York: Macmillan & The Free Press.

McGoldrick, M., Pearce, J. K., & Giordano, J. (Eds.). (1982). *Ethnicity and family therapy*. New York: Guilford.

Simpson, J. A., & Weiner, E.S.C. (Eds.). (1989). *The Oxford English dictionary* (2nd ed.). Oxford: Oxford University Press.

Tajfel, H. (1982). Social psychology of intergroup attitudes. *Annual Review of Psychology, 33*, 1–39.

Angela M. White

PROXEMICS—Refers to the perception and use of personal and interpersonal space in interactions. Certain norms seem to exist concerning the use of distance or closeness in social interactions. In this regard, Hall (1976) was among the first who identified distance zones that seemed to be exemplified in culture within the United States. These were *intimate* (contact to 18 inches), *personal* (from 1½ to 4 feet), *social* (from 4 to 12 feet), and *public* as in speeches or lectures, greater than 12 feet (Sue & Sue, 1990). *Proxemics* is related to other basic aspects of communication such as *kinesics* (body gestures and movements while conveying messages) or *paralanguage* (vocal cues, volume of speech, timing of speaking or not speaking). However, *proxemics* (or in this context, space in communication) may be a major initial goal of attaining multicultural counseling competency, as many different cultures have different rules for personal space considerations.

References

Hall, E. T. (1976). *Beyond culture*. New York: Anchor Press/Doubleday.

Sue, D. W., & Sue, D. (1990). *Counseling the culturally different: Theory and practice* (2nd ed.). New York: Wiley.

Matthew R. Mock

PSYCHOMETRIC EQUIVALENCE—Refers to a yardstick or metric that "can be used to measure the same concept in two or more cultures" (Okazaki & Sue, 1995, p. 371). *Psychometric equivalency* holds whenever a statistical parameter (e.g., a test mean, an item variance, a factor loading) is shown to be similar across cultures. Historically, *metric, scalar,* and *factorial equivalency* have been presented as synonyms for, or subclasses of, *psychometric equivalency* (see CULTURAL EQUIVALENCE). Today, clearer distinctions are made among *relational, factorial, structural,* and *measurement equivalency*, which are roughly associated with *correlation/regression analysis, factor analysis, structural equation modeling,* and *item response theory*, respectively (Hui & Triandis, 1985). To understand structural and measurement equivalency, it helps to draw a distinction between *latent constructs* (or factors) and their *overt indicators* (or observed variables). Following Drasgow (1987), most psychometricians now described the relation of a latent construct with its indicators as a topic of measurement equivalency. In contrast, the relation of one latent construct with other latent constructs is called *structural equivalency* (Van de Vijver & Leung, 1997). For example, measurement equivalence explores the relationship between a latent construct (e.g., depression) and its indicators (insomnia, social isolation, negative affect) across two or more cultures. Measurement equivalency asks: Does the construct of depression have the same pattern of indicators across cultures? In other words, structural equivalency addresses the question of whether depression means the same thing across cultures by indexing depression's relationship with other relevant constructs (anxiety, finances, lithium) across cultures. Subcategories aside, it is important to note that none of the above statistical techniques assume or guarantee that equivalency across cultures can be achieved. The techniques simply render statistical parameters (e.g., regression weights) in one group that can then be compared with the same parameter in another group. Such comparisons are empirical, numerical, and usefully scientific. Even so, most psychometricians admit that they cannot quantify all conceivable forms of equivalence. For this and other reasons (Darlington, 1971), psychometric equivalency and nonequivalency remain somewhat wedded to policy decisions regarding fairness and bias.

References

Darlington, R. B. (1971). Another look at "cultural fairness." *Journal of Educational Measurement, 8,* 71–82.

Drasgow, F. (1987). Study of the measurement bias of two standardized psychological tests. *Journal of Applied Psychology, 19,* 19–29.

Hui, C. H., & Triandis, H. C. (1985). Measurement in cross-cultural psychology. *Journal of Cross-Cultural Psychology, 16,* 131–152.

Okazaki, S., & Sue, S. (1993). Methodological issues in assessment research with ethnic minorities. *Psychological Assessment, 7,* 367–375.

Van de Vijver, F., & Leung, K. (1997). Methods and data analysis of comparative data research. In J. Berry, Y. H. Poortinga, & J. Pandey (Eds.), *Handbook of cross-cultural psychology.* Boston: Allyn and Bacon.

William Peter Flannery

PUERTO RICAN—A term describing individuals who were born on the island of Puerto Rico, who trace their ancestors to Puerto Rico, or who identify with Puerto Rican culture and traditions. Puerto Rican cultural and racial ancestry may be a mixture of native indigenous "Taino," Spanish, African, and other European groups. This mixture of races contributes to the diversity within Puerto Ricans, yet a common cultural heritage fosters values such as allocentrism, belief in spirituality, dignity of the individual, respect for authority, control of aggression, and close ties with extended family to include a network of "kin" (Garcia-Preto, 1982).

Reference

Garcia-Preto, N. (1982). Puerto Rican families. In M. McGoldrick, J. K. Pearce, & J. Giordano (Eds.), *Ethnicity and family therapy* (pp. 164–186). New York: Guilford.

Sandra I. Lopez-Baez

R

RACE—*Race* is a controversial concept the origin of which can be traced to the Swedish taxonomist Carolus Linnaeus (1735; Montague, 1974), who said that human beings come from four types: *Americanus*, *Asiaticus*, *Africanus*, and *Europeaeus*. Genetic studies by contemporary scientists indicate that traits assumed to be factors of "race" (i.e., hair texture, skin color, eye color, and facial features) are basically superficial and thus make the attempt to classify *Homo sapiens* into "races" a futile exercise (Rogers, 1952). While many scientists believe *race* cannot be accurately defined (Allport, 1958; Montague, 1974), they also concede that this concept will continue to be used to categorize people into one of four groups: Asian, Black, White, or American Indian. Migrations and contact between human populations have caused the human gene pools to be mixed to a degree that is sufficient to make racial classifications inaccurate and unscientific. Wright (1994) wrote, "Whatever the word 'race' may mean elsewhere in the world or to the world of science, it is clear that in America the categories are arbitrary, confused and hopelessly intermingled" (p. 53). Although many educational, governmental, and military institutions still use racial classifications and identities, new data on genetics makes such classifications scientifically meaningless.

References

Allport, G. W. (1958). *The nature of prejudice*. New York: Doubleday Anchor.
Montague, A. (1974). *Man's most dangerous myth: The fallacy of race* (5th ed.). London: Oxford University Press.
Rogers, J. A. (1952). *Nature knows no color line*. New York: Helga M. Rogers.
Wright, L. (1994, July 25). One drop of blood. *The New Yorker*, 46–55.

Lawrence W. Young, Jr.

RACIAL/ETHNIC PRIDE—The knowledge, acceptance, and perpetuation of the total range of contribution from one's racial/ethnic group; from this recognition comes empowerment. Racial/ethnic pride is intricately woven into universal human experiences that are earmarked as vibrant, multidimensional, and adaptable for ongoing life-affirming patterns for future generations (Rogers, 1952, 1971). With respect to Americans of African descent, this has led to determining an acceptable name: African Americans (Browder, 1992). Recognition and acceptance of the appellation *African American* by people of African descent has evolved out of necessity. Historically biased nomenclatures that are inappropriate, inaccurate, and insensitive to the existence and contributions of an entire race of people have necessitated a reclaiming of self-identity, self-pride, and a positive self-image. Because of the diverse populations and varied geographical homelands of Africans in the diaspora, maintaining a sense of self-knowledge and self-acceptance has been minimized and deliberately discouraged by historians and chroniclers (Browder, 1992). However, through preserved oral and written history by African peoples (e.g., Fanon, 1967), much of the pride and recognition comes from the knowledge of African roots producing knowledge, beauty, and spiritual concepts that are enjoyed and practiced throughout today's world. Science, technology, arts, and religions commonly bear fundamental elements from Egypt, Kimet, Mali, Ghana, Songhai, Punt, Ethiopia, and the Zulu and Zimbabwean Empires (Browder, 1992). The cultural bindings that promote racial/ethnic pride for African Americans includes: gatherings and rituals; various rites of passage (e.g., birth, marriage, graduations, promotions, and death); music, motion, rhythm, and entertainment; and creative innovations in language usage.

References

Browder, A. T. (1992). *Nile Valley contributions to civilization*. Washington, DC: The Institute of Karmic Guidance.
Fanon, F. (1967). *A dying colonialism*. New York: Grove Press.
Rogers, J. A. (1952). *Nature knows no color-line*. New York: Helga M. Rogers.
Rogers, J. A. (1971). *From "Superman" to man*. New York: Helga M. Rogers.

Tengamana Mapule Thumbutu

RACISM—Used first by anthropologist Ruth Benedict in the 1940s, *racism* was influenced by the French word *racisme* (Benedict, 1943; Goldberg, 1993). The central tenet of racism as used by Benedict is built on either real or perceived biological distinctions among groups of people. Since biological distinctions were not made prior to the nineteenth century, racism did not exist prior to that time. Slavery and other social injustices did occur, but they were not based upon biological distinctions, therefore, they did not constitute racism. Between 1853 and 1857, Count de Gobineau published the "Essay on the Inequality of Human Races." This essay is considered to be the classic writing, which established racist thought (Benedict, 1943). Only the dominant group can practice racism. Subordinate groups cannot practice racism, because racism is a politically based phenomenon that combines prejudice and discriminatory exclusion. The political construct of racism can be observed historically by Ammon's Law (nineteenth-century Europe), which proposed that *long-heads* were superior to *narrow-heads* (Benedict, 1943), and by Nazi Germany during World War I and World War II, who did not subject their Japanese Allies to racist exclusion (Goldberg, 1993). The immigrant groups to the United States during the twentieth century who endured racism upon their arrival to the United States present a more modern example of the political nature of racism. Racism can be practiced on the individual or the societal level. At the individual level, racism is directed towards a specific person. At the societal level, institutional racism occurs in the policies, norms, and laws which are ingrained into the social fabric of either the institution or the society, in either a blatant or subtle manner. This institutional racism either directly or indirectly harms the subordinate group(s). A person who believes he/she is a nonracist may be guilty of perpetuating institutional racism whether or not it is acknowledged (Rothenberg, 1995). In the United States, a distinction must be made between *old-fashioned racism* and *modern racism* (McConahay, 1986). Old-fashioned racism is an ideology used to justify past oppression such as stereotypes, segregation, and overt discrimination. Modern racism is ''the expression in terms of abstract ideological symbols and symbolic behaviors of the feeling that Blacks (or other subordinate groups) are violating cherished values in the racial status quo'' (McConahay & Hough, 1976). Whether the distinction between old-fashioned racism and modern racism is generalizable to countries outside of the United States has yet to be determined by academicians.

References

Benedict, R. (1943). *Race and racism*. Great Britain: University Press.
Goldberg, D. T. (1993). *Racist culture: Philosophy and the politics of meaning*. Cambridge, MA: Blackwell.
McConahay, J. B. (1986). Modern racism, ambivalence, and the Modern Racism Scale. In J. F. Dovidio & S. L. Gaertner (Eds.), *Prejudice, discrimination and racism* (pp. 91–125). New York: Academic Press.
McConahay, J. B., & Hough, J. C. (1976). Symbolic racism. *Journal of Social Issues, 32*, 23–45.
Rothenberg, P. S. (1995). *Race, class and gender in the United States: An integrated study* (3rd ed.). New York: St. Martin's Press.

John Johnson

REFUGEE—Someone who flees one country to live in another country due to ''natural disasters such as drought or famine or because of political, religious, or racial repression'' (Huang, 1989, p. 278). *Refugees* should not be confused with *immigrants*, who travel to another country in a planned fashion. Such planning is most frequently preceded by months or years of learning about the customs and manners of the host country; refugees tend to need to flee their country of origin in a very brief period, so such acculturative steps are not made. As a consequence, refugees often experience psychological adjustment problems, such as depression (Kinzie, Sack, Angell, Manson, & Rath, 1986), withdrawal (Sack, Angell, Kinzie, & Rath, 1986), and identity development (Tobin & Freidman, 1984). Moreover, those Southeast Asian refugees who were exposed to war in their countries of origin were found to experience enduring effects of posttraumatic stress disorder (Abe, Zane, & Chun, 1994; Kinzie, Sack, Angell, Clarke, & Rath, 1989). However, these reactions were found among those who were directly exposed to war and who were among their country's lower socioeconomic backgrounds. The Vietnamese immigrants who came right after the fall of South Vietnam, and who were among the economically and educationally elite of the country, tended to have relatively few problems of adjustment (Lee & Zhan, 1998; Sokoloff, Carlin, & Pham, 1984).

References

Abe, J. S., Zane, N. W., & Chun, K. (1994). Differential responses to trauma: Migration-related discriminants of post-traumatic stress among Southeast Asian refugees. *Journal of Community Psychology, 22*, 121–135.

Huang, L. N. (1989). Southeast Asian refugee children and adolescents. In J. T. Gibbs, L. N. Huang, & Associates (Eds.), *Children of color: Psychological interventions with minority youth* (pp. 278–321). San Francisco: Jossey-Bass.

Kinzie, J. D., Sack, W. H., Angell, R. H., Clarke, G., & Rath, B. (1989). A three-year follow-up of Cambodian young people traumatized as children. *Journal of American Academy of Child and Adolescent Psychiatry, 28*, 501–504.

Kinzie, J. D., Sack, W. H., Angell, R. H., Manson, S., & Rath, B. (1986). The psychiatric effects of massive trauma on Cambodian children: The children. *Journal of the American Academy of Child Psychiatry, 25*, 370–376.

Lee, L. C., & Zhan, G. (1998). Psychosocial status of children and youths. In L. C. Lee & N.W.S. Zane (Eds.), *Handbook of Asian American psychology* (pp. 137–163). Thousand Oaks, CA: Sage.

Sack, W. H., Angell, R. H., Kinzie, J. D., & Rath, B. (1986). The psychiatric effects of massive trauma on Cambodian children: The family, the home, and the school. *Journal of the American Academy of Child Psychiatry, 25*, 377–383.

Sokoloff, B., Carlin, J., & Pham, H. (1984). Five-year follow-up of Vietnamese refugee children in the United States. *Clinical Pediatrics, 10*, 565–570.

Tobin, J. J., & Friedman, J. (1984). Intercultural and developmental stresses confronting Southeast Asian refugee adolescents. *Journal of Operational Psychiatry, 15*, 39–45.

Jeffery Scott Mio

RESISTANCE AND IMMERSION STAGE—A stage of identity development proposed by Atkinson, Morten, and Sue (1989) that suggests that the individual who has been exposed to either some sort of racist incident or an extremely fulfilling positive experience with his/her own ethnic group rejects the majority group and entirely immerses him-/herself into his/her own racial/

ethnic group. The rejection of the majority group comes in the form of the perception that the majority group is oppressive, so all representations of the group are rejected in favor of one's own group. With respect to other ethnic minority groups, there tends to be a conflict between one's desire to feel empathy to other groups that may have experienced the same degree of oppression by the dominant society and one's developing ethnocentrism. This stage is similar to Cross's (1971, 1995) *Immersion–Emersion Stage* for African Americans, Ponterotto's (1988) *Immersion Stage* for ethnic minorities, and Helms's (1990, 1995) *Immersion/Emersion Stage* or *Status* for Whites.

References

Atkinson, D. R., Morten, G., & Sue, D. W. (1989). *Counseling American minorities: A cross-cultural perspective* (3rd ed.). Dubuque, IA: Brown.

Cross, W. E., Jr. (1971). The Negro-to-Black conversion experience: Toward a psychology of Black liberation. *Black World, 20,* 13–27.

Cross, W. E., Jr. (1995). The psychology of nigrescence: Revising the Cross model. In J. G. Ponterotto, J. M. Casas, L. A. Suzuki, & C. M. Alexander (Eds.), *Handbook of multicultural counseling* (pp. 93–122). Thousand Oaks, CA: Sage.

Helms, J. E. (Ed.). (1990). *Black and White racial identity: Theory, research, and practice.* Westport, CT: Greenwood Press.

Helms, J. E. (1995). An update of Helms's White and people of color racial identity models. In J. G. Ponterotto, J. M. Casas, L. A. Suzuki, & C. M. Alexander (Eds.), *Handbook of multicultural counseling* (pp. 181–198). Thousand Oaks, CA: Sage.

Ponterotto, J. G. (1988). Racial consciousness development among White counselor trainees. *Journal of Multicultural Counseling and Development, 16,* 146–156.

Jeffery Scott Mio

REVERSE RACISM—*Racism* has been defined as any attitude, action, or institutional structure that subordinates people because of their color (see RACISM). Racism is not simply a matter of attitudes; actions and institutional structures can also be a form of racism. Racism involves having the *power* to carry out systematic discriminatory practices through the major institutions of our society (Feagin & Vera, 1955; Franklin, 1991). The term *reverse racism* would imply that societal victims of racism would amass the wherewithal to impose racist actions, attitudes, or institutional structures that subordinate White Americans in the manner that people of color had traditionally been subordinated. While it may be possible for an individual (a person of color) to so impact another individual (a White American), the likelihood of any such large-scale movement is remote, if not impossible. The major obstacle to such a turn of events is control of institutions of power. To carry out systematic discrimination against Whites, thus, would require control over major institutions, including but not limited to courts, police, government, finance, housing, employment, and education. There is no known instance in the United States where such unchallenged control has ever existed. Thus, while people of color may be prejudiced, may despise or hate, or may even discriminate, they lack the power and authority to carry out a racist imperative: to systematically subordinate, marginalize, or proscribe the lives of White Americans (Williams, 1991). In sum, reverse racism may be defined as a "straw man," an imaginary opposite to White racism.

References

Feagin, J., & Vera, H. (1955). *White racism.* New York: Routledge.
Franklin, R. S. (1991). *Shadows of race and class.* Minneapolis: University of Minnesota Press.
Williams, P. J. (1991). *The alchemy of race and rights.* Cambridge, MA: Harvard University Press.

Lawrence W. Young, Jr.

S

SANSEI—Third generation Japanese American. According to the Japanese language, individuals who immigrated to the United States are called *Issei*, or "first generation." The children of the *Issei* were referred to as *Nisei*, which means "second generation." American and European languages would typically refer to the *Nisei* generation as "first generation of Americans," because this generation was the first to be born in the United States. The *Sansei* were the children of the *Nisei*, born and educated in the United States (Mish, 1994).

Reference

Mish, F. C. (Ed.). (1994). *Merriam-Webster's collegiate dictionary* (10th ed.). Springfield, MA: Merriam-Webster.

Patricia J. Matsumoto

SANTERIA—A religion based on Yoruba traditions and spiritual beliefs of West African slaves, brought to Cuba over a 350-year slave period. Forbidden to practice their own religion, slaves pretended to adopt the Roman Catholic saints, but secretly assigned their names and images to various Yoruba gods. In this way, they were able to continue worshipping their own *orishas* (spirits or deities), while appearing to conform outwardly to Catholic ceremonies, holidays, and religious festivals (Murphy, 1993). During the Mexican Revolution of 1910, an interesting discovery was made, illustrating the flexible nature of this new, hybrid religion. Similar to the way early Spanish missionaries smashed all the Aztec gods when taking over the area, Mexican Native Americans during the revolution stormed the Catholic churches and overturned religious statues. What they found embedded inside these statues of Roman Catholic saints were small sculptures of the native Mexican gods (Curry, 1997). Other characteristics of this religion that arose due to their need for secrecy include many different rituals, based in Yoruba culture and customs, preserved through generations in secret initiations and ceremonies (Brandon, 1993). This religion is practiced currently by many people of Puerto Rican, Cuban, and Dominican descent. *Santeria* was originally called *Lucumi*.

References

Brandon, G. (1993). *Santeria from Africa to the new world: The dead sell memories.* Bloomington and Indianapolis: Indiana University Press.
Curry, M. C. (1997). *Making the gods in New York.* New York and London: Garland.
Murphy, J. M. (1993). *Santeria: African spirits in America.* Boston: Beacon.

Cindy Yee

SCIENTIFIC RACISM—The (mis)use of biological, sociological, psychological, archaeological, or anthropological sciences to subordinate a person or group based on their race or color. *Scientific racism* has a long history in the Western world and has been the main rationale for colonialism and genocide. European countries embraced scientific racism to "prove" White superiority over the world's people of color and to justify their subordination of those people in Africa, Asia, and the Americas. Scientific racism involves such spurious claims as: European man evolved thousands of years before African man; White brains are larger than Black brains; no civilization existed in Africa before White colonialism; Blacks have a "criminal gene" that Whites do not possess; and, of course, the recent Bell Curve theory of Whites being more intelligent than Blacks (Herrnstein & Murray, 1994). The persistence of efforts to prove "scientifically" White superiority over the centuries is testament to the power of racist beliefs.

Reference

Herrnstein, R. J., & Murray, C. A. (1994). *The bell curve: Intelligence and class structure in American life.* New York: The Free Press.

Lawrence W. Young, Jr.

SCIENTISM—An exaggerated trust in and dependence on the methods of natural science applied to all areas of investigation, as in philosophy, the social sciences and the humanities. Scientism in the examination of people and cultures becomes problematic in that the variations in and between groups are so great that model building or comparative standards tend to yield skewed results. Outlaw (1990) quoted Frank B. Livingstone, who said "Yesterday's science is today's common sense and tomorrow's nonsense" (p. 65). Thus, *scientism* in relation to issues of cross-cultural understanding, particularly in classifications of "race," can create confusion and inappropriate assumptions and designations. Outlaw further states that in eighteenth-century Europe, "evidence from geology, zoology, anatomy and other fields of scientific enquiry were assembled to support a claim that racial classifications would help explain many human differences. . . . First drawing on the rising authority of science as the realization and guardian of systematic, certain knowledge, there was the legitimization of race as a gathering concept'' (pp. 62–63). David Theo Goldberg, the editor of *Anatomy of Race*, states in that volume, ''classification is central to scientific methodology and scientific method, in turn, was taken to furnish the ideal model for rationality. The capacity for rationality, however, was considered the mark of humanity. It seemed obvious, then, that the anthropological ordering into a system of races, in terms of rational capacity would establish a hierarchy of humankind. The race represented by the classifiers was considered to stand at the hierarchical apex. The rational hierarchy was thought to be revealed through its physical-natural correlates: skin color, head shape, body size, smell, hair texture and so on. This engendered a metaphysical pathos, an aesthetic empathy or aversion. Because it was putatively natural, this pathos was considered rational'' (p. 302).

References

Goldberg, D. T. (1990). (Ed.). *Anatomy of racism*. Minneapolis: University of Minnesota Press.
Outlaw, L. (1990). Toward a critical theory of ''race.'' In D. T. Goldberg (Ed.), *Anatomy of racism* (pp. 58–82). Minneapolis: University of Minnesota Press.

Lawrence W. Young, Jr.

SELF CONCEPT—Has a long history in psychology. Most of the literature recognizes that the *self* is a concept that is very personal, yet arises from interactions with others (Triandis, 1989). Schweder and Bourne (1984) found that individuals are defined by their social relationships, and that the concept of the self as being comprised of enduring traits is subordinated to the terms of their relationships. As a basis for motivated behaviors, *self concept* has several components: physical, social, cognitive, and spiritual. Clearly, how individuals view themselves has implications for cross-cultural psychology. Self concept is often thought of as encompassing three dimensions: private, public, and collective (Baumeister, 1986; Greenwald & Pratkanis, 1984). The *private self* includes traits or behaviors the individual holds about her/himself; the *public self* is a generalized concept of how others characterize her/him; and the *collective self* involves the concept of the individual held by a group, or groups, of others (Triandis, 1989). The more individualistic the culture, generally, the more private self is emphasized; whereas individuals in collective cultures sample the collective self more frequently (Trafimow, Triandis, & Goto, 1991). Self concept is a universal phenomenon seen in all cultures. However, how the self is developed depends highly on cultural norms and standards. Markus and Kitayama (1994) found that the self is constructed and framed according to specific cultural dimensions. They state that ''the exact functional role that the person assigns to other people when defining the self depends on culturally shared assumptions about the separation or connectedness between the self and others'' (p. 226). Thus, the self is motivated by either independent or interdependent relationships with others (Markus & Kitayama, 1994). Independent self concept is seen to arise from individualist cultures, and the interdependent self is a result of having come from a collectivistic culture. Thus, while some cultures define *self concept* more in relation to others, other cultures develop a self based on individual perceptions. Other researchers have looked at the concept of "real" versus "ideal" self concept. DeGooyer and Williams (1992) found that the distance between real self and ideal self was smaller in the U.S. sample than the distance between real and undesired self, while the Japanese sample expressed a real self as being equidistant between ideal and undesired self. This finding, according to the authors, has implications for motivation, happiness, and self-esteem.

References

Baumeister, R. F. (1986). *Public self and private self.* New York: Springer-Verlag.

DeGooyer, M. J., & Williams, J. E. (1992). A comparison of self-concepts in Japan and the United States. In S. Iwawaki, Y. Kashima, & K. Leung (Eds.), *Innovations in cross-cultural psychology* (pp. 279–288). Amsterdam: Swets & Zeitlinger B. V.

Greenwald, A. G., & Pratkanis, A. R. (1984). The self. In R. S. Wyer & T. K. Srull (Eds.), *Handbook of social cognition* (Vol. 3, pp. 129–178). Hillsdale, NJ: Erlbaum.

Markus, H. R., & Kitayama, S. (1994). A collective fear of the collective: Implications for selves and theories of selves. *Personality and Social Psychology Bulletin, 20,* 568–579.

Schweder, R. A., & Bourne, E. J. (1984). Does the concept of the person vary cross-culturally? In R. A. Schweder & R. A. LeVine (Eds.), *Cultural theory* (pp. 158–199). New York: Cambridge University Press.

Trafimow, D., Triandis, H. C., & Goto, S. G. (1991). Some tests of the distinction between the private self and the collective self. *Journal of Personality and Social Psychology, 60,* 649–655.

Triandis, H. S. (1989). The self and social behavior in differing cultural contexts. *Psychological Review, 96,* 506–520.

Sharon G. Goto

SELF-DETERMINATION—The ability of a person or a group to exert his/her/its will and create his/her/its destiny. It is the ability to maximize one's potential, to use one's physical, psychological, and material resources for maximum benefit. *Self-determination* involves the ability to develop a positive identity and self-concept and the ability to marshal resources necessary to achieve desired and desirable goals. Self-determination in the Black community embodies Black solidarity, Black self-help, and self-reliance as a community. This includes control of schools, economics, and local politics. Cross (1984) takes a more extreme position. He states that Black self-determination should be a withdrawal from the main United States system of government, culminating even in the creation of a separate Black state. Ironically, self-determination, a concept that has roots in the very foundation of the American nation, when employed by Black Americans, is viewed by the general public as subversive, leftist, and anti-American.

References

Cross, T. (1984). *The Black power imperative*. New York: Faulkner.
Feagin, J., & Vera, H. (1995). *White racism*. New York: Routledge.
Franklin, R. S. (1991). *Shadows or race and class*. Minneapolis: University of Minnesota Press.

Lawrence W. Young, Jr.

SELF-DISCLOSURE—Information about oneself communicated to another person (Cozby, 1973). The use of the term and the construct it represents presents a normative theory of communication. It was made most popular by adherents of the Third Force humanistic psychology movement during the 1960s and 1970s. Jourard and others (Jourard, 1971) developed an ideology of relationships which included a primary role for self-disclosure, feedback, and sensitivity to the disclosures of others in the development of interpersonal understanding. The term *self-disclosure* is used to describe "the process of sharing information, thoughts, and feelings about one's self in ways that contribute to the growth of a relationship" (Crable, 1981, p. 111). The basic parameters of self-disclosure are the breadth or amount of information disclosed, the depth or intimacy of information disclosed, and the duration of time spent describing each item of information. The instruments which have been used to assess self-disclosure measure the sharing of the known self in content areas, including attitudes and opinions, tastes and interests, work, money, personality, and body to target persons including mother, father, best opposite-sex friend, and best same-sex friend. Jourard (1971) asserts that self-disclosure—the ability to disclose to at least one "significant" other—is directly related to one's mental health (i.e., it is in fact a prerequisite for a healthy personality). Bochner (1984), however, believes that self-disclosure is an overrated activity which has enjoyed uncritical acceptance. He notes that there is "no firm empirical basis for endorsing unconditional openness" and that a more grounded evaluation of the data suggests "at most a restrained attitude toward the efficacy of self-disclosure" (p. 608). The linkage between mental health and self-disclosure is a problematic one, because it represents a culture-bound value that is biased against diverse cultural criteria of normality or the desirability of self-disclosure. Sue and Sue (1990) note that this generic characteristic of counseling, which values verbal expressiveness and openness as markers of insight and therapeutic progress, conflicts with the values of clients from traditional Asian cultural backgrounds, which discourage revealing personal or social information to anyone outside the family. Similarly, American Indian and Latino individuals are more likely to share intimate information only with close friends. Vontress (1976) believes that African Americans are particularly hesitant to disclose to White Americans due to racism's residue of distrust and resentment. Self-disclosure to a White counselor would be regarded as an unhealthy and risky move against the backdrop of oppression. The history of discrimination and prejudice that all peoples of color have experienced would lead to interracial encounters characterized initially by caution, due to the sociopolitical considerations. Another component of the context of mental health services provision which may be antithetical to different cultural norms and values is the tradition of conversation and communication direction from client to counselor. For many clients of non-Anglo ethnic and racial backgrounds, this initial role would be uncomfortable and perceived as disrespectful. Communication theories that add to our understanding of the process of increasing intimacy in relationships include those of *social penetration* (Miller & Sunnafrank, 1982) and *social exchange* (Taylor & Altman, 1987). Miller and Sunnafrank contend that different kinds of information are shared in the process of self-disclosing in interpersonal relationships: *cultural, sociological, and psychological,* in that order. He states that *cultural information* is the most general and basic and gives us an initial ability to predict how an individual might respond based on cultural norms. *Sociological information* is somewhat more personal than *cultural knowledge,* enabling us to know both how to behave in various circumstances and what to predict the other may do, but it remains still fairly general and abstract. *Psychological information* is the most intimate and specific, and allows us to know or predict individual traits, feelings, attitudes, and other important personal data. *Social penetration* is the process of moving from cultural knowledge to psychological knowledge. Another point of emphasis in *social penetration theory* is its emphasis on joint effects of verbal and nonverbal communication elements, another domain of cross-cultural differences with which counseling professionals must be familiar. Taylor and Altman's (1987) *social exchange theory* also speaks of this increasingly intimate progression of knowledge of other, and suggests that as relationships develop, communication moves from the less personal to the more personal and intimate levels, involving the exchange of information and feelings, and the sharing of activities. They hypothesize that relationship growth is a joint result of reward/cost factors, personality characteristics, and contextual circumstances. Relationships will be sustained if in this exchange they continue to provide rewards, and they will be discontinued if they become relatively costly.

References

Bochner, A. P. (1984). The functions of human communicating in interpersonal bonding. In C. C. Arnold & J. W. Bowers (Eds.), *Handbook of rhetorical and communication theory* (pp. 544–621). Boston: Allyn & Bacon.

Cozby, P. W. (1973). Self-disclosure: A literature review. *Psychological Bulletin, 79,* 73–91.

Crable, R. E. (1981). *One to another: A guidebook for interpersonal communication.* New York: Harper and Row.

Jourard, S. M. (1971). *The transparent self*. New York: Van Nostrand Reinhold.

Miller, G. R., & Sunnafrank, M. J. (1982). All is for one but one is not for all: A conceptual perspective of interpersonal communication. In F.E.X. Dance (Ed.), *Human communication theory: Comparative essays* (pp. 220–242). New York: Harper & Row.

Sue, D. W., & Sue, D. (1990). *Counseling the culturally different: Theory and practice* (2nd ed.). New York: Wiley.

Taylor, I., & Altman, D. A. (1987). Communication in interpersonal relationships: Social penetration processes. In M. E. Roloff & G. R. Miller (Eds.), *Interpersonal processes: New directions in communication research* (pp. 257–277). Newbury Park, CA: Sage.

Vontress, C. E. (1976). Racial and ethnic barriers in counseling. In P. Pedersen, W. J. Lonner, & J. G. Draguns (Eds.), *Counseling across cultures* (pp. 87–106). Honolulu, HI: East–West Center.

Christine A. Bates

SELF-FULFILLING PROPHECY—Coined by Merton in 1949 to identify a belief that comes true as a function of people acting as if the belief were true (Johnson, 1992). Researchers have demonstrated that our beliefs about others lead us to treat them in certain ways and this, in turn, causes them to fulfill the prophecy that is contained in our beliefs (Merton, 1968). Beliefs about the characteristics and actions of others often come from our culture, family, or the status we hold (Johnson, 1992). These beliefs often become stereotypes that influence how we interact with others about whom we have a particular belief. Darley and Fazio (1980) argued that certain conditions in a social interaction must be met in order for a self-fulfilling prophecy effect to occur: (a) a perceiver forms an expectancy about another person; (b) the perceiver's behavior is congruent with the expectancy; (c) the person who is the subject of the perception interprets this behavior; (d) the subject responds according to expectancy; (e) the perceiver interprets this behavior; and (f) the individual interprets his/her own behavior, completing the cycle. Illustrative of this cycle is the belief within the dominant White culture in the U.S. that Blacks are childlike and inferior. A teacher subscribing to this belief may consciously or unconsciously lower his/her expectations for Black students in his/her charge. The students, sensing this low expectation, incorporate the expectations into their behavioral repertoire and perform accordingly in academic matters. Finally, the teacher observes the lower academic performance and feels justified in his/her initial beliefs. Ultimately, negative beliefs that the dominant group holds regarding nondominant groups or their members can suppress that member or group's upward mobility and quality of life. The manifestation of social control is known as social oppression, which in effect forecloses educational, social, political, and economic opportunities to nondominant groups and their members. Johnson (1992) has identified the academic tracking system as an instrument of social oppression. Johnson contends that this system has its basis in stereotypes in American society and results in the disproportionate placement of minorities into vocational curricula and their White counterparts into academic or college preparatory curricula.

References

Darley, M. J., & Fazio, R. H. (1980). Expectancy confirmation processes arising in the social interaction sequence. *American Psychologist, 35*, 867–881.

Johnson, G. A. (1992). *Human arrangements* (3rd ed.). Orlando, FL: Harcourt Brace Jovanovich.

Merton, R. K. (1968). *Social theory and social structure* (enlarged ed.). New York: The Free Press.

Lonnie Duncan

SELF-STEREOTYPING [AKA AUTO-STEREOTYPING]—A form of self-categorization (Turner, Hogg, Oakes, Reicher, & Wetherell, 1987). A cognitive process, *self-stereotyping* is a framework of generalizations in which an individual perceives the general characteristics of the self as being the same as the characteristics of the in-group (Simon & Hamilton, 1994). Self-stereotyping provides individuals a framework for the categorization of their own attitudes, values, and behaviors in order to either discriminate themselves from out-group members or, conversely, cohere themselves more closely to the in-group. Similar to Tversky's (1977) proposition that there is an interrelation between the categorization and the similarity of objects, self-stereotyping may be both a result of self-categorization and may be a cause of it (Simon & Hamilton, 1994). Thus, self-stereotyping may both affect and be affected by the ways in which an individual identifies with the in-group. As with *heterostereotyping* (or stereotyping of out-group members), self-stereotyping ignores present-tense, individual variability (McNabb, 1986) and, instead, applies the characteristics of the in-group to the self. Furthermore, Simon and Hamilton (1994) found that the degree of self-stereotyping has an inverse relationship with in-group size and status. Thus, when the in-group is small and of low status—relative to the majority out-group—self-stereotyping will be greater. Additionally, self-stereotypes have been found to be more positive in nature than stereotypes of members of the out-group (also called *heterostereotypes*; Marin & Salazar, 1985). Self-stereotyping has also been discussed in terms of cultural variables. Self-identity varies between individualistic and collectivistic cultures. Individuals from individualistic cultures value uniqueness, personal achievement, and individual values, whereas collectivists focus on group achievement, cohesion, and shared values (Gudykunst & Ting-Toomey, 1988). Thus, self-stereotyping takes on different dimensions and importance within different cultures. Specifically, self-stereotyping is thought to be greater within collectivistic cultures, since identity with the in-group is stronger (Iwao & Triandis, 1993). Because group affiliation is the core determinant of the self in collectivistic cultures, application of in-group characteristics is more salient within those cultures than within individualistic cultures. Self-stereotyping suffers from the same handicaps of validity that heterostereotyping does (Iwao & Triandis, 1993). In other words, although self-stereotypes may have a "kernel of truth" to them, they are, again, based on the perceptions of in-group behavior, attitudes, and values, and suffer from similar consequences of misperception.

References

Gudykunst, W. B., & Ting-Toomey, S. (1988). *Interpersonal communication*. Newbury Park, CA: Sage.

Iwao, S., & Triandis, H. C. (1993). Validity of auto- and hetero-stereotypes among Japanese and American students. *Journal of Cross-Cultural Psychology, 24,* 428–444.

Marin, G., & Salazar, J. M. (1985). Determinants of hetero- and autostereotypes: Distance, level of contact and socioeconomic development in seven nations. *Journal of Cross-Cultural Psychology, 16,* 403–422.

McNabb, S. L. (1986). Stereotypes and interaction conventions of Eskimos and non-Eskimos. In Y. Y. Kim (Ed.), *Interethnic communication: Current research.* Newbury Park, CA: Sage.

Simon, B., & Hamilton, D. L. (1994). Self-stereotyping and social context: The effects of relative in-group size and in-group status. *Journal of Personality and Social Psychology, 66,* 699–711.

Turner, J. C., Hogg, M. A., Oakes, P. J., Reicher, S. D., & Wetherell, M. S. (1987). *Rediscovering the social group: A self-categorization theory.* Oxford: Basil Blackwell.

Tversky, A. (1977). Features of similarity. *Psychological Review, 84,* 327–352.

Sharon G. Goto

SEXISM—The belief that one sex (usually male) is naturally superior to the other and should dominate most important areas of political, economic, and social life (Hirsch, Kett, & Trefil, 1988). It is also the act of (usually by men) intentionally or unintentionally inequitably distributing resources, refusing to share power, maintaining unresponsive and inflexible institutional policies, procedures and practices, and imposing its culture on the other sex (usually women) for their supposed benefit. Actions are justified by punishing, blaming, and/or helping the other sex (women). These behaviors are most often attributed to men for their general position within the nation's *macroculture* (see entry) and their power within the political, social, and economic systems.

Reference

Hirsch, E. D., Kett, J. F., & Trefil, J. S. (1988). *The dictionary of cultural literacy.* Boston: Houghton Mifflin.

Adelaida Santana Pellicier

SEXUAL DYSFUNCTION—Is described as "impairment or difficulty that affects *sexual functioning* or produces *sexual pain*" (McCammon, Knox, &

Schacht, 1993, p. 532). According to the American Psychiatric Association (1987), *sexual dysfunction* may occur in any phase of the human sexual response (HSR) and usually involves a disruption in the subjective experience of desire or pleasure and/or the objective physiological elements of sexual functioning. Before the mid-1950s, sexual dysfunctions were considered symptoms of personality disorders. Several HSR models have been proposed to describe the possible events which occur when an individual moves from a state of nonarousal to the period following orgasm (Beach, 1956; Ellis, 1906; Kaplan, 1979, Masters & Johnson, 1966; Stayton, 1992). Despite the major criticisms (Robinson, 1976; Tavris, 1992; Tiefer, 1991), Masters and Johnson's four-stage model of the human sexual response cycle (HSRC), which includes excitement, plateau, orgasm, and resolution, has received the most professional visibility. It is around these stages that the *Diagnostic and Statistical Manual of Mental Disorders* (DSM-IV, American Psychiatric Association, 1994) categorizes sexual dysfunction (disorders of sexual desire, arousal, orgasm, and sexual pain). In addition to describing sexual dysfunction as a problem with sexual response or sexual pain, timing and situational factors are also considered (Masters & Johnson, 1970). Time of onset difficulties include *primary dysfunction*, which is a sexual problem that is always experienced, and *secondary dysfunction*, which is a sexual problem that may be experienced now or is experienced periodically between periods of satisfactory sexual functioning. An individual may also have a *situational dysfunction*, which occurs when a sexual problem develops in one situation but not another, or a *total dysfunction*, which occurs when a sexual problem is experienced in all situations. *Sexual dysfunction* is also classified by whether it is caused primarily by organic (or biological) or psychosociocultural factors (Masters & Johnson, 1970). In most cases, however, a sexual dysfunction results from an interaction of factors (Goldman, 1992; Hawton, 1985).

References

American Psychiatric Association. (1987). *Diagnostic and statistical manual of mental disorders* (3rd ed.). Washington, CD: Author.

American Psychiatric Association. (1994). *Diagnostic and statistical manual of mental disorders* (4th ed.). Washington, DC: Author.

Beach, F. A. (1956). Characteristics of masculine sex drive. In M. R. Jones (Ed.), *Nebraska Symposium on Motivation* (Vol. 4, pp. 1–32). Lincoln: University of Nebraska Press.

Ellis, H. (1906). *Studies in the psychology of sex* (7 vols.). New York: Random House.

Goldman, H. H. (1992). *Review of general psychiatry* (3rd ed.). Norwalk, CT: Appelton & Lange.

Hawton, K. (1985). *Sex therapy: A practical guide*. Oxford: Oxford University Press.

Kaplan, H. S. (1979). *Disorders of sexual desire*. New York: Simon & Schuster.

McCammon, S. L., Knox, D., & Schacht, C. (1993). *Choices in sexuality*. St. Paul, MN: West.

Masters, W. H., & Johnson, V. E. (1966). *Human sexual response*. Boston: Little, Brown.

Masters, W. H., & Johnson, V. E. (1970). *Human sexual inadequacy*. Boston: Little, Brown.

Robinson, P. (1976). *The modernization of sex*. New York: Harper and Row.

Stayton, W. R. (1992). A theology of sexual pleasure. *SIECUS Report, 20*, 9–15.

Tavris, C. (1992). *The mismeasure of woman*. New York: Simon & Schuster.

Tiefer, L. (1991). Historical, scientific, clinical, and feminist criticisms of "The Human Sexual Response Cycle" model. In J. Bancroft (Ed.), *Annual review of sex research* (vol. 2, pp. 1–23). Lake Mills, IA: Society for the Scientific Study of Sex.

Monica D. Lange

SHAMAN—A healer, male or female, who has a supernatural contact with spirits that assist healers in their powers to conduct good and evil (Harner, 1973). Historically, shaman originated from within hunting and gathering civilizations but now can be found among many cultures. The word "shaman" originated in Siberia from the Tungusic word "saman" meaning "to raise oneself or enter an ecstatic state." Ecstatic in this sense refers to a heightened emotional state. The shaman is given supernatural powers by guardian spirits but may have inherited the role, self-selected it, or received it through initiatory illness. However, it is more common to inherit the position through sickness than through lineage. Often, a self-selected shaman's powers are perceived as weaker than the powers of a shaman chosen by the spirits or one who inherited the position. A shaman's powers include healing (retrieval of lost souls), extraction, and divination through visions or dreams. These visions come to the shaman after days of self-sacrifice, such as fasting, praying, or isolation; through spirit possession; and through journeys to other dimensions, referred to as soul flight. Visions can be related to anything and some include: location of game or enemies, cause of sicknesses, and sources for cures. In rituals and ceremonies, shaman conduct seances, call on spirits, and display their spirit-given powers, which can be entertaining, yet serious (for example, walking barefoot across hot coals). Some anthropologists have related the shaman's powers to higher cognitive abilities, and others have considered the powers to be similar to psychotherapeutic cures (Honigmann, 1973).

References

Harner, M. (1973). *Hallucinogens and shamanism*. Oxford: Oxford University Press.

Honigmann, J. (1973). *Handbook of social and cultural anthropology*. Chicago: Rand McNally.

Joseph E. Trimble and Heather K. Mertz

SHAMANISM—A religion of the Ural-Altaic peoples of Northern Asia and Europe, and characterized by a belief that the unseen world of gods, demons, and ancestral spirits are responsive only to the Shamans (see SHAMAN). Shamanism can be defined also as any religion similar to shamanism. The North American form of shamanism is characterized by the use of the mediumistic trance (Merriam-Webster, 1986). Nanda (1991) described shamanism as a religion that serves a variety of activities for those ethnic groups who participate in this religion. Shamanism serves to cure the sick, reveal things to other ethnic group members, and read fortunes. Shamanism has been known to cure the sick through its rhythmic rituals, which is often cathartic to those involved. It also serves to integrate functions of a society by its wide variety of symbolic acts which bring together several different beliefs and religious practices (De-Rios & Winkleman, 1989). The rhythmic and energetic nature of some shaman rituals can be found in many Christian churches, particularly those that have similar rhythmic and energetic worship services. Such services have been shown to relieve psychosocial stress in some and help to prevent and alleviate psycho-somatic illnesses in others (Horwatt, 1988). Many Native American ceremonies involve participants donning ceremonial garb and paying homage to many spir-its, as is the tradition of shamanism (Nanda, 1991). Shamanism can be char-acterized as the belief system that undergirds the practice and also as the specific rituals which it shares with many other religions.

References

De-Rios, M. D., & Winkleman, M. (1989). Shamanism and altered states of conscious-ness. *Journal of Psychoactive Drugs, 21,* 1–7.
Horwatt, K. (1988). The Shamanic complex in the Pentecostal church. *Ethos, 16,* 128–145.
Merriam-Webster, A. (1986). *Webster's third new international dictionary* (Vol. III). Chicago: Encyclopedia Britannica.
Nanda, S. (1991). *Cultural anthropology* (4th ed.). Belmont, CA: Wadsworth.

Lonnie Duncan

SHAME—A public loss of face in Asian countries. Many perceive this concept to be equivalent to the concept of *guilt* in Western societies. However, *shame* has a more collectivistic connotation. Shon and Ja (1982) directly equate shame with *tiu lien*, the Chinese term for social loss of face. Hu (1956) has asserted that the dread caused by loss of *lien* has an even greater central nervous system effect upon Chinese than the dread caused by fear. According to Shon and Ja (1982), ''The concepts of shame and loss of face involve not only the exposure of your actions for all to see, but also the withdrawal of the family's, commu-nity's, or society's confidence and support. In societal structures where inter-dependence is so important, the actual or threatened withdrawal of support may shake the individual's basic trust that there will be others to rely upon and raise his or her existential anxiety of being truly alone to face life'' (p. 215). Thus, shame can be a powerful form of social control; it is a much more important concept than *guilt*, which tends to be more individualistic in nature.

References

Hu, H. C. (1956). The Chinese concepts of face. In D. G. Haring (Ed.), *Personal char-acter and cultural milieu* (pp. 447–467). Syracuse, NY: Syracuse University Press.

Shon, S. P., & Ja, D. Y. (1982). Asian families. In M. McGoldrick, J. K. Pearce, & J. Giordano (Eds.), *Ethnicity and family therapy* (pp. 208–228). New York: Guilford.

Jeffery Scott Mio

SICK—*Webster's Third New International Dictionary* (1986) defines *sick* as: (1) affected with disease; not well or healthy; (2) spiritually or morally unsound or corrupt; (3) affected by some strong emotion to the degree that one becomes nauseated; and (4) mentally or emotionally unsound or disordered. Being in a state of sickness includes any condition that is not within the normal range of mental, moral, or spiritual health as this range is dictated, generally, by the powerful and influential members of a given society (Parson, 1951). Sick people have an obligation to get well because being sick is undesirable, both for the individual and for society. The power to define what constitutes sickness is of critical importance in the diagnosis of mental illness, since the dominant culture sets the norm by which each of its members is judged (Solomon, 1992). It follows that in a multiethnic society, the margin for error is greater when diagnosing mental illness. Solomon (1992) suggested that people from different cultures express the same feelings in different ways. They also express feelings that may suggest different symptoms in different cultures. For example, in depression a person is unable to cope with daily life, yet individuals of different backgrounds may express depressive behaviors in ways that contradict normal expression in a given culture or society. In societies where extraverted behaviors are the norm, a depressed person may become introverted; where introversion is the norm, a depressed person may become extraverted. One whose culture condones the full expression of introversion is at risk of being misdiagnosed as manic in settings outside of one's cultural group. Given the sociopolitical nature of the act of defining, sick can be defined as a state of being abnormal as defined by the society in which a person finds himself/herself. Within a societal context, sickness can be defined in a spiritual, moral, biological, or emotional state.

References

Parsons, T. (1951). *The social system*. New York: The Free Press.
Solomon, A. (1992). Clinical diagnosis among diverse populations: A multicultural perspective. *Families in Society, 73,* 371–377.
Merriam-Webster, A. (1986). *Webster's third new international dictionary* (Vol. III). Chicago: Encyclopedia Britannica.

Lonnie Duncan

SITUATIONAL ETHNICITY—A term that suggests individuals can and do choose, within certain constraints, a variety of identities. Individuals may seek to maximize their options and use ethnic identity if they see an advantage in doing so; and the use of situational ethnic identity is fluid and flexible. For instance, one may emphasize his/her Asian American identity with other Asian

Americans while downplaying it in the presence of other ethnic groups. In the presence of other Italian Americans, the Italian part of one's identity may become more salient than one's membership in the more general White racial group (Smith, 1991). An individual may invoke a situational use of his or her ethnic identity for the purpose of dealing with life events that may be stressful (Smith, 1985). For instance, an African American, Hispanic, Native American, or Asian American, who in the past has demonstrated little visible allegiance to or identification with his/her respective cultures, will, under attack (e.g., after experiencing severe ethnic discrimination), heighten his/her identification with his/her ethnic group, often seeking emotional and instrumental support from the group. Situational use of ethnicity is similar to what Lyman and Douglass (1973) call *ethnic impression management* with an example of an individual who was born in Puerto Rico, educated in Europe, and of Vizcayan Basque ancestry. Depending upon the situation, he/she may be a Vizcayan, a Spanish Basque, or a Puerto Rican.

References

Lyman, S. M., & Douglass, W. A. (1973). Ethnicity: Strategies of collective and individual impression management. *Social Research, 40*, 344–365.
Smith, E. J. (1985). Ethnic minorities: Life stress, social support and mental health issues. *The Counseling Psychologist, 13*, 537–579.
Smith, E. J. (1991). Ethnic identity development: Toward the development of a theory within the context of majority/minority status. *Journal of Counseling and Development, 70*, 181–188.

Elsie J. Smith

SOCIAL CONTROL—Refers to control of a person or persons by the social group as well as society in which one or one's group holds membership (Chafe, 1995). These external controls refer to social processes in which people conform to norms or rules that reward them with status, prestige, money, and freedom. Vander Sanden (1990) identified three main types of social control processes operating in society: (1) those that lead us to internalize society's expectations; (2) those that structure our social experiences; and (3) those that utilize formal and informal social sanctions. Social control also refers to any methods and strategies that regulate behavior in a society (Vander Sanden, 1990). Hirschi (1969), in formulating *micro-social control theory*, stated that the relationship between people and conventional society consists of four bonds: belief, attachment, commitment, and involvement. *Belief* refers to the extent to which conventional norms are internalized; *commitment* refers to the extent to which social rewards are tied to conformity; *attachment* is a person's sensitivity to the opinions of others (i.e., the more people are concerned with the respect and status afforded to them by others, the more they are subjected to social control); and *involvement* refers to the amount of time people spend on conventional activities (i.e., the greater the extent of one's involvement in conventional activities, the less time one has to break the social norms of a given society. Social control is a process by which an individual or individuals are obligated or feel compelled, either by external forces or internal processes, to follow prescribed social norms. This control can come from society, one's cultural group, family, or community. Social control is effected through the control and manipulation of rewards and penalties for following or not following a prescribed social norm.

References

Hirschi, T. (1969). *Cause of delinquency.* Berkeley: University of California Press.
Vander Sanden, W. J. (1990). *Sociology the core* (2nd ed.). New York: McGraw-Hill.

Lonnie Duncan

SOCIAL NORMS—Rules, spoken or unspoken, indicating how individuals are expected to behave in specific situations (Baron & Byrne, 1991). According to the social learning theory of prejudice, social norms have been shown to influence the behaviors and attitudes that an individual may hold about another individual who is perceived to be different from themselves (Sherif, Harvey, White, Hood, & Sherif, 1961). These attitudes and behaviors usually are learned from an individual's reference group. The individual's reference group prescribes whom a group member should like or dislike and determines what practices are fair or unfair in relation to out-group members (Greenberg & Cohen, 1982). These rules and expectations are reinforced by rewards and punishment for noncompliance (Baron & Byrne, 1991). The process of conforming whereby a person changes his/her attitude is said to be a result of an individual complying with social norms. Often, conformity is based on the individual knowing or observing the rules and regulations set by society or the individual's reference group (Greenberg & Cohen, 1982). This process of conforming to social norms has influenced work productivity (Roethlisberger & Dixon, 1939), treatment of employees (Garvin, 1986), and the development of stereotypes (Wyer, 1988). Social norms can be characterized as norms that are learned by an individual's reference group or society that affect how he or she interacts with nongroup members, and that contribute to the values and beliefs that an individual may hold.

References

Baron, R. A., & Byrne, D. (1991). *Social psychology: Understanding human interaction* (6th ed.). Needham Heights, MA: Allyn and Bacon.
Garvin, D. A. (1986). Quality problems, policies, and attitudes in the United States and Japan: An explorative study. *Academy of Management Journal, 29,* 653–673.
Greenberg, J., & Cohen, R. L. (1982). *Equity and justice in the social behavior.* New York: Academic Press.
Roethlisberger, F. G., & Dickerson, W. J. (1939). *Management and the worker.* Cambridge, MA: Harvard University Press.
Sherif, M., Harvey, O. J., White, B. J., Hood, W. E., & Sherif, C. W. (1961). *Intergroup conflict and the robbers' cave experiment.* Norman, OK: Institute of Group Relations.

Wyer, R. S., Jr. (1988). Social memory and social judgment. In P. R. Solomon, G. R. Goethals, C. M. Kelley, & B. R. Stephens (Eds.), *Perspectives on memory research* (pp. 241–270). New York: Springer-Verlag.

Lonnie Duncan

SOCIAL PROCESS—The interaction between two individuals which sets the stage, to some degree, for a fluid, shared consciousness that structures their actions (Couch, 1992). Historically, the term *social process* has not been defined in much of the social science literature, because the field has lacked sound methodological techniques for observing social process (Buban, 1986). In efforts to understand the elements of "sociation," Miller (1975) initiated a study (reported in Couch, 1992) to examine characteristics that are necessary for a social process exchange to occur. Miller's results indicated that there are six elements needed for an exchange: mutual awareness, acknowledgment of the recipient, mutual presence, mutual understanding, clear intentions, and congruent verbal or behavioral responses. Aside from the elements of social processing, other salient factors became instrumental in describing the social process. For example, the form (or forms) used in exchanges affects the social process outcome. The elementary form is the most basic type of social process (Couch, 1992) and it involves a courtesy exchange between two people that is reciprocal and complementary. A participant is allowed time to express him/herself without being interrupted and the same respect is granted for the other participant. A complex form contains more than one social process during an exchange. A participant can initiate an exchange but may not receive any feedback for the response. The other participant may also choose to engage in another activity. Another characteristic that has affected social actions (processing) is the influence of a social past. Hall (1987) and Couch (1992) have concluded that one's shared history or social past will determine the complexity (i.e., elementary or complex form) and intensity (engaging or disengaging) of the relationship. Equally important to one's understanding of social process is one's ability to understand the effects of culture and contextualism on the verbal and nonverbal responses. Culture can serve as a lens through which information is filtered and thus it is important for people to get clarification for responses when they are unsure about the meaning of a concept. Contextualism is also important because words and behaviors can be ambiguous, and understanding one's words and behaviors within the context of their use can help elucidate the meaning and rationale for their use. Together the elements of sociation, types of relational forms, and an understanding of culture and contextualism are beneficial for participants who are engaged in social processes.

References

Buban, S. L. (1986). Studying social processes: Chicago and Iowa. In C. J. Couch, S. L. Saxton, & M. A. Katovich (Eds.), *Schools revisited* (pp. 25–38). Greenwich, CT: JAI Press.

Couch, C. J. (1992). Toward a formal theory of social processes. *Symbolic Interaction,*
    15, 117–134.
Hall, P. M. (1987). Interactionism and the study of social organization. *Sociological*
    Quarterly, 27, 1–22.

Bryant Ford

SOCIAL STRATIFICATION—A hierarchically organized structure of social
inequality (Jary & Jary, 1991). Jary and Jary noted that in geology, the term
refers to a layered structuring, but in sociology the layers consist of social
groups, and the emphasis is on the ways in which inequalities between groups
are structured and persist over time. The layers that make up the strata include
qualitative characteristics such as ethnicity, race, caste, socioeconomic status,
and gender. Ogbu (1994) has posited a definition of social stratification that
states that social stratification occurs when a member from a social group is
ranked or placed within that ranked group. Furthermore, Ogbu reported that the
maintenance of social stratification is the result of an arrangement of social
groups/categories in a hierarchical order of subordination and domination in
which some groups, so organized, have unequal access to the society's fundamental resources. Historically, the origin of social stratification is hazy, however,
social scientists speculate that social stratification has been a subject of academic
inquiry for the past few decades (Plotnicov, 1996). Much of the work conducted
on social stratification is attributed to three key figures—Karl Marx, Max Weber,
and Ralf Durkheimer—who each shared in shaping comprehension of this concept (Jenkins, 1991). Researchers also propose that two factors—the increase of
human population and the economic stability of a society—contribute to the
understanding of social stratification (Beeghley, 1989). Jary and Jary (1991)
reported that mobility and change are important social stratification characteristics. Mobility and change refer to the upward and downward movements along
the social stratification index. Movement within the social strata is contingent
upon the rewards dispensed by society (Plotnicov, 1996). Plotnicov also stated
that these rewards are based on the work and status of individuals; however,
they are not always dispensed equally due to the qualitative characteristics that
shape social stratification. Additionally, Plotnicov reported that those members
at the top layers of the social strata fair economically better than does the rest
of the social strata, and, therefore, work diligently at convincing everyone that
social hierarchies are important so that they may maintain their status and position within society.

References

Beeghley, L. (1989). *The structure of social stratification in the United States.* Needham
    Heights, MA: Allyn and Bacon.
Jary, D., & Jary, J. (Eds.). (1991). *Collins dictionary of sociology* (Vol. 1). New York:
    HarperCollins.

Jenkins, R. (1991). Disability and social stratification. *British Journal of Sociology, 42*, 557–580.

Ogbu, J. (1994). Racial stratification and education in the United States: Why inequality persists. *Teachers College Record, 96*, 264–298.

Plotnicov, L. (1996). Social stratification. *Encyclopedia of cultural anthropology* (Vol. 4, pp. 1205–1210). New York: Holt.

Bryant Ford

SOCIOECONOMIC STATUS (SES)—*Social status* (Hollingshead & Redlich, 1958) is often seen as one *sociocultural variable* that contributes to our understanding of psychopathology. Social scientists have long held that *socioeconomic status* (SES) will influence a family's "social environment, lifestyle, level of education attained, and occupational aspirations" (Gibbs & Huang, 1989, p. 10). Recently researchers (Anderson, Bastida, Kramer, Williams, & Wong, 1995) revealed that measures of SES do not fully capture lifetime exposure to deprived conditions. Blau and Graham's study (cited in Anderson, et al., 1995) point out that racial differences in assets and wealth are more striking than income as a measure of SES for African Americans. Boyd-Franklin (1989) states there is also an interaction effect between SES, racism, and discrimination particularly for African Americans. Boyd-Franklin concludes the perceptions of middle-class Black couples sense of their position in society will be contaminated by their experiences of racism and discrimination. For example, middle-class Blacks may feel that they are in a "privileged position vis-à-vis the Black community, but they may have received little acknowledgment in white society. . . . This pattern is experienced by Black people at all socioeconomic levels and often leads to a feeling of dissatisfaction" (pp. 231–232).

References

Anderson, N. B., Bastida, E., Kramer, B. J., Williams, D., & Wong, M. (1995). Panel II: Macrosocial and environmental influences on minority health. *Health Psychology, 14*, 601–612.

Boyd-Franklin, N. (1989). *Black families in therapy: A multisystems approach.* New York: Guilford.

Gibbs, J. T., & Huang, L. N. (1989). A conceptual framework for assessing and treating minority youth. In J. T. Gibbs, L. N. Huang, & Associates (Eds.), *Children of color: Psychological interventions with minority youth* (pp. 1–29). San Francisco: Jossey-Bass.

Hollingshead, A. B., & Redlich, F. C. (1958). *Social class and mental illness: A community study.* New York: Wiley.

Leslie C. Jackson

SOJOURNER—Literally, to dwell in a place as a temporary resident or as a stranger (Siu, 1952). Historically, *Sojourner Truth* (originally named Isabella Baumfree) was an Abolitionist, women's rights activist, and preacher who suffered terrible cruelties as a slave. In 1843, she claimed a voice from God told her to take the name "Sojourner" and to travel across the United States to show people their sins and to be a sign from God to end slavery. When Sojourner asked the Lord for a second name, she claimed He gave her the name "Truth" because she was to tell everyone the truth about slavery (Claflin, 1987). For nearly 20 years, Sojourner Truth traveled across the country speaking out on slavery and women's rights. The term *sojourner* described the status of Chinese in the United States during the second half of the nineteenth century and first half of the twentieth century. For these 100 years, Chinese were characterized as aliens who were "nonassimilable" and "incompatible with the American character" (Wang, 1991). During this period of time, public policy toward Chinese was based on the image of sojourners as individuals clinging to the culture of their own ethnic group and psychologically unwilling to organize themselves as permanent residents in the country of their sojourn. Public policies toward sojourners developed from prevailing cultural and biological perspectives of race, which prevented Chinese from being considered as immigrants, permanent settlers, or naturalized citizens (Lyman, 1974; Siu, 1952). Until the 1965 Amendments to the Immigration and Nationality Act eliminated remaining restrictions on Asian immigrantion, Chinese residents in the United States were conveniently described as sojourners and designated as strangers who spend many years of their lifetime in a foreign country without being assimilated by it (Siu, 1952; Wang, 1991; Ward & Kennedy, 1993). Bonacich (1972, 1973) used sojourner as an explanation of an outlook of immigrants who have economic objectives similar to a sojourner: a person who, as the economic middleman, expects to leave the host country and seek occupations and trades which require little fixed investment; a person who has little reason to develop lasting relationships with members of the surrounding society and has strong incentives to maintain ethnic ties. Bonacich proposed a sojourner theory to explain why certain groups (Jews) have been associated with particular economic positions in societies and why this has engendered hostility towards them. The implications of Bonacich's theory to explain relationships between African American communities and Jewish business middlemen have been of interest in recent years (Cherry, 1990). Church (1982) discussed issues of personal adjustment processes sojourners undergo.

References

Bonacich, E. (1972). A theory of ethnic antagonism: The split labor market. *American Sociological Review, 37*, 547–559.

Bonacich, E. (1973). A theory of middleman minorities. *American Sociological Review, 38*, 583–594.

Cherry, R. (1990). Middleman minority theories: Their implications for Black–Jewish relations. *Journal of Ethnic Studies, 17*, 117–138.

Church, A. T. (1982). Sourjourn adjustment. *Psychological Bulletin, 91*, 540–572.

Claflin, B. E. (1987). *Sojourner Truth and the struggle for freedom*. New York: Eisen, Durwood.

Lyman, S. (1974). Institutional racism: Social discrimination and the legitimation of the ghetto, 1910–1943. In S. Lyman (Ed.), *Chinese Americans* (pp. 86–118). New York: Random House.

Siu, P. C. (1952). The sojourner. *American Journal of Sociology, 58,* 34–44.

Wang, L.L.C. (1991). Roots and changing identity of the Chinese in the United States. *Daedalus, 120,* 181–206.

Ward, C., & Kennedy, A. (1993). Where's the "culture" in cross-cultural transition? *Journal of Cross-Cultural Psychology, 24,* 221–249.

MaryAnna Domkos-Cheng Ham

SORCERY—Derived from the French term *sors,* or "spell," and refers to the casting of spells or the use of charms to influence emotions, thoughts, moods, and health (Guiley, 1991). Guiley reported that although sorcery has been practiced for centuries, no definite date on its origin exists. For some time, sorcery has eluded definition in much of the literature, because it has been used interchangeably with the term *witchcraft.* Although *sorcery* and witchcraft share similar characteristics, such as the belief in the "supernatural and mystical power" and the integration into cosmology (Marwick, 1970), there are some qualitative distinctions between the two. For example, sorcery was related as a practice associated with religion and was used to protect people and livestock against disaster, outsiders, and enemies, redressing wrongs, and meeting out justice (Guiley, 1991). However, Guiley stated that around 6 B.C., Christianity was developing and the popularity of sorcery decreased subsequently, altering people's perceptions about the practice of sorcery (i.e., sorcery became known as a demonizing religion). Unlike sorcery, the origins of witchcraft are hazy, and its practices have been around much longer. Witchcraft has always been associated with negativity, and it has generated very little support from mainstream societies. Fortune (1932) suggested that another qualitative difference between sorcery and witchcraft is that men practice sorcery while women practice witchcraft. Further, Fortune noted that historically sorcerers were men in various societies (e.g., herbalists and healers) who possessed powers that could not be explained by ordinary or traditional means. Sorcery is still practiced in many cultures around the world, and it is perceived as an alternative religion garnering modest attention from various societies. Additionally, the practice of sorcery varies across cultures because the model of transmitting information from generation to generation has been either amended or deleted through oral traditions.

References

Fortune, R. F. (1932). *Sorcerers.* New York: Dutton.

Guiley, R. E. (1991). Sorcery. *The encyclopedia of witches and witchcraft* (Vol. 1, pp. 320–321). New York: Facts on File.

Marwick, M. (Ed.). (1970). *Witchcraft and sorcery.* Middlesex, England: Penguin Books.

Bryant Ford

SOUL LOSS—Refers to one losing his or her soul, often causing illness to or within the individual. Soul loss often manifests as a depression, although symptoms may vary by culture and include: loss of sensation, fainting spells, self-deprivation, and memory loss. Most often one loses his or her soul after experiencing an emotionally traumatic event. Spirits, sorcerers, or witches also may steal the soul while the person is sleeping (the soul wanders above the body), while yawning (the spirit may enter through the mouth and take the soul), or sneezing (the person may expel his or her soul). Other times, soul loss occurs from being frightened or startled suddenly, and the soul flees, possibly returning. The Mohave American Indians experience soul loss as *ghost-weylak*, which occurs after a family death through the individual's dreams (Devereux, 1937). The soul of a Seminole (*soloipi*) also will wander through dreams and may be persuaded to stay with the dead (Capron, 1953). According to Johnson and Johnson (1965), the fear, anxiety, and stress associated with soul loss can sometimes develop into problems of alcoholism, vandalism, suicide, or family abandonment. Treatment of soul loss requires one's soul to be recaptured by a shaman, who must reintroduce it to the individual's body (see SHAMAN).

References

Capron, L. (1953). The medicine bundles of the Florida Seminole and the Green Corn Dance (Anthropological Paper No. 35). *Bureau of American Ethology Bulletin, 151*, 159–210.

Devereux, G. (1937). Mohave soul concepts. *American Anthropologist, 39*, 417–422.

Johnson, L. G., & Johnson, C. A. (1965). Totally discouraged: A depression syndrome of the Dakota Sioux. *Transcultural Psychiatric Research, 1*, 141–143.

Joseph E. Trimble and Heather K. Mertz

SOUTH ASIAN—A socially constructed category for those people living in the Southwestern region of the Asian continent who have both ethnic and cultural connections to the country of India. These countries include India, Pakistan, Sri Lanka, Nepal, and Burma. South Asians are of Dravidian and Aryan ancestry. While the term *Asian Indian* is still popularly used and accepted, historical and cultural traits of Asian Indians are from other surrounding countries as well. In the United States, South Asians have had an interesting history regarding their struggle with racial identification. Takaki (1989) wrote:

Asian Indians were Caucasian. Would they be entitled to naturalized citizenship in the U.S.? Seeking to set forth a distinction between Asian Indians and white Americans, the Asiatic Exclusion League conceded in 1910 that students of ethnology all agreed "the Hindus" were "members of the same family" as Americans of European ancestry. But "as a matter of fact," the league argued, the people of the U.S. were "cousins, far removed, of the Hindus of the northwest provinces." The forefathers of white Americans "pressed to the west, in the everlasting march of conquest, progress and civilization," while the "forefathers of the Hindus went East and became enslaved, effeminate, cast ridden and degraded.'' The Western Aryans became the "Lords of Creation," while the Eastern Aryans became the "slaves of Creation." (p. 298)

Reference

Takaki, R. (1989). *Strangers from a different shore*. New York: Penguin Books.

Lui Amador and Anita Jain

SOUTHEASTERN ASIAN—A person who was born or has familial roots in Southeast Asia. Geographically, Southeast Asia includes Myanmar (formerly Burma), Thailand, Malaysia, Singapore, Brunei, Indonesia, Laos, Cambodia, Vietnam, and the Philippines. The region has great geographical diversity. It is composed of many islands, and except for Laos, all have a shoreline. Southern China and Eastern Tibet were the source of the region's population. The largest ethnic group are brown-skinned Malay from Southern China that now live in Malaysia, Brunei, Indonesia, and the Philippines. Major religions in Southeast Asia include Buddhism, Hinduism, Islam, and Christianity. Philippine's majority has been Christianized (more than 90 percent) when the Spanish dominated the nation. Vietnam has also significant numbers of people who accept Christianity, mostly following the Catholic faith from their years of French colonization. Missionaries from various Western countries have influenced many in Southeastern Asian to convert to Christianity. The majority of Southeastern Asian immigrants came after the end of the Vietnam War in 1975 (see INDOCHINESE REFUGEES). The education system in the United States had to adjust to three distinct backgrounds: (1) refugees without formal education, (2) those with some formal education, and (3) those who had extensive formal education. However, because most Southeast Asians arriving in the United States did not know English, they were initially treated very similarly by the educational system. According to Gall and Gall (1993), 87.5 percent of all Southeastern Asian students come from homes where a non-English language is spoken.

Reference

Gall, S. B., & Gall, T. L. (1993). (Eds.). *Statistical record of Asian Americans*. Detroit: Gale Research, Inc.

Rakefet Richmond

SOVEREIGNTY—The earliest use of the term dates back to 1340 (Simpson & Weiner, 1989). *Sovereignty* is the process by which a state (i.e., territory of land) governs itself by functioning autonomously and defending it from the influence of other states (Philpott, 1995). Sovereignty has also been defined as an essential condition for political order (Crick, 1968). Crick concluded that the phenomenon and concept of sovereignty is best understood historically, since it originated as an expression of the search for a purely secular basis for authority within the new state. Once a state has gained sovereignty, Philpott (1995) noted that there are three characteristics that are essential to its survival: Authority (the right to command and the right to be obeyed by its inhabitants), supremacy (status and how it is perceived by other states), and territoriality (boundaries of the state). Another component of sovereignty is the ability of a state to establish and maintain internal control within (i.e., against domestic and foreign enemies). A lack of internal control will leave territories subject to invasions from more powerful states. Internal and external control are very important characteristics of a sovereign state because loss of such control can lead to domination by another state in the form of slavery and even death (Brown, 1992). Attaining sovereignty is an important issue for states because sovereignty serves as a mechanism for obtaining and maintaining national culture and identity. The identity and culture of a state is manifested through language, values, and ethnicity, and without sovereignty, states are subject to the culture of other states. Brown (1992) concluded that sovereignty is simply human rights and that without sovereignty, human rights not only are abused, but they are nonexistent. The notion of sovereignty can be applied to sovereignty of issues within psychology. In other words, *conceptual domains* in psychology are the functional equivalents to *territorial domains* in the literal sense of sovereignty. For example, developmental psychologists would not want behavioral pharmacologists to speak for the developmental psychology community. Similarly, those interested in multicultural issues would not want those unfamiliar with such issues to speak for the multicultural community. Thus, many see multicultural issues to be the sovereignty of the multicultural community. This is not to exclude anyone from discussing the issue, but if one were to want to speak for the multicultural community, one would need to gain some expertise in the area in order to gain credibility on the topic (Mio & Iwamasa, 1993; Parham, 1993).

References

Brown, W. (1992). Sovereignty and human rights. *Beijing Review, 35,* 8–12.

Crick, B. (1968). Sovereignty. *International encyclopedia of the social sciences* (Vol. 15, pp. 77–82). New York: The Free Press.

Mio, J. S., & Iwamasa, G. (1993). To do, or not to do: That is the question for White cross-cultural researchers. *The Counseling Psychologist, 21,* 197–212.

Parham, T. A. (1993). White researchers conducting multicultural counseling research: Can their efforts be "mo betta?" *The Counseling Psychologist, 21,* 250–256.

Philpott, D. (1995). Sovereignty: An introduction and brief history. *Journal of International Affairs, 48,* 353–368.

Simpson, J. A., & Weiner, E.S.C. (Eds.). (1989). *The Oxford English dictionary* (2nd ed.). Oxford: Oxford University Press.

Bryant Ford

SPIRIT INTRUSION—The invasion of evil witches, ghosts, or spirits into one's body manifesting into a disease or illness (Clement, 1932). Symptoms of spirit intrusion can include depression, hallucinations, and somatic complaints (Jilek & Jilek-Aal, 1971). Spirit intrusion among the Ojibwa Indians conflicts with the overall goal of achieving a satisfying life. This conflict can involve fear

and anxiety about failing to meet one's expectations, or guilt associated with
past immoral behavior which results in illness (Hallowell, 1963). Among the
Northwest Coast Salish people of the United States, the possession of *schwas*
is responsible for the depression brought on by hopelessness, failure, and frustration within the society (Jilek, 1974). In addition, Eskimos in the eastern subarctic regions refer to spirit intrusion as *quissaatug*, which commonly includes
depression, but also retraction, indolence, and mania (Vallee, 1966).

References

Clement, F. (1932). Primitive concepts of disease. *University of California Archaeology
    and Ethology, 32*, 185–252.
Hallowell, A. (1963). Ojibwa world view and disease. In I. Galdston (Ed.), *Man's image
    in medicine and anthropology* (pp. 258–315). New York: International Univer-
    sities Press.
Jilek, W. (1974). Indian healing power: Indigenous therapeutic practices in the Pacific
    Northwest. *Psychiatric Annals, 4*, 13–21.
Jilek, W., & Jilek-Aall, L. (1971). A transcultural approach to psychotherapy with Ca-
    nadian Indians: Experiences from the Fraser Valley of British Columbia. In *Psy-
    chiatry (Part II) Proceedings of the Fifth World Congress of Psychiatry* (Excerpta
    Medica International Congress Series, No. 274). Mexico City, Mexico.
Vallee, F. (1966). Eskimo theories of mental illness in the Hudson Bay region. *Anthro-
    pologica, 8*, 53–83.

Joseph E. Trimble and Heather K. Mertz

STATUS/ROLE—*Status* and *role* are two distinct terms although they often
are used interchangeably in much of the social science literature. No existing
research explains the origin of status in the social sciences; nevertheless, there
is a breadth of research addressing the topic. Status is defined as a position
occupied by an individual in a social system (Johnson, 1995), and it frequently
derives from class positions, but it may be achieved independent of economic
standing (Frank, Lachman, Smith, Swenson, Wanner, & Wells, 1986). Status
can also be defined in relation to groups and situations (Omodei, 1982). Omodei
suggested that status groups are people within a political community who share
some level of access to valued rights and privileges; that is, they are a group of
people who share similar status situations. Omodei noted also that status situations are the configurations of rights and privileges claimed by the group. The
term role, however, was introduced to the social sciences in a couple of ways;
in the discipline of psychology, it was introduced through the cross-disciplinary
efforts of a number of social and clinical psychologists (Sarbin, 1968), while in
sociology, it was borrowed from the [theater] "stage" (Turner, 1968). Role is
defined as a set of behaviors performed by an individual in a particular situation
with the idea that people will adjust their behaviors according to the response
they receive from others (Frank et al., 1986). Turner (1968) defined role by
identifying certain "elements" or concepts that are found in various definitions
of the term. Examples include: (a) a comprehensive pattern for behavior and

attitudes; (b) a strategy for coping with a recurrent situation; (c) a socially identifiable entity; (d) a chance for individuals to occupy roles of other individuals; and (e) a major basis for identifying and placing people in society. Although there is no single definition for role, these elements clearly represent a complete and comprehensive description of the term. More important, the definition of status and role mentioned support the view that a status is attained and a role is assigned or assumed. As regards to culture, status and role have considerable implications, because the terms help define people and systems in many societies. The effects of status on culture (i.e., societal or ethnic) is significant, because status has roots in social stratification, a system used for classifying people by status. Status is often attained primarily through economic criteria. However, the rewards and privileges that are associated with status are determined by qualitative characteristics (i.e., race, ethnicity, caste, etc.). Role also has considerable cultural implications, because many roles are evaluated by their status in a culture. A role valued in one culture is not necessarily accorded reciprocity in another culture because of the social stratification (level of prestige) and inequitable dispensing of rewards. Status and role are important terms in the social science literature; they are instrumental in providing a framework for conceptualizing rank and positions within societies. Although universal definitions do not exist for these terms, societies must be aware of the potential danger in assuming that these terms have similar definitions and can be applied cross-culturally because of differences in language and practice of customs.

References

Frank, A. W., Lachman, R., Smith, D. W., Swenson, J. V., Wanner, R., & Wells, A. (Eds.). (1986). *The encyclopedic dictionary of sociology* (Vol. 1). Guilford, CT: Dushkin.

Johnson, A. G. (1995). *The Blackwell dictionary of sociology: A user's guide to sociological language* (Vol. 1). Cambridge, MA: Blackwell.

Omodei, R. A. (1982). Beyond the new-Weberians' concept of status. *Australian and New Zealand Journal of Sociology, 18*, 196–213.

Sarbin, T. (1968). Roles. *International encyclopedia of the social sciences* (pp. 546–552). New York: Macmillan.

Turner, R. H. (1968). Roles. *International encyclopedia of the social sciences* (pp. 552–557). New York: Macmillan.

Bryant Ford

STEREOTYPE—A set of oversimplified generalizations of characteristics that typify a person, group, or situation. The term originates from a nineteenth-century printing process through which duplicates were made from a caste or mold rather than from the original. The term was adopted by social scientists to describe the process by which individuals develop attitudes and judgments about an entire group based, usually, on limited information and experience with a member from a particular group or situation. Lippmann (1922) stated that stereotypes are the subtlest and most pervasive of all influences, because people imagine most things before experiencing them. One rationale for stereotypes is based in a cognitive explanation claiming stereotypes as necessary and inevitable coping mechanisms for avoiding cognitive overload (Brown, 1965). Stereotypes can be negative or positive but can almost always have negative effects if additional information is not acquired and the stereotype is used to predict behaviors (Atkinson, Morten, & Sue, 1993). Positive stereotypes are perpetuated by a "kernel of truth" found in most overgeneralized behaviors and characteristics. This "truth" can help individuals gauge the appropriate behavior for interaction, and they can become stigmatizing and harmful to future interactions if previous attitudes and conceptions are not adjusted. Ridley (1995) suggested that stereotypes can be very damaging when used to address or describe individuals or groups that are assumed to be inferior. Further, Ridley noted that stereotype leads to *self-fulfilling prophecy* (see entry), and that those who use stereotypes are dogmatic and unyielding in the face of disconfirming information. Stereotypes are usually difficult to change and are often represented on racist, sexist, and/or homophobic continua. McCauley, Stitt, and Segal (1980) concluded that stereotypes are typical of the types of generalizations made in other cognitive domains.

References

Atkinson, D. R., Morten, G., & Sue, D. W. (1993). Defining populations and terms. In D. R. Atkinson, G. Morten, & D. W. Sue (Eds.), *Counseling American minorities: A cross-cultural perspective* (4th ed., pp. 3–18). Madison, WI: Brown and Benchmark.
Brown, R. (1965). *Social psychology.* New York: The Free Press.
Lippman, W. (1922). *Public opinion.* New York: The Free Press.
McCauley, C., Stitt, C. L., & Segal, M. (1980). Stereotyping: From prejudice to prediction. *Psychological Bulletin, 87,* 195–208.
Ridley, C. R. (1995). *Overcoming unintentional racism in counseling and therapy: A practitioner's guide to intentional interventions.* Thousand Oaks, CA: Sage.

Leon Caldwell

SUBSTANCE ABUSE—Any use of alcohol or other mood-altering drug that has an undesired effect on the user's life or the lives of others (Lewis, Dana, & Blevins, 1994). The negative effects of the substance may involve impairment of physiological, psychological, social, or occupational functioning. Among the psychoactive substances associated with abuse are alcohol, sedative hypnotics, opioids, amphetamines, cannabis, cocaine, and tobacco. *Substance abuse* plays a role in some of society's most pressing concerns, including accidents, violence, criminal behavior, family problems, and productivity loss. The dollar costs of alcohol abuse alone in American society—which includes medical care and loss of productivity—range between $100 and $200 billion per year. Alcohol causes some 150,000 premature deaths a year, perhaps half from the increased likelihood of accidents and violence and the other half from the various diseases the drug causes. Of all drugs, however, cigarettes cause the greatest loss of life over the long run. The Surgeon General of the United States estimates that over 400,000 Americans die prematurely every year as a conseequence of cigarette smoking (Goode, 1993). Thus, substance abuse is not limited to the use of illegal substances. In fact, the cost of alcohol and tobacco to American society is far greater than the cost of all illegal drugs combined. The American Psychiatric Association (1994) proposes diagnostic criteria for what it calls "psychoactive substance abuse." This revision signified a move away from its earlier diagnostic criteria focused on the abuse of specific drugs. According to these criteria, a diagnosis of psychoactive substance abuse must include at least one of the following two criteria: (1) continued use despite knowledge of having a persistent or recurrent social, occupational, psychological, or physical problem that is caused or exacerbated by use of the psychoactive substance; and (2) recurrent use in situations in which use is physically hazardous (e.g., driving while intoxicated).

References

American Psychiatric Association. (1994). *Diagnostic and statistical manual of mental disorders* (4th ed.). Washington, DC: Author.

Goode, E. (Ed.). (1993). *Drugs, society, and behavior*. Guilford, CT: Dushkin.

Lewis, J. A., Dana, R. Q., & Blevins, G. A. (1994). *Substance abuse counseling* (2nd ed.). Monterey, CA: Brooks/Cole.

Gerardo M. Gonzalez

SYNERGETIC ARTICULATION AND AWARENESS—A stage of development in Atkinson, Morten, and Sue's (1993) racial identity model. The adaptation to a different culture and redefining one's identity is a gradual process and is hypothesized to involve a number of stages. While there is variation among identity stage models, the following stages are commonly included in most stage models: (1) an identification with the dominant culture (*preencounter* or *conformity stages*), where the dominant culture is preferred over one's own cultural group; (2) a *dissonance stage*, which is characterized by confusion and conflict towards the dominant cultural system and one's own cultural system; (3) a *resistance and immersion stage*, where there is a rejection of the dominant society in favor of one's own cultural values and norms; (4) an *introspection stage*, where there is a questioning of the value of both the dominant culture and one's own culture; and (5) a *synergetic articulation and awareness stage*, where an individual begins to develop a cultural identity that integrates elements of both cultures (Atkinson et al., 1993; McFadden, 1993; Pedersen, 1994, Sue & Sue, 1990). An individual experiencing *synergetic articulation and awareness* has achieved a healthy and secure sense of cultural identity. He/she is able to feel autonomous with the dominant culture while also freely embracing his/her own cultural heritage. Conflicts encountered during the previous stages have been resolved, allowing his/her ability to feel a sense of confidence. Acceptable and unacceptable elements of both cultures are able to be highlighted and ana-lyzed critically. Thus, the individual is able to see things more objectively and decide what is right for him/herself as a person. Those who have reached this stage often learn much about themselves as individuals as well as their rela-tionship to different cultures (Pedersen, 1994; Sue & Sue, 1990). As clients in a counseling situation, those who reach the synergetic articulation and awareness stage often display strong psychological resources and are motivated to act to-wards community and societal change concerning all forms of oppression. The preferred counselors for these clients are ones who can share, understand, and accept the clients' worldviews rather than those who simply share their race or ethnic identities (Sue & Sue, 1990).

References

Atkinson, D. R., Morten, G., & Sue, D. W. (Eds.). (1993). *Counseling American minor-ities* (4th ed.). Madison, WI: Brown & Benchmark.
McFadden, J. (1993). *Transcultural counseling*. Alexandria, VA: American Counseling Association.
Pedersen, P. (1994). *A handbook for developing multicultural awareness*. Alexandria, VA: American Counseling Association.
Sue, D. W., & Sue, D. (1990). *Counseling the culturally different: Theory and practice* (2nd ed.). New York: Wiley.

Lisa Frye

T

TABOO BREAKING—The breaking of a taboo that results in punishment that manifests in an illness, death, or other hardship (Levinson & Ember, 1996). The word "taboo" comes from the Polynesian term *tapu* or *tabu*, which means "sacred" or "defiled" (Barnard & Spencer, 1996). Violation of prohibited norms results in a gradual onset of symptoms that can include loss of appetite, insomnia, headaches, tiredness, mood swings, and seizures. Taboos often associated with this illness include those that are sexual or sexually aggressive, homicidal (Hallowell, 1936), or deceptive (Ritzenhaler, 1963) in nature. Similarly, sibling (brother–sister) incest in Navajo mythology is referred to as "moth sickness" (Kaplan & Johnson, 1964). In Freudian terms, LaBarre (1964) explains the illness as a result of anxiety between the superego and ego upon confession of guilt.

References

Barnard, A. & Spencer, J. (1996). *Encyclopedia of social and cultural anthropology.* London: Routledge.

Hallowell, A. (1936). Psychic stresses and culture patterns. *American Journal of Psychiatry, 92,* 1291–1310.

Kaplan, B., & Johnson, D. (1964). The social meaning of Navajo psychopathology and psychotherapy. In A. Kiev (Ed.), *Magic, faith and healing studies in primitive psychiatry today* (pp. 203–229). New York: The Free Press.

LaBarre, W. (1964). Confession as cathartic therapy in American Indian tribes. In A. Kiev (Ed.), *Magic, faith and healing: Studies in primitive psychiatry today* (pp. 36–49). New York: The Free Press.

Levinson, D., & Ember, M. (1996). *Encyclopedia of cultural anthropology.* New York: Henry Holt.

Ritzenthaler, R. (1963). Primitive therapeutic practices among the Wisconsin Chippewa.

In I. Galdston (Ed.), *Man's image in medicine and anthropology* (pp. 316–334). New York: International Universities Press.

                               Joseph E. Trimble and Heather K. Mertz

TAÍNO—The name given by Christopher Columbus to the group of Arawak Indians whom he first met, because *taíno* (meaning "peace") was how they greeted him. Many believe that the Taino Indians died due to hunger, overwork, or suicide as a result of the Spanish invasion (Garcia-Preto, 1996). "Their numbers were decimated within a century by illness, malnutrition, overwork, and social collapse precipitated by Spanish colonization of their islands" (Naylon, 1996, p. 195). Despite their decimation at the hands of the Spanish conquerors, there remain many remnants of the Taino Indians in Puerto Rico, such as Puerto Rican skin color, hair texture, and other physical characteristics (Garcia-Preto, 1996). Moreover, many common English words are derivatives of the Taino language, such as *canoa* (canoe), *tobaco* (tobacco), *hamaca* (hammock), *sābana* (savanna), and *maiz* (maize or corn; Hauberg, 1974).

References

Garcia-Preto, N. (1996). Puerto Rican families. In M. McGoldrick, J. Giordano, & J. K. Pearce (Eds.), *Ethnicity and family therapy* (2nd ed., pp. 183–199). New York: Guilford.

Hauberg, C. A. (1974). *Puerto Rico and the Puerto Ricans*. New York: Twayne.

Naylon, J. E. (1996). Taínos. In B. A. Tenenbaum, G. M. Magassy, M. Karasch, J. J. TePaske, & R. L. Woodward, Jr. (Eds.), *Encyclopedia of Latin American history and culture* (Vol. 2, pp. 492–493). New York: Charles Scribner's Sons.

                               Cindy Yee and Jeffery Scott Mio

TALL POPPY SYNDROME—The origins of *tall poppy syndrome* can be traced to Roman times, when, according to the historian Livy, the elder Tarquinius walked through his garden, chopping off the tops of the tallest poppies. His son, Sextus Tarquinius, received the symbolic message and killed the leaders of the state Gabii, thus rendering it unresisting into the hands of the Roman king (Feather, 1989). Helmreich, Aronson, and LeFan (1970) found that in the United States, when a highly competent person makes a mistake, people of average self-esteem find them significantly more attractive than before their fall. On the other hand, people of high or low self-esteem were more attracted to a highly competent person who did not take a fall, and people were also more attracted to incompetent persons who had not made a blunder other than towards those who had fallen. Similarly, in Australia, it has been found that people often gain satisfaction in seeing a person of high status brought down (Feather, 1989). In some Asian cultures, individuals are expected to conform to group norms in terms of actions, status, and beliefs (Markus & Kitayama, 1991). In fact, any aspect of the individual that stands out from the group is thought to be undesirable, and perhaps even dangerous (Feather & McKee, 1993). Overall, then, it appears that most people find it satisfying (and perhaps attractive) when a person of high status is brought down. On the other hand, research has continued to try to determine what in particular accounts for the differences observed in attitudes towards the tall poppy after a blunder. As sugested above (Helmreich et al., 1970), self-esteem may account for some of the differences within cultures. Feather and McKee (1993) have postulated that self-construal (based on work by Markus & Kitayama, 1991) may also be important in the way that people view the "fall from favor." They found that nationality (Japanese) and interdependent self-construal were correlated with a desire to see the tall poppy fall from his or her high position. Feather and other researchers (e.g., Feather, 1989; Feather & McKee, 1993) have suggested that there are numerous other possibilities that may influence attitudes towards the fall of the tall poppy and that additional research in various cultures would be beneficial.

References

Feather, N. (1989). Attitudes towards the high achiever: The fall of the tall poppy. *Australian Journal of Psychology, 41*, 239–267.

Feather, N., & McKee, I. (1993). Global self-esteem and attitudes toward the high achiever for Australian and Japanese students. *Social Psychology Quarterly, 56*, 65–76.

Helmreich, R., Aronson, E., & LeFan, J. (1970). To err is humanizing—sometimes: Effects of self-esteem, competence, and a pratfall in interpersonal attraction. *Journal of Personality and Social Psychology, 16*, 259–264.

Markus, H., & Kitayama, S. (1991). Culture and the self: Implications for cognition, emotion, and motivation. *Psychological Review, 98*, 224–253.

Devin Marsh

TEJANO—One of the most popular styles of music, especially in Mexico and the Southwest, which has roots in traditional folk songs of Colombian origin, and Mexican polkas. Added are elements of country, pop, rock, and Afro-Cuban sounds (Peña, 1999). This style of music gained a broader acceptance with the popularity and tragic death of music star Selena Perez.

Reference

Peña, M. (1999). *Música tejana: The cultural economy of artistic transformation.* College Station: Texas A & M University Press.

Cindy Yee

TEST BIAS (CULTURE BIAS)—Is technically defined as "differential validity of a given interpretation of a test score for any definable, relevant subgroup of test takers" (Cole & Moss, 1989, p. 205). During World War I, psychologists were asked to help screen and classify Army personnel with the use of intelligence tests. Later, the use of psychological testing was expanded to industry and education. One of the major problems associated with the use of such tests is that these tests were not standardized on, or written by, a diverse population

256 THIRD WORLD

but were used to measure the intelligence of these populations. The fight against inappropriate use of intelligence testing began early in the 1920s with Dr. Horace Mann Bond and continued into the 1970s when protest from Black psychologists, sociologists, and other educators forced the United States to ban the general use of intelligence tests. Another problem with intelligence tests is the inability to answer the question, "What is intelligence?" For many years, psychology used the circular definition of intelligence being "what intelligence tests measure" (Stratton & Hayes, 1988, p. 92) in lieu of a better answer. Most dictionaries tend to define intelligence as the ability to understand the world enough to problem solve in new situations; however, most tests are not able to measure this well. The issue with *test bias* in intelligence testing is that everyone's "world" (experience) is different and thus problem-solving in one culture may be different than problem-solving in another. The term is most commonly used when discussing intelligence tests but can also be used to discuss differential scores on other tests, such as locus of control, developmental, sexuality, femininity–masculinity, etc.

References

Cole, N., & Moss, P. (1989). Bias in test use. In R. L. Linn (Ed.), *Educational measurement* (3rd ed., pp. 201–220). New York: American Council on Education and Macmillan.
Stratton, P., & Hayes, N. (1988). *A student's dictionary of psychology*. New York: Edward Arnold.

Christine C. Iijima Hall

THIRD WORLD—Refers to the economically and technologically underdeveloped or developing countries of Africa, Asia, Latin America, and Oceania, collectively. Usually regarded as one entity with common characteristics such as high birth rate, economic dependence on advanced industrialized countries, and widespread poverty contrasted with a wealthy, ruling elite, *Third World* countries are also unmistakably differentiated by the varying degrees of their economic development. According to Chaliand (1997), in 1952 Alfred Sauvy, a French demographer, coined the phrase "le tiers monde" or "the Third World," denoting the "third estate" which referred to the commoners in France prior to and throughout the French Revolution. According to Sauvy, his purpose for introducing the expression "le tiers monde" was to contrast it with the "first estate," comprising priests, and the "second estate," comprising nobles. He observed that the Third World, like the third estate, is "nothing and wants to be something" and suggested the destiny of the third estate is revolution. He added that the Third World, like the third estate, is nonaligned, and belongs neither to the capitalist, Western industrialized block of nations, or *First World*, nor to the communist, Eastern industrialized block of nations, or *Second World*. Since the 1950s, industrialized countries have exploited the land, the natural resources, and the residents of Third World countries, which has created vast wealth for the West and impoverishment and loss of self sufficiency for Third World citizens (Seabrook, 1993). It is their desire for the luxuries enjoyed by the West and the promise of development assistance that contributes to the vulnerability of Third World countries to this exploitation. However, because the West's wealth is dependent on the Third World's exploitation, the continuation of the disproportionate distribution of resources and riches is virtually guaranteed (Seabrook, 1993).

References

Chaliand, G. (1997). *Third world.* Available on Internet: http://www.infoasis.com.
Seabrook, J. (1993). *Victims of development.* New York: Verso Books.

Monica D. Lange

TRIBALISM—The representation or tribal identity of a tribe or ethnocentric organization by its members that have moved away from their native land into a larger multicultural society. Tribalism is the manner in which members still maintain a strong sense of loyalty to tribe or organization by upholding tribal values and traditions. This ''detribalization'' usually has been related to the expansion of urban and industrial societies and government regulation. For example, in the sixteenth century, the United States government began driving Native Americans off their tribal lands in hopes of ''Americanizing'' them (McNickle, 1973). The U.S. government created and established treaties and acts that pushed the Indians further westward off their native lands and onto reservations. This detribalization of Native Americans stemmed from the belief that Native Americans were inferior to the White people who were colonizing America. Many of these Indian tribes, separated and dispersed, still exist today practicing their tribal beliefs. For the most part, members do uphold strong ties to their native society and resist acculturation (Lewis, 1968). Strong ethnic identification and sense of loyalty to their culture have contributed substantially to the survival of Native Americans and tribalism (McNickle, 1973).

References

Lewis, I. M. (1968). Tribal society. In *International encyclopedia of social sciences* (Vol. 16, pp. 146–151). New York: The Macmillian Company & The Free Press.
McNickle, D. (1973). *Native American tribalism.* London: Oxford University Press.

Joseph E. Trimble and Heather K. Mertz

U

UNDERPRIVILEGED—The experience of being below an assumed standard of living which is the social norm. Being underprivileged encompasses class and socioeconomic status. The term was first used in 1896 by Barnes in the *Princetonian* (Salzman, Smith, & West, 1996) to describe children who were excluded from an activity afforded to wealthy children. In contemporary literature, *underprivileged* refers to not having the same entitlements nor opportunities as those in mainstream America. Class and economic status are central themes to being underpriveleged. Education, economic condition, and other social variables are predicates for the label of underprivileged. References to underprivileged usually describes a group (e.g., youth, urban poor).

Reference

Salzman, J., Smith, D., & West, C. (Eds.). (1996). *Encyclopedia of African American culture*. New York: Simon & Schuster Macmillan.

Leon Caldwell

UNIVERSALISM—A belief in the universal existence of and meaning ascribed to behaviors across ethnocultural groups. It is contrasted with *cultural relativism*, which is a recognition of essential differences between different cultural groups. These terms are derived from Kelly's (1955) *Personal Construct Theory*. As described by Betancourt and Lopez (1993), *cultural relativism* holds that "culture has largely been ignored in mainstream psychology and . . . theories do not include cultural variables and findings or principles are thought to apply to individuals everywhere" (p. 632). Fowler and Richardson (1996) acknowledge that "inattention to cultural factors in the vast majority of studies represents a tacit statement of universality" (p. 610). Others (Jahoda, 1988; Sue & Sue,

1990) say that *universalism* represents a Eurocentric perspective and is a form of *cultural imperialism* that discounts the legitimacy of other ways of life. Post modern and social constructionist theorists would concur that standards of rationality and value are arbitrary to a particular culture (Gergen, 1994). At the other end of the argument are *universalists* such as Schwartz (1992, 1994), who based his work on Rokeach's (1973) values survey. Schwartz developed a values instrument which he and others have empirically tested and concluded represents 10 values which are universal in "contents and structure . . . and hence . . . basic . . . to the nature of the human condition" (p. 42). Among the 10 values is universalism described as "understanding, appreciation, tolerance and protection for the welfare of *all* people and for nature" (p. 22). Fowler and Richardson (1996) argue that relativism cannot be used to defend principles to which multiculturalists subscribe, those of cultural equality, tolerance, and respect and that these are in fact universalist beliefs.

References

Betancourt, H., & Lopez, S. R. (1993). The study of culture, ethnicity, and race in American psychology. *American Psychologist, 48*, 629–637.

Fowler, B. J., & Richardson, F. C. (1996). Why is multiculturalism good? *American Psychologist, 51*, 609–621.

Gergen, K. (1994). Exploring the postmodern: Perils or potentials. *American Psychologist, 49*, 412–416.

Kelly, G. A. (1955). *The psychology of personal constructs*. New York: Norton.

Jahouda, G. (1988). J'Accuse. In M. H. Bond (Ed.), *The cross-cultural challenge to social psychology* (pp. 86–95). Newbury Park, CA: Sage.

Rokeach, M. (1973). *The nature of human values*. New York: The Free Press.

Schwartz, S. H. (1992). Universals in the content and structure of values: Theoretical advances and empirical tests in 20 countries. In M. Zanna (Ed.), *Advances in experimental social psychology* (vol. 25, pp. 1–65). Orlando, FL: Academic Press.

Schwartz, S. H. (1994). Are there universal aspects in the structure and contents of human values? *Journal of Social Issues, 50*, 19–45.

Sue, D. W., & Sue, S. (1990). *Counseling the culturally different: Theory and practice* (2nd ed.). New York: Wiley.

Michele Harway

V

VIETNAMESE—The dominant ethnic group of Vietnam. *Vietnamese* is also an *Austro-Asiatic* language, related to *Khmer* and other languages of Southeast Asia. In addition to Vietnamese, the primary languages spoken in Vietnam include French, Chinese, English, Khmer, and tribal dialects. Vietnamese is written in Roman script, with special characters for tonal inflections. Present-day Vietnam was part of Chinese empires for most of its history. Europeans arrived in the sixteenth century, converting many Vietnamese to Christianity. In addition to Christianity, religious affiliations represented in Vietnam include Buddhism, Confucianism, Taoism, Muslim, and animism. France consolidated Vietnam into its holdings in Indochina in the late nineteenth century. After World War II, the *Viet Minh*, a coalition of nationalists and communists took control of the Northern half of Vietnam. After a 10-year-long war, the independent states of North Vietnam—led by Chinese backed communists—and South Vietnam—led by French supported nationalists—were estabished. The French later withdrew, and the United States came to the support of South Vietnam in its war against the North. After devastating losses, U.S. forces withdrew from Vietnam, and the South Vietnamese government fell to the communist North Vietnam forces in 1975. Many South Vietnamese fled to the United States and other Western countries and thousands more, including escapees known as the *boat people*, fled to refugee camps elsewhere in Southeast Asia. In 1964, there were only 603 Vietnamese in the United States that had come from South Vietnam. They were mainly language teachers, diplomats, and students (Takaki, 1989). Although tens of thousands of Vietnamese had entered the United States before the end of the Vietnam War, the withdrawal of U.S. troops from Vietnam set off a wave of Southeast Asian refugees. Unlike the Asian immigrants from other countries living in the United States, these Vietnamese did not have a choice when they came, as they were driven away by the events of the war. In 1975 alone, 130,000 Vietnamese had been admitted into the United States (Kitano & Daniels, 1988). Most of the people who fled were military personnel and their families. They were generally Christian, educated families coming from urban areas, such as Saigon, and approximately half were female. During the reconstruction period after the war, the second wave of immigration began. These people mainly fled by boat to refugee camps in Southeast Asia. In 1977, 1978, and 1979, the numbers of people who had escaped from Vietnam were 21,000, 106,500, and 159,000, respectively. In the years following, thousands more left Vietnam as well. Most of the people in these groups of refugees did not speak English. They were educated professionals as well as farmers and fishermen coming from rural and small coastal areas. Forty percent were ethnic Chinese that had become targets for discrimination under the new communist leadership. Soon after this second wave of Vietnamese refugees fled their country, an orderly departure program was established. In 1979, the United States agreed to allow 20,000 Vietnamese, whose family members were already in the United States, to enter the country annually (Takaki, 1989). As of 1985, there were 643,000 Vietnamese living in the United States. Forty percent of these immigrants settled in California, with large concentrations in Orange County, Los Angeles County, and San Jose. Other geographic locations with large communities of Vietnamese include Houston, Texas, and Washington, D.C. In recent years, the psychological literature addressing Vietnamese mental health concerns has increased (e.g., Felsman, Leong, Johnson, & Felsman, 1990; Flaskerud & Anh, 1988; Matsuoka, 1993). Many such theorists have documented the unique experiences of the group, particularly the issue of refugee status. For example, because of the war experiences and separation from families, refugees have experienced a high incidence of traumatic symptoms and psychological stress (Flaskerund & Anh, 1988).

References

Felsman, J. K., Leong, F. L., Johnson, M. C., & Felsman, I. C. (1990). Estimates of psychological distress among Vietnamese refugees: Adolescents, unaccompanied minors and young adults. *Social Science and Medicine, 31*, 1251–1256.

Flaskerud, J., & Anh, N. T. (1988). Mental health needs of Vietnamese refugees. *Hospital and Community Psychiatry, 39*, 435–437.

Kitano, H. L., & Daniels, R. (1988). *Asian Americans: Emerging minorities.* Englewood Cliffs, NJ: Prentice-Hall.

Matsuoka, J. (1993). Demographic characteristics as determinants in qualitative differences in the adjustment of Vietnamese refugees. *Journal of Social Service Research, 17*, 1–21.

Shepherd, J. (1992). Post-traumatic stress disorder in Vietnamese women. Special issue. Refugee women and their mental health: Shattered societies, shattered lives. II. *Women and Therapy, 13*, 281–296.

Takaki, R. (1989). *Strangers from a different shore: A history of Asian Americans.* New York: Penguin Books.

Christine Yeh

VISIBLE RACIAL/ETHNIC GROUPS (VREG)—A term used when referring to Asians, African Americans, Hispanics, and Native Americans to potentially replace *minorities* which often implies an ethnocentric comparison often in relation to the White majority (Helms, 1990). Helms has used the expression *VREG* to discuss racial and ethnic identity models, diagnoses, research, and therapist–client perspectives. Ethnic groups are oftentimes identified through cultural facets such as language, accent, religion or beliefs, customs, and celebrations. Ethnic characteristics can oftentimes be traced to national origins or geographic regions. *Visible racial/ethnic groups* (VREG) has often been used in reference to members of groups readily identified by distinctive physical characteristics perceived as different from members of dominant or majority society. Such visible racial, ethnic attributions have referred to skin color, hair texture, body structure, shape of the head, eyes or nose, and eye color (Axelson, 1993; Mio & Morris, 1990). It must be noted that the pseudoscientific subdivision of people via race has perpetuated barriers and divisiveness between them. It has influenced the operation of psychological mechanisms that have contributed to oppression and racism.

References

Axelson, J. (1993). *Counseling and development in a multicultural society.* Monterey, CA: Brooks/Cole.

Helms, J. E. (1990). Three perspectives on counseling and psychotherapy with visible racial/ethnic group clients. In F. C. Serafica, A. Schwebel, R. Russell, P. Isaac, & L. Myers (Eds.), *Mental health of ethnic minorities* (pp. 171–202). New York: Praeger.

Mio, J. S., & Morris, D. R. (1990). Cross-cultural issues in psychology training programs: An invitation for discussion. *Professional Psychology, 21,* 434–441.

Matthew R. Mock

W

WHITE—A general ethnic term that describes anyone whose ancestry traces to the Caucasians, a collective of ancient tribes who lived in the Caucasus Mountains, a range located between the Black and Caspian Seas in what is today Russia. The description is, of course, based upon skin color. The *Oxford English Dictionary* (2nd ed.) places the first written use of the term "white" in de Acosta's (1590) *The Natural and Moral History of the Indies*, in which the term "white" describes the residents of "temperate countries." Charante (1671) used "white" to distinguish people who were not descended from the Spanish Moors, and Nesse (1680) drew the distinction between "blacks" and "whites," suggesting that "whites" were descended from Seth, the third son of Adam and Eve, whereas "blacks" were the "cursed brood of Cain," the eldest son of Adam and Eve who murdered his brother Abel, and was punished by being physically marked and condemned to a life of wandering. It was not until 1795 that Blumenbach (in the third edition of *On the Natural Variety of Mankind*) argued that "whites" were descended from the Caucasus peoples. Shortly after that, the theory was advanced that the Caucasus tribes migrated westward to populate a region that encompasses Europe, Greenland, Northern Africa, and Southwestern Asia. This theory has now been discredited, but the classification of a person whose ancestry originates from this region as Caucasian remains. This classification scheme may be fairly accurate, as, of the five classical ethnic groups (Caucasian, Ethiopian, Mongolian, Malayan, and American), Caucasians generally have the lightest-colored skin. This is likely attributable to climate. The Caucasian region tends to be the coldest of the five, and it is thought that light-colored skin is least vulnerable to frostbite. If anything, the Caucasian region has been expanded in recent times. For example, Finns, orginally considered to be Mongols (and hence related to the Japanese, Chinese, and other

Oriental groups), are now grouped with Caucasians. Unlike other ethnic terms based upon color (e.g., Negro), White has been in continual use as a descriptor of Caucasians since the 1600s. While there have been derogatory terms applied to Whites throughout the ages (e.g., honkey, whitey), Caucasians themselves have not adopted alternative descriptive terms. One movement that arose in the late 1980s and early 1990 to refer to Whites as European Americans or People of European Descent here in America has not seemed to resonate with the country as the term African Americans has in replacing the former term Blacks.

References

Blumenbach, J. F. (1795). *On the natural variety of mankind* (3rd ed.) (Trans. 1865 by T. Bendyshe). London: Anthropological Society of London.

Charante, A. (1671). *A letter in answer to diverse curious questions concerning the religion, manners, and customs of Muley Arxid, King of Tafiletta*. London: Moses Pitt.

de Acosta, J. (1590). *The natural and moral history of the Indies* (Trans. 1880 by C. R. Markham). New York: Burt Franklin.

Nesse, C. (1680). *A complete and compendius church-history*. London: Sampson & Wilkins.

Craig D. Parks

WHITE IDENTITY DEVELOPMENT—A process of realization and awareness experienced by White people as they interact with people of different cultural backgrounds and experience multiculturalism in their lives. *White identity development*, unlike *ethnic identity development*, assumes White people are a part of the dominant culture and possess certain unearned privileges based on their white skin color (McIntosh, 1988). As a result, White peoples' identity development process may depend on intentional and/or frequent contact, or critical incidents experienced with people of color throughout their lives. Several researchers have defined *White identity development* in terms of stage models. Helms suggests "a healthy white identity develops via a two phase process, abandonment of racism and evolution of a non-racist identity" (Helms, 1992, p. 24). Other stage models, including the Helms model, typically assume that Whites have a lack of awareness of self as a racial being (Helms, 1990) or attempt to ignore race and whiteness by focusing on a person's "humanness" (Terry, 1975). Through interaction with people of color, Whites become aware intellectually of themselves as racial beings (Carney & Kahn, 1984; Hardiman, 1982; Helms, 1984). A period of dissonance occurs in the third and fourth stages of several models, where Whites experience conflict, guilt, and anger over their understanding of themselves racially and others in society (Carney & Kahn, 1984; Helms, 1984; Kovel, 1970). Next, Whites often over-identify with people of color in order to deal with inner conflict (Carney & Kahn, 1984; Helms, 1984; Kovel, 1970; Terry, 1975). The final stage(s) involve(s) internalizing one's own identity as a White person and developing antiracist tendencies and healthy interactions with people of color. The progression of development envisioned by these models is not necessarily linear so that "in reality the movement may be more complex, marked by loops into previous stages at various choice points" (Sabnani, Ponterotto, & Borodovsky, 1991, p. 82). Some have proposed that White identity development is not linear at all; rather, they suggest that Whites can be at any given level of racial consciousness or lack of consciousness at any time (Rowe, Bennet, & Atkinson, 1994). Furthermore, these researchers believe that viewing White identity development "as a process parallel to minority identity development is not merited" (Rowe et al., 1994, p. 131). Nevertheless, recognition and development of a healthy White identity may have positive impact on the emotional development (Karp, 1981), mental health (Pettigrew, 1981), and socialization of Whites (Dennis, 1981).

References

Carney, C. G., & Kahn, K. B. (1984). Building competencies for effective cross-cultural counseling: A developmental view. *The Counseling Psychologist, 12*, 111–119.

Dennis, R. (1981). Socialization and racism: The White experience. In B. Bowser & R. Hunt (Eds.), *Impacts of racism on White Americans* (pp. 71–86). Beverly Hills, CA: Sage.

Hardiman, R. (1982). White racial identity development: A process model for describing the racial consciousness of White Americans. *Dissertation Abstracts International, 43*, 104A (University Microfilms No. 82–10330).

Helms, J. E. (1984). Toward a theoretical explanation of the effects of race on counseling: A Black and White model. *The Counseling Psychologist, 12*, 153–165.

Helms, J. E. (1990). *Black and White racial identity: Theory, research, and practice.* Westport, CT: Greenwood Press.

Helms, J. E. (1992). *A race is a nice thing to have: A guide to being a White person or understanding the White persons in your life.* Topeka, KS: Content Communications.

Karp, J. (1981). The emotional impact and model for changing racist attitudes. In B. Bowser & R. Hunt (Eds.), *Impacts of racism on White Americans* (pp. 87–96). Beverly Hills, CA: Sage.

Kovel, J. (1970). *White racism: A psychohistory.* New York: Pantheon.

McIntosh, P. (1988). White privilege and male privilege: A personal account of coming to see correspondences through work in women's studies. *Wellesley College Center for Research on Women, 3*, 163–165.

Pettigrew, T. (1981). The mental health impact. In B. Bowser & R. Hunt (Eds.), *Impacts of racism on White Americans* (pp. 97–118). Beverly Hills, CA: Sage.

Rowe, W., Bennet, S., & Atkinson, D. (1994). White racial identity models: A critique and alternative proposal. *The Counseling Psychologist, 22*, 129–146.

Sabnani, H., Ponterotto, J., & Borodovsky, L. (1991). White racial identity development and cross-cultural counseling training: A stage model. *The Counseling Psychologist, 19*, 76–102.

Terry, R. W. (1975). *Whites only.* Grand Rapids, MI: Eerdmans.

William E. Kratt

WHITE PRIVILEGE—Whites (European Americans) have a privileged status in the society of the United States without necessarily acknowledging that status and without having done anything to earn or justify such an elevated status (Frankenberg, 1993; McIntosh, 1988; Roediger, 1994). The claim is that Whites are not taught to recognize the many privileges heaped upon them that are not granted to nonwhites. A further claim is that some Whites work hard to protect their privileged status, and other Whites are in denial about their privileged status, and this serves to protect their high status. Whether consciously or not, Whites may have deeply entrenched the process of White privilege so that it has become institutionalized in the fabric of U.S. society. It is assumed to be a monumental task to uncover all the hidden aspects of White privilege and over-turn them. According to Obear, Dalpes, and Scott (1990), the following are some of the privileges Whites enjoy: (1) White means growing up in an affirming world where White is the norm; (2) Whites are taken more seriously and given more credibility; (3) Whites serve less time for the same crime; (4) Whites can choose when/if to speak out about racism; (5) Whites are viewed as an individual first, not a member of the White race; (6) standardized tests are based on White culture; (7) Whites control societal institutions; (8) products are designed for White needs; (9) Whites have higher life expectancy; and (10) Whites do not have to realize that racism exists.

References

Frankenberg, R. (1993). *White women, race matters: The social construction of White-ness*. Minneapolis: University of Minnesota Press.

McIntosh, P. (1988). *White privilege and male privilege: A personal account of coming to see correspondences through work in women's studies*. Paper presented at the Annual Convention for the Massachusetts Center for Research on Women, Wellesley College, Boston.

Obear, K., Dalpes, P., & Scott, J. (1990). *The human advantage*. San Diego: Culture Plunge Consultants.

Roediger, D. R. (1994). *Towards the abolition of whiteness: Essays on race, politics, and working class history*. New York: Verso.

Yoshito Kawahara

WHITE RACISM—A system of socially organized attitudes, ideas, and prac-tices that deny to people of color the dignity, opportunities, and rewards ac-corded White Americans (Feagin & Vera, 1995). White racism motivates a range of negative attitude and actions against people of color. These acts range from passively watching the racist acts of others, to social exclusion, to murder. *In-dividual* and *institutional racism* are two levels of manifestations of White ra-cism. Individual racism occurs at the personal level while institutional racism is more prevalent and ingrained in the social context of the United States (Jones, 1981). Although White racism is not exclusive to the United States, the U.S. system of White racism has profound psychological implications for Whites and for people of color. The system of White racism is assumed to be based on a false sense of intellectual and biological superiority despite the absence of a rational basis or proof for the assumption. Whites erroneously conceive and perceive themselves to be intellectually and socially superior to other groups. This error in self-perception often leaves no other option for Whites but to continue the myth of White superiority as a protection against the reality of their intellectual and social abilities. For other groups who are subjected to the overwhelming reinforcement of White racism found in the social sciences, the media, and the political structure, White racism can have a deleterious effect on their development of a positive self-image. Implicit in the ideology of White racism is other group inferiority. Authors have postulated that White racism is part of the White socialization process. Jones (1981) conceptualized White racism as operating at three levels: individual, institutional, and cultural. These conceptualizations include ethnocentrism, racial superiority, and the broad-based ideology of cultural centrism (see ETHOCENTRISM). Recent investigations of White racism have focused on its psychological and social effects on Whites (Jones, 1981, 1997).

References

Feagin, J., & Vera, H. (1995). *White racism*. New York: Routledge.
Jones, J. M. (1981). The concept of racism and its changing reality. In B. P. Bowser & R. G. Hunt (Eds.), *Impacts of racism on White Americans* (pp. 27–49). Beverly Hills, CA: Sage.
Jones, J. M. (1997). *Prejudice and racism* (2nd ed.). New York: McGraw-Hill.

Leon Caldwell

WINDIGO PSYCHOSIS (WITIKO, WIITIKO, WHITIKO, OR WEN-DIGO)—A deep depression involving delusions and cannibalism; commonly found among the young males of the Ojibwa, Algonquin, and Cree Indian tribes. Both the Ojibwa and Algonquin tribes believe that Windigo is a flesh-eating spirit. Windigo originated from beliefs in witchcraft, sorcery, and ancestral revenge where the soul was viciously stolen or possessed by the Windigo spirit. During the middle to late 1800s, an unidentified psychologist observed this strange behavior and probably referred to it as "windigo psychosis," and the label withstood time (Teicher, 1960; Landes, 1938). In 1928, J. E. Saindon, a missionary among the Cree Indians, was the first to document windigo psychosis as a sickness (Marano, 1982). According to Landes (1938), windigo psychosis occurs in two stages. The first stage involves a depression or sadness that develops into other symptoms, such as delusions, distaste of food, and homicidal thoughts. The second stage, although rare, begins if treatment does not occur. In this second stage, the afflicted person kills and eats his friends and family. The person then blames the Windigo spirit for his behavior and continues cannibalism until he is eventually killed. Landes (1938) has suggested that the psychosis is related to failure at hunting and fear of starvation, which destroys the male ego and self-esteem causing the depression. In addition, the Ojibwa place great importance on teaching young males to abstain from eating and to develop superior hunting skills. These skills teach male children the importance of food and their responsibility as adults to provide it. These pressures result in dependency upon food, parents, and self in later adulthood, but also result in frustration and aggression from parental denial of necessities of food and support. According to Parker (1960) and Landes (1938), windigo psychosis could result from this conflict between unmet needs and failing ego defenses. This disorder also has been related to the harsh conditions of North American subarctic regions, nutritional deficiency or food scarcity, and sleep deprivation (see ARCTIC HYSTERIA).

References

Landes, R. (1938). The abnormal among the Ojibwa Indians. *Journal of Abnormal and Social Psychology, 33,* 14–33.

Marano, L. (1982). Windigo psychosis: The anatomy of an emic–etic confusion. *Current Anthropology, 23,* 385–412.

Parker, S. (1960). The wittiko psychosis in the context of Ojibwa personality and culture. *American Anthropologist, 64,* 603–623.

Teicher, M. I. (1960). Windigo psychosis: A study of a relationship between belief and behavior among the Indians of Northeastern Canada. In V. F. Ray (Ed.), *Proceedings of the 1960 Annual Spring Meeting of the American Ethnological Society.* Seattle: University of Washington Press.

Joseph E. Trimble and Heather K. Mertz

WITCHCRAFT—The innate ability to inflict harm upon those deemed to be bewitched. *Witchcraft* is the practice of witches. The act of witchcraft is a psychic act of which evil thoughts are cast upon the victim—the bewitched (Buhrmann, 1987). Not to be confused with *sorcery*, which usually refers to men (see entry), witchcraft is understood to be a power of a witch. Witches are rarely men and are given wicked and evil powers at birth that then can be passed down only to their daughters. Although sorcery and witchcraft is driven by antisocial feelings, the witch is permanently malicious as a result of inheriting her unconscious and unwillful powers (Buhrmann, 1987). Nonbelievers have referred to witchcraft as a superstition, myth, and folklore. Witchcraft as it is known in Western society has its origins in medieval Europe. The Witch Burning of Salem, Massachusetts, is the most famous case of the public's fear and sentiment associated with witchcraft. Judeo-Christian dichotomies of good and evil, God and the devil, set up the social fear of witches and other such paranormal and phenomenological behaviors and events. However, in many non-Western cultures, witchcraft serves a distinct social role from law and order to spiritual healing. Witches are always feared and are distinct, for the most part, from *traditional healers*. The spells of witches are usually in retribution for disturbing a spirit or an ancestor of a witch. Traditional healers are reluctant to treat witches' spells for fear the witch may cast a spell on them. The power of a witch is so feared, it is believed that to kill her is the only way to remove a spell. Witchcraft practices can be found in contemporary cultures throughout the world. In the United States, there have been reported rises in satanic and demonic cult activity, usually involving teens claiming practices in witchcraft. Witchcraft is distinct from traditional healing, Shamanism, folk medicine, or magic, which are viewed as holistic health approaches. There have been investigations of psychological explanations for witchcraft, such as Arctic hysteria (Zellar, 1990; see ARCTIC HYSTERIA). Others have investigated behavioral aspects of teens practicing witchcraft (Burket, Myers, Lyles, & Cerrera, 1994). Terms relevant to witchcraft include occultism, Shamanism, Satanism, traditional healing, sorcery, traditional African religions, medieval history, myth, faith healing, cultism, superstition, paranormal, voodooism, and spiritual healing. Competent cross-cultural psychological interventions will be informed by the client's own cultural beliefs or by manifestations that the client holds.

References

Burket, R. C., Myers, W. C., Lyles, W. B., & Cerrera, F. (1994). Emotional and behavioral disturbances in adolescents involved in witchcraft and Satanism. *Journal of Adolescence, 17*, 41–52.

Buhrmann, M. V. (1987). The feminine of witchcraft: I. *Journal of Analytical Psychology, 32*, 139–156.

Zeller, A. C. (1990). Arctic hysteria in Salem? *Anthropologica, 32*, 239–264.

Leon Caldwell

WOMEN—Generally used to refer to adult females (*Merriam-Webster's Collegiate Dictionary*, 1993). Its origins derive from the Old English word *wifman*, a combination of *wif* (woman) and *man* (human being), which pluralized eventually became *women* (Barnhart, 1988; Morris & Morris, 1962). The term is generally identified as analogous to the term *men* used to refer to human males. Women are generally assigned to this "female" category—as opposed to the "male" category—at birth, based on a number of biological variables (e.g., appearance of external genitals; Hyde, 1991). However, although this term is often thought of as "neutral," denoting simply biological sex, the label "woman" denotes more than simple biology and reproductive capability. Merriam-Webster's (1993) third entry for the term defines woman as having a "distinctly feminine nature" (p. 1360). Psychological research supports this notion that more than simple biology is assumed when using the term woman. Gender stereotyping often leads people to assume a large number of very specific behaviors, attitudes, and characteristics based on stereotypic femininity when identifying someone as a woman (Broverman, Vogel, Broverman, Clarkson, & Rosenkrantz, 1972; Deaux, Winston, Crowley, & Lewis, 1985). In her discussion of research in this area, Matlin (1996) categorized those terms associated with women as emphasizing a concern for relationships with others. Niemann and colleagues (1994), however, have found that these gender stereotypes differ greatly depending on ethnicity, revealing that gender and race interact in determining images of women. Researchers have shown that women have a number of issues in common based on their gender. However, research has also shown that women vary greatly among themselves, and that differences within each sex are generally greater than any differences found between the two sexes (Matlin, 1996). Thus, although identification of someone as a woman is often crucial to her experiences in society, this term provides more limited information regarding her as an individual than has often been assumed.

References

Barnhart, R. K. (Ed.). (1988). *The Barnhart dictionary of etymology*. New York: H. W. Wilson.

Broverman, I. K., Broverman, D. M., Clarkson, F. E., Rosenkrantz, P. S., & Vogel, S. R. (1972). Sex-role stereotypes: A current appraisal. *Journal of Social Issues, 28*, 59–78.

Deaux, K., Winston, W., Crowley, M., & Lewis, L. (1985). Level of categorization and content of gender stereotypes. *Social Cognition, 3*, 145–167.

Hyde, J. S. (1991). *Half the human experience: The psychology of women* (4th ed.). Lexington, MA: D.C. Heath.

Matlin, M. (1996). *The psychology of women* (3rd ed.). New York: Harcourt, Brace.

Merriam-Webster's collegiate dictionary (10th ed.). (1993). Springfield, MA: Merriam-Webster.

Morris, W., & Morris, M. (1962). *Morris dictionary of word and phrase origins*. New York: Harper & Row.

Niemann, Y. F., Jennings, L., Rozelle, R. M., Baxter, J. C., & Sullivan, E. (1994). Use of free responses and cluster analysis to determine stereotypes of eight groups. *Personality and Social Psychology Bulletin, 20*, 379–390.

Laurie A. Roades

WORLDVIEW—A frame of reference which consists of the unique assumptions, understandings, interpretations, and beliefs an individual holds about life, particularly about the individual's relationship to the people, institutions, and phenomena within her/his environment. Although the concept of *worldview* has existed for some time (Pepper, 1942), it was identified as an important aspect of cross-cultural counseling by Sue (1978), who described the need for counselors to understand their own worldviews as well as their clients' in order for effective counseling to occur. Sue (1978) initially discussed differences in worldview from locus of control and locus of responsibility dimensions. Ibrahim (1991) confirmed the importance of this concept for psychotherapy, stating that "worldview has been identified as a critical variable that can ease or obstruct the process of counseling" (p. 14). Ibrahim (1985, 1991) expanded the conceptualization of worldview to include an individual's values, beliefs, assumptions, attitudes, and behaviors. Sodowsky and Johnson (1993) state further that worldview relates to "individual perceptions and to social, moral, religious, educational, economic, or political inputs shared with other members of one's reference group" (p. 59). For members of ethnic minorities, "a strong determinant of wordview is very much related to racism and the subordinate position assigned to them in society" (Sue & Sue, 1990, p. 137). Other forms of oppression and societal discrimination against an individual's class, gender, religion, sexual orientation, and other aspects of one's identity will also profoundly influence one's worldview. The complexity of individual identity inevitably enters into each client's—and each counselor's—worldview. A culturally sensitive counselor would consider client problems and potential solutions within the contexts of the client's worldview (Ibrahim, 1984). Normality and health need to be judged with some attention to what is "normal" and "healthy" for an individual within his or her own framework (Sue & Sue, 1990). It may even be postulated that people enter into counseling because some aspect of their worldview has not been functioning effectively (Frank & Frank, 1991). The counselor's role may be to help a client develop a more viable way of understanding and interacting with the world through cognitive reframing, adopting new behaviors, facilitating a corrective emotional experience, or other interventions (Trevino, 1996).

References

Frank, J. D., & Frank, J. B. (1991). *Persuasion and healing: A comparative study of psychotherapy* (3rd ed.). Baltimore, MD: Johns Hopkins University Press.

Ibrahim, F. A. (1984). Cross-cultural counseling and psychotherapy: An existential-psychological approach. *International Journal for the Advancement of Counseling, 7,* 159–169.

Ibrahim, F. A. (1985). Effective cross-cultural counseling and psychotherapy: A framework. *The Counseling Psychologist, 13,* 625–638.

Ibrahim, F. A. (1991). Contribution of cultural worldview to generic counseling and development. *Journal of Counseling and Development, 70,* 13–19.

Pepper, S. C. (1942). *World hypotheses: A study in evidence.* Berkeley: University of California Press.

Sodowsky, G. R., & Johnson, P. (1993). Worldviews: Culturally learned assumptions and values. In P. B. Pedersen & J. C. Carey (Eds.), *Multicultural counseling in schools: A practical handbook* (pp. 59–79). Boston: Allyn and Bacon.

Sue, D. W. (1978). Eliminating cultural oppression in counseling: Toward a general theory. *Journal of Counseling Psychology, 25,* 419–428.

Sue, D. W., & Sue, D. (1990). *Counseling the culturally different: Theory and practice* (2nd ed.). New York: Wiley.

Trevino, J. G. (1996). Worldview and change in cross-cultural counseling. *The Counseling Psychologist, 24,* 198–215.

Kelly D. Willson

Y

YAVIS—First mentioned by Schofield (1964) who noted that at that time it was regarded as the ideal psychotherapy patient's "diagnosis." The acronym stands for *Young, Attractive, Verbal, Intelligent*, and *Successful*, criteria that specify the characteristics of highly desirable patients. Patient characteristics are among the types of criteria professionals may use to make decisions regarding whether and how to treat. Other characteristics are: the psychological situation with which the client presents; impressions or assumptions about the environment; and resources of the client; and criteria generated by the service organization or therapy context in which the professional practices. YAVIS criteria highlight the tendency of therapists to seek "good" patients, motivated individuals who do not want to experience the psychological distress for which they are seeking treatment, persons who will demand less than more deeply disturbed patients, and those who will cooperate with the recommendations of the professional and try to get well. Hence, the "best" client is believed to be one who is educated, psychologically minded, articulate, introspective, and intellectually, interpersonally, and socioeconomically advantaged. This illustrates the nature of a therapy that values these characteristics as a primarily White, middle-class activity which tends to "discriminate against people from different minority groups or those from lower-socioeconomic classes" (Sue, 1981, p. 28). These preferences and stereotypes of therapists may explain the finding that there is a significant relation between social class variables such as age, race, education, income, diagnosis, and motivation, and referral for psychotherapy (Garfield, 1986, p. 214). There is also a relation between these client factors and the kind and type of modality and therapy context to which a client may be referred. The notion of YAVIS suggests that there exists a set of therapist stereotypes that believe that certain client variables and factors influence and predict a positive therapeutic outcome. Negative stereotypes of those who are aged, economically disadvantaged or poor, disabled, or members of ethnic or cultural minorities may have a profound effect on clinical decisions regarding therapeutic responses or the enthusiasm level of effort to respond to those needs. It may lead to rejection of potential clients, referral to other professionals, or early termination and therapeutic failure, all in spite of the negative relation between economic disadvantage, minority status, and indices of mental disorders (Lorion & Parron, 1985).

References

Garfield, S. L. (1986). Research on client variables in psychotherapy. In S. L. Garfield & A. E. Bergin (Eds.), *Handbook of psychotherapy and behavior change* (pp. 87–106). New York: Wiley.

Lorion, R. P., & Parron, D. L. (1985). Countering the countertransference: A strategy for treating the untreatable. In P. Pedersen (Ed.), *Handbook of cross-cultural counseling and therapy* (pp. 79–86). Westport, CT: Greenwood Press.

Schofield, W. (1964). *Psychotherapy: The purchase of friendship*. Englewood Cliffs, NJ: Prentice-Hall.

Sue, D. W. (1981). *Counseling the culturally different: Theory and practice*. New York: Wiley.

Christine A. Bates

YONSEI—Fourth generation Japanese American (Kitano, 1976; Kitano & Daniels, 1995). According to the Japanese language, individuals who immigrated to the United States are called *Issei*, or "first generation." The children of the *Issei* were referred to as *Nisei*, which means "second generation." American and European languages would typically refer to the *Nisei* generation as "first generation of Americans," because this generation was the first to be born in the United States. The *Sansei* were the children of the *Nisei*, and the *Yonsei* are the children of the *Sansei*. The root of *Yonsei* has an interesting history. The Japanese language counting system that produced the terms *Issei*, *Nisei*, and *Sansei* should logically produce the term *Shisei* for the fourth generation. However, the root *shi* in the Japanese language also means "death," so an alternative counting system was utilized to describe the fourth generation (Benjamin Tsutomu and Patricia Kimiko Matsumoto, personal communication, May 4, 1996). *Yon* means "four" in this alternative counting system. However, the children of the *Yonsei*, or the fifth generation, will revert back to the original counting system and be referred to as *Gosei* (Kitano & Daniels, 1995). However, Kitano (1976) predicts that keeping track of generational terms may give way to a newer designation, as he states, "the generational terms may be less meaningful as newer generations are born (the *Yonsei*, or fourth generation) and new *Issei* arrive from Japan. The term *Nikkei*, which includes all of the generations, may become more appropriate" (p. 5).

References

Kitano, H.H.L. (1976). *Japanese Americans: The evolution of a subculture* (2nd ed.). Englewood Cliffs, NJ: Prentice-Hall.

Kitano, H.H.L., & Daniels, R. (1995). *Asian Americans: Emerging minorities* (2nd ed.). Englewood Cliffs, NJ: Prentice-Hall.

Patricia J. Matsumoto and Jeffery Scott Mio

Selected Bibliography

Abudarham, S. (Ed.). (1987). *Bilingualism and the bilingual: An interdisciplinary approach to pedagogical and remedial issues*. Berkshire, Great Britain: Nfer-Nelson.

Agger-Gupta, N. (Ed.). (1997). *Terminologies of diversity 97: A dictionary of terms for individuals, organizations & professions* (rev. ed.). Alberta, Canada: Alberta Community Development.

Allport, G. W. (1954). *The nature of prejudice*. Reading, MA: Addison-Wesley.

Asante, M. K. (1987). *The Afrocentric idea*. Philadelphia: Temple University Press.

Asante, M. K. (1988). *Afrocentricity*. Trenton, NJ: Africa World Press.

Atkinson, D. R., Morten, G., & Sue, D. W. (1993). *Counseling American minorities: A cross-cultural perspective* (4th ed.). Madison, WI: Brown & Benchmark.

Auerbach, S. (Ed.). (1994). *Encyclopedia of multiculturalism*. North Bellmore, NY: Marshall Cavendish.

Axelson, J. A. (1993). *Counseling and development in a multicultural society*. Monterey, CA: Brooks/Cole.

Banks, J. R. (1994). *Multiethnic education: Theory and practice*. Needham Heights, MA: Allyn & Bacon.

Barringer, H. R., Gardner, R. W., & Levin, M. J. (1993). *Asian and Pacific Islanders in the United States*. New York: Russell Sage Foundation.

Bean, F. D., & Tienda, M. (1987). *The Hispanic population of the United States*. New York: Russell Sage Foundation.

Bernal, M., & Castro, F. (1994). Are clinical psychologists prepared for service and research with ethnic minorities? Report of a decade of progress. *American Psychologist, 49*, 797–805.

Berry, J. W., & Annis, R. C. (Eds.). (1988). *Ethnic psychology: Research and practice with immigrants, refugees, native people, ethnic groups and sojourners*. Berwyn, PA: Swets North America.

Berry, J. W., Dasen, P. R., & Saraswathi, T. S. (Eds.). (1997). *Handbook of cross-cultural psychology. 2. Basic processes and human development* (2nd ed.). Needham Heights, MA: Allyn & Bacon.

Berry, J. W., Poortinga, Y. H., & Pandey, J. (Eds.). (1997). *Handbook of cross-cultural psychology. 1. Theory and method* (2nd ed.). Needham Heights, MA: Allyn & Bacon.

Berry, J. W., Poortinga, Y. H., Segall, M. H., & Dasen, P. R. (Eds.). (1992). *Cross-cultural psychology: Research and applications*. Cambridge: Cambridge University Press.

Berry, J. W., Segall, M. H., & Kagitcibasi, C. (Eds.). (1997). *Handbook of cross-cultural psychology. 3. Social behavior and applications* (2nd ed.). Needham Heights, MA: Allyn & Bacon.

Betancourt, H., & Lopez, S. R. (1993). The study of culture, ethnicity, and race in American psychology. *American Psychologist, 48*, 629–637.

Bhawuk, D. P., & Brislin, R. (1992). The measurement of intercultural sensitivity using the concepts of individualism and collectivism. *International Journal of Intercultural Relations, 16*, 413–436.

Boyd-Franklin, N. (1989). *Black families in therapy: A multisystems approach*. New York: Guilford.

Brislin, R. (1993). *Understanding culture's influence on behavior*. Fort Worth, TX: Harcourt, Brace.

Brislin, R. W. (1981). *Cross-cultural encounters: Face-to-face interaction*. New York: Pergamon.

Brislin, R. W. (Ed.). (1990). *Applied cross-cultural psychology*. Newbury Park, CA: Sage.

Broverman, I. K., Broverman, D. M., Clarkson, F. E., Rosenkrantz, P. S., & Vogel, S. R. (1970). Sex-role stereotypes and clinical judgments on mental health. *Journal of Consulting Psychology, 34*, 1–7.

Burch, E. (1988). *The Eskimos: Echoes of the ancient world*. Norman: University of Oklahoma Press.

Burlew, A.K.H., Banks, W. C., McAdoo, H. P., & Azibo, D. A. (Eds.). (1992). *African American psychology: Theory, research, and practice*. Newbury Park, CA: Sage.

Camilli, G., & Shepard, L. A. (1994). *Methods for identifying biased test items*. Thousand Oaks, CA: Sage.

Carmichael, S., & Hamilton, C. V. (1967). *Black power: The politics of liberation in America*. New York: Random House.

Casas, J. M., Ponterotto, J. G., & Gutierrez, J. M. (1986). An ethical indictment of counseling research and training: The cross-cultural perspective. *Journal of Counseling and Development, 64*, 347–349.

Cheatham, H. E., & Associates (Eds.). (1991). *Cultural pluralism on campus*. Washington, DC: American College Personnel Association.

Church, A. T. (1982). Sojourner adjustment. *Psychological Bulletin, 91*, 540–572.

Comas-Diaz, L., & Greene, B. (Eds.). (1994). *Women of color: Integrating ethnic and gender identites in psychotherapy*. New York: Guilford.

Comas-Diaz, L., & Griffith, E.E.H. (Eds.). (1988). *Clinical guidelines in cross-cultural mental health*. New York: Wiley.

Cordasco, F. (1976). *Bilingual schooling in the United States: A sourcebook for educational personnel*. New York: McGraw-Hill.

Cross, W. E. (1971). The Negro-to-Black conversion experience: Toward a psychology of Black liberation. *Black World, 20*, 13–27.

Cross, W. E. (1978). The Thomas and Cross models of psychological nigrescence: A literature review. *Journal of Black Psychology, 4*, 12–31.

Cross, W. (1991). *Shades of Black: Diversity in African-American identity.* Philadelphia: Temple University Press.

D'Andrea, M., & Daniels, J. (1991). Exploring the different levels of multicultural counseling training in counselor education. *Journal of Counseling and Development, 70*, 78–85.

De Varona, F. (1996). *Latino literacy: The complete guide to our Hispanic history and culture.* New York: Henry Holt.

Deloria, V., Jr., & Lytle, C. M. (1983). *American Indians, American justice.* Austin: University of Texas Press.

Dovidio, J. F., & Gaertner, S. L. (1986). *Prejudice, discrimination, and racism.* Orlando, FL: Harcourt, Brace, & Jovanovich.

Du Bois, W.E.B. (1969). *The souls of Black folk.* New York: New American University Press.

Durham, W. H. (1991). *Coevolution: Genes, culture, and human diversity.* Stanford, CA: Stanford University Press.

Essandoh, P. K. (1996). Multicultural counseling as the "Fourth Force": A call to arms. *The Counseling Psychologist, 24*, 126–137.

Faludi, S. (1991). *Backlash: The undeclared war against American women.* New York: Crown.

Franklin, R. S. (1991). *Shadows of race and class.* Minneapolis: University of Minnesota Press.

Funderburg, L. (1994). *Black, White, other: Biracial Americans talk about race and identity.* New York: Morrow.

Gaw, A. C. (Ed.). (1993). *Culture, ethnicity, and mental illness.* Washington, DC: American Psychiatric Press.

Gibbs, J. T., & Huang, L. N. (1989). *Children of color: Psychological interventions with minority youth.* San Francisco: Jossey-Bass.

Gilligan, C. (1982). *In a different voice: Psychological theory and women's development.* Cambridge, MA: Harvard University Press.

Goldberg, D. T. (1990). (Ed.). *Anatomy of racism.* Minneapolis: University of Minnesota Press.

Gordon, A., & Newfield, C. (1996). *Mapping multiculturalism.* Minneapolis: University of Minnesota Press.

Grier, W. H., & Cobb, P. M. (1968). *Black rage.* New York: Bantam Books.

Guthrie, R. V. (1976). *Even the rat was white: A historical view of psychology.* New York: Harper.

Helms, J. E. (1986). Expanding racial and identity theory to cover counseling process. *Journal of Counseling Psychology, 33*, 62–64.

Helms, J. E. (1990). *Black and White racial identity: Theory, research and practice.* Westport, CT: Greenwood Press.

Helms, J. E. (1992). *A race is a nice thing to have: A guide to being a White person or understanding the White persons in your life.* Topeka, KS: Content Communications.

Helms, J. E. (1995). An update of Helms's White and people of color racial identity models. In J. G. Ponterotto, J. M. Casas, L. A. Suzuki, & C. M. Alexander (Eds.), *Handbook of multicultural counseling* (pp. 181–198). Thousand Oaks, CA: Sage.

Herbst, P. H. (1997). *The color of words: An encyclopedic dictionary of ethnic bias in the United States*. Yarmouth, ME: Intercultural Press.

Herrnstein, R. J., & Murray, C. A. (1994). *The bell curve: Intelligence and class structure in American life*. New York: The Free Press.

Hirsch, E. D., Kett, J. F., & Trefil, J. S. (1988). *The dictionary of cultural literacy*. Boston: Houghton Mifflin.

Hofstede, G. (1980). *Culture's consequences: International differences in work-related values*. London: Sage.

Honigmann, J. J. (Ed.). (1973). *Handbook of social and cultural anthropology*. Chicago: Rand McNally.

Hui, C. H., & Triandis, H. C. (1985). Measurement in cross-cultural psychology. *Journal of Cross-Cultural Psychology, 16*, 131–152.

Ibrahim, F. A. (1985). Effective cross-cultural counseling and psychotherapy: A framework. *The Counseling Psychologist, 13*, 625–638.

Ivey, A., Ivey, M., & Simek-Morgan, L. (1993). *Counseling and psychotherapy: A multicultural perspective* (3rd ed.). Boston: Allyn & Bacon.

Iwamasa, G. Y. (1996). Introduction to the special series: Ethnic and cultural diversity in cognitive and behavioral practice. *Cognitive and Behavioral Practice, 3*, 209–213.

Jones, A. C. (1985). Psychological functioning in Black Americans: A conceptual guide for use in psychotherapy. *Psychotherapy: Theory, Research, Practice, Training, 22*, 363–369.

Jones, J. M. (1997). *Prejudice and racism* (2nd ed.). New York: McGraw-Hill.

Jones, R. L. (Ed.). (1972). *Black psychology*. New York: Harper and Row.

Kitano, H.H.L. (1997). *Race relations* (5th ed.). Upper Saddle River, NJ: Simon & Schuster.

Kluckhohn, F., & Strodtbeck, F. (1961). *Variations in value orientations*. New York: Harper & Row.

Kroeber, A. L., & Kluckhohn, C. (1952). *Culture: A critical review of concepts and definitions*. New York: Vintage Books.

LaFromboise, T. D., Coleman, H., & Gerton, J. (1993). Psychological impact of biculturalism: Evidence and theory. *Psychological Bulletin, 14*, 395–412.

LaFromboise, T. D., & Foster, S. L. (1992). Cross-cultural training: Scientist-practitioner model and methods. *The Counseling Psychologist, 20*, 427–489.

Landrine, H. (Ed.). (1995). *Bringing cultural diversity to feminist psychology: Theory, research, and practice*. Washington, DC: American Psychological Association.

Landy, D. (1977). *Culture, disease, and healing*. New York: Macmillan Publishing Co.

Lee, L. C., & Zane, N.W.S. (Eds.). (1998). *Handbook of Asian American psychology*. Thousand Oaks, CA: Sage.

Leong, F.T.L. (1995). History of Asian American psychology. *Asian American Psychological Association Monograph Series, 1*.

Leong, F.T.L., & Kim, H.H.W. (1991). Going beyond cultural sensitivity on the road to multiculturalism: Using the intercultural sensitizer as a counselor training tool. *Journal of Counseling and Development, 70*, 112–118.

Levinson, D. (1994). *Ethnic relations: A cross-cultural encyclopedia*. Santa Barbara, CA: ABC-CLIO.

Levinson, D., & Ember, M. (Eds.). (1986). *Encyclopedia of cultural anthropology*. New York: Holt.

Lonner, W., & Malpass, R. (1994). *Psychology and culture*. Boston: Allyn & Bacon.

Lonner, W. J. (1985). Issues in testing and assessment in cross-cultural counseling. *The Counseling Psychologist, 13*, 599–614.

Lòpez, S. R. (1989). Patient variable biases in clinical judgment: Conceptual overview and methodological considerations. *Psychological Bulletin, 106*, 184–203.

Majors, R., & Billson, J. M. (1992). *Cool pose: The dilemmas of Black manhood in America*. New York: The Free Press.

Malgady, R. G., Rogler, L. H., & Constantino, G. (1989). Ethnocultural and linguistic bias in mental health evaluation of Hispanics. *American Psychologist, 42*, 228–234.

Marin, G., & Van Oss Marin, B. (1991). *Research with Hispanic populations*. Newbury Park, CA: Sage.

Markus, H. R., & Kitayama, S. (1991). Culture and the self: Implications for cognition, emotion, and motivation. *Psychological Review, 98*, 224–253.

Marsella, A. J. (1993). Sociocultural foundations of psychopathology: An historical overview of concepts, events and pioneers prior to 1970. *Transcultural Psychiatric Research Review, 30*, 97–142.

Marsella, A. J., & White, G. M. (Eds.). (1982). *Cultural conceptions of mental health and therapy*. Boston: D. Reidel.

Martin, J. N. (1989). Intercultural communication competence. *International Journal of Intercultural Relations, 13*, 227–328.

McConahay, J. B., & Hough, J. C. (1976). Symbolic racism. *Journal of Social Issues, 32*, 23–45.

McGoldrick, M., Giordano, J., & Pearce, J. K. (Eds.). (1996). *Ethnicity & family therapy* (2nd ed.). New York: Guilford.

McIntosh, P. (1988). White privilege and male privilege: A personal account of coming to see correspondences through work in women's studies. *Wellesley College Center for Research on Women, 3*, 163–165.

Mio, J. S., & Iwamasa, G. (1993). To do, or not to do: That is the question for White cross-cultural researchers. *The Counseling Psychologist, 21*, 197–212.

Mio, J. S., & Morris, D. R. (1990). Cross-cultural issues in psychology training programs: An invitation for discussion. *Professional Psychology: Research and Practice, 21*, 434–441.

Myers, L. J., Speight, S. L., Highlen, P. S., Cox, C. I., Reynolds, A. L., Adams, E. M., & Hanley, C. P. (1991). Identity development and worldview: Toward an optimal conceptualization. *Journal of Counseling and Development, 70*, 54–63.

Novas, H. (1994). *Everything you need to know about Latino history*. New York: Penguin.

Ogbu, J. W. (1994). Social stratification and education in the United States: Why inequality persists. *Teachers College Record, 96*, 264–298.

Olson, J. S., & Wilson, R. (1984). *Native Americans in the twentieth century*. Champaign: University of Illinois Press.

Padilla, A. M. (Ed.). (1995). *Hispanic psychology: Critical issues in theory and research*. Thousand Oaks, CA: Sage.

Paniagua, F. (1994). *Assessing and treating culturally diverse clients*. Thousand Oaks, CA: Sage.

Parham, T. A. (1989). Cycles of psychological nigrescence. *The Counseling Psychologist, 17*, 197–226.

Parham, T. A. (1993). White researchers conducting multicultural counseling research: Can their efforts be "mo betta"? *The Counseling Psychologist, 21,* 250–256.

Pedersen, P. (1994). *A handbook for developing multicultural awareness* (2nd ed.). Alexandria, VA: American Counseling Association.

Pedersen, P. (Ed.). (1998). *Multiculturalism as a fourth force.* Philadelphia: Taylor and Francis.

Pedersen, P., Draguns, J., Lonner, W., & Trimble, J. (Eds.). (1996). *Counseling across cultures* (4th ed.). Thousand Oaks, CA: Sage.

Pedersen, P. B. (1991). Multiculturalism as a generic approach to counseling. *Journal of Counseling & Development, 70,* 6–12.

Pedersen, P. B. (Ed.). (1985). *Handbook of cross-cultural counseling and therapy.* Westport, CT: Greenwood Press.

Pedersen, P. B., & Ivey, A. E. (1993). *Culture-centered counseling and interview skills.* Westport, CT: Praeger.

Pettigrew, T. (1964). *A profile of the American Negro.* New York: Van Nostrand Reinhold.

Phinney, J. S. (1990). Ethnic identity in adolescents and adults: Review of research. *Psychological Bulletin, 108,* 499–514.

Pinderhughes, E. (1989). *Understanding race, ethnicity, & power: The key to efficacy in clinical practice.* New York: The Free Press.

Ponterotto, J. G. (1988). Racial consciousness development among White counselor trainees. *Journal of Multicultural Counseling and Development, 16,* 146–156.

Ponterotto, J. G., Casas, J. M., Suzuki, L. A., & Alexander, C. M. (Eds.). (1995). *Handbook of multicultural counseling.* Thousand Oaks, CA: Sage.

Ponterotto, J. G., & Pedersen, P. B. (1993). *Preventing prejudice: A guide for counselors and educators.* Newbury Park, CA: Sage.

Pope-Davis, D. P., & Coleman, H. (1997). *Multicultural counseling competencies.* Thousand Oaks, CA: Sage.

Ridley, C. R. (1995). *Overcoming unintentional racism in counseling and therapy: A practitioner's guide to intentional intervention.* Thousand Oaks, CA: Sage.

Ridley, C. R., Mendoza, D. W., & Kanitz, B. E. (1994). Multicultural training: Reexamination, operationalization, and integration. *The Counseling Psychologist, 22,* 227–289.

Roediger, D. R. (1994). *Towards the abolition of whiteness: Essays on race, politics, and working class history.* New York: Verso.

Rogler, L. H., Malgady, R. G., Constantino, G., & Blumenthal, R. (1987). What do culturally sensitive mental health services mean? *American Psychologist, 42,* 565–570.

Root, M.P.P. (Ed.). (1992). *Racially mixed people in America.* Newbury Park, CA: Sage.

Root, M.P.P. (Ed.). (1996). *The multiracial experience: Racial borders as the new frontier.* Thousand Oaks, CA: Sage.

Rothenberg, P. S. (1995). *Race, class and gender in the United States: An integrated study* (3rd ed.). New York: St. Martin's Press.

Salzman, J., Smith, D., & West, C. (Eds.). (1996). *Encyclopedia of African American culture.* New York: Simon & Schuster.

Simpson, J. A., & Weiner, E.S.C. (Eds.). (1989). *The Oxford English dictionary* (2nd ed.). Oxford: Oxford University Press.

Smith, E. J. (1991). Ethnic identity development: Toward the development of a theory within the context of majority/minority status. *Journal of Counseling and Development, 70,* 181–188.

Smith, K. (1995). *The Harlem cultural/political movements, 1960–1970: From Malcolm X to "Black is beautiful."* New York: Gumbs & Thomas.

Snipp, C. M. (1989). *American Indians the first of this land.* New York: Russell Sage Foundation.

Spickard, P. R. (1989). *Mixed blood: Intermarriage and ethnic identity in twentieth-century America.* Madison: University of Wisconsin Press.

Steinberg, S. (1989). *Race, ethnicity and class in America.* Boston: Beacon.

Stonequist, E. (1935). The problem of the marginal man. *American Journal of Sociology, 41,* 1–12.

Sue, D. W. (1990). Culture-specific strategies in counseling: A conceptual framework. *Professional Psychology: Research and Practice, 21,* 424–433.

Sue, D. W., Bernier, J. E., Durran, A., Feinberg, L., Pedersen, P., Smith, E. J., & Vasquez-Nutall, E. (1982). Position paper: Cross-cultural counseling competencies. *The Counseling Psychologist, 10,* 45–52.

Sue, D. W., Carter, R. T., Casas, J. M., Fouad, N. A., Ivey, A. E., Jensen, M., La-Fromboise, T., Manese, J. E., Ponterotto, J. G., & Vazquez-Nutall, E. (1998). *Multicultural counseling competencies: Individual and organizational development.* Thousand Oaks, CA: Sage.

Sue, D. W., & Sue, D. (1990). *Counseling the culturally different: Theory and practice* (2nd ed.). New York: Wiley.

Sue, S., Fujino, D. C., Hu, L. T., Takeuchi, D. T., & Zane, N.W.S. (1991). Community mental health services for ethnic minority groups: A test of the cultural responsiveness hypothesis. *Journal of Counseling Psychology, 59,* 533–540.

Sue, S., & Morishima, J. K. (1990). *The mental health of Asian Americans.* San Francisco: Jossey-Bass.

Sue, S., & Zane, N. (1987). The role of culture and cultural techniques in psychotherapy: A critique and reformulation. *American Psychologist, 42,* 37–45.

Suzuki, L. A., Meller, P. J., & Ponterotto, J. G. (Eds.). (1996). *Handbook of multicultural assessment: Clinical, psychological, and educational applications.* San Francisco: Jossey-Bass.

Takaki, R. (Ed.). (1994). *From different shores: Perspectives on race and ethnicity in America* (2nd ed.). New York: Oxford University Press.

Tavris, C. (1992). *The mismeasure of woman.* New York: Simon & Schuster.

Thomas, A., & Sillen, S. (1972). *Racism and psychiatry.* New York: Brunner/Mazel.

Triandis, H. C. (1978). Some universals of social behavior? *Personality and Social Psychology, 4,* 1–16.

Triandis, H. C. (1989). The self and social behavior in differing cultural contexts. *Psychological Review, 96,* 506–520.

Triandis, H. C. (1995). *Individualism and collectivism.* Boulder, CO: Westview.

Triandis, H. C., & Berry, J. W. (Eds.). (1980). *Handbook of cross-cultural psychology. 2. Methodology.* Boston: Allyn & Bacon.

Triandis, H. C., Bontempo, R., Villareal, M. J., Asai, M., & Lucca, N. (1988). Individualism and collectivism: Cross-cultural perspectives on self–ingroup relationships. *Journal of Personality and Social Psychology, 54,* 323–338.

Triandis, H. C., & Brislin, R. W. (Eds.). (1980). *Handbook of cross-cultural psychology. 5. Social psychology.* Boston: Allyn & Bacon.

Triandis, H. C., & Draguns, J. G. (Eds.). (1980). *Handbook of cross-cultural psychology. 6. Psychopathology.* Boston: Allyn & Bacon.

Triandis, H. C., & Heron, A. (Eds.). (1981). *Handbook of cross-cultural psychology. 4. Developmental issues.* Boston: Allyn & Bacon.

Triandis, H. C., & Lambert, W. W. (Eds.). (1980). *Handbook of cross-cultural psychology. 1. Perspectives.* Boston: Allyn & Bacon.

Triandis, H. C., Leung, K., Villareal, M. J., & Clack, F. L. (1985). Allocentric versus idiocentric tendencies: Convergent and discriminant validation. *Journal of Research in Personality, 19,* 395–415.

Triandis, H. C., & Lonner, W. (Eds.). (1980). *Handbook of cross-cultural psychology. 3. Basic processes.* Boston: Allyn & Bacon.

Trimble, J. E., Fleming, C. M., Beauvais, F., & Jumper-Thurman, P. (1996). Essential cultural and social strategies for counseling Native American Indians. In P. B. Pedersen, J. G. Draguns, W. J. Lonner, & J. E. Trimble (Eds.), *Counseling across cultures* (4th ed.). Thousand Oaks, CA: Sage.

Vecoli, R. J. (Ed.). (1995). *Gale encyclopedia of multicultural America.* New York: Gale Research.

Vontress, C. E. (1971). Racial differences: Impediments to rapport. *Journal of Counseling Psychology, 18,* 7–13.

White, J. L., & Parham, T. A. (1990). *The psychology of Blacks: An African-American perspective* (2nd ed.). Englewood Cliffs, NJ: Prentice-Hall.

Willie, C. V., Kramer, B. M., & Brown, B. S. (Eds.). (1973). *Racism and mental health.* Pittsburgh, PA: University of Pittsburgh Press.

Winthrop, R. H. (Ed.). (1991). *Dictionary of concepts in cultural anthropology.* Westport, CT: Greenwood Press.

Wrenn, C. G. (1962). The culturally encapsulated counselor. *Harvard Educational Review, 32,* 444–449.

Zambrana, R. E. (Ed.). (1995). *Understanding Latino families: Scholarship, policy and practice.* Thousand Oaks, CA: Sage.

Index

About the Contributors

Phillip D. Akutsu is an Assistant Professor at the Pacific Graduate School of Psychology and a Staff Research Associate with the Center for Mental Health Services Research at the University of California, Berkeley. Dr. Akutsu's research interests involve examining the financing, organization, and delivery of mental health services to ethnic minority populations in the private and public sectors.

Lui Amador is the Coordinator of California State Polytechnic University, Pomona's Asian & Pacific Islander Student Center.

Patricia Arredondo is Founder and President of Empowerment Workshops, Inc. in Boston. Her work addresses organizational and individual change through a focus on diversity and multiculturalism. Dr. Arredondo is the author of numerous publications, including "Successful Diversity Management Initiatives" and in the counseling field, "Operationalization of the Multicultural Counseling Competencies," among others. She is Past-President of the Association of Multicultural Counseling and Development and the National Hispanic Psychological Association of Massachusetts. She is a Fellow of APA Division 45 and holds an honorary doctorate from the University of San Diego.

Lori Barker-Hackett is an Associate Professor of Psychology in the Behavioral Sciences Department at California State Polytechnic University, Pomona. She is a Licensed Clinical Psychologist and also works part-time as a Therapist and Clinical Supervisor at Cal Poly Pomona's Counseling and Psychological Services Center. Her primary areas of interest include cultural diversity, community psychology, and child/adolescent psychology.

Honora Kwon Batelka has participated in research exploring multiracial individuals and ethnicity, and in research examining adoptive families. She has interests in minority adolescents and mental health and plans to attend graduate school in education.

Christine A. Bates is currently in private practice in Orange, California. Areas of clinical interest include life-span development and adult psychotherapy issues. She also consults and presents to organizations dealing with issues of communication, team building, and conflict management.

Fred Beauvais is a Senior Research Associate with the Tri-Ethnic Center for Prevention Research at Colorado State University. For the last 20 years he has been examining substance abuse and other adolescent problems among American Indian youth. This work has included research on epidemiology, etiology, prevention, treatment, and program evaluation. His most recent work has been an exploration of problems experienced by Indian high school dropouts.

La Verne A. Berkel is a doctoral candidate in Pennsylvania State University's Counseling Psychology Program. Her research interests include the relationship between domestic violence and religious variables, and health practices among African Americans. After completion of her internship at the University of Maryland's Counseling Center, she hopes to obtain a faculty position in Counseling Psychology.

Leon Caldwell is an Assistant Professor of Educational Psychology at the University of Nebraska at Lincoln. His research interests include multicultural counseling, career counseling, ethical decision making, and Black males.

Harold E. Cheatham is a Professor of Counseling and Educational Leadership and Dean of the College of Health, Education, and Human Development at Clemson University in South Carolina. He attained Professor Emeritus status at The Pennsylvania State University and has held faculty positions at Case Western Reserve University, where he also was Director of University Counseling, and at the U.S. Coast Guard Academy. He is a member of the Honor Society of Phi Kappa Phi and in 1993, the American College Personnel Association (ACPA) honored Dr. Cheatham with the Contribution to Knowledge Award and with induction as a Senior Scholar. He served as National President of ACPA from 1995 to 1996. Dr. Cheatham is author of numerous publications and editor or coeditor of two books. He was recognized in the American Psychological Association Division 17 journal as a Pioneer in Multicultural Counseling in 1996.

S. Andrew Chen is a Professor and a former Head of the Department of Counseling and Education at Slippery Rock University. His teaching experience includes Hofstra University, Emporia State University of Kansas, and Oxford University, England. Dr. Chen has written numerous articles and given frequent presentations on cultural diversity, violence, ethnic identity, language rights, and multicultural education. His publications include *Reason to Hope: The Psychological Perspectives of Violence and Youth* (co-authored three chapters), *Asian Americans in Pennsylvania*, *Identity of Chinese American Youth*, and *In Pursuit of Justice*.

A. Timothy Church is a Professor in the Department of Counseling Psychology at Washington State University. His cross-cultural research interests include the cross-cultural and cross-language generalizability of personality and emotion dimensions and concepts, determinants of subjective well-being across cultures, culture-relevant assessment, and dimensions of culture. He is currently a consulting editor for the *Journal of Cross-Cultural Psychology*.

James Fuji Collins is an Assistant Professor in the Department of Psychology at Central Washington University in Ellensburg, Washington. He was formerly the Director of Children, Youth & Family Services, Richmond Area Multi-Services (RAMS) in San Francisco. While at RAMS, he was on the faculty of the National Asian American Psychology Training Center, an APA-approved internship site, the first training program in the United States to focus on the development of psychologists with expertise in working with Asian populations. His interests include biracial and multi-ethnic identity development, counseling across cultures, and children and adolescent development.

Madonna G. Constantine is an Associate Professor in the Department of Counseling and Clinical Psychology at Teachers College, Columbia University. Her professional interests include multicultural issues in counseling, training, and supervision; professional development issues, particularly issues related to psychology internship training and people of color; and the vocational and psychological issues of underserved populations.

Lonnie Duncan is a Counseling Psychologist at the Counseling and Student Development Center at Northern Illinois University. His research interests are in the interaction between race, class, and gender on the help-seeking behavior of African Americans and culturally sensitive therapeutic approaches to therapy for African American depressed clients.

Ruben J. Echemendia is Director of the Psychological Clinic and Clinical Associate Professor of Psychology at The Pennsylvania State University. His research interests involve clinical neuropsychology, mild head injury in athletes, and issues of diversity including the use of neuropsychological practices with ethnic minority populations.

William Peter Flannery is in an NIMH-funded postdoctoral training program in emotion research at the University of California, Berkeley. Dr. Flannery's research interests include acculturation, mood regulation, and cross-cultural methodology.

Bryant Ford is a doctoral candidate in Psychology at the University of Wisconsin–Madison, completing his internship at Michigan State University's Counseling Center. His research interests are in the areas of life-span development of Black males and vocational development.

Deborah Kirby Forgays is currently an Assistant Professor in the Department of Psychology at Western Washington University. Her research interests include cross-cultural expression of type A behavior, alcohol use/abuse in adolescents, and personality and health issues in women.

Lisa Frye is an active advocate for battered women and volunteers at a shelter for battered women and their children. She has a strong interest in social and cross-cultural psychology and hopes to pursue these interests as a graduate student.

Mary Fukuyama has been on the staff of the University of Florida Counseling Center for the past 15 years. She has published in the areas of multicultural training and Asian American issues. She has served as training director and taught graduate courses for students in Counselor Education and Counseling Psychology. Her most recent work is focused on integrating spiritual issues into counseling.

Gerardo M. Gonzalez is Professor and Associate Dean in the College of Education at the University of Florida. Dr. Gonzalez's work has been presented in numerous scholarly publications, including *Journal of Alcohol and Drug Education*, *Journal of Drug Issues*, *Journal of College Student Development*, *International Journal of the Addictions*, and *International Review of Education*. In addition to his work in substance abuse prevention, Dr. Gonzalez is active in multicultural counseling and education issues. He was founder and first president of the Association of Hispanic Faculty at the University of Florida.

Sharon G. Goto is an Assistant Professor of Psychology at Pomona College, where her research focuses on cultural diversity issues. Specifically, she is interested in cross-cultural interpersonal interactions both within and beyond the workplace, and strategies that foster success for ethnic minorities. Her research has concentrated largely on Asian American populations. She is currently working on a collaborative project that looks at Asian American perceptions of racism and its effects on subjective well-being. She currently teaches an Asian American

Psychology course and is developing a course looking at the Asian American experience within organizations.

Christine C. Iijima Hall is currently Senior Associate Dean of Instruction at Glendale Community College, Arizona. She was the first female president of the Asian American Psychological Association. Dr. Hall has authored books, chapters, and journal articles on multiracial identity, ethnic women and body image, and the need for psychology to diversify its profession in teaching, research, and practice. Dr. Hall has appeared on television, radio, and in magazines on the topic of diversity.

MaryAnna Domokos-Cheng Ham is an Associate Professor and the Director of the Marriage and Family Program in the Department of Counseling and School Psychology, Graduate College of Education, University of Massachusetts at Boston. Her research interests, teaching, and writing include multicultural issues, empathy, ethics, and marriage and family therapy. She has co-authored a book and written journal articles in those areas, and presented her ideas and research at numerous meetings.

Michele Harway is Director of Research and Core Faculty at Phillips Graduate Institute (formerly California Family Study Center), an accredited graduate program in marriage and family therapy in Encino, California. She is also a member of the Consulting Faculty at the Fielding Institute and maintains a small private practice as a Licensed Psychologist and a Licensed Marriage, Family, and Child Counselor. Dr. Harway is the author or editor of six books, including *Treating the Changing Family: Handling Normative and Unusual Events* (1996), *Spouse Abuse: Assessing and Treating Battered Women, Batterers and Their Children* (1994, with M. Hansen), and *Battering and Family Therapy: A Feminist Perspective* (1993, with M. Hansen).

Susanna A. Hayes is an Associate Professor of Psychology at Western Washington University, with primary concentration on the graduate programs in mental health and school counseling. Before joining the faculty at Western Washington University, she worked as a counselor and educator on the Colville Reservation for eight years and for the Saginaw Board of Education (Michigan) for three years. She also develops and delivers training for managers of Washington State Department of Social and Health Services.

Gayle Y. Iwamasa is an Assistant Professor in the Graduate Psychology Department at the University of Indianapolis. She conducts research on acculturation and ethnic identity, mentoring and clinical training, and on mood and anxiety disorders among ethnic minorities. Dr. Iwamasa is also a licensed psychologist, supervises clinical practica, and teaches at the undergraduate and graduate level. She is currently President of the Asian American Psychological

Association, and is President of the Asian American Special Interest Group of the Association for Advancement of Behavior Therapy.

Leslie C. Jackson is an Associate Professor of Psychology at Georgia State University. Besides teaching, clinical work, and training, she has developed an expertise working with cultural and self-esteem issues of women of color. This expertise has led to a recent book contract with Guilford Publications to be the senior co-editor of a book on clinical work with African American women. She was recently elected to the Board of Directors of Womanline, Dayton, Ohio. She consults regularly with their Women's Clinic staff regarding both diversity and clinical issues.

Anita Jain is pursuing her Ph.D. in Cultural Studies at Claremont Graduate University.

John Johnson is currently volunteering with the Los Angeles County Probation Department while waiting to enter the Peace Corps. He is interested in race relations and plans to study race relations either in graduate school or in seminary.

Jonathan Kaplan is scheduled to graduate from the University of California, Los Angeles' Ph.D. program in Clinical Psychology in 1999. His research interests revolve around cross-cultural and interethnic issues related to mental health. Specifically, he is interested in the area of cross-cultural adaptation. While at UCLA, he has worked with Dr. Hector Myers and Dr. Stanley Sue at the National Research Center on Asian American Mental Health.

Yoshito Kawahara is a Professor of Psychology at Mesa College in San Diego, California. His research interests are in culturally based values, although he has recently been studying ethnic/gender perspectives in counseling preferences. His values research has compared (1) Asian Americans to European Americans, (2) Chinese Americans, Japanese Americans, and Korean Americans with one another, (3) mainland Chinese with Chinese Americans, and (4) Japanese Americans who either have been or have not been in the American concentration camps during World War II. His analyses were conducted across generations, gender, and situations.

Arlene B. Kelly is an Assistant Professor in the Department of Deaf Studies at Gallaudet University. She teaches courses related to Deaf Culture and Deaf Studies. She is a doctoral student in American Studies at the University of Maryland–College Park, where she is developing an ethnographic study of Deaf female American Sign Language teachers for her dissertation. Her other research interests include linguistics of American Sign Language and other sign languages, acquisition of receptive and expressive fingerspelling skills, historical linguistics, women's studies, and cultural studies.

Kelley R. Kenney is a Full Professor and Counselor at Kutztown University. She also serves as an Adjunct Professor for the graduate Counseling Psychology program of Chestnut Hill College in Philadelphia. Dr. Kenney has close to 20 years of counseling, supervision, teaching, and consultation experience. She is currently co-authoring a book entitled *Counseling Multiracial Families*. She is active on a national level with the American Counseling Association, and in July 1998 began her term as Treasurer for the North Atlantic Region American Counseling Association. She will serve as Chair of the North Atlantic Region American Counseling Association for 2000–2001.

Randi I. Kim is currently an Assistant Professor in the Department of Psychology, Clinical/Counseling Program, at California State University, Humboldt. Her research and teaching interests include multicultural/cross-cultural counseling, career development and decision-making, and social cognition. Additional areas of teaching interest include counseling theories, clinical/counseling practicum, research methods, personality, abnormal psychology, and introductory psychology.

Julie Eiko Kobayashi-Woods is a psychologist and Coordinator of Training at the Counseling Center at Loyola College in Maryland. She also maintains a part-time private practice in the Baltimore area. Her primary interests include multicultural issues, in particular Asian/Asian Americans, women's issues, training, supervision, and educational programming on sexual assault awareness.

William E. Kratt is the Coordinator of Leadership and Diversity Programs at California State Polytechnic University, Pomona. He has conducted a number of workshops on White racial identity in the Southern California area.

Melissa Lamson is a Research Associate with Empowerment Workshops, Inc., Boston. Her areas of interest are cross-cultural and diversity factors in healthcare and ethnographic approaches to working with urban students of color.

Monica D. Lange is an Adjunct Faculty member in Psychology at California State University, Fullerton, California State University, Long Beach, El Camino College, and California State Polytechnic University, Pomona. She specializes in feminist and sociocognitive psychology and relationship therapy. Her research interests focus on issues of social cognition, including attributions in couple communication, the influence of beliefs in critical thinking, and the influence of beliefs and traditions on attributions.

Irene W. Leigh was the third Deaf teacher of the Deaf at the Lexington School for the Deaf in New York City. She is a Professor in the Department of Psychology at Gallaudet University with primary responsibility in the doctoral program in Clinical Psychology. Her current research interests include socialization, identity, and depression.

Arleen C. Lewis is Director of the School Counseling Program and Professor of Psychology at Western Washington University. She is also an Associate of the Center for Cross-Cultural Research. Her current research interests involve peer helping networks and peer helping program effectiveness.

Sandra I. Lopez-Baez is a Professor, Program Director, and Coordinator of the Post Master's Clinical Track in the Counseling and Human Development Department at Walsh University in North Canton, Ohio. She is also an Adjunct Professor in the Behavioral Sciences Department at Northeastern Ohio University's College of Medicine in Rootstown, Ohio. Dr. Lopez-Baez is also an Associate at Rogativa Center, a center that conducts research, provides consultation, and delivers serves to individuals and groups.

Devin Marsh is currently a graduate student in the Clinical Psychology Ph.D. program at Washington State University. He is a recipient of a Ford Foundation Fellowship for Minorities. He plans to pursue a career in teaching, research, and clinical work with ethnic minority and cross-national populations.

Patricia J. Matsumoto is a State of Washington Certified Mental Health Counselor and a Certified Ethnic Minority Mental Health Specialist. Her research and clinical interests include multicultural counseling, supervision, consultation, and education. She is particularly interested in racial self-hatred, cultural conflict, life transitions, and the development of cultural awareness and sensitivity.

Heather K. Mertz is a graduate student in the Department of Psychology at Western Washington University. Currently, she is collaborating with a few faculty and staff at Western Washington on studies involving student alcohol consumption and normative approaches to prevention.

Jeffery Scott Mio is a Professor of Psychology in the Behavioral Sciences Department at California State Polytechnic University, Pomona. He is also the Director of the Master's of Science Program in Psychology at Cal Poly Pomona. His research interests are in the teaching of cross-cultural issues and in how metaphors are used in political persuasion.

Matthew R. Mock is Program Supervisor of the Family, Youth and Children's Service for the City of Berkeley Mental Health Division. He is also Director and Associate Professor of the Cross-Cultural Program with the Graduate School of Professional Psychology at J. F. Kennedy University. He is an officer with the Asian American Psychological Association and Co-Chair of the Ethnic Diversity Committee for the California Psycholgical Association.

John Moritsugu is Professor of Psychology, Pacific Lutheran University, Tacoma, Washington. Dr. Moritsugu has taught psychology for over 20 years, offering courses in the Asian American Experience for most of that time. He has written on minority status and community psychology, co-edited texts on preventive psychology, and served in the governance structure of the American Psychological Association and the Asian American Psychological Association.

Fred Ninonuevo is a clinical psychologist of Filipino descent. He has a private practice in Minneapolis, Minnesota, specializing in mental health service delivery with urban, inner-city Native Americans, who comprise up to 90 percent of his clients. He is also a Community Faculty Instructor in the Psychology Department at Metropolitan State University.

Don Operario is enrolled in the Personality–Social Psychology doctoral program at the University of Massachusetts at Amherst to learn more about people's reactions to stereotyping and prejudice. Guided by mentors Susan Fiske and William Cross, Jr., Mr. Operario's research addresses power and intergroup relations, focusing on the psychological consequences of stigmatized group membership.

Craig D. Parks is an Associate Professor in the Department of Psychology at Washington State University. His research interests address group processes, especially conflict resolution and group decision making. He has published research on, and continues to investigate, cultural differences in conflict resolution. He also studies strategic behavior in conflict, and discussion process and content in decision-making groups.

Paul Pedersen is a Professor of Education in Human Studies at the University of Alabama–Birmingham, having taught at Syracuse University, the University of Hawaii, the University of Minnesota, and for five years at universities in Indonesia and Malaysia. He is a Fellow in Divisions, 9, 17, and 45 of the American Psychological Association, and was director of an NIMH training grant in Hawaii for four years. He has written or edited 26 books, 44 chapters, and 76 articles.

Adelaida Santana Pellicier is an Associate Professor in the Department of Educational Psychology, Northern Arizona University. Her teaching interests are in multicultural counseling, adolescent psychology, and women. She has also taught Spanish Language at the university level.

Patricia Taimanglo Pier is a Clinical Therapist for a private mental health agency in Hawaii. She is also an Adjunct Faculty member of Heritage College in Washington, teaching courses for a Master's level Counselor Education Program in Maui, Hawaii. She is a Chamorro woman who has diverse interests that include multicultural counseling, cultural and community trauma, training and consulting with school personnel, and Pacific Islanders. She enjoys working with children, adolescents, families, and groups.

Raechele L. Pope is an Assistant Professor of Higher Education at Teachers College, Columbia University. Her research interests are focused on multicultural organization development in higher education, multicultural competence for higher education administrators, psychosocial development of students of color, and emergent and transformative models for leadership development. Dr. Pope has served as a private consultant on leadership and multicultural issues in higher education, private industry, and nonprofit and governmental agencies.

Amy L. Reynolds is an Assistant Professor of Counseling Psychology at Fordham University in New York City. Her research interests are primarily in the area of multicultural counseling, training, and supervision. Her writing has focused on such topics as identity development, gay, lesbian, and bisexual issues, multicultural issues on college campuses, multicultural counseling and training, as well as multicultural competence.

Rakefet Richmond, a native of Israel, has interests in multicultural studies and marriage and family studies. She is in the graduate program at Indiana State University and hopes to serve immigrants and other families and individuals from diverse backgrounds.

Laurie A. Roades is an Assistant Professor of Psychology in the Behavioral Sciences Department at California State Polytechnic University, Pomona. Her teaching and research interests are in the psychology of women, in gender and ethnic issues in clinical diagnosis and treatment, and in allies across traditional demographic lines of demarcation.

Maria Rodriguez is an Associate Professor in the Department of SEEK at Hunter College of The City University of New York. Her teaching and counseling endeavors have focused on facilitating the career and educational development of academically and economically disadvantaged college students. Dr. Rodriguez's research and publication efforts have supported the importance of developing relevant career interventions for this student population and assessing the impact of those interventions on students' career maturity. Additionally, she is involved in assessing the use of instructional technology in career planning courses and assessing the adequacy of career information resources for ethnic and racial minorities.

Grace Powless Sage lives in Arlee, Montana, and teaches classes at the Salish–Kootenai College; in the summer she teaches at the University of Alaska, Fairbanks. Her research interests involve studies on the prevention and treatment of alcoholism and drug use among American Indians and Alaska Natives.

Azara L. Santiago-Rivera is an Associate Professor in the Department of Latin American and Caribbean Studies and in the Department of Counseling Psychology at SUNY–Albany. Her research interests include gender differences in the appraisal of and responses to stressful life events. Another area of research interest involves multicultural counseling issues and includes counseling the bilingual Spanish-speaking client. Also, she is pursuing a new area of research involving the study of the effects of environmental contamination on the psychological and physical well-being of individuals.

Douglas Y. Seiden is President of the Cross-Cultural Behavior Therapy Special Interest Group of the Association for Advancement of Behavior Therapy, and works as a Staff Psychologist for the Coney Island Hospital Department of Psychiatry's School-Based Mental Health Program. He has authored and co-authored articles and presentations on the history of behavioral and cognitive therapies in France, cross-cultural functional analysis, behavioral approaches to the culture-bound syndromes, the teaching of cross-cultural abnormal psychology, and method factors in research on facial emotion recognition.

Elsie J. Smith is a Fellow of the American Psychological Association. She has published in the area of cross-cultural psychology and is currently working on a theory of ethnic identity development.

David Sue is Professor of Psychology at Western Washington University where he has served as the Chairperson of the Mental Health Counseling Program for the past 12 years. He is an Associate of the Center for Cross-Cultural Psychology and has research interests in multicultural counseling and Asian American personality.

Karen L. Suyemoto is an Assistant Professor in Counseling Psychology at Northeastern University. Her areas of interest include ethnic identity development in multiracial individuals, feminist and gender issues, constructivistic approaches to psychotherapy, and the relationship of anger to psychopathology and self-destructive behavior. Recent publications have appeared in *Clinical Psychology Review* and *Psychotherapy*.

Tengemana Mapule Thumbutu is a Public Affairs Assistant in the College of Letters, Arts, and Social Sciences at California State Polytechnic University, Pomona. In this capacity, she has extensive day-to-day contact with students and has developed an extensive applied knowledge concerning values of today's students. Her commitment to education also involves community activism, civic organizations, church affiliations, and family support and activities.

Pamela Jumper Thurman, a Western Cherokee, has worked with American Indian mental health and substance abuse programs in a professional capacity for about 15 years. She has developed and/or consulted on the evaluation component of several programs across the United States and has served as a Research Associate on various research grants. She has published two Drug and Alcohol Prevention Curricula and several articles on cultural issues, solvent abuse, suicide, and substance abuse research, treatment, and prevention.

Stella Ting-Toomey is Professor of Speech Communication at California State University, Fullerton. She is the author and editor of 11 books. Three recent book titles are *Communicating Effectively with the Chinese* (co-authored); *The Challenge of Facework: Cross-Cultural and Interpersonal Issues*; and *Building Bridges: Interpersonal Skills for a Changing World* (co-authored). She has published extensively on cross-cultural facework, intercultural conflict, Asian communication patterns, and the effective identity negotiation model. She has lectured widely throughout the United States, Asian, and Europe on the topic of intercultural facework management. She is an experienced trainer in the area of transcultural communication competence.

Ivory Achebe Toldson, a Counseling Psychology Ph.D. student at Temple University in Philadelphia, works for a community-based mental health facility in an impoverished African American area, Mr. Toldson has an abiding interest in the mental health concerns of the socially and economically disenfranchised. The concentration of his dissertation research is African American adolescent males with diagnosed conduct disorder. His other areas of interest include college student personnel, substance abuse treatment, African American epistemological constructs, and the ecological etiopathogenesis of African American antisocial behavior.

Saundra Tomlinson-Clarke is an Associate Professor and the Director of Training/Program Coordinator of the Program in Counseling Psychology, Department of Educational Psychology at Rutgers, The State University of New Jersey. Her research interests and publications focus on multicultural counseling, counselor bias and clinical judgments, and the psychosocial development of college students.

Joseph E. Trimble is a Professor of Psychology at Western Washington University, where he has been a faculty member since 1978. Throughout his academic career, he has focused his efforts on promoting and conducting psychological research with indigenous, ethnic populations, especially American Indians. In the past two decades, he has been working on drug abuse prevention and intervention research models with native youth. He has presented over 200 papers and invited lectures at professional meetings and has generated over 130 publications dealing with topics concerning psychology and culture.

Beverly J. Vandiver is an Assistant Professor of Counseling Psychology in the Department of Counselor Education, Counseling Psychology, and Rehabilitation Services at The Pennsylvania State University. Her research and writings focuses on multicultural mental health issues, scale development, and career development, particularly for African Americans and women.

Christopher J. Weiss is an Academic Counselor with the Office of Supportive Services at Syracuse University. He is completing his doctoral studies in Counselor Education while working full-time at Syracuse University. His dissertation and research interests focus on alliance formation in cross-cultural and multicultural counseling interactions. Mr. Weiss has also facilitated a number of community dialogues on racism and racial healing, working through the Interreligious Council of Central New York.

Angela M. White is a Counseling Psychology doctoral candidate at The Pennsylvania State University. Her research interests include cultural/ethnic minority issues in help-seeking and psychological service utilization, nontraditional (culturally relevant) modes of psychological service delivery, and support service development for cultural minorities within college and university settings.

Kelly L. Willson is a Senior Staff Psychologist at the University of Iowa Counseling Service, working with undergraduate, graduate, and professional students. In addition to her work as an individual and group therapist, she conducts outreach programs, workshops, supervision, and training in the areas of White racial identity/White racism, and sexual identity. Dr. Willson serves as a liason to the University of Iowa's Gay, Lesbian, Bisexual, Transgender student group and faculty/staff association.

M. D'André Wilson is a doctoral candidate in Counseling Psychology at The Pennsylvania State University. He is a Predoctoral Intern at Counseling and Psychological Services on the Penn State campus. His research interests are in the areas of cross-cultural clinical supervision, multicultural counseling, gay, lesbian, and bisexual issues, and domestic violence.

Cindy Yee is a certified professional and substance abuse counselor from Scottsdale, Arizona. Ms. Yee has worked as a therapist in various settings, with children, adolescents, adults, and families. She is working on her doctorate in Counseling Psychology at the University of Memphis. As a second-and-a-half generation Chinese American, her research areas of interest include multicultural counseling, ethnic identity development, multiethnic issues and concerns, transracial adoptions, mentoring, and spirituatlity.

Christine Yeh is an Assistant Professor in the Department of Counseling and Clinical Psychology at Teachers College, Columbia University. She has conducted research in the areas of Asian American psychology with particular focus on ethnic and gender role identity development, identity conflict, barriers to mental health utilization, and health and healing from a traditional Asian perspective.

Lawrence W. Young, Jr. has written editorial columns for newspapers across the country and was American correspondent for AFROMART, which is published in London. Mr. Young has published articles on intercultural communications, racism, African American culture, and health issues that confront the Black community that have appeared in *Black Issues in Higher Education* and *Black Opinion*.

Gangaw Zaw, a native of Myanmar, is currently in the Masters in Experimental Psychology Program at Loma Linda University in California. She is interested in political, psychological, and legal issues.

ISBN 0-313-29547-6

90000>

EAN

9 780313 295478

HARDCOVER BAR CODE